SIXTEEN TEACHERS TEACHING

D1563441

SIXTEEN TEACHERS TEACHING

Two-Year College Perspectives

EDITED BY
PATRICK SULLIVAN

UTAH STATE UNIVERSITY PRESS
Logan

© 2020 by University Press of Colorado

Published by Utah State University Press
An imprint of University Press of Colorado
245 Century Circle, Suite 202
Louisville, Colorado 80027

All rights reserved
Manufactured in the United States of America

The University Press of Colorado is a proud member of the Association of University Presses.

The University Press of Colorado is a cooperative publishing enterprise supported, in part, by Adams State University, Colorado State University, Fort Lewis College, Metropolitan State University of Denver, Regis University, University of Colorado, University of Northern Colorado, University of Wyoming, Utah State University, and Western Colorado University.

∞ This paper meets the requirements of the ANSI/NISO Z39.48-1992 (Permanence of Paper)

ISBN: 978-1-60732-902-2 (paperback)
ISBN: 978-1-60732-930-5 (ebook)
https://doi.org/10.7330/9781607329305

Library of Congress Cataloging-in-Publication Data

Names: Sullivan, Patrick, 1956– editor.
Title: 16 teachers teaching : two-year college perspectives / edited by Patrick Sullivan.
Other titles: Sixteen teachers teaching
Description: Logan : Utah State University Press, an imprint of University Press of Colorado [2020] | Includes bibliographical references and index.
Identifiers: LCCN 2020010027 (print) | LCCN 2020010028 (ebook) | ISBN 9781607329022 (paperback) | ISBN 9781607329305 (ebook)
Subjects: LCSH: Composition (Language arts)—Study and teaching (Higher) | English language—Rhetoric—Study and teaching (Higher) | Community college teachers. | Community colleges. | Junior colleges.
Classification: LCC PE1404 .A15 2020 (print) | LCC PE1404 (ebook) | DDC 428.0071—dc23
LC record available at https://lccn.loc.gov/2020010027
LC ebook record available at https://lccn.loc.gov/2020010028

Front-cover illustration: *Jump Into It*, 2017, ink on paper, Bonnie Rose Sullivan. Back-cover photo by Dan Long.

Whoever you are
and wherever you may be,
if you are looking for inspiration about teaching,
this book is for you.

***

And to
Susan,
Bonnie Rose,
Nicholas,
Marigold Hope
and
Baby Beluga

"When the morning stars sang together,
and all the sons of God shouted for joy"
—Book of Job

American colleges and universities must envision a much larger role for higher education in the national life. They can no longer consider themselves merely the instrument for producing an intellectual elite; they must become the means by which every citizen, youth, and adult is enabled and encouraged to carry his education, formal and informal, as far as his native capacities permit.

This conception is the inevitable consequence of the democratic faith; universal education is indispensable to the full and living realization of the democratic ideal. No society can long remain free unless its members are freemen, and men are not free where ignorance prevails. No more in mind than in body can this Nation or any endure half slave, half free. Education that liberates and ennobles must be made equally available to all. Justice to the individual demands this; the safety and progress of the Nation depend upon it. America cannot afford to let any of its potential human resources go undiscovered and undeveloped.

—The Truman Commission Report, 1947

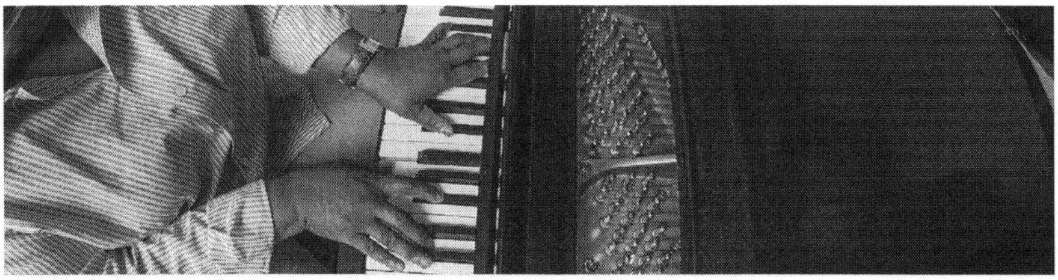

CONTENTS

SIXTEEN TEACHERS TEACHING

Introduction

DEMOCRACY'S UNFINISHED BUSINESS

Patrick Sullivan

I am what time, circumstance, history, have made of me, certainly, but I am, also, much more than that. So are we all.
—James Baldwin

It is a great pleasure to welcome you to these pages.

Readers of this book have a number of appealing prospects before them. Perhaps foremost among these is the opportunity to visit the classrooms of fellow English teachers and see firsthand how a group of acclaimed professionals in our discipline put together their classes, design their reading and writing assignments, and theorize their work as writing instructors.

Readers also have the opportunity—which is very rare in our profession—to visit classrooms of English teachers who teach at open-admissions two-year colleges, where 41 percent of all undergraduates in America now enroll (American Association of Community Colleges 2020; Hassel and Giordano 2013).[1] To my knowledge, there has never been a scholarly book quite like this one, offering readers wisdom, expertise, and a warmly personal welcome and sense of common purpose gathered from English teachers at the two-year college. It is certainly time we had one.

DOI: 10.7330/9781607329305.c000

As readers will see, the individuals featured here are all deeply committed to the art of teaching, and most have spent decades honing their craft. Most are well known and highly respected scholars as well. Because these individuals teach at two-year colleges, they have spent their careers teaching three, four, or even five sections of writing classes each semester. Considered cumulatively, there is an impressive (and perhaps unprecedented) abundance of pedagogical expertise, teaching knowledge, and classroom experience reflected in these pages. Because these individuals routinely teach first-year composition and developmental classes, their areas of expertise align precisely with what English teachers at all levels of instruction spend most of their time doing: teaching reading, writing, and thinking.

This book also provides readers with the opportunity to see social justice work in action. The modern community college was created in 1947 by the Truman Commission to be—by mission and mandate—a social justice institution. The landmark book-length study produced by the Truman Commission that created the modern community college, known popularly as the Truman Commission Report (and officially titled *Higher Education for Democracy: A Report of the President's Commission on Higher Education*), is one of the most important documents ever produced about education in America (President's 1947). Crucially for our purposes here, the commission urged the nation to address "democracy's unfinished business": structural patterns of inequality related to class, race, and gender. The primary means for addressing this unfinished business was through radically expanded access to higher education (President's 1947, 12). What the Truman Commission candidly acknowledged in 1947 still holds true today:

> By allowing the opportunity for higher education to depend so largely on the individual's economic status, we are not only denying to millions of young people the chance in life to which they are entitled; we are also depriving the Nation of a vast amount of potential leadership and potential competence which it sorely needs. (President's 1947, 29)

Before open-admissions institutions began appearing in great numbers across the nation in the late 1960s, colleges in America were "bastions of privilege" and not "engines of opportunity" (Bowen, Kurzweil, and Tobin 2005, 135). Figure 0.1 gives readers a glimpse into that fraught, tumultuous moment in our history when access to higher education became a civil rights issue—contested in boardrooms, in state and federal legislatures, and in the streets. Figure 0.1 is an artifact from the City University of New York (CUNY) system archive where open-admissions policies were pioneered in the 1960s and early 1970s by African American

Figure 0.1. "Fiscal Crisis of 1976: Big PSC [Professional Staff Congress] street rally near City Hall against cuts to CUNY." Source: CUNY Digital Historical Archive, http://cdha.cuny.edu/items/show/5642. Used with permission of the CUNY Digital History Archive and the Professional Staff Congress.

and Latinx activists (Kynard 2013; Smitherman 1977), by student activism, and by individuals like Mina Shaughnessy, Marilyn Sternglass, and David Lavin (Lavin, Alba, and Silberstein 1981).

Figure 0.2, taken from table 302.20 from the National Center for Education Statistics (NCES) *Digest of Education Statistics* (Snyder, de Brey, and Dillow 2017), suggests the revolutionary nature of this enterprise. The key data points for our purposes here are the long strings of "—" and "†" notations for Black and Hispanic students during the 1960s—and then the sudden jump in enrollment beginning in the early 1970s, when open-admissions policies were established across the nation at public two-year colleges. These symbols represent data that is either not available (—) or not applicable (†). We also see comparable numbers related to gender and family income during this time (Cahalan et al. 2018). This data set documents a dramatic change in college enrollment patterns in America. We must be careful about evaluating these data and drawing correlational or causal relationships from them. Nonetheless, and without attempting to simplify this complex historical moment, we can say that the Civil Rights movement, African American and Latinx activism (Kynard 2013, 151; Smitherman 1977), the Black Arts Movement (BAM) (Kynard 2014, 122), the Women's Movement, other progressive social movements, the G.I. Bill, state and federal financial aid programs, along with postwar optimism and prosperity

DIGEST *of* EDUCATION STATISTICS

2016 Tables and Figures | All Years of Tables and Figures | Most Recent Full Issue of the Digest

◀ Previous Page | Download Excel (83KB)

Table 302.20. Percentage of recent high school completers enrolled in 2- and 4-year colleges, by race/ethnicity: 1960 through 2015

[Standard errors appear in parentheses]

Year	Percent of recent high school completers[1] enrolled in college[2] (annual data)					3-year moving averages[3]: Percent of recent high school completers[1] enrolled in college[2]					3-year moving averages[3]: Difference between percent enrolled		
	Total	White	Black	Hispanic	Asian[4]	Total	White	Black	Hispanic	Asian[4]	White-Black	White-Hispanic	White-Asian[4]
1	2	3	4	5	6	7	8	9	10	11	12	13	14
1960[5]	45.1 (2.16)	45.8 (2.24)	— (†)	— (†)	— (†)	46.6 (1.52)	47.7 (1.58)	— (†)	— (†)	— (†)	— (†)	— (†)	— (†)
1961[5]	48.0 (2.12)	49.5 (2.22)	— (†)	— (†)	— (†)	47.4 (1.22)	48.7 (1.28)	— (†)	— (†)	— (†)	— (†)	— (†)	— (†)
1962[5]	49.0 (2.08)	50.6 (2.19)	— (†)	— (†)	— (†)	47.4 (1.22)	48.6 (1.27)	— (†)	— (†)	— (†)	— (†)	— (†)	— (†)
1963[5]	45.0 (2.12)	45.6 (2.21)	— (†)	— (†)	— (†)	47.5 (1.18)	48.5 (1.23)	— (†)	— (†)	— (†)	— (†)	— (†)	— (†)
1964[5]	48.3 (1.92)	49.2 (2.01)	— (†)	— (†)	— (†)	48.5 (1.10)	49.2 (1.15)	— (†)	— (†)	— (†)	— (†)	— (†)	— (†)
1965[5]	50.9 (1.73)	51.7 (1.81)	— (†)	— (†)	— (†)	49.9 (1.03)	51.0 (1.08)	— (†)	— (†)	— (†)	— (†)	— (†)	— (†)
1966[5]	50.1 (1.74)	51.7 (1.82)	— (†)	— (†)	— (†)	51.0 (1.01)	52.1 (1.06)	— (†)	— (†)	— (†)	— (†)	— (†)	— (†)
1967[5]	51.9 (1.44)	53.0 (1.52)	— (†)	— (†)	— (†)	52.5 (0.82)	53.8 (0.87)	— (†)	— (†)	— (†)	— (†)	— (†)	— (†)
1968[5]	55.4 (1.41)	56.6 (1.50)	— (†)	— (†)	— (†)	53.6 (0.81)	55.0 (0.86)	— (†)	— (†)	— (†)	— (†)	— (†)	— (†)
1969[5]	53.3 (1.36)	55.2 (1.43)	— (†)	— (†)	— (†)	53.5 (0.80)	54.6 (0.85)	— (†)	— (†)	— (†)	— (†)	— (†)	— (†)
1970[5]	51.7 (1.38)	52.0 (1.46)	— (†)	— (†)	— (†)	52.9 (0.79)	53.8 (0.83)	— (†)	— (†)	— (†)	— (†)	— (†)	— (†)
1971[5]	53.5 (1.35)	54.0 (1.42)	— (†)	— (†)	— (†)	51.5 (0.78)	51.9 (0.83)	— (†)	— (†)	— (†)	— (†)	— (†)	— (†)
1972	49.2 (1.33)	49.7 (1.45)	44.6 (4.74)	45.0 (12.85)	— (†)	49.7 (0.77)	50.5 (0.83)	38.4 (3.26)	49.9 (8.76)	— (†)	12.1 (3.36)	‡ (†)	— (†)
1973	46.6 (1.31)	47.8 (1.43)	32.5 (4.40)	54.1 (11.89)	— (†)	47.8 (0.76)	48.2 (0.83)	41.4 (2.68)	48.8 (7.04)	— (†)	6.8 ! (2.81)	‡ (†)	— (†)
1974	47.6 (1.30)	47.2 (1.42)	47.2 (4.69)	46.9 (11.79)	— (†)	48.3 (0.75)	48.7 (0.82)	40.5 (2.69)	53.1 (6.72)	— (†)	8.3 ! (2.82)	‡ (†)	— (†)
1975	50.7 (1.29)	51.1 (1.40)	41.7 (4.81)	58.0 (11.14)	— (†)	49.1 (0.75)	49.1 (0.82)	44.5 (2.78)	52.7 (6.44)	— (†)	‡ (†)	‡ (†)	— (†)
1976	48.8 (1.33)	48.8 (1.45)	44.4 (4.94)	52.7 (10.52)	— (†)	50.1 (0.75)	50.3 (0.82)	45.3 (2.78)	53.6 (6.18)	— (†)	‡ (†)	‡ (†)	— (†)
1977	50.6 (1.30)	50.8 (1.42)	49.5 (4.70)	50.8 (10.43)	— (†)	49.9 (0.75)	50.1 (0.83)	46.8 (2.73)	48.8 (6.18)	— (†)	‡ (†)	‡ (†)	— (†)
1978	50.1 (1.29)	50.5 (1.42)	46.4 (4.55)	42.0 (11.06)	— (†)	50.0 (0.75)	50.4 (0.82)	47.5 (2.69)	46.1 (6.14)	— (†)	‡ (†)	‡ (†)	— (†)
1979	49.3 (1.29)	49.9 (1.42)	46.7 (4.73)	45.0 (10.37)	— (†)	49.6 (0.75)	50.1 (0.82)	45.2 (2.65)	46.3 (6.32)	— (†)	‡ (†)	‡ (†)	— (†)
1980	49.3 (1.31)	49.8 (1.44)	42.7 (4.48)	52.3 (11.39)	— (†)	50.8 (0.75)	51.5 (0.83)	44.0 (2.64)	49.6 (6.25)	— (†)	7.5 ! (2.76)	‡ (†)	— (†)
1981	53.9 (1.31)	54.9 (1.45)	42.7 (4.48)	52.1 (10.73)	— (†)	51.3 (0.76)	52.4 (0.84)	40.3 (2.53)	48.7 (6.13)	— (†)	12.2 (2.66)	‡ (†)	— (†)
1982	50.6 (1.38)	52.7 (1.54)	35.8 (4.39)	43.2 (10.37)	— (†)	52.4 (0.80)	54.2 (0.90)	38.8 (2.61)	49.4 (6.44)	— (†)	15.4 (2.76)	‡ (†)	— (†)
1983	52.7 (1.41)	55.0 (1.57)	38.2 (4.41)	54.2 (11.69)	— (†)	52.8 (0.81)	55.5 (0.90)	38.0 (2.50)	46.7 (6.16)	— (†)	17.5 (2.66)	‡ (†)	— (†)
1984	55.2 (1.39)	59.0 (1.57)	39.8 (4.21)	44.3 (10.00)	— (†)	55.1 (0.82)	57.9 (0.92)	39.9 (2.58)	49.3 (6.38)	— (†)	18.0 (2.74)	‡ (†)	— (†)

Figure 0.2. from , National Center for Education Statistics, Department of Education, table 302.20. Percentage of recent high school completers enrolled in two- and four-year colleges, by race/ethnicity: 1960 through 2015. Prepared: July 2016. Source: https://nces.ed.gov/programs/digest/d17/tables/dt17_302.20.asp

during this period helped generate a foundational event in American history: the birth of the modern open-admissions community college and the beginning of what would become the eventual democratization of our system of higher education (Boggs 2011; Lavin, Alba, Silberstein 1981; Pickett 1998; see also Anyon 1980; Armstrong and Hamilton 2013; Calhoon-Dillahunt 2018; Karabel 2005).

TEACHER-SCHOLAR-ACTIVIST

> *It's amazing how raw this is for me, because . . . there were so many people, when I was a high school dropout, or I was a teenage mom, or I was a community college student, who had just given up on me and written me off. And I tell you, we can't write people off. We can't decide that they're* done. *What we have to do is figure*

> *out how to put them back on track, and get them in the pipeline, and on the road to success and that road is going to look different for everybody. There are different ways of doing and being.*
>
> —Rep. Jahana Hayes (D-CT)[2]

Access to higher education at two-year colleges continues to be a contested, high-stakes civil rights and social justice issue today. A select list of notable recent developments in this regard would include the following:

- Florida's Senate Bill 1720 in 2013 (Hassel et al. 2015)
- Connecticut's PA 12–40 legislation in 2014 (Sullivan 2015a)
- Wisconsin's higher education restructuring, which began in 2017 (Hassell 2018; Kaufman 2018; Lafer 2017, 44–77)
- Growing impatience with two-year college success and graduation rates among legislators and politicians (Attewell et al. 2006; Flores 2011; Bailey, Jaggers, and Jenkins 2015; Schnee 2014; Schnee and Shakoor 2017; see also Sternglass 1997)
- Proposals to move to a performance-funding model for community colleges that link government funding to community college completion rates (Bailey, Jaggars, and Jenkins 2015; Fain 2018)
- Controversies about assessment practices that can imperil access to higher education, especially for nontraditional students, in a variety of ways (Belfield and Crosta 2012; Belfield 2014; Hassel and Giordano 2011; Hassel and Giordano 2015; Klausman et al. 2016; Scott-Clayton 2012)
- State legislatures systematically disinvesting in higher education across the nation (Mitchell et al. 2018)
- Cuts to and reformulations of financial aid formulas and eligibility requirements
- The federal government working with an outdated assessment model to measure the effectiveness of open admissions institutions. The Integrated Postsecondary Education Data System (United States 2020), uses the following metrics to measure the effectiveness of community colleges: first time, full-time; 3 years to complete; graduation (United States). These metrics are obviously adapted from a traditional, four-year residential model. The most current data using IPEDS calculates student "success" at community colleges at 25% (American 2020). Using the Voluntary Framework of Accountability (American 2012)—a system developed by community college professionals which measures success for all entering students, provides *six years to completion,* and tracks *nine separate outcomes*—calculates student success at 59% (American 2020). As the authors of *The Voluntary Framework of Accountability: Developing Measures of Community College Effectiveness and Outcomes* (2012) note, "traditional measures address only a fraction of the ways students succeed in community colleges" (5).

All of this emphatically affirms that politics, ideology, economics, and history continue to play a decisive role in the lives of English teachers at the two-year college—as they always have, of course, and as they undoubtedly always will (Said 1996; Sen 1999). Although this volume focuses on what teachers do inside the classroom, it has become increasingly clear that teachers at the two-year college must also be active outside the classroom as well (Sullivan 2015b). In fact, the work teachers do *outside* the classroom may be at least as important for their students and institutions as the work they do *inside* the classroom (Toth, Sullivan, and Calhoon-Dillahunt 2019, 405; Lee and Kahn 2020).

New teachers of writing at all levels of instruction, and especially those teaching at the two-year college, are entering a complex, highly politicized, and often contentious professional environment (Bousquet 2008; Giroux 2014; Newfield 2011, 2016). It is imperative that new English faculty members—even if they teach at four-year institutions (Calhoon-Dillahunt et al. 2017)—become knowledgeable about the history of the community college and the many crucially important issues related to open-admissions institutions currently being debated at academic conferences, in the pages of professional journals, and in state legislatures. In response to these pressing political and economic conditions, a number of scholars have advocated that English teachers at two-year colleges position themselves as teacher-scholar-*activists*. This is scholarship that all new two-year college English teachers should be familiar with.[3]

Christopher Mullin, in a policy brief written for the American Association of Community Colleges, sums up the current situation this way: "In policy conversations, especially those concerned with policies related to access and choice, there is a silent movement to redirect educational opportunity to 'deserving' students" (2012a, 4). Of course, most community college professionals believe that *all* students are deserving, no matter how unimpressive their placement scores may be or how modest their high school transcripts are. Given the right kinds of support and opportunity, most community college teachers believe that *all* students are capable of great things—and, of course, we see this kind of achievement and transformation enacted every day in our classrooms.

A recent special issue of *Teaching English at the Two-Year College* devoted to academic freedom provides an important overview of these political and economic complexities, all of which have profound implications for anyone teaching English at the two-year college (Lynch-Biniek and Hassel 2018). Mike Rose's book *Back to School* (2012) also examines the many complex, often hidden dynamics at play in the lives of individual community college students and adult learners attending adult education programs. Rose's book helps us understand what is at stake with open-admissions policies and what can potentially be lost when access to higher education is restricted or compromised.

An important new social justice organization—the Hope Center for College, Community, and Justice—has recently been founded by a group of community leaders, scholars, and researchers to address these issues. This action research and advocacy group builds on Sara Goldrick-Rab's research on food and housing insecurity on college campuses (Goldrick-Rab 2016; Goldrick-Rab et al. 2016). This group's work focuses on conditions outside of the college classroom that affect student achievement: "Too many students leave college without credentials because life, logistics, and a lack of money got in the way" (Hope 2019). The Hope Center agenda includes addressing food and housing insecurity and revising financial aid formulas. This organization is also engaged in public relations work, seeking to modernize the public perception of college students and to reshape higher education policy and practice. Their website is located here: https://hope4college.com.

My home institution, Manchester Community College in Manchester, Connecticut, recently opened a food pantry on campus, and we were astonished to discover how many of our students used this support service (Moore 2019; Goldrick-Rab, Cady, and Coca 2018). When finances are tight—as they often are for a significant cohort of two-year college students—many students are forced to go hungry in order to make ends meet (Goldrick-Rab et al. 2018). Sara Goldrick-Rab's work has helped us understand how these powerful, often invisible economic conditions shape students' lives and learning. These material conditions complicate in profound ways any simplistic numbers-driven understanding of retention and completion rates at two-year colleges (see Sullivan 2017a, 205–240 and 323–340).

All of this work suggests that there are powerful, structural, and systemic conditions outside the classroom that affect student performance, attendance, persistence, and success. Some of these are economic, of course (Case and Deaton 2020; Chetty et al. 2016; Goldrick-Rab 2016; Kalleberg 2011; Lafer 2017; Mullin 2012b; Mullin 2017; Piketty 2014, 2020; Rose 2012; Sen 1999; Sullivan 2017a). Others are related to race and racism, along with other forms of oppression like misogyny, homophobia, and xenophobia (Alexander 2012; Bateman, Katznelson, and Lapinski 2018; Diangelo 2018; Dunbar-Ortiz 2015; Ginwright 2015; Hung et al. 2019; Inoue 2015, 2019a; Kendi 2016; Rothstein 2004; Treuer 2019; Waite 2017; Whitman 2017). Scholars using critical race theory

(CRT) have documented the many ways that racism (and other forms of oppression) affect academic achievement in America (Crenshaw et al. 1996; Delgado and Stefancic 2017; Ladson-Billings 1998). This is work all two-year college teachers must be familiar with.

Recent work in our discipline has brought attention to the role that positionality, privilege, identity formation, and racism play in student engagement, achievement, persistence, and learning. This work includes Asao Inoue's book *Antiracist Writing Assessment Ecologies: Teaching and Assessing Writing for a Socially Just Future* (2015) and his 2019 CCCC keynote address (2019a) and landmark articles in *Teaching English in the Two-Year College* (*TETYC*) including "The Risky Business of Engaging Racial Equity in Writing Instruction: A Tragedy in Five Acts" by Taiyon J. Coleman, Renee DeLong, Kathleen Sheerin DeVore, Shannon Gibney, and Michael C. Kuhne (2016, reprinted in this volume); Mara Lee Grayson's "Race Talk in the Composition Classroom: Narrative Song Lyrics as Texts for Racial Literacy" (2017); and "A Critical Race Analysis of Transition-Level Writing Curriculum to Support the Racially Diverse Two-Year College" by Jamila Kareem (2019). Scholarship informed by CRT candidly addresses the long history of racism and violence in America and seeks to examine the many ways that racism—along with other forms of physical and psychological violence—continues to silence, marginalize, and disadvantage students in academic settings.

One of the core principles of CRT is that "racism is ordinary, not aberrational—'normal science,' the usual way society does business, the common, everyday experience of most people of color in this country" (Delgado and Stefancic 2017, 8). Richard Rothstein's (2017) book *The Color of Law: A Forgotten History of How Our Government Segregated America* provides one powerful example of this lethal condition, documenting the many ways that federal, state, and local governments helped segregate American neighborhoods beginning in the 1930s. As Rothstein notes, "Today's residential segregation in the North, South, Midwest, and West is not the unintended consequence of individual choices and of otherwise well-meaning law or regulation but of unhidden public policy that explicitly segregated every metropolitan area in the United States" (2017, viii). These segregated neighborhoods—along with the segregated school systems that accompany them—continue to plague us today and play a key role in student academic achievement and success. CRT scholars note that race is often an "absent presence" in discussions of educational achievement (Prendergast 1998). Despite this absence, race and racism nonetheless play a central role in student learning and persistence in community college classrooms across America.

CRT also complicates theoretical models for teaching and encouraging resilience (Masten 2015) and "grit" (Duckworth 2016). Dispositional characteristics like persistence and perseverance are essential for success in any endeavor, of course. But we must also acknowledge the role that social conditions like poverty, economic inequality, and racism play in our understanding of these concepts (McGee and Stovall 2015; Rose 2018; Schreiner 2017; see also Kidd, Palmeria, and Aslinab 2013; Mullainathan and Shafir 2014). A focus on grit as a key to student success overlooks the role that privilege plays in individual lives. It also draws attention away from structural inequities that impact the lives of many students in our classrooms. McGee and Stovall (2015) urge us to build theoretical models of resiliency and grit that also account for the "*vulnerability* of people of color who are burdened by unique and often underexamined levels of risk" and exposure to trauma (492). While we must always help promote agency, self-determination, self-authorship (Baxter Magolda 2004), self-efficacy (Bandura 1997), and positive identity development (Ginwright 2010), we must also acknowledge "the systematic inequality and interlocking systems of oppression" that affect student learning on our campuses as well (Velez and Spencer 2018, 75; see also Kareem 2018). One way we can begin countering these oppressive systems is to develop *culturally sustaining pedagogies* in our classrooms and campuses (Aronson and Laughter 2016; Ladson-Billings 1995, 1998). As Paris and Alim (2017) note in the introduction to their book *Culturally Sustaining Pedagogies* the key question for educators today is not "What is the purpose of schooling?" but, rather, "What is the purpose of schooling *in pluralistic societies?*" (1). Culturally sustaining pedagogies seek to foster and sustain "linguistic, literate, and cultural pluralism" in all educational spaces (Paris and Alim 2017, 1).

As Thomas Piketty (2020) notes, "Every human society must justify its inequalities: unless reasons for them are found, the whole political and social edifice stands in danger of collapse. Every epoch therefore develops a range of contradictory discourses and ideologies for the purpose of legitimizing the inequality that already exists or that people believe should exist" (1). These explanations are ideologically driven, of course, and the current narrative explaining inequality in America is built around a deified business model that celebrates freedom, choice, and the opportunities the marketplace provides (Friedman 1990; Hayek 2007, 2011). In this theoretical model, the market is self-sustaining and self-correcting, and success or failure is explained by luck, choice, and personal responsibility. This model does not take into account, however, systemic oppression and unequal opportunity, and thus conceals from view very powerful forces shaping the lives of students and citizens (Bourdieu 2010; Bourdieu and Passeron 2000; Hung et al. 2019; Sen 1999; Sullivan 2017a). One of the primary goals of our pedagogy, our committee work, and our engagement off campus—in everything we do, in fact, as citizens and teachers—must be to dismantle these systems of oppression.

EDUCATION THAT LIBERATES AND ENNOBLES

A great nation is a compassionate nation.
—Martin Luther King Jr.

The documented record of the modern community college in the service of the public good can only be regarded as inspiring—and revolutionary. Since 1947, millions of students have graduated from two-year colleges who never would have had the opportunity to attend college without them (Attewell and Lavin 2007; Attewell et al. 2006). For the academic year 2017–2018, for example, 852,504 associate's degrees were awarded nationwide, along with 579,822 certificates (American Association of Community Colleges 2020). Since 1947, the modern two-year college has actively helped disrupt entrenched social inequalities and subvert conditions that reproduce very old and pernicious patterns of privilege and privation (Attewell and Lavin 2007; Bourdieu and Passeron 2000; Sullivan 2017a; Cahalan et al. 2018). The modern two-year college is founded on the transformative power of personal agency (Bandura 1997), self-authorship (Baxter Magolda 2004), and the belief in new beginnings, fresh starts, and second and third chances (Rose 2012). It is an institution built on the understanding that anything is possible for individual students, no matter where they may come from or what their past might seem to predict. As the many stories about students shared by teachers and by student contributors themselves in this volume suggest, given the right kind of support and opportunity, students who attend two-year colleges create futures for themselves that are, to borrow a phrase from Russian Nobel Laureate Svetlana Alexievich (n.d.), "impossible to imagine or invent" (Sullivan 2017a, 15–142; Sullivan 2019).

The Truman Commission emphasizes this point on virtually every page of its report, but perhaps nowhere more memorably than here:

> American colleges and universities must envision a much larger role for higher education in the national life. They can no longer consider themselves merely the instrument for producing an intellectual elite; they must become the means by which every citizen, youth, and adult is enabled and encouraged to carry his education, formal and informal, as far as his native capacities permit.

> This conception is the inevitable consequence of the democratic faith; universal education is indispensable to the full and living realization of the democratic ideal. No society can long remain free unless its members are freemen, and men are not free where ignorance prevails. No more in mind than in body can this Nation or any endure half slave, half free. Education that liberates and ennobles must be made equally available to all. Justice to the individual demands this; the safety and progress of the Nation depend upon it. America cannot afford to let any of its potential human resources go undiscovered and undeveloped. (President's 1947, 101)

Readers can see this revolutionary work firsthand in this book as it is realized today in English classrooms across the nation. This work is perhaps best understood, following the Truman Commission, as liberating and ennobling. It is devoted to the foundational belief in human dignity and potential, and to James Baldwin's core assertion about the luminous potential that resides in us all: "I am what time, circumstance, history, have made of me, certainly, but I am, also, much more than that. So are we all" (1998, 810). The modern open-admissions two-year college is devoted to precisely this proposition.

DEMOCRACY IN ACTION

> *The classroom remains the most radical space of possibility in the academy.*
>
> —bell hooks

One strength of this book is the great diversity of students acknowledged and represented. By design and necessity, this diversity informs in profound ways the teaching practices described here. We live in a vibrant, complex, transnational, translingual era—a "highly plural and interdependent world," in the words of philosopher Martha Nussbaum (1997, 299; see also Young 2009; hooks 2003; Canagarajah 2013; Paris and Alim 2017). For this reason, the perspectives and experiences of two-year college English teachers are particularly valuable for our profession. The modern open-admissions two-year college is one of the most dynamically diverse public institutions in America. The two-year college currently enrolls roughly half of all students of color (Native American, Hispanic, African American, and Asian/Pacific Islanders), 39 percent of all first-generation college students, along with large numbers of single parents, veterans, multilingual and Generation 1.5 students, immigrants, students with disabilities, and students with prior bachelor's degrees (American Association of Community Colleges 2020). These institutions have become key sites where classist, racist, and sexist structures in America are challenged and disrupted. As Nell Ann Pickett famously observed, community colleges are "democracy in action" (1998, 98).

One essential site on campus where this important work is accomplished is in gateway English classes—first-year composition classes and developmental reading and writing courses. There is much we can learn, therefore, from the teachers featured in this book, not only about teaching reading and writing, but also about promoting diversity, access, and social justice in our profession (Freire 1994; Tinberg 1997; Shaughnessy 1979; Sternglass 1997; Goldblatt 2007; Steele 2010; Stuber 2011).

The intended audience for this book is anyone teaching reading and writing, grades 6–14. I have endeavored to make this volume as pragmatic and classroom-centered as possible and to provide a variety of accessible entry points for readers. When contributors discuss theory and scholarship, I have encouraged them to talk about how they translate this theory into practice in their classrooms (Larson 2018; Reynolds 2005; Tinberg 1997).

Perhaps most importantly, there is a great deal of hope, optimism, and joy expressed by our contributors about the work they do and the students they work with. This enthusiasm for teaching at the two-year college is often unacknowledged in many public and scholarly discussions of open-admissions institutions, so it is a very real pleasure to document—and to submit for the public record—evidence of the passion and hope that courses through so much of what English teachers bring to their work as educators at the two-year college. Teachers at all levels of instruction can draw inspiration from this commitment to potential and possibility (Duncan-Andrade 2009; Dweck 2007; Schnee and Shakoor 2017).

Secondary school teachers can draw insight and inspiration from the teachers featured in this book because our contributors all teach classes that most high school graduates will take when they get to college (Hansen and Farris 2010; Sullivan and Tinberg 2006). This book therefore offers high school teachers an extraordinary opportunity to learn firsthand about the kind of work their students will be doing in college. Since institutional alignment and college readiness continue to be urgent professional concerns, secondary English teachers can use this book as a kind of practical guide to college readiness.[4] This book can help further our understanding of the best ways to help high school students prepare for college—and thrive once they get there.

This book is also designed, of course, for teachers of English at two-year colleges. This includes colleagues new to the profession or in graduate school training to be English teachers, as well as seasoned veterans looking for new ideas, inspiration, and sources for professional renewal and growth. There is a rich abundance of practical advice in these pages, including writing assignments and classroom activities that can be put to use in classrooms on Monday morning when you meet your classes. Since roughly half of all basic writing and first-year composition classes are now taught at two-year colleges by two-year college writing teachers (Hassel and Giordano 2013), the need for this kind of book—and the sharing of pragmatic classroom advice, experience, and wisdom—is obvious.

We also bear witness in these pages to examples of two-year college teachers finding ways to stay current with scholarship and to stay actively engaged with the discipline despite busy teaching schedules and heavy workloads. It is my hope that these examples of professional engagement will inspire others to find ways to become involved with scholarship, research, and disciplinary knowledge-making. This work has the potential to enrich an educator's teaching practice in profound ways, as it has for me and for all of the teachers featured here. This book is also designed to be a companion volume to *Teaching Composition at the Two-Year College*, a book in Bedford/St. Martin's Professional Resources Series (Sullivan and Toth 2016). Both books are designed to provide professional development opportunities for two-year college faculty.

There is also an urgent need for a book like this in graduate schools preparing future teachers of English. The complex nature of this need is articulated perhaps most eloquently in the recent "TYCA Guidelines for Preparing Teachers of English in the Two-Year College" (Calhoon-Dillahunt et al. 2017; see also Jensen and Toth 2017; Toth and Jensen 2017; Lovas 2002). This document calls for individuals who design graduate programs for training writing teachers and others who work as teachers, scholars, and researchers at four-year institutions to make the two-year college visible:

> Given the growth of community colleges, both in terms of enrollment and prominence in national education policy, now is the time to call on graduate programs to take seriously the work of educating future faculty for the full range of institutional contexts in which they might teach. The millions of students whose first experiences with postsecondary writing are in two-year college English classrooms deserve to learn with engaged professionals who employ context-appropriate best practices in our field. (Calhoon-Dillahunt et al. 2017, 550)

This book is designed to directly address this urgent need.

Teachers of writing at four-year institutions can draw wisdom and inspiration from this book as well because it features some of the most accomplished, reflective, and highly successful teacher-scholar-activists in our field. Regardless of where we may teach, all of us have something we can learn from the extraordinary educators featured in these pages.

If we believe, following Ken Bain, that the creation of a successful classroom learning environment is "an important and serious intellectual (or artistic) act," and perhaps even "a kind of scholarship" (2004, 49), then that understanding is certainly realized in important ways by the teachers featured here. This book has been designed to be a source of inspiration and hope to English teachers at all levels of instruction as they go about their daily work in the classroom.

CELEBRATION

> *Teaching is the greatest act of optimism.*
> —Colleen Wilcox

A book like this can be assembled in many different ways. Nonetheless, and to offer readers full transparency, once I had the original idea for this book and began thinking about who to invite to contribute, the list of contributors essentially assembled itself. Given how well-known most of these individuals are, how comprehensively they have demonstrated their commitment to the craft of teaching, and how actively involved they have been as scholars and researchers, our list of contributors represents a consensus group of key disciplinary leaders in our profession today. Each contributor embodies the aspirational ideal of the two-year college teacher-scholar-activist. Each contributor is also committed to the profoundly transformative role that education can play in students' lives. Each contributor has also embraced the inescapably political nature of all literacy work.

The inspiration for this volume comes from a book I have long admired: Richard Straub and Ronald Lunsford's *12 Readers Reading* (1995). Straub and Lunsford's book features disciplinary leaders talking collaboratively, collegially, and candidly about teaching and writing. A recent companion volume to Straub and Lunsford's book, *First-Year Composition: From Theory to Practice* (2014) edited by Deborah Coxwell-Teague and Ronald Lunsford, inspired me to assemble a two-year college version of these books.

Both Straub and Lunsford's book and Coxwell-Teague and Lunsford's volume feature well-known compositionists and scholars. I have adopted a modified version of this model. It is a great honor to include work in this book featuring some of the most engaged, innovative, highly respected two-year college teachers currently at work today. This group includes Peter Adams, Jeff Andelora, Helane Adams Androne, Taiyon J. Coleman, Renee DeLong, Kathleen Sheerin DeVore, Shannon Gibney, Joanne Baird Giordano, Holly Hassel, Jeff Klausman, Michael C. Kuhne, Hope Parisi, and Howard Tinberg. Holly is the current editor of *Teaching English at the Two-Year College*, and Hope is the current co-editor of *The Journal of Basic Writing*. Readers will be spending time in distinguished company, indeed, and they will have the chance to visit the classrooms of accomplished professionals in our field.

Readers will also have the opportunity to consider Taiyon J. Coleman, Renee DeLong, Kathleen Sheerin DeVore, Shannon Gibney, and Michael C. Kuhne's landmark essay on race and diversity at the two-year college, "The Risky Business of Engaging Racial Equity in Writing Instruction: A Tragedy in Five Acts." This essay was originally published in *Teaching English at the Two-Year College* (*TETYC*) and won the 2017 Mark Reynolds Prize from *TETYC*. This essay is essential reading for anyone teaching at a two-year college. Kathleen Sheerin DeVore has written a new postscript for this volume—updating the social justice work this group of educators has been pursuing and describing the reception this essay received at their home institution and across the nation.

I have also included two chapters written by teachers working with the Accelerated Learning Program (ALP), a corequisite model for teaching developmental reading and writing developed by Peter Adams and his colleagues at the Community College of Baltimore County (CCBC). This approach to developmental education, which mainstreams basic writing students with a peer cohort of FYC students, is one of the most important curricular innovations in the history of developmental education. The ALP model has been adopted by more than three hundred schools around the country, and to date, eight states have launched wide-scale adoptions of co-requisite models like ALP: Arkansas, California, Colorado, Connecticut, Indiana, Michigan, Texas, and West Virginia (Adams et al. 2009; "ALP" 2019; Cho et al. 2012). Additionally, California's recent AB 705 legislation, which took effect January 1, 2018, has mandated a corequisite model like ALP as the default developmental option in California (California 2018). Under this legislation, the burden of proof now shifts to colleges to prove that students should *not* be in a transfer-level course.

One of the founders of this curricular model, Peter Adams, has written a chapter for us. Another chapter is provided by Jamey Gallagher, who Peter recommended as both an accomplished teacher and an individual who is deeply knowledgeable about developments with ALP at CCBC and across the nation. ALP is poised to become the new "normal" in developmental education nationwide and these chapters can serve as a resource for teachers looking to understand how this approach works and how to implement ALP in their classrooms and on their campuses. Readers who wish to learn more about ALP and Peter's approach to teaching reading and writing can consult his new textbook, *The Hub: A Place for Reading and Writing* (2020).

To add additional perspective, I have included chapters authored by two newer voices in the field. Brett Griffiths is a recent PhD, active with NCTE's Two-Year College English Association (TYCA), and a member of TYCA's Research Committee (I am also a member of this committee). In addition to 16 years of experience teaching college-level writing and a PhD in English and Education, Brett draws on previous professional experience as a teacher and scholar, including eight years working as a crisis intervention specialist. Brett currently directs The Reading and Writing Studios at Macomb Community College, a large community college located north of Detroit. Her chapter advocates for compassion in pedagogy as a means toward fostering student learning and growth.

Darin Jensen has also been teaching for many years at a variety of institutions. He has taught in high schools, as a Teaching Assistant, as an ESL instructor, and as an English teacher. He is, he suggests, a "well-travelled nomad teacher." Like Brett, Darin is a recent PhD, active with TYCA, and already widely published. Until very recently, Darin was a part-time instructor, and I asked him to share with us the challenges of teaching from a non-tenure track position. His chapter provides readers with a candid, often humorous, no-holds-barred overview of the field of two-year college teaching from the perspective of an adjunct professor—an enterprise that is complex, daunting, and inspiring all at the same time. Readers will be happy to learn that Darin has been hired full-time and is now teaching at Des Moines Area Community College in Iowa.

To add variety, and to provide opportunities for knowledge building that do not rely exclusively on single-authored or coauthored academic essays, I have also included a number of interviews in this book—with Helane Adams Androne, Jeff Andelora, and Howard Tinberg. I have always admired the interview Howard conducted with Ira Shor (Tinberg 1999a, 1999b), and I have had an interest in helping liberate academic writing from the restrictive single model we currently employ almost exclusively—the seven-thousand-word thesis-driven essay with citations (Sullivan 2014, 2015c; Smith 2019a, 2019b). I admire how collaborative, dialogic, and fluid Howard's interview with Ira is, and I have sought to capture some of that spirit in the interviews featured here. There are many ways to produce knowledge, and it is my hope that readers will find that these interviews offer an engaging and accessible way to talk about teaching and learning.

COMMUNITY COLLEGE STUDENTS

Listening with an open heart, we are able to keep compassion alive.
—Thich Nhat Hanh

Another unique feature of this book is that readers get to hear directly from two-year college students themselves about effective teaching. I invited a number of two-year college students (mostly from my home institution, Manchester Community College in Manchester, Connecticut) to share their thoughts about effective teaching strategies at the two-year college. Readers will find these student-authored chapters distributed throughout the book. By including student perspectives, I am seeking to honor calls by Susanmarie Harrington, Wendy Bishop, bell hooks, Alison Cook-Sather, Cornelius Minor, Django Paris, and H. Samy Alim, and others for scholarship that is, to use Bishop's phrase, "student-present" (1993, 199). This type of research, Harrington suggests, devotes "serious attention to student voices" (1999, 96–97). In *We Got This.: Equity, Access, and the Quest to Be Who Our Students Need Us to Be*, Cornelius Minor suggests that great teaching begins with *listening*: "authentic listening and the actions that result from it" are "the most radical of all teacher behaviors" (2018, 15; see also 9–24, 77–100). Culturally sustaining pedagogies are built around the core belief in the transformative power of listening to students, in all their great variety (Paris and Alim 2017). These student-authored chapters have precisely this focus. In this way, following Sheryl Fontaine and Susan Hunter (1993), we are helping students "write themselves into the story" of teaching and learning at the two-year college.

As a teacher of English myself, I continue to be astonished by how much I learn from my students—about courage, strength, and hope, about living in the world, and about so many other things as well. Although I have been teaching at a community college for many years now, I continue to be deeply thankful for these gifts. Teaching at a two-year college is a humbling, inspiring, and rewarding enterprise. I encourage teachers at all levels of instruction to welcome the profound gifts we receive from our students—opportunities for learning, growth, and personal transformation.

Readers interested in learning more about community college students are invited to visit the Community College Success Stories Project, an archive of essays written by community college students about their journeys to and from open-admissions institutions. This project is designed to help students write themselves into the story of the two-year college. I designed and created this website, which officially launched in 2018, with the support of a 2016 Conference on College Composition and Communication (CCCC) Research Award Grant from the National Council of Teachers of English (NCTE). The goal of the Community College Success Stories Project is to build an archive of thousands of stories written by community college students that can be searched and accessed by new and returning community college students looking for inspiration and direction, and by scholars, researchers, and teachers interested in learning more about students who attend open-admissions institutions. The homepage for the project is here: https://www.communitycollegesuccessstories.org/. This project privileges writing by community college students themselves, and therefore provides a unique, personal, and rare glimpse into the kinds of lives being lived right now by students at two-year colleges in America. The database is fully searchable, so individuals interested in learning more about community college students can personalize their search depending on their needs and interests. This site has the potential to be a very valuable resource for teachers new to the two-year college and can supplement the contents of this book in productive ways. I cordially invite teachers to help strengthen this archive by encouraging their own students to submit essays for this project.

Another unique feature of this book is the photo essay documenting everyday campus life at the two-year college produced by Dan Long, my colleague at Manchester Community College. These photos were all taken at MCC, and they are dispersed throughout the book at the beginning of most chapters. These photos document the experience of community college students in all its vitality and variety. We see individuals—most of whom are community college students—baking bread, playing the piano, browsing through books at the library, working on the wheel in a ceramics class, studying, strolling to class, tending to plants at MCC's community garden, and graduating. We even have a photo of fresh produce taken at MCC's farmer's market. Our goal with these photos, as with this book in general, is to help readers see beyond reductive caricatures and to understand the two-year college in fresh new ways—as a site devoted to agency, personal transformation, and equality of opportunity. These images appear in black and white in the print edition of the book and in full color in the electronic version.

AN ABUNDANCE OF RICHES

> *I tell my students, "When you get these jobs that you have been so brilliantly trained for, just remember that your real job is that if you are free, you need to free somebody else. If you have some power, then your job is to empower somebody else."*
> —Toni Morrison

Part I of this book is designed to provide readers with a general introduction to teaching English at the two-year college. It features Darin Jensen's essay about the joys and challenges of teaching at a two-year college as an adjunct professor along with my interview with Helane Adams Androne (Androne 2014; Androne 2016). These chapters are followed by our first two student contributors, Bridgette Stepule and Lydia Sekscenski, who offer advice to teachers at the two-year college about effective teaching. One of the reasons we begin the book with Darin's essay is because he offers readers a candid, heartfelt introduction to teaching at the two-year college, but also because most writing courses across the nation are now taught by adjunct faculty at both two- and four-year institutions. These teachers are the new teaching majority (Kezar and Maxey 2014a; Kezar and Maxey 2014b; Klausman 2018; see also Kalleberg 2011; Lafer 2017). By beginning the book with Darin's essay, I seek to honor—and enact a form of solidarity with—our part-time colleagues. I also seek to publicly acknowledge the important—but underappreciated and certainly undercompensated—work of our adjunct faculty.

Part II of the book focuses on two vitally important aspects of teaching at the two-year college—teaching with compassion and teaching with scholarship and theory (see Bain 2004). This chapter includes Brett Griffiths's essay about the transformative power of empathy and compassion in the classroom and in writing centers, and Jeff Klausman's essay about the essential role that theory and scholarship play in his pedagogy and teaching practice. These essays are followed by my interview with Jeff Andelora, who has combined compassion and theory in his own teaching practice in inspiring ways. This interview is followed by two more student perspectives, written by Darlene Pierpont and Kevin Rodriguez, which address compassion and theory.

Part III of the book is devoted to examining equity and social justice at the two-year college. This section includes Holly Hassel's essay about social justice and open-admissions institutions and Hope Parisi's essay about *inversive teaching*, which invites teachers at the two-year college to think in innovative new ways about *presence* and *absence* in the classroom. At its core, inversive teaching is about accommodating for the disparate impacts of racialized educations, K–12, and those leading from the range of challenges, obstacles, and obligations our diverse students face. Parisi suggests that the community college classroom must become the epitome for "making room." This section also features a student essay written by Lauren Sills that addresses issues of diversity, equity, and community. We conclude this section with Taiyon J. Coleman, Renee DeLong, Kathleen Sheerin DeVore, Shannon Gibney, and Michael C. Kuhne's essay about race, equity, and white institutional, pedagogical, and curricular heternomativity at the two-year college, "The Risky Business of Engaging Racial Equity in Writing Instruction: A Tragedy in Five Acts." Social and cultural identity positions have become an important issue in our discipline, in part because of this essay. Taiyon J. Coleman, Kathleen Sheerin DeVore, Shannon Gibney, Michael C. Kuhne, and Valérie Déus's new book on the subject of racial equity in the college writing classroom, *Working Toward Racial Equity in First-Year Composition: Six Perspectives* (2019) is essential reading for all teachers at the two-year college.

Part IV offers readers a group of essays devoted to developmental education. Writing teachers at two-year colleges are routinely called upon to teach basic reading and writing courses, and these chapters provide readers of the book with a kind of professional summit meeting on developmental curriculum. Readers will be learning from a group of experienced, accomplished developmental educators—Jamey Gallagher, Joanne Baird Giordano, and Peter Adams. The approaches to teaching developmental reading and writing in these chapters reflect the most current scholarly advances in the field today. Included with these essays is an important student-authored chapter written by a former developmental student, Jamil Shakoor, who began his academic career at Kingsborough Community College, City University of New York (CUNY), in Brooklyn, New York, as a developmental student in 2008. Jamil has very positive things to say about developmental education and what developmental courses have meant to him. Jamil has since earned a bachelor's degree in psychology from Queens College, CUNY. He has also coauthored a scholarly essay about his experience as a developmental writing student with his former teacher, Emily Schnee, an English professor at Kingsborough Community College in (Schnee and Shakoor 2017).

The need for professional development material like this related to developmental education is urgent, especially in graduate school. Peter Adams notes in his chapter that as he has been visiting campuses around the nation as a consultant for the Accelerated Learning Program, he has asked faculty and staff to respond to a variety of survey questions before he meets with them to discuss the ALP model. Thus far, he has surveyed 361 basic writing faculty teaching at forty different institutions. The most significant question on his survey has turned out to be this: "Which of the following best describes your graduate preparation to teach basic writing?" Of the 343 English faculty who have responded to this question, 267, or 78 percent, had taken *no* courses in their graduate programs to prepare them to teach basic writing (see also Jensen and Ely 2017). It is my hope that the section in this book focusing on developmental education will provide important professional development opportunities for those new to basic reading and writing and those unfamiliar with the ALP model.

Part V, which serves as the conclusion for the book, features a deeply heartfelt "call out" to English teachers by MCC student Leah McNeir along with an interview with Howard Tinberg, who has been an inspiration and role model for many of us who teach English at two-year colleges. It is an honor to have Howard providing the final words in this volume.

CONCLUSION

> *Democracy has to be born anew every generation, and education is its midwife.*
> —John Dewey

This book celebrates the joys of teaching at the two-year college. It is my hope that readers will feel the same sense of gratitude, honor, and hopefulness that I feel about my job. Teaching English at the two-year college is a grand, high-stakes enterprise—with profound implications for the health and vitality of our democracy. The American community college is not just a convenient alternative to traditional four-year colleges. It is a social justice institution—where we enact our most foundational ideals about freedom, equity, and opportunity.

To members of our profession who don't routinely read academic books and journals—this book is for you. I have often heard colleagues admit, "I don't read scholarship." When I ask them why, I hear very good reasons: "It's inaccessible." "It's never written about students like mine." "It always seems to be written by theorists rather than actual classroom teachers." "It never contains anything I can actually use in my own classes on Monday morning when I meet my students." This is feedback that deserves careful attention (Toth and Sullivan 2016). Building on this wisdom, I have endeavored to address these concerns in this book by asking contributors to focus as much as possible on pragmatic classroom activities and assignments. It is my hope that these efforts will offer reluctant scholars an entry point, a way to begin engaging our ongoing scholarly conversation about the art of teaching English.

I dedicate this book to classroom English teachers across America, grades 6–14, especially to those of you who work at open-admissions two-year colleges. Thank you for all that you do.

NOTES

1. A note about terminology: the vast majority of public two-year colleges are open-admissions institutions. Most of these public two-year institutions refer to themselves as "community colleges." "Open-admissions institution," "community college," and "two-year college" have thus come to be used interchangeably, as they are throughout this book.
2. Quoted in Newfield "Crisis."
3. To avoid disrupting the flow of the narrative too much by including lengthy parenthetical citations, I am employing footnotes in a few places here to direct readers to additional readings and citations. For more discussion of the emerging teacher-scholar-activist professional identity model, please see Tinberg 1997; Lewiecki-Wilson and Sommers 1999; Lovas 2002; Andelora 2005; Andelora 2008; Kroll 2012; Andelora 2013; Sullivan 2015b; Griffiths 2017; Jensen, Sullivan, and Toth 2017; Suh and Jensen 2017; Sullivan 2017a; Sullivan 2017b; Warnke and Higgins 2018; Toth, Sullivan, and Calhoon-Dillahunt 2019; Jensen, Sullivan, and Toth 2019; see also Alford and Kroll 2001; Bousquet 2008; Adler-Kassner 2008; Adler-Kassner 2012; Ravitch 2013; Scott 2015; Welch and Scott 2016; Adler-Kassner 2017.
4. See Pope 2001; Blau 2003; Sullivan and Tinberg 2006; Sullivan 2009; Hansen and Farris 2010; Sullivan, Tinberg, and Blau 2010; Council 2011; Tinberg and Nadeau 2011; Smith 2012; Gale and Parker 2014; Ruecker 2015; Sullivan 2016; Smith 2017; Sullivan, Tinberg, and Blau 2017; Carillo 2018.

REFERENCES

Adams, Peter. 2020. *The Hub: A Place for Reading and Writing.* Boston: Bedford/St.Martin's.

Adams, Peter, Sarah Gearhart, Robert Miller, and Anne Roberts. 2009. "The Accelerated Learning Program: Throwing Open the Gates." *Journal of Basic Writing* 28 (2): 50–69.

Adler-Kassner, Linda. 2008. *The Activist WPA: Changing Stories about Writing and Writers.* Logan: Utah State University Press.

Adler-Kassner, Linda. 2012. "The Companies We Keep or the Companies We Would Like to Try to Keep: Strategies and Tactics in Challenging Times." *WPA: Writing Program Administration* 36 (1): 119–140.

Adler-Kassner, Linda. 2017. "Because Writing Is Never Just Writing: CCCC Chair's Address." *College Composition and Communication* 69 (2): 317–140.

Adler-Kassner, Linda, and Elizabeth Wardle, eds. 2015. *Naming What We Know: Threshold Concepts in Writing Studies.* Logan: Utah State University Press.

Alexander, Michelle. *The New Jim Crow: Mass Incarceration in the Age of Colorblindness.* New York: New Press, 2012.

Alexievich, Svetlana. n.d. "A Search for Eternal Man: In Lieu of Biography." *Voices from Big Utopia.* Accessed May 8, 2020. http://www.alexievich.info/indexEN.html.

Alford, Barry, and Keith Kroll, eds. 2001. *The Politics of Writing in the Two-Year College.* Portsmouth, NH: Boynton/Cook.

ALP (Accelerated Learning Program). 2019. *Accelerated Learning Program.* http://alp-deved.org/.

American Association of Community Colleges. 2012. *The Voluntary Framework of Accountability: Developing Measures of Community College Effectiveness and Outcomes.* Washington, DC: American Association of Community Colleges.

American Association of Community Colleges. 2020. "2020 Community College Fast Facts." American Association of Community Colleges. https://www.aacc.nche.edu/research-trends/fast-facts/.

Andelora, Jeffrey. 2005. "The Teacher/Scholar: Reconstructing Our Professional Identity in Two-Year Colleges." *Teaching English in the Two-Year College* 32 (3): 307–322.

Andelora, Jeffrey. 2008. "Forging a National Identity: TYCA and the Two-Year College Teacher-Scholar." *Teaching English in the Two-Year College* 35 (4): 350–362.

Andelora, Jeffrey. 2013. "Teacher/Scholar/Activist: A Response to Keith Kroll's 'The End of the Community College English Profession.'" *Teaching English in the Two-Year College* 40 (3): 302–307.

Androne, Helane Adams. 2014. *Multiethnic American Literature: Essays for Teaching Context and Culture.* Jefferson, NC: McFarland.

Androne, Helane Adams. 2016. *Ritual Structures in Chicana Fiction.* New York: Palgrave Macmillan.

Anyon, Jean. 1980. "Social Class and the Hidden Curriculum or Work." *The Journal of Education* 162 (1): 67–92.

Armstrong, Elizabeth A., and Laura T. Hamilton. 2013. *Paying for the Party: How College Maintains Inequality.* Cambridge, MA: Harvard University Press.

Aronson, Brittany, and Judson Laughter. 2016. "The Theory and Practice of Culturally Relevant Education: A Synthesis of Research Across Content Areas." *Review of Educational Research* 86 (1): 163–206.

Attewell, Paul, and David E. Lavin. 2007. *Passing the Torch: Does Higher Education for the Disadvantaged Pay Off Across the Generations?* New York: Russell Sage.

Attewell, Paul, David Lavin, Thurston Domina, and Tania Levey. 2006. "New Evidence on College Remediation." *The Journal of Higher Education* 77 (5): 886–924.

Bailey, Thomas R., Shanna Smith Jaggars, and Davis Jenkins. 2015. *Redesigning America's Community Colleges: A Clearer Path to Student Success.* Cambridge, MA: Harvard University Press.

Bain, Ken. 2004. *What the Best College Teachers Do.* Cambridge, MA: Harvard University Press.

Baldwin, James. 1998. "Introduction to Notes of a Native Son, 1984." *Collected Essays,* edited by Toni Morrison, 808–813. New York: Library of America.

Bandura, Albert. 1997. *Self-Efficacy: The Exercise of Control.* New York: W. H. Freeman.

Bateman, David, Ira Katznelson, and John S. Lapinski. 2018. *Southern Nation: Congress and White Supremacy after Reconstruction.* Princeton, NJ: Princeton University Press.

Baxter Magolda, Marcia B. 2004. *Making Their Own Way: Narratives for Transforming Higher Education to Promote Self-Development.* Sterling, VA: Stylus.

Belfield, Clive R. 2014. *Improving Assessment and Placement at Your College: A Tool for Institutional Researchers.* New York: Columbia University, Teachers College, Community College Research Center.

Belfield, Clive R., and Peter M. Crosta. 2012. *Predicting Success in College: The Importance of Placement Tests and High School Transcripts.* New York: Columbia University, Teachers College, Community College Research Center.

Bishop, Wendy. 1993. "Students' Stories and the Variable Gaze of Composition Research." In *Writing Ourselves into the Story: Unheard Voices from Composition Studies,* edited by Sheryl Fontaine and Susan Hunter, 197–214. Carbondale: Southern Illinois University Press.

Blau, Sheridan. 2003. "Performative Literacy: The Habits of Mind of Highly Literate Readers." *Voices from the Middle* 10 (3): 18–22.

Boggs, George R. 2011. "The American Community College: From Access to Success." *About Campus* 16 (2): 2–10. https://doi.org/10.1002/abc.20055.

Bourdieu, Pierre. 2010. "The Forms of Capital." In *Cultural Theory: An Anthology*, edited by Imre Szeman and Timothy Kaposy, translated by Richard Nice, 81–93. Malden. MA: Wiley-Blackwell.

Bourdieu, Pierre, and Jean-Claude Passeron. 2000. *Reproduction in Education, Society and Culture.* 2nd ed., translated by Richard Nice. Thousand Oaks, CA: Sage.

Bousquet, Marc. 2008. *How the University Works: Higher Education and the Low-Wage Nation.* New York: NYU Press.

Bowen, William, Martin Kurzweil, and Eugene Tobin. 2005. *Equity and Excellence in American Higher Education.* Charlottesville: University of Virginia Press.

Cahalan, Margaret, Laura W. Perna, Mike Yamashita, J. Wright, and Sureima Santillan. 2018. *2018 Indicators of Higher Education Equity in the United States: Historical Trend Report.* Washington, DC: The Pell Institute for the Study of Opportunity in Higher Education, Council for Opportunity in Education (COE), and Alliance for Higher Education and Democracy of the University of Pennsylvania (PennAHEAD).

California Community Colleges. 2018. "What Is AB 705?" State of California. http://pell institute.org/downloads/publications-Indicators_of_Higher_Education_Equity_in _the_US_2018_Historical_Trend_Report.pdf.

Calhoon-Dillahunt, Carolyn. 2018. "2018 CCCC Chair's Address: Returning to Our Roots: Creating Conditions and Capacity for Change." *College Composition and Communication* 70 (2): 273–293.

Calhoon-Dillahunt, Carolyn, Darin L. Jensen, Sarah Z. Johnson, Howard Tinberg, and Christie Toth. 2017. "TYCA Guidelines for Preparing Teachers of English in the Two-Year College." *College English* 79 (6): 550–560.

Canagarajah, Suresh. 2013. *Translingual Practice: Global Englishes and Cosmopolitan Relations.* New York: Routledge.

Carillo, Ellen C. 2018. Teaching Readers in Post-Truth America. Logan: Utah State University Press.

Case, Anne, and Angus Deaton. 2020. *Deaths of Despair and the Future of Capitalism.* Princeton: Princeton University Press.

Chetty, Raj, David Grusky, Maximilian Hell, Nathaniel Hendren, Robert Manduca, and Jimmy Narang. 2016. "The Fading American Dream: Trends in Absolute Income Mobility Since 1940." National Bureau of Economic Research, Working Paper 22910.

Cho, Sung-Woo, Elizabeth Kopko, Davis Jenkins, and Shanna Smith Jaggars. 2012. "New Evidence of Success for Community College Remedial English Students: Tracking the Outcomes of Students in the Accelerated Learning Program (ALP)." CCRC Working Paper no. 53.

Coleman, Taiyon J., Renee DeLong, Kathleen Sheerin DeVore, Shannon Gibney, and Michael C. Kuhne. 2016. "The Risky Business of Engaging Racial Equity in Writing Instruction: A Tragedy in Five Acts." *Teaching English in the Two-Year College* 43 (4): 347–370.

Cook-Sather, Alison. 2006. "Sound, Presence, and Power: 'Student Voice' in Educational Research and Reform." *Curriculum Inquiry* 36 (4): 359–390.

Cook-Sather, Alison, Catherine Bovill, and Peter Felten. 2014. *Engaging Students as Partners in Learning and Teaching: A Guide for Faculty.* San Francisco: Jossey-Bass.

Council of Writing Program Administrators, National Council of Teachers of English, National Writing Project. 2011. "Framework for Success in Postsecondary Writing." *WPA Council.* Accessed May 8, 2020. http://wpacouncil.org/files/framework-for-success -postsecondary-writing.pdf.

Coxwell-Teague, Deborah, and Ronald F. Lunsford, eds. 2014. *First-Year Composition: From Theory to Practice.* Anderson, SC: Parlor Press.

Crenshaw, Kimberle, Neil Gotanda, Gary Peller, and Kendall Thomas, eds. 1996. *Critical Race Theory: The Key Writings That Formed the Movement.* New York: New Press.

Delgado, Richard, and Jean Stefancic. 2017. *Critical Race Theory: An Introduction.* 3rd ed. New York: New York University Press.

DeLong, Renee, Taiyon J. Coleman, Kathleen Sheerin DeVore, Shannon Gibney, Michael C. Kuhne, and Valérie Déus. 2019. *Working Toward Racial Equity in First-Year Composition: Six Perspectives.* New York: Routledge.

Dewey, John. 1980. "The Need of an Industrial Education in an Industrial Democracy." *The Middle Works of John Dewey, 1899–1924.* Vol. 10, edited by Jo Ann Boydston, 137–143. Carbondale, IL: Southern Illinois University Press.

Duckworth, Angela. 2016. *Grit: The Power of Passion and Perseverance.* New York: Scribner.

Duncan, Greg J., and Richard J. Murnane, eds. 2011. *Whither Opportunity?: Rising Inequality, Schools, and Children's Life Chances.* New York: Russell Sage.

Duncan-Andrade, Jeffrey M. 2009. "Note to Educators: Hope Required When Growing Roses in Concrete." *Harvard Educational Review* 79 (2): 181–194.

Dweck, Carol. 2007. *Mindset: The New Psychology of Success.* New York: Ballantine.

Fain, Paul. June 12, 2018. "As California Goes?" *Inside Higher Ed.*

Flores, Roy. February 17, 2011. "False Hope," *Inside Higher Ed.*

Fontaine, Sheryl, and Susan Hunter. 1993. *Writing Ourselves Into the Story: Unheard Voices from Composition Studies.* Carbondale: Southern Illinois University Press.

Friedman, Milton, and Rose Friedman. 1990. *Free to Choose: A Personal Statement.* New York: Harvest.

Freire, Paulo. 1994. *Pedagogy of the Oppressed.* Revised 20th anniversary edition. New York: Continuum.

Gale, Trevor, and Stephen Parker. 2014. "Navigating Change: A Typology of Student Transition in Higher Education." *Studies in Higher Education* 39 (5): 734–753.

Ginwright, Shaun A. 2009. *Black Youth Rising: Activism and Radical Healing in Urban America.* New York: Teachers College Press.

Ginwright, Shaun A. 2015. *Hope and Healing in Urban Education.* New York: Routledge.

Giroux, Henry R. 2014. *Neoliberalism's War on Higher Education.* Chicago: Haymarket.

Goldblatt, Eli. 2007. *Because We Live Here: Sponsoring Literacy Beyond the College Curriculum.* New York: Hampton.

Goldin, Claudia, and Lawrence F. Katz. 2010. *The Race between Education and Technology.* Cambridge, MA: Belknap Press.

Goldrick-Rab, Sara. 2016. *Paying the Price: College Costs, Financial Aid, and the Betrayal of the American Dream.* Chicago: University of Chicago Press.

Goldrick-Rab, Sara, Robert Kelchen, Douglas N. Harris, and James Benson. 2016. "Reducing Income Inequality in Higher Education: Experimental Evidence on the Impact of Financial Aid on College Completion." *American Journal of Sociology* 121 (6): 1762–1817.

Goldrick-Rab, Sara, Clare Cady, and Vanessa Coca. 2018. *Campus Food Pantries: Insights from a National Survey.* Hope Center for College, Community and Justice. https://hope4college.com/wp-content/uploads/2018/10/2018-CUFBA-Report-web3.pdf.

Goldrick-Rab, Sara, Jed Richardson, J. Schneider, Clare Cady, and Daphne Hernandez. 2018. *Basic Needs Insecurity in Massachusetts Public Colleges and Universities.* Wisconsin HOPE Lab. https://hope4college.com/wp-content/uploads/2018/10/StillHungryMA-4-1.html.

Grayson, Mara Lee. 2017. "Race Talk in the Composition Classroom: Narrative Song Lyrics as Texts for Racial Literacy." *Teaching English in the Two-Year College* 45 (2): 47–68.

Griffiths, Brett. 2017. "Professional Autonomy and Teacher-Scholar-Activists in Two-Year Colleges: Preparing New Faculty to Think Institutionally." *Teaching English in the Two-Year College* 45 (1): 143–167.

Hansen, Kristine, and Christine R. Farris, eds. 2010. *College Credit for Writing in High School: The "Taking Care of" Business.* Urbana, IL: NCTE.

Harrington, Susanmarie. 1999. "The Representation of Basic Writers in Basic Writing Scholarship, or Who Is Quentin Pierce?" *Journal of Basic Writing* 18 (2): 91–107.

Hassel, Holly. April 19, 2018. "Reflections on Leaving Wisconsin, or Ghosting UW, Heartbreak Edition." *HollyJHassel* (blog), https://hollyjhassel.wordpress.com/2018/04/19/reflections-on-leaving-wisconsin-or-ghosting-uw-heartbreak-edition/.

Hassel, Holly, and Joanne Baird Giordano. 2011. "First-Year Composition Placement at Open-Admission, Two-Year Campuses: Changing Campus Culture, Institutional Practice, and Student Success." *Open Words: Access and English Studies* 5 (2): 29–59.

Hassel, Holly, and Joanne Baird Giordano. 2013. "Occupy Writing Studies: Rethinking College Composition for the Needs of the Teaching Majority." *College Composition and Communication* 65 (1): 117–139.

Hassel, Holly, and Joanne Baird Giordano. 2015. "The Blurry Borders of College Writing: Remediation and the Assessment of Student Readiness." *College English* 78 (1): 656–680.

Hassel, Holly, Jeff Klausman, Joanne Baird Giordano, Margaret O'Rourke, Leslie Roberts, Patrick Sullivan, and Christie Toth. 2015. "TYCA White Paper on Developmental Education Reforms." *Teaching English in the Two-Year College* 42 (3): 227–243.

Hassel, Holly, Mark Reynolds, Jeff Sommers, and Howard Tinberg. 2019. "Editorial Perspectives on Teaching English in the Two-Year College: The Shaping of a Profession." *College English* 81 (4): 314–338.

Hayek, F. A. 2007. *The Road to Serfdom: Text and Documents: The Definitive Edition,* ed. Bruce Caldwell. Chicago: University of Chicago Press.

Hayek, F. A. 2011. *The Constitution of Liberty: The Definitive Edition,* edited by Ronald Hamowy. Chicago: University of Chicago Press.

hooks, b. 1994. *Teaching to Transgress: Education as the Practice of Freedom.* New York: Routledge.

hooks, bell. 2003. *Teaching Community: A Pedagogy of Hope.* New York: Routledge.

The Hope Center for College, Community, and Justice. 2019. https://hope4college.com/.

Hung, Man, William A. Smith, Maren W. Voss, Jeremy D. Franklin, Yushan Gu, and Jerry Bounsanga. 2020. "Exploring Student Achievement Gaps in School Districts across the United States." *Education and Urban Society* 52 (2): 175–193. doi:10.1177/0013124519833442.

Inoue, Asao B. 2015. *Antiracist Writing Assessment Ecologies: Teaching and Assessing Writing for a Socially Just Future.* Anderson, SC: Parlor Press.

Inoue, Asao B. 2019a. "2019 CCCC Chair's Address: How Do We Language So People Stop Killing Each Other, or What Do We Do about White Language Supremecy?" *College Composition and Communication* 71 (2): 352–369.

Inoue, A.B. 2019b. *Labor-Based Grading Contracts: Building Equity and Inclusion in the Compassionate Writing Classroom.* Fort Collins, CO: WAC Clearinghouse.

Jensen, Darin, and Susan Ely. 2017. "A Partnership Teaching Externship Program: A Model That Makes Do." *Teaching English in the Two-Year College* 44 (3): 247–263.

Jensen, Darin, Patrick Sullivan, and Christie Toth. 2017. "Teacher-Scholar-Activist: Making a Scene." *4c4Equality: Writing Networks for Social Justice,* edited by Liz Lane and Don Unger, "Writing Networks for Social Justice." (print ed. September 2017, online ed. May 2018). *Constellations: A Cultural Rhetorics Publishing Space.* http://constell8cr.com/4c4e/.

Jensen, Darin, Patrick Sullivan, and Christie Toth, eds. 2019. Teacher-Scholar-Activist. https://teacher-scholar-activist.org/.

Jensen, Darin, and Christie Toth. 2017. "Unknown Knowns: The Past, Present, and Future of Graduate Preparation for Two-Year College English Faculty." *College English* 79 (6): 561–592.

Kalleberg, Arne L. 2011. *Good Jobs, Bad Jobs: The Rise of Polarized and Precarious Employment Systems in the United States, 1970s to 2000s.* New York: Russell Sage.

Karabel, Jerome. 2005. *The Chosen: The Hidden History of Admission and Exclusion at Harvard, Yale, and Princeton.* New York: Houghton Mifflin.

Kareem, Jamila M. 2018. "Transitioning Counter-Stories: Black Student Accounts of Transitioning to College-Level Writing." *Journal of College Literacy and Learning* 44: 15–35.

Kareem, Jamila. 2019. "A Critical Race Analysis of Transition-Level Writing Curriculum to Support the Racially Diverse Two-Year College." *Teaching English in the Two-Year College* 46 (4): 271–296.

Kaufman, Dan. 2018. *The Fall of Wisconsin: The Conservative Conquest of a Progressive Bastion and the Future of American Politics.* New York: Norton.

Kendi, Ibram X. 2016. *Stamped from the Beginning: The Definitive History of Racist Ideas in America.* New York: Nation Books.

Kezar, Adrianna, and Daniel Maxey. 2014a. *An Examination of the Changing Faculty: Ensuring Institutional Quality and Achieving Desired Student Learning Outcomes.* Council for Higher Education Accreditation Occasional Paper. https://www.chea.org/userfiles/Conference%20Presentations/Examination_Changing_Faculty_2013.pdf.

Kezar, Adrianna, and Daniel Maxey. 2014b. *Dispelling the Myths: Locating the Resources Needed to Support Non-Tenure-Track Faculty.* The Delphi Project on the Changing Faculty and Student Success, Pullias Center for Higher Education, University of Southern California. https://pullias.usc.edu/wp-content/uploads/2013/10/DelphiProject-Dispelling_the_Myths.pdf.

Kidd, Celeste, Holly Palmeria, and Richard N. Aslinab. 2013. "Rational Snacking: Young Children's Decision-Making on the Marshmallow Task Is Moderated by Beliefs about Environmental Reliability." *Cognition* 126 (1): 109–114.

Klausman, Jeffrey. 2018. "The Two-Year College Writing Program and Academic Freedom: Labor, Scholarship, and Compassion." *Teaching English in the Two-Year College* 45 (4): 385–405.

Klausman, Jeffrey, Leslie Roberts, Joanne Baird Giordano, Brett Griffiths, Patrick Sullivan, Wendy Swyt, Christie Toth, Anthony Warnke, and Amy L. Williams. 2016. "TYCA White Paper on Placement Reform." *Teaching English in the Two-Year College* 44 (2): 135–157.

Kroll, Keith. 2012. "The End of the Community College Profession." *Teaching English in the Two-Year College* 40 (2): 118–129.

Kynard, Carmen. 2013. *Vernacular Insurrections: Race, Black Protest, and the New Century in Composition-Literacies Studies.* Albany: State University of New York Press.

Ladson-Billings, Gloria. 1995. "Toward a Theory of Culturally Relevant Pedagogy." *American Educational Research Journal* 32 (3): 465–491.

Ladson-Billings, Gloria. 1998. "Just What Is Critical Race Theory and What's It Doing in a Nice Field Like Education?" *Qualitative Studies in Education* 11 (1): 7–24.

Ladson–Billings, Gloria. 2006. "It's Not the Culture of Poverty, It's the Poverty of Culture: The Problem with Teacher Education." *Anthropology and Education Quarterly* 37 (2): 104–109.

Lafer, Gordon. 2017. *The One Percent Solution: How Corporations Are Remaking America One State at a Time.* Ithaca, NY: ILR Press.

Larson, Holly. 2018. "Epistemic Authority in Composition Studies: The Tenuous Relationship between Two-Year College Faculty and Knowledge Production." *Teaching English in the Two-Year College* 46 (2): 109–136.

Lavin, David E., Richard D. Alba, and Richard A. Silberstein. 1981. *Right Versus Privilege: The Open Admissions Experiment at the City University of New York.* New York: Free Press.

Layton, Marilyn Smith. 2005. "Lives Worth Fighting For." *The Profession of English in the Two-Year College,* edited by Mark Reynolds and Sylvia Holladay-Hicks, 27–37. Portsmouth, NH: Boynton/Cook.

Lee, Jonghwa, and Seth Kahn. 2020. Activism and Rhetoric: Theories and Contexts for Political Engagement, 2nd ed. New York: Routledge.

Lewiecki-Wilson, Cynthia, and Jeff Sommers. 1999. "Professing at the Fault Lines: Composition at Open Admissions Institutions." *College Composition and Communication* 50 (3): 438–462.

Lovas, John. 2002. "All Good Writing Develops at the Edge of Risk." *College Composition and Communication* 54 (2): 264–288.

Lynch-Biniek, Amy, and Holly Hassel, eds. 2018. "Academic Freedom, Labor, and Teaching English in the Two-Year College." Special issue of *Teaching English in the Two-Year College* (4): 330–442.

Masten, Ann S. 2015. *Ordinary Magic: Resilience in Development.* New York: Guilford Press.

McGee, Ebony O., and David Stovall. 2015. "Reimagining Critical Race Theory in Education: Mental Health, Healing, and the Pathway to Liberatory Praxis." *Educational Theory* 65 (5): 491–511. https://doi.org/10.1111/edth.12129.

Minor, Cornelius. 2018. *We Got This.: Equity, Access, and the Quest to Be Who Our Students Need Us to Be.* Portsmouth, NH: Heinemann.

Mitchell, Michael, Michael Leachman, Kathleen Masterson, and Samantha Waxman. 2018. *Unkept Promises: State Cuts to Higher Education Threaten Access and Equity.* Washington, DC: Center on Budget and Policy Priorities.

Moore, Maya. June 14, 2019. "As Food Insecurity Bill Slips in Under Radar, Advocates Hope for Further Action." *CT Mirror.* https://ctmirror.org/2019/06/14/as-food-insecurity-bill-slips-in-under-radar-advocates-hope-for-further-action/.

Mullin, Christopher. 2012a. "Why Access Matters: The Community College Student Body." American Association of Community Colleges, Policy Brief 2012-01PBL.

Mullin, Christopher. 2012b. "Student Success: Institutional and Individual Perspectives." *Community College Review* 40 (2): 126–144.

Mullin, Christopher. 2017. *When Less is More: Prioritizing Open Access.* American Association of Community Colleges. https://www.aacc.nche.edu/wp-content/uploads/2017/10/Prioritizing_Access_Final.pdf.

Newfield, Christopher. 2011. *Unmaking the Public University: The Forty-Year Assault on the Middle Class.* Cambridge, MA: Harvard University Press.

Newfield, Christopher. 2016. *The Great Mistake: How We Wrecked Public Universities and How We Can Fix Them.* Baltimore, MD: Johns Hopkins University Press.

Newfield, Christopher. April 9, 2019. "The Crisis of Higher Ed Realpolitik: A Visit to Connecticut," *Remaking the University* (blog). http://utotherescue.blogspot.com/2019/04/the-crisis-of-higher-ed-realpolitik.html.

Nussbaum, Martha C. 1997. *Cultivating Humanity: A Classical Defense of Reform in Liberal Education.* Cambridge, MA: Harvard University Press.

Paris, Django, and H. Samy Alim. 2017. *Culturally Sustaining Pedagogies: Teaching and Learning for Justice in a Changing World.* New York: Teachers College Press.

Pickett, Nell Ann. 1998. "The Two-Year College as Democracy in Action." *College Composition and Communication* 49 (1): 90–98.

Piketty, Thomas. 2014. *Capital in the Twenty-First Century.* Cambridge, MA: Belknap Press.

Piketty, Thomas. 2020. *Capital and Ideology.* Cambridge, MA: Belknap Press.

Pope, Denise Clark. 2001. *"Doing School": How We Are Creating a Generation of Stressed-Out, Materialistic, and Miseducated Students.* New Haven, CT: Yale University Press.

Prendergast, Catherine. 1998. "Race: The Absent Presence in Composition Studies." *College Composition and Communication* 50 (1): 36–53.

President's Commission on Higher Education. 1947. "Higher Education for Democracy: A Report of the President's Commission on Higher Education." In *Establishing the Goals,* 5–103. Vol. 1 of *The Truman Commission Report.* New York: Harper & Brothers.

Ravitch, Diane. 2013. *Reign of Error: The Hoax of the Privatization Movement and the Danger to America's Public Schools.* New York: Knopf.

Reynolds, Mark. 2005. "Two-Year College Teachers as Knowledge Makers." In *The Profession of English in the Two-Year College*, edited by Mark Reynolds and Sylvia Holladay-Hicks, 1–15. Portsmouth, NH: Boynton/Cook.

Rose, Mike. 2012. *Back to School: Why Everyone Deserves a Second Chance at Education.* New York: New Press.

Rose, Mike. 2018. "Why Teaching Kids to Have 'Grit' Isn't Always a Good Thing." *Washington Post,* 14 May: n.p., https://www.washingtonpost.com/news/answer-sheet/wp/2015/05/14/why-teaching-kids-to-have-grit-isnt-always-a-good-thing/.

Rothstein, Richard. 2004. *Class and Schools: Using Social, Economic, and Educational Reform to Close the Black–White Achievement Gap.* New York: Teachers College Press.

Rothstein, Richard. 2017. *The Color of Law: A Forgotten History of How Our Government Segregated America.* New York: Liveright.

Ruecker, Todd. 2015. *Transiciones: Pathways of Latina and Latinos Writing in High School and College.* Logan: Utah State University Press.

Said, Edward. 1996. *Representations of the Intellectual: The 1993 Reith Lectures.* Reprint, New York: Vintage.

Schnee, Emily. 2014. "A Foundation for Something Bigger: Community College Students' Experience of Remediation in the Context of a Learning Community." *Community College Review* 42 (3): 242–261.

Schnee, Emily, and Jamil Shakoor. 2017. "Self/Portrait of a Basic Writer: Broadening the Scope of Research on College Remediation." *Journal of Basic Writing* 35 (1): 85–113.

Schreiner, Laurie A. 2017. "The Privilege of Grit." *About Campus* 22: 11–20. https://doi.org/10.1002/abc.21303.

Scott, Tony. 2015. "Writing Enacts and Creates Identities and Ideologies." In *Naming What We Know: Threshold Concepts in Writing Studies,* edited by Linda Adler-Kassner and Elizabeth Wardle, 48–50. Logan: Utah State University Press.

Scott-Clayton, Judith. 2012. "Do High Stakes Placement Exams Predict College Success?" CCRC Working Paper No. 41. New York: Columbia University, Teachers College, Community College Research Center.

Sen, Amartya. 1999. *Development as Freedom.* New York: Anchor.

Shaughnessy, Mina P. 1979. *Errors and Expectations: A Guide for the Teacher of Basic Writing.* New York: Oxford University Press.

Smith, Cheryl Hogue. 2012. "Interrogating Texts: From Deferent to Efferent and Aesthetic Reading Practices." *Journal of Basic Writing* 31 (1): 59–79.

Smith, Cheryl Hogue. 2017. "Aesthetic Reading: Struggling Students Sensing Their Way to Academic Success." *Journal of Basic Writing* 36 (2): 26–53.

Smith, Cheryl Hogue. 2019a. "All Truly Great Thoughts Are Conceived While Walking: Academic Inclusion through Multimodal Walkabouts." *Teaching English in the Two-Year College* 47 (1): 18–21.

Smith, Cheryl Hogue. 2019b. "Fractured Reading: Experiencing Students' Thinking Habits." *Teaching English in the Two-Year College* 47 (1): 22–35.

Smitherman, Geneva. 1977. *Talkin and Testifyin: The Language of Black America.* Detroit: Wayne State University Press.

Snyder, Thomas D., Cristobal de Brey, and Sally A. Dillow. 2017. *Digest of Education Statistics 2016* (NCES 2017-094). National Center for Education Statistics, Institute of Education Sciences, US Department of Education. Washington, DC.

Spencer, Margaret Beale. 2008. "Fourth Annual Brown Lecture in Education Research—Lessons Learned and Opportunities Ignored Since *Brown v. Board of Education*: Youth Development and the Myth of a Color-Blind Society." *Educational Researcher* 37 (5): 253–266. Doi:10.3102/0013189X08322767.

Steele, Claude M. 2010. *Whistling Vivaldi: How Stereotypes Affect Us and What We Can Do.* New York: W. W. Norton.

Sternglass, Marilyn. 1997. *Time to Know Them: A Longitudinal Study of Writing and Learning at the College Level.* Mahwah, NJ: Lawrence Erlbaum Associates.

Straub, Richard, and Ronald Lunsford. 1995. *12 Readers Reading: Responding to College Student Writing.* Cresskill, NJ: Hampton.

Stuber, Jenny M. 2011. *Inside the College Gates: How Class and Culture Matter in Higher Education.* New York: Rowman and Littlefield.

Suh, Emily, and Darin Jensen. 2017. "Building Professional Autonomy: A Way Forward in Hard Times." *Journal of Developmental Education* 41 (1): 28–29.

Sullivan, Patrick. 2009. "An Open Letter to Ninth Graders." *Academe* (January–February). https://www.aaup.org/article/open-letter-ninth-graders#.XVK0olB7mi5.

Sullivan, Patrick. 2014. *A New Writing Classroom: Listening, Motivation, and Habits of Mind.* Logan: Utah State University Press.

Sullivan, Patrick. 2015a. "Ideas about Human Possibilities: Connecticut's PA 12-40 and Basic Writing in the Era of Neoliberalism." *Journal of Basic Writing* 34 (1): 44–80.

Sullivan, Patrick. 2015b. "The Two-Year College Teacher-Scholar-Activist." *Teaching English in the Two-Year College* 42 (4): 227–243.

Sullivan, Patrick. 2015c. "The UnEssay: Making Room for Creativity in the Composition Classroom." *College Composition and Communication* 67 (1): 6–34.

Sullivan, Patrick. 2016. "An Open Letter to High School Students about Reading." *Academe* (May-June). https://www.aaup.org/article/open-letter-high-school-students-about-reading#.XVK0k1B7mi4.

Sullivan, Patrick. 2017a. *Economic Inequality, Neoliberalism, and the American Community College.* New York: Palgrave Macmillan.

Sullivan, Patrick. 2017b. "Shaping the Public Narrative about Teaching and Learning." *Liberal Education* 103 (3/4): 68–71. https://www.aacu.org/liberaleducation/2017/summer-fall/Sullivan. Reprinted in *Tomorrow's Professor,* Stanford University's online faculty development e-newsletter, April 9, 2018, https://tomprof.stanford.edu/posting/1636.

Sullivan, Patrick. 2019. *The Community College Success Stories Project: Celebrating America's Community Colleges and the Students Who Attend Them.* https://www.communitycollegesuccessstories.org/home.html.

Sullivan, Patrick. 2020. "The World Confronts Us with Uncertainty." In *(Re)Considering What We Know: Learning Thresholds in Writing, Composition, Rhetoric, and Literacy,* edited by Linda Adler-Kassner and Elizabeth Wardle, 113–134. Logan: Utah State University Press.

Sullivan, Patrick, and Christie Toth, eds. 2016. *Teaching Composition at the Two-Year College.* Bedford/St.Martin's Professional Resources series. New York: Bedford/St. Martin's.

Sullivan, Patrick, and Howard Tinberg, eds. 2006. *What Is "College-Level" Writing?* Urbana, IL: NCTE.

Sullivan, Patrick, Howard Tinberg, and Sheridan Blau, eds. 2010. *What Is "College-Level" Writing? Volume 2: Assignments, Readings, and Student Writing Samples.* Urbana, IL: NCTE.

Sullivan, Patrick, Howard Tinberg, and Sheridan Blau, editors. 2017. *Deep Reading: Teaching Reading in the Writing Classroom.* Urbana, IL: NCTE.

Tinberg, Howard. 1997. *Border Talk: Writing and Knowing in the Two-Year College.* Urbana, IL: NCTE.

Tinberg, Howard. 1999a. "An Interview with Ira Shor—Part I." *Teaching English in the Two-Year College* 27 (1): 51–60.

Tinberg, Howard. 1999b. "An Interview with Ira Shor—Part II." *Teaching English in the Two-Year College* 27 (2): 161–175.

Tinberg, Howard, and Jean-Paul Nadeau. 2011. "Contesting the Space between High School and College in the Era of Dual-Enrollment." *College Composition and Communication* 62 (4): 704–725.

Treuer, David. 2019. *The Heartbeat of Wounded Knee: Native America from 1890 to the Present.* New York: Riverhead Books.

Toth, Christie, Brett Griffiths, and Kathryn Thirolf. 2013. "Distinct and Significant: Professional Identities of Two-Year College English Faculty." *College Composition and Communication* 65 (1): 90–116.

Toth, Christie, and Darin Jensen, eds. 2017. "Symposium: Guidelines for Preparing Teachers of English in the Two-Year College." *Teaching English in the Two-Year College* 45 (2): 29–46.

Toth, Christie, and Patrick Sullivan. 2016. "Toward Local Teacher-Scholar Communities of Practice: Findings from a National TYCA Survey." *Teaching English in the Two-Year College* 43 (3): 247–263.

Toth, Christie, Patrick Sullivan, and Carolyn Calhoon-Dillahunt. 2016. "A Dubious Method of Improving Educational Outcomes: Accountability and the Two-Year College." *Teaching English in the Two-Year College* 43 (4): 391–410.

Toth, Christie, Patrick Sullivan, and Carolyn Calhoon-Dillahunt. 2019. "Two-Year College Teacher-Scholar-Activism: Reconstructing the Disciplinary Matrix of Writing Studies." *CCC* 71 (1): 86–116.

United States, Department of Education, National Center for Education Statistics. 2020. Integrated Postsecondary Education Data System (IPEDS). Washington, DC: Department of Education. https://nces.ed.gov/ipeds/.

Velez, Gabriel, and Margaret Beale Spencer. 2018. "Phenomenology and Intersectionality: Using PVEST as a Frame for Adolescent Identity Formation amid Intersecting Ecological Systems of Inequality." In *Envisioning the Integration of an Intersectional Lens in Developmental Science*, edited by Carlos E. Santos and Russell B. Toomey, 161, 75–90. San Francisco: Jossey-Bass.

Waite, Stacey. 2017. *Teaching Queer: Radical Possibilities for Writing and Knowing.* Pittsburgh: University of Pittsburgh Press.

Warnke, Anthony, and Kirsten Higgins. 2018. "A Critical Time for Reform: Empowering Interventions in a Precarious Landscape." *Teaching English in the Two-Year College* 45 (4): 361–384.

Welch, Nancy, and Tony Scott. 2016. *Composition in the Age of Austerity.* Logan: Utah State University Press.

Whitman, James Q. 2017. *Hitler's American Model: The United States and the Making of Nazi Race Law.* Princeton, NJ: Princeton University Press.

Young, Vershawn Ashanti. 2009. "'Nah, We Straight': An Argument Against Code Switching." *JAC* 29 (1/2): 49–76. *JSTOR*, www.jstor.org/stable/20866886. Accessed 9 May 2020.

Young, Vershawn Ashanti, Rusty Barrett, Y'Shanda Young-Rivera, and Kim Brian Lovejoy. 2018. *Other People's English: Code-Meshing, Code-Switching, and African American Literacy.* Anderson, SC: Parlor.

PART I

An Introduction to Teaching Writing at the Two-Year College

1

DISPATCHES FROM BARTERTOWN

Building Pedagogy in the Exigent Moment

Darin L. Jensen

Abstract: This essay explores the challenge of engaging in authentic critical literacy work while being positioned as contingent labor in the neoliberal community college. The author offers a set of principles that help him engage in literacy work while negotiating the significant systemic and ideological challenges faced in the twenty-first-century writing classroom.

> *"There is no such thing as a single-issue struggle because we do not live single-issue lives."*
> —Audre Lorde (n.p.)

THE LANDSCAPE AND SOME QUESTIONS

This volume's call to examine teaching writing in the two-year college is an important one. Nearly half of all first-year writing courses are taught at the two-year college, and I imagine that a high percentage of the two million students who take developmental education classes annually do so at a community college (Lovas 2002, Saxon et. al. 2005). What's more, the two-year college engages students who are the least visible and most often relegated to the sidelines. In fact, a quick look at the American Association of Community Colleges' *Fast Facts* reveals that two-year colleges teach a diverse body of students, including 40 percent of first-time freshmen, a majority of Hispanic and Native American students, and a

DOI: 10.7330/9781607329305.c001

significant numbers of black and Asian students (AACC 2018). The two-year college is inarguably one of the most important sites for education in the United States. If we are going to examine teaching writing in the community college, there are three broad sites of inquiry in which to aim our work:

1. What does it mean to teach in the community college in the twenty-first century?
2. What does it mean to teach a writing course in the twenty-first century? How do we undertake the task well? What are the best practices?
3. What does it mean to teach as an adjunct in the community college in this moment? This last question is crucial because over three-fourths of postsecondary teachers are contingent faculty (Curtis 2014).

THE TWENTY-FIRST CENTURY COMMUNITY COLLEGE

I confess that I love the community college. At its best, it is an agile institution that meets the needs of a community and helps prepare citizens to make those communities better. But we must be honest; The community college has always had tension in its mission. The tension is complex. Part of it sits in the space between work for transfer and work for vocation. Part of it sits in the notion of the purpose of the community college. What is it for? At this moment, the answer is that the community college is largely an institution guided by neoliberal ideology—the notion that everything is a market and that all education is job preparation (see Caplan 2018). Students are customers. Colleges partner with businesses to train employees to enter the market. We are either creating students who can immediately enter the workplace with a vocation or we are creating students who will transfer to a university to receive more training to be a technocrat and then enter the economy. We talk about competition and marketability rather than the public good and community.

But is that all that the two-year college is for? The short answer for me is: I hope not. Community colleges have a long association with the democratization of education with open access and being able to represent students who are not traditionally represented in post-secondary education. However, as Barry Alford mentions in "Composition in the New Gilded Age," it seems almost quaint to hear education and democracy in the same sentence (Alford 2017). Recently, Patrick Sullivan wrote an entire book on neoliberalism in the community college that examines this tension (see Sullivan's *Economic Inequality* 2017), and Nancy Welch and Tony Scott recently edited the collection *Composition in the*

Age of Austerity (2016), which examines the influences of neoliberalism on education. These works point to our political moment wherein ideological and budgetary forces seemingly are aligned against affordable and accessible education and seem to be headed toward crisis. Decades of neoliberal ideology have undermined faith in public institutions and the institutions themselves. Sadly, arguments about the public good of education belong in the same quaint club Alford describes.

The moment the community college finds itself in is one where state legislatures demand evidence of persistence and completion, where developmental education is under attack as a barrier to success, more than three-fourths of the instructional workforce is contingent, and funding for community colleges has decreased by nearly 40 percent over the last three decades (Harbour 2014). It's tough. Even so, students are still coming through the doors and they want to learn and they still believe in the power of education in some fashion. Working with those students, who have wildly different levels of preparation and who live under the exigent conditions of austerity and the pernicious ideology of neoliberalism, is what's on the table. High stakes indeed.

These exigent circumstances have led me to think of the community college, and educational institutions in general, as *Bartertown*, the fictional town in *Mad Max: Beyond Thunderdome*. Bartertown is out in the wasteland and its primary purpose is trade and income generation. Bartertown is the raw market—everything is a market without any of the shiny varnish we have in our world. Anything can be had for a price. And under Bartertown is the *Underworld*, which provides power to Bartertown through methane generation—literally pig shit. The Underworld is staffed by those who "ask" for work. No one would want to ask for work there, but it is all some can get. It's not too much of a stretch to see Bartertown and the Underworld as symbols for the neoliberal community college—devoted to economic output with a vast underworld of exploited adjunct laborers keeping it functioning.

TEACHING WRITING IN THE TWENTY-FIRST CENTURY

Considering our notion of Bartertown, what does it mean to be a writing teacher, especially in the two-year college? I always think of Mike Rose's *Lives on the Boundary* when I start to think about what it means to teach writing. Early in his book, Rose takes on the notion of literacy crises. He gives a succinct account of how before World War II, most students read at a fourth-grade level, and then we needed more as a society (Rose 1990, 6). He tells us that compulsory high school education wasn't demanded until the late 1970s (1990, 6). His point is that rather than a literacy crisis or series of literacy crises, what we've really had occurring in the United States is an opening up of literacy and the opportunity to become literate. The last three US presidents (Clinton, Bush, and Obama) all called for post-secondary education on a much wider scale. Of course, they couched it in neoliberal terms: We are preparing human resources for the market, we are working to be more competitive, etc. But the fact remains that we are teaching more people—and more people who would not otherwise be included in education than we ever have before in the United States, and the community college is a major facilitator of that labor. Neoliberal or not, the community college has been an influence for the public good. What, then, is the role of the language teacher?

For me, what it means to be a writing/language teacher in the two-year college is a need to be true to an ideology and practice of education that prepares students in ways that will help them employ literacy for their own benefit and for the benefit of their community. The driving ideological framework I use comes from critical pedagogy—scholars and teachers like bell hooks, Audre Lorde, Patrick Finn, Paolo Friere, and Carmen Kynard. hooks encapsulates this idea when she calls for "teaching that enables transgressions—a movement against and beyond boundaries" so that "education is a practice of freedom" (hooks 2014, 12). I envision an education that benefits students and their local communities as they define that benefit. Importantly, I consider local contexts just as essential for teaching in the community college. I contrast this localism with the drive for fitting out students as technocrats and cogs in a globalized service economy. This ideological orientation in the classroom is an enormous commitment. I take seriously hooks' notion that teaching is sacred in the sense that it is work that is set apart and dedicated to one purpose. Unfortunately, being part of those local contexts and being able to dedicate oneself to the work is made more difficult without a permanent position and work.

WHAT DOES IT MEAN TO BE AN ADJUNCT? AN EXAMINATION OF THE HUSTLE

The most important thing in understanding my current life as an adjunct is to understand the difference between the Work and the Hustle. I earnestly listen to the advice of Carmen Kynard's mentor, who reminded her: "do not confuse work with the job" (Kynard 2017). The Work is that of critical literacy; helping students critically engage with language to empower themselves and experience education that liberates and ennobles. This Work is what the Truman Commission described in 1947: the democratization of higher education for broader equality. It is also the work of those who see language teaching as being able to build powerful literacy (see Finn 2009), being able to transgress and challenge systems and leading to *conscientization*—the Frierian process of developing critical awareness in social reality through reflection and engagement. I teach to do the Work. The Work can happen in community literacy centers, activist organizations, within religious organizations, and more, but I have learned to do the Work in the classroom.

The Hustle refers to the actions I have to take to keep my life going. In the fall of 2017, the Hustle was teaching five sections of composition at two different campuses for $13,500 before taxes. The Hustle is learning where the copy machine is and when I can make copies in order to get around the requirement of sending everything to the copy center for tracking purposes. The Hustle is finding an empty room where I can meet with students because I don't have an office. The Hustle is submitting to redundant training on technology or Title IX training that might be construed as more about creating a shield for the institution than making sure things are equal. The Hustle is all of these things and a thousand more that we learn to do and put up with so we can do the Work.

Let me be clear: full-timers do the Hustle too, but they do it with benefits, a retirement match, and guaranteed income. If you are on the tenure track, there's a Hustle with all of that, too (see Kynard 2017). But the Hustle a contingent faculty member does is raw and near the edge of collapse and ruin—financial, mental, emotional, spiritual. Many educators have read the recent stories of adjuncts and sex work or adjuncts living in cars (Gee 2017). All of this is the Hustle in the neoliberal community college landscape where funding has been cut for decades and the majority of instructional staff are part of the "just-in-time" gig economy, and it is part of devaluing those who do the Work. If you are lucky like me, you have a spouse who has a job with benefits and you aren't likely to miss a meal or essential health care. But if you don't have that, it's bleak out there. It's easy to feel Marc Bousquet's assertion in *How the University Works* that PhDs are the waste product of the university (Bousquet 2008).

The situation is dire. Carmen Kynard is right that academia is a hustle, just as Bousquet is right that PhD students are the waste product of a broken system. To return to my metaphor, they are what powers

Bartertown. Alford is right that composition has entered a New Gilded Age, and Shor is right, on some level, when he asserts that mass education has failed (Shor, *Teacher-Scholar-Activist* comment 2018). But Rose is also right that two-year colleges are great second-chance institutions, and Sullivan is right that we need to attend to the democratic vision espoused in the Truman condition (Sullivan 2017). Duffy is also right that first-year writing classes are a site of development for democratic citizens (Duffy 2012). These thinkers are right, but it's hard to live in Bartertown on the edge of civilization and do the Work of teaching literacy and focusing education on democratic principles when you know you're working in a broken system that doesn't value your work or worth. This tension of two competing realities and ideologies is what adjuncts who teach first-year writing and are interested in the Work of democratic critical education must navigate every day of their lives.

THE PRINCIPLES OF TEACHING THE WORK

All of that being said, and my position within the Education Industrial Complex accounted for, I still love the Work and believe there are principles for enacting it in a writing classroom in the two-year college. In this section, I lay out some principles that I follow in teaching that I believe get at the notion of powerful literacy.

Inquiry-Based Writing Classrooms

I have found that many of my students do not know why they are at a community college or that they know in a tangential way. They might know that they want to be a nurse or get some classes under their belt to transfer on to a four-year school or take enough courses to get a job as a welder, but many more do not know what they want to do. And because two-year colleges have many first-generation students enrolled, it may be that they haven't had discussions about the purpose of education in their homes or communities. I was a first-generation student and my parents didn't talk to me about college; they talked to me about getting to work after high school. What this means in my classroom is that my students have not thought about the purpose of education very often. If I ask, they often talk about the economic capital to be gained from a college education—they have been indoctrinated into neoliberal logics of market-based education and competition almost totally. They haven't ever talked about becoming a better person through education. And only rarely have they said they want to get an education to give back to their community. I find this alarming. And that alarm has shaped my pedagogy in the writing classroom.

I want my students to begin to think about why they are in college and what the point of an education is. To do this work, I begin many of my classes with a definition essay; students should define education. What does it mean for them? For their community? What is the etymology of education? Of student? We then have a conversation. To help facilitate that thinking and discussion, I have been using John Duffy's short essay "Virtuous Arguments" on the purpose of first-year writing. Duffy makes the argument that first-year writing is one of the only places in our culture where we can learn to discuss the issues of the day, treat argument as testing out ideas, and where we might develop the thinking required of citizens (Duffy 2012). He contrasts the first-year writing course with what he calls *toxic rhetoric*—"rhetorical tactics of misinformation, demonization, incendiary metaphors, and poisonous historical analogies" that debase public discourse (Duffy 2012, n.p.). He contrasts the development of thinking that can happen in first-year writing with the sound bites on cable news and talk radio. I make an argument to the students that his essay is a definition of first-year writing. We discuss the essay and his arguments. We think about his audience; is it students? Teachers? How would you change the argument to be aimed at the students as an audience? After that, we write our own definition essay for education. I have models that I've saved over the years and I write the essay too, making sure that they see my rough draft.

The reasoning behind this assignment is that I want them to think about why they are spending money, probably going into debt, spending time, and spending energy on college classes. I know that I didn't have anyone talk to me about things like this, and having an explicit discussion about it allows students to looking at their own motivations for their work. I think of this as a vital inquiry into values. In the past, I've built a whole course around that inquiry.

Another thing I know about my students is that most of them have had some bad experiences in school. They have faced terrible, burned-out teachers, racist systems, rote curricula, and life circumstances that have made school experiences trying. And my students often hate English classes. The act of listening to their definitions of education and then asking about what they think education should be, and why, allows them to process the experiences they've had in meaningful ways that help them mature. We often read work from Mike Rose about education, along with Sandra Cisneros and Sherman Alexie. I choose these works because they create a theme that allows students to build and scaffold knowledge. I choose these works because students will read them and because they can find themselves in the work. Cisneros' characters in *House on Mango Street* deal with the oppression of school, with the world telling them that education isn't necessary. My students can write about that and compare it to their own lives. They can see the lengths that Junior goes to in the *Absolute True Diary of a Part-Time Indian* to get access to education and to have a chance. My students see and understand these texts as jumping-off points for inquiry and writing.

Language Politics in First-Year and Basic Writing

One of the things I do on the first day of my writing class is to ask my students what good English is. It's one of my favorite questions. It never changes; someone says "proper," another says "good grammar." And so it goes, right? This exercise leads to a discussion of standard-English ideology, dialects, code switching, registers, and how power is maintained through language. I believe this conversation belongs in the first-year writing classroom and in the basic writing classroom. Many of my students speak in a dialect or an accent and many have stories of being punished in some way because of it. On the first day of my English class, especially if it's basic writing, students are bringing the weight of their experiences with language to the classroom. Deconstructing standard-English ideology and the notion of code switching seems revolutionary to many of my students. Often, this conversation is the first time that anyone has ever had their home language or their community's dialect honored. I talk about my own code-switching from working-class English—my "mislearned grammar" or that my father says "warsh" instead of "wash," or that I mispronounced a bunch of words because I'd only seen them in books and never heard them spoken—to using academic English with folks at the university. We talk about when we should deploy our different registers and how we know to make these choices—which, of course, are rhetorical choices. And they already know these things; they just didn't know they were doing complex linguistic and rhetorical work. We get to work articulating these choices and applying terminology to them. We theorize what we already do with language to legitimize their own language practices. It's intellectual work and it's the work of critical literacy and conscientization because the students become conscious of their own literacy practices and of the structures that have imposed other literacy practices upon them. (Friere 2010).

MATERIAL IN THE FIRST-YEAR AND BASIC WRITING CLASSROOM IN THE TWO-YEAR COLLEGE

One of the things I hadn't thought about as a teacher was the cost of my curriculum for the student. It wasn't something that came up as a graduate teaching assistant.[1] However, I have become keenly aware of the material I require. When I first started teaching composition as a graduate teaching assistant, I used the book the program administrator gave me. It wasn't good or bad. It felt like training wheels and I used it because I was supposed to and it was easy. However, when I started teaching writing on a community college campus, I quickly found out that my students couldn't afford the book, didn't have the book because their financial aid hadn't come in yet, or bought the wrong used version of the book online. It was frustrating. What's more, I had a huge book with an MLA guide, a grammar handbook, and more assignments (color coded, no less) than I could assign in a quarter or semester. The students complained about the book's cost and about how much the bookstore paid them when they sold it back. Over time, it didn't seem like a very good system. On top of that, the more I read and the more I taught, the more I went away from the writing assignments and readings in the book.

Finally, I took the plunge; I got rid of the book. I told my students they would have to print some PDFs and online essays that I assigned. For the citation work, I had them use Purdue Online Writing Lab—after all, it's more likely that learning to use that site is a transferable skill that develops digital literacy than it is likely that students will keep and use the handbook. As for citations, Zotero and any number of free software programs exist to help students manage citations and bibliographies. Most of my students will never create another bibliography after college. They won't get their knickers in a twist when MLA 27 comes out and changes things once again. What they need is access to the idea that good research provides its sources.

Even if I assign a small book now, I make sure there are ample used copies available and wait several weeks to start using them so that students have time to get the money together and have it shipped to them. I abhor customized and consumable textbooks and I won't use them, as I think they take advantage of the students. I won't use the big, expensive composition books, as they are wasted too. I see these as part of the Education-Industrial Complex (Adler-Kassner 2017) and the material choices in my classroom is one of the places where I can resist it. Seriously, develop your own material. Make as much of it free or as cheap as possible. And frankly, as more bookstores go to rentals that give nothing back to the student and don't even allow the buying and selling of used books, making materials may become ever more important. If your college has an assigned book, tell your students to take it back, close your door, and teach reading and writing without it. I know this might mean that there isn't a swanky party at a conference hosted by a textbook publisher, but trust me, your students will be better for it.

Authentic Objectives

Every college writing course has objectives. They are probably held within several pages of stuffy writing that is put into binders for the Higher Learning Commission. There are goals and objectives, outcomes, and best practices. And they are good, if sometimes too abstract. When I was a full-time faculty member, I helped write these documents, and as an adjunct I have been handed these documents along with model syllabi as a way to discipline and shape the teaching I do. But I remember the very first time I ever heard about an outcome in a writing course. I was a student in an English comp I class in a small college, and we were writing our evaluations of the instructor. The adjunct instructor was a poet who had terrific energy. We wrote a great deal in several genres and we became better writers. The students were happy with the course and with how the instructor had treated them as human beings. One student, an adult learner who had spent his life working for the railroad, wrote that the instructor had "taught him to write like a motherfucker." I totally got what he was saying—he felt empowered by the class; he felt inspired and strengthened by the reading and writing that he had done. "What a great compliment," I thought. I wish I'd had the courage to write something so honest. I found out years later that the adjunct had almost been fired for that comment. I was shocked. To this day, if a student wrote that on one of my evaluations, I'd be proud because I can hear it as the working-class shout-out that it is. Of course, I'd want to talk to the student about audience awareness; but nevertheless, I'd feel like I'd done my job because the student was engaged in the work of writing.

In *Literacy with an Attitude* Patrick Finn talks about teaching literacy in ways that liberates versus literacy that domesticates (Finn 2009). I think back on my fellow student's comment and read it as a proclamation that he felt liberated. I think that should be our outcome. It should especially be our outcome when students come to us bearing the weight of standardized writing, standard-English ideology, and prescriptivism—all cloaked, of course, in the five-paragraph essay. This argument isn't to say that the careful thinking about objectives in the composition classroom isn't important; it is. However, I've had objectives that give the number of pages a student should write in a semester along with prescriptive directions and a call to have all essays be "thesis-driven," whatever that means. When objectives take on a disciplining and narrowing effect, my argument is that they can only result in domesticating literacy; creating the kind of literacy that reproduces the very social inequalities that we so often say we are interested in addressing.

Reading and Literacy

During my time as a teacher I've had students tell me that zombies were real and that was why the Chernobyl area was closed off from people. Apparently, the radioactive cloud "zombified" the leftover mammals. Neat. I've had students tell me that evolution wasn't a thing, that vaccines caused autism, that the earth was flat, that 9/11 was an inside job, that the Sandy Hook massacre was a hoax, and that the Illuminati were real and that they run everything. When we talk about writing instruction, sometimes we talk about triaging—that is, determining the priority of work to be done based on the severity of the condition. I have to be honest, prescriptive grammar and MLA citation style are pretty far down on the list. With the beliefs above being far more common than I ever thought they would be, I realized that what I had to privilege was literacy, reading critically and deeply, discussion, and writing to know and understand. Again, I am in the world of the Thunderdome—a land decimated by nuclear war. It doesn't look as dramatic as the Australian desert does in the film, but are the defunding of education, the attack on expertise and science, and the embracing of neoliberal ideology across society any less destructive?

These principles, instituting an inquiry-based classroom, making explicit the politics of language, using affordable materials that don't support the Education-Industrial Complex, building authentic objectives, and concentrating on literacy, form the basis of all writing classes I teach. I shamelessly use whatever materials I find out in the world. If you are an adjunct or if you're teaching five classes per semester, or both, you must repurpose whatever you find to aid your students in the classroom.

FINAL THOUGHTS

To return to Kynard, she writes in her blog that she "love[s] the WORK that I do as a college educator teaching first-generation, racially marginalized, urban young people of color. I enjoy fighting for my own language, narrative, geographies, epistemologies, and styles in my research and scholarship. That's the WORK . . . surviving the academy as a job is a whole other game though. I call this job a hustle, quite deliberately pushing against the snobbery and tomfoolery that would suggest what we do and what we are about is any different from corporate America" (Kynard 2017). I am with her in this. I believe in the Work of literacy in the two-year college writing classroom. Mark Reynolds and Sylvia Holladay-Hicks famously wrote that the two-year college profession is a distinct and significant profession (Reynolds and Holladay-Hicks 2005, ix). I agree. It is distinct because it happens in the two-year college—an institution that has the potential for progressive pedagogy in the Deweyan sense. It is a powerful possibility and one that keeps exploited adjuncts coming back. And simultaneously, Kynard is right to call out the corporatized education that is beholden to neoliberal logics and enmeshed fully in the education industrial complex.

I want to return to our questions, which, like an academic at a conference, I have avoided answering succinctly and clearly: (1) What does it mean to teach in the community college in the twenty-first century? It means to teach in a neoliberal institution with a contested mission. A person who teaches in the community college must negotiate both the democratic purpose and potential of the community college and the drive for consumer-based technocratic education beholden to an unequal globalized economy that sees students as widgets rather than citizens.

(2) What does it mean to teach a writing course in the twenty-first century? How do we undertake the task well? What are best practices? Teaching writing in the twenty-first century should mean a deep engagement with critical literacies and pedagogies in service of authentic learning outcomes that see education as a progressive endeavor with the potential to liberate and ennoble. In practice, it means negotiating outcomes that discipline and narrow our work.

(3) What does it mean to teach as an adjunct in the community college in this moment? This last question is crucial as over three-fourths of faculty are contingent. To teach as an adjunct in the community college is to realize that one is in the Underworld shoveling the shit to make Bartertown (the neoliberal college) function. To teach at the community college means to engage in the hustle in hopes that some of the Work can get done. I do not recommend it. Get another job if you can. Find another way to do real work. But if you are down there in Bartertown, concentrate on the Work and get what you can through the Hustle.

I began this chapter with an epigraph from Audre Lorde. In an address to Harvard she argued that there were no single issues because no one lives a single-issue life. I see her 1982 remarks as an early notion of intersectionality—the idea that there is a complex manner in which oppression is interweaved, overlaps, and intersects. Likewise, there is no single issue in teaching writing at the two-year college. The issues of teaching students who face an array of systemic oppression is interwoven with what Keith Kroll calls the end of the two-year college English profession (Kroll 2012). What we are at the two-year college, as Hassel and Giordano brilliantly assert, is the teaching majority (Hassel and Giordano 2013). And we are under-resourced and underemployed and undervalued (by both the profession and discipline and the institutions in which we work) as we simultaneously engage with students who most need what we can offer in writing instruction—critical thinking, deep reading, inquiry, argument. These facts intersect and make teaching in the two-year college, especially as an adjunct, a difficult and often dispiriting task. The Hustle is a drag. I stay because I believe in the Work. I stay because I stupidly hope that reform and change are possible. I stay because my students sometimes write and say things that are beautiful and true. I stay because many of my students value me and they value that I see them not as cogs, but as real people.

My chapter is not entirely hopeful. We are in a moment that can break spirits and challenge notions of community and public good. If you can do the Work, do it with open eyes in a way that honors students and the potential of the community college. Barry Alford writes in the introduction to *The Politics of Writing in the 2-Year College* that the essays in his book "mean everything" and that "these essays mean nothing" (2001, v). He goes on to explain that they can mean everything because they "bring the voices of practitioners too often silent [. . .] to bear in ways that challenge" our universalized concepts of writing and that they mean nothing because "two-year college faculty seldom benefit from the effort to publish" (2001, v). I will not benefit from this publication as traditional academics do either—there is no tenure, and publication isn't needed for most two-year college jobs. But I write it to bear witness to my effort and the Work, and because I imagine my witness is the witness of many who labor as I do. This chapter is posted from Bartertown; It means nothing. It means everything.

NOTE

1. See Jensen and Toth's *Unknown Knowns* 2017 for a discussion of the intermittent and troubling history of graduate preparation to teach in the two-year college.

REFERENCES

Alford, Barry. 2001. "Introduction." In *The Politics of Writing in the Two-Year College.* Edited by Barry Alford and Keith Kroll, v–viii. Portsmouth, NH: Boynton/Cook.

Alford, Barry. 2017. "Composition in the New Gilded Age." *Teacher-Scholar-Activist*. https://teacher-scholar-activist.org/2017/12/28/composition-in-the-new-gilded-age/.
Adler-Kassner, Linda. 2017. "Because Writing Is Never Just Writing: 2017 CCCC Chair's Address." *College Composition and Communication* 69 (2): 317–340.
American Association of Community Colleges. 2018. "Fast Facts 2018." https://www.aacc.nche.edu/research-trends/fast-facts/
Bousquet, Marc. 2008. *How the University Works: Higher Education and the Low-Wage Nation*. New York: NYU Press.
Caplan, Bryan. January/February 2018. "The World Might Be Better Off without College for Everyone." *Atlantic*. https://www.theatlantic.com/magazine/archive/2018/01/whats-college-good-for/546590/.
Curtis, John W. 2014. "The Employment Status of Instructional Staff Members in Higher Education, Fall 2011." https://www.aaup.org/sites/default/files/files/AAUP-InstrStaff2011-April2014.pdf. Washington, DC: American Association of University Professors.
Duffy, John. March 2012. "Virtuous Arguments." *Inside Higher Education*. https://www.insidehighered.com/views/2012/03/16/essay-value-first-year-writing-courses.
Finn, Patrick J. 2009. *Literacy with an Attitude: Educating Working-Class Children in Their Own Self-Interest*, 2nd ed. Albany, NY: SUNY Press.
Freire, Paulo. 2010. *Pedagogy of the Oppressed*. New York: Bloomsbury Publishing USA.
Gee, Alastair. September 28, 2017. "Outside in America: Facing Poverty, Academics turn to Sex Work and Sleeping in Cars." *The Guardian*. https://www.theguardian.com/us-news/2017/sep/28/adjunct-professors-homeless-sex-work-academia-poverty.
Harbour, Clifford P. 2014. *John Dewey and the Future of Community College Education*. New York: Bloomsbury Publishing USA.
Hassel, Holly, and Joanne Baird Giordano. 2013. "Occupy Writing Studies: Rethinking College Composition for the Needs of the Teaching Majority." *College Composition and Communication* 65 (1): 117–139.
hooks, bell. 1994. *Teaching to Transgress*. New York: Routledge.
Jensen, Darin, and Christie Toth. 2017. "Unknown Knowns: The Past, Present, and Future of Graduate Preparation for Two-Year College English Faculty." *College English* 79 (6): 561–592.
Kynard, Carmen. 2017. "Academia as a Hustle Part I." *Education, Liberation & Black Radical Traditions for the Twenty-First Century* (blog). http://carmenkynard.org/academia-as-a-hustle-part-i/.
Kroll, Keith. 2012. "The End of the Community College Profession." *Teaching English in the Two-Year College* 40 (2): 118–129.
Lorde, Audre. February 1982. "Learning from the 60s." Address, Harvard University. Black Past. http://www.blackpast.org/1982-audre-lorde-learning-60s.
Lovas, John. 2002. "All Good Writing Develops at the Edge of Risk." *College Composition and Communication* 54 (2): 264–288.
Reynolds, Mark, and Sylvia A. Holladay. 2005. "Introduction." *The Profession of English in the Two-Year College*. Edited by Mark Reynolds and Sylvia Holladay-Hicks, ix–x. Portsmouth, NH: Boynton/Cook.
Reynolds, Mark, and Sylvia A. Holladay-Hicks, eds. 2005. *The Profession of English in the Two-Year College*. Portsmouth, NH: Boynton/Cook.
Rose, Mike. 1990. *Lives on the Boundary*. New York: Penguin Books.
Saxon, D. P., M. P. Sullivan, H. R. Boylan, and D. F. Forest. 2005. "Developmental Education Facts, Figures, and Resources." *Research in Developmental Education* 19 (4): 1–4.
Sullivan, Patrick. 2017. *Economic Inequality, Neoliberalism, and the American Community College*. New York: Palgrave MacMillan.
Welch, Nancy, and Tony Scott. 2016. *Composition in the Age of Austerity*. Logan: Utah State University Press.

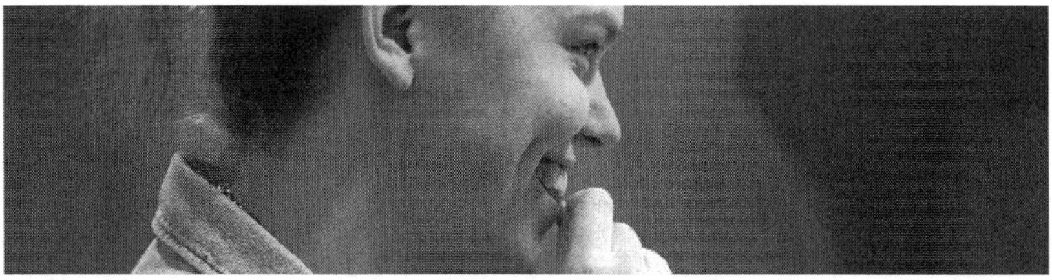

2

TEACHING AS CELEBRATION

An Interview with Helane Adams Androne

Patrick Sullivan

Helane Adams Androne [introducing herself to readers]: I'm a west coast transplant happily living in greater Cincinnati, Ohio. I grew up in San Diego, California, which always leads to the question: "What are you doing in *Ohio*?" I typically reply, with a sheepish shrug, that I actually like seasons, and it's relatively mild in southwest Ohio (though I still don't drive in snow if I can help it). To be fair, I spent seven years living in Seattle, Washington—in all its extraordinary beauty—before I arrived in Ohio, so I had a chance to get a little more chill and a lot more rain.

I am a lover of good food (read: less of a foodie than a food snob) and good stories. That's the epitome of fun for me—food and stories. I enjoy stories of all sorts, but I'm particularly into stories that intersect the real and fantastic. I see artists as both chroniclers and prophets of our time, so my love of stories varies from "high-brow" to geek-lit. I've written about race and rites in Toni Morrison and Ana Castillo and Gloria Anzaldúa. But I'm also into how those same ideas emerge in science fiction, fantasy, fairytales and mythologies. Supers with their backstories, gods with their vices, frighteningly prophetic futures, and the aesthetic tech of steampunk are mad fun. I enjoy stories in literary styles that entangle history, culture, and language in stylish and unexpected ways. Think Octavia Butler. And Shakespeare. And Yoda.

My academic journey includes earning a degree in literature/writing from the University of California at San Diego, an MAT (Masters in Teaching) in English and doctorate in English as well from the University of Washington—without a single cup of coffee, by the way. Now,

DOI: 10.7330/9781607329305.c002

I'm an affiliate in Black World Studies; Latin American, Latino/a and Caribbean Studies; Women's, Gender, and Sexuality Studies; and American Studies programs within Miami's Global and Intercultural Studies Department at one of Miami's regional open admissions campuses. I have taught beginning composition, ethnic American (African American, Latinx, and multi-ethnic) literatures, Integrative Studies, Liberal Studies, Women's Studies, and graduate-level courses for K–12 teachers in the Ohio Writing Project, which I directed at Miami for 4 1/2 years.

Students in my classes can expect deep-diving community-building activities (with and without tech) because it's difficult to share your thinking or create a safe space without feeling like you know the people with whom you're sharing. And because of my experience in a National Writing Project model, they can also expect to write as a space from where to think, explore, and find their unique voices. Much of what I believe I do well in a classroom is a direct result of understanding the role and value of classroom community alongside the sort of best practice exchanges that happened in the Ohio Writing Project. There are many ways to experience and teach course content, but the bridge between my research and pedagogy is built upon respect for the creative, healing power of those who dare to write.

TRANSLATION

Patrick: Helane, it is a great honor to be speaking with you today. One goal we have for this book is to offer readers a warmly personal glimpse into the classrooms of our colleagues teaching at open-admissions two-year colleges. As a classroom teacher, what have you found most appealing, personally meaningful, and rewarding about working at an open-admissions two-year college?

Helane: Hi Pat, thank you for the opportunity to talk about teaching in this context.

I'm afraid I have a rather complex response to this question that involves my own undergraduate and graduate student experience. When I thought about where I wanted to teach upon completion of graduate school, I considered first where I came from. I had attended some very good schools. As an undergraduate I attended a research university, which I am grateful for, but part of that experience was the overwhelming size and scope. It was beautiful, well-resourced and had amazing faculty. But as a student, I found it difficult to navigate and I was convinced that only perhaps four of my professors knew my name over the course of the entire time I attended. I was an outgoing student from a relatively educated family, but I still found the experience daunting. I could imagine a similar experience for students with less connection to education, less ability to navigate, particularly those students like myself, who might see very few faces like their own. I was rather sure that I wanted to have the opportunity to know my students.

Second, at one point during my undergraduate life, the university raised tuition 300 percent. Since my family was not quite categorized as middle class, that sent me looking elsewhere for low-level required courses I needed to complete the degree. I found myself at a local community college for a semester. That experience was eye-opening. I was in smaller courses with students at so many different levels, and with instructors who didn't make assumptions about us, since we all came with so many different stories. It was disconcerting and rich at the same time. I was humbled and astonished. That experience showed me something about what can happen in a smaller setting as well as how different we could be in a single classroom. I wasn't the "only" of any sort there.

Once I went off to graduate school to pursue my master's in teaching English and then the PhD, I found myself operating in a kind of strange translation process within my home community. How could I explain what I was doing, what I was studying, and the implications of it to the people I cared about? What good was it all to them? I quickly realized that while I deeply enjoyed the rigor of what I was doing, I wanted desperately for it to matter to those for whom graduate education was still foreign or seemingly unattainable—or even of little interest. I was beginning to wonder how I might bridge that space between what I was learning and what difference I could make.

I decided finally, and quite emphatically, that I didn't want to teach students like me and those I'd attended school with—those who had supposedly made the "right" choices all along, who had moved through the system without a distraction, lots of whom had had opportunities handed to them and success assumed. I wanted something different. When I stumbled upon an open-access mostly two-year degree regional campus in Ohio that honors providing students with a broad-based liberal educational foundation, I was both surprised and excited. I would have the opportunity to do the kind of work that I loved with access to extensive university resources, but I would be able to teach all kinds of students—traditional and nontraditional. It was exactly what I was looking for.

THE "TYPICAL" COMMUNITY COLLEGE CLASSROOM

Patrick: Thank you for feeling that way! I had a similar experience myself. I started my academic life as a high school dropout who ran away from home at age 16. A community college saved my life. Although I attended a number of other great institutions, I never felt as welcome or as comfortable as I did at my humble little community college, which still feels like home to me. Transitioning to our next question; given what you've said here about students, what do you enjoy most about the students you work with at your institution?

Helane: Wow, that's a wonderful testimony to the benefit of open-access . . . and I think your story is a familiar one that leads to my answer. Something I love about my students is the multi-level diversity—the sort that extends, if it doesn't completely obliterate the check boxes typical of more deliberate university-level recruitment efforts. My classes look like a hodge-podge of pluralistic heaven.

Sitting in my classes, I've had traditional well-prepared students next to veterans, next to parents, next to grandparents, next to ex-convicts, next to business owners, next to community leaders, next to high school students trying to get ahead. It's a subversive, exciting space that operates against expectations. Some drive Maseratis, some drive beaters, others don't drive. Some are bidialectal and can code-switch into Appalachian or African American or Latinx, or Chinese dialects. Some are trying to save money, some are trying again. What makes it work is the attitude of the students; they are there because they know they need to be. I'm excited because such classes are spaces that make room for ideas in ways that we're still struggling to do in this country. I'm proud of that. And that means my job has been both invigorating and excruciating at times. It has been utterly time-consuming even as it's been mind-blowingly meaningful.

Patrick: I love that phrase: "a hodge-podge of pluralistic heaven." And your description of the "typical" community college classroom may be the best (and funniest and most generous and most accurate) one I've ever read. Thank you for that. My next question is this: Many newly minted teachers coming out of graduate school will be teaching at two-year colleges for the first time. Some readers of this book will also be seasoned teachers looking for new ideas and professional renewal. Can you give us three pieces of wisdom, perspective, or advice about two-year colleges and two-year college students that will help teachers at the two-year college thrive and enjoy teaching at these kinds of institutions?

Helane: First, in these spaces it's best to understand going in that you have to teach students more than content or traditional skills. You have to be willing to help them locate their celebrations along with their challenges. Some students won't struggle so much with recognizing what is difficult for them; they need to recognize their celebrations to motivate them to keep going. For them, it means everything to have someone find the unexpected in their work. You can't ever really go wrong in that sense. While it may seem, however, that we all love to celebrate, many find it uncomfortable at first. They won't be used to anyone finding their successes because they have been trained to prepare for the discussion of their failures and challenges. Defy that.

Another thing that has empowered my students has been to explain to them how multiple learning styles work—not to pigeon-hole them or to necessarily determine how you will teach (always teach creatively to accomplish the objectives of a course), but to help explain how some assessments of success have been more about how well one adapted to a particular style of learning. If students have determined that they "aren't good at writing," as a simple fact of how "smart" and therefore capable they are, it's going to be an uphill battle changing their mind about that when it may be true that their skill level is low. I have found that just knowing about different ways of being "smart" has empowered my students to believe that they are in fact always learning in different ways at different times and for different reasons. I have seen how helping students to find ways to access their own comfort-level with learning can be motivation enough to try again.

Finally, model the behaviors you want to teach. We can forget, in our rush toward content and depth, that these students are learning the "how" of doing this work as well. Model and share your writing process, your navigation and access of resources, even good basic communication practices—not as instructions only, but in and how you work with the students. Let them see you do what you're asking them to do. Tell them about the stumbling blocks and frustrations and how you moved through those to solve problems. It excites me when students exhibit real learning, which requires curiosity, struggle, and a certain comfort with the progress that comes with failure.

TEACHING "IN THE PLURAL"

Patrick: Can you talk us through how you theorize your writing courses? What scholarship has been important to you as you go about your work teaching writing and reading? What scholarly sources most foundationally inform your work and daily teaching practice?

Helane: This is tough. So how I teach crosses several traditions—from traditional composition theory to ritual and performance studies. Several scholarly texts have framed my approach(es) to teaching, but I can name just a few here: Linda Brodkey's *Writing Permitted in Designated Areas Only* was a text that influenced my perception of writing and its connection to purposeful citizenship as a motivator for students; Paulo Freire's *Pedagogy of the Oppressed* was amazing to me in how it could articulate the positionality of students all over the world in relationship to educational practices; John C. Bean's *Engaging Ideas* was important to my development of assessment techniques; discussions about and connections to the National Writing Project helped me to solidify my understanding of the connections between reading and writing in ways that hadn't been made obvious in my traditional training. There have been texts that articulate other nuances about identity and voice in the classroom, and scholars like bell hooks and Audre Lorde have been important voices for how I've considered the safety and importance of self-expression in the classroom. Richard Schechner, Victor Turner, and Mircea Eliade have been important influences on how I view and handle performance and how I value certain experiences in my classroom as well.

Patrick: That's a great list. I'm interested in hearing more about your experience with the National Writing Project, but first I'd like to ask how you translate this theory into practice in the classroom, a key concern for two-year college teachers. How do you build your writing classes? How do you design writing assignments and thematic units? How do you pick your readings? And can you share with us an assignment or two that you are currently using in your classroom?

Helane: Wow, that's a loaded question!

How do you build your writing classes? How do you design writing assignments and thematic units?

I would say I've used a process-oriented framework for building writing classes. We have a rather standardized curriculum built for beginning composition courses, but our approach can vary a bit. We used to have two required composition courses, both at the 100 level with the first focusing upon "the principles and practices of rhetoric . . . for producing writing that is effective . . ." The second is similar, but is designed in a context that introduces students to the critical study of literature. I have most often taught the latter of the two. The concept of "text" is broadly defined in these classes, so it includes literary, disciplinary, public, and popular texts; print and digital texts; and visual, video, and aural texts as well as verbal print text. The course includes four overlapping units that we have called "inquiries" during which students explore the relationship between reading and writing, how knowledge and meaning are constructed, as well as how to engage in literary analysis. Our key outcomes are to help students:

- Write with a sophisticated understanding of how texts work—how texts hold multiple meanings and have multiple effects depending on audience, context, and methodological perspective.
- Engage in critical, close reading, making arguments using textual citation as evidence.
- Understand the complexity of texts—how texts hold multiple meanings and produce multiple effects depending on audience, context, and methodological approach or perspective.
- Conduct research-based inquiries into the rhetorical, literary, historical, and/or cultural contexts of a particular text or group of texts, employing various literary and rhetorical methods for invention, analysis, and argument.
- Write effectively for specific audiences, purposes, and contexts, especially for academic contexts and disciplinary audiences.
- Locate, evaluate, integrate, and cite sources effectively and ethically.
- Practice close, critical editing of writing according to audience, purpose, and context.
- Articulate and reflect critically on reading and composing practices, including rhetorical decisions about the production and delivery of writing. (Gruwell and Frey 2014)

Each inquiry scaffolds the next, though there is room for variation. The first inquiry is about close critical reading and reader response. Students are asked to apply the skills from their prior composition course in their reading, but also to begin participating in reader response methods for considering texts. They can choose their text for their essay assignment at the end of the inquiry unit (one major work or a set of smaller works). Then, they do a larger project that includes research methods and a bit more creativity. It is a cultural/historical project that includes a research proposal, a two-part exploration of the conventions of a genre, and a multi-genre project (see Tom Romano's work) geared toward an audience outside of academia. Finally, their last project requires reflection and revision. They are to write a detailed reflection on the corpus of their coursework, but they also are to spend significant time on significant revision of a project or essay.

How do you pick your readings?

For this kind of work, I typically choose readings that reflect a variety of interests, experiences, creative choices, and certainly popular culture. I prefer familiar texts when I teach writing—mythologies or fairytales, movies, TED talks, graphic novels/comics, flash fiction, and the like. I want these texts to speak to the variety of interests in the class, but I also want to avoid intimidating texts at the start. By that I don't mean they aren't just as challenging in detail and/or assumptions, but I find that there is as much fodder for analysis in accessible, popular texts as anywhere. This also gets to my general desire to bridge the kind of thinking we do in college with what matters most to students' interests and in their communities.

And can you share with us an assignment or two that you are currently using in your classroom?

In my courses, I always allow for choices in assignments and that's been taken up as important in our standardized versions of these courses. Some version of the cultural historical project is my favorite because it encourages students to explore a genre based on a topic they decide on. They get to think about genre and the conventions ~~of~~ attached to them, to think about how those operate to create meaning and an experience for readers, and they get a more thoughtful and guided exposure to genres they might not otherwise consider. This project also works nicely because it opens the opportunity for students to explore workplace genres, which makes it easier for them to connect their work in the course to work they might be doing in their current and future fields of expertise.

Because of administrative duties and my role in teaching literature more specifically, I haven't taught composition as regularly these days, but the notion of student choice is a consistent one in my courses, as is the idea of applicable inquiry. I prefer to use projects in my courses that allow for extended thinking and application of skills, revision, and celebration. I have a project that I've written about and that I've shared with other instructors and programs. It's called the Applied Learning Project (see my book *Teaching Multiethnic Literatures* for a chapter on this one, but I can provide some details about it). The ALP asks students to draw connections between the issues and topics covered in a course and their own disciplinary/career interests to create an artifact of use outside our academic space . . .

Patrick: Yes, I found that project fascinating. I was impressed with how many choices you provide students in terms of the artifacts they could produce as the culminating project—everything from lesson plans to brochures to a propaganda poster. The chart you prepared for your online students about those options is wonderful (pp. 110–112). In the introduction you wrote for *Multiethnic American Literatures*, you talk about teaching "in the plural" (2). I'm wondering if you can tell us a little bit about how you developed this idea and if you see any ways to enact this principle in writing courses? Also, teaching "in the plural" seems especially crucial for two-year college teachers, who are typically working with a very diverse student body and astonishing variety in students' lived human experience. Is there anything particularly important about this idea in your view as it applies to teaching at the two-year college?

Helane: The concept of teaching in the plural emerges from the understanding that American identity is inherently pluralized and, therefore, much of what we do will and should deliberately reflect that. American literatures are the result of people interacting on a scale and in a space like never before, with world-changing results—from exciting, unparalleled intersections in cultural exchange and production to riotous, unhinged and traumatic violence. Texts chronicle "us" in a variety of ways. Teaching in the plural demonstrates a way to approach these realities: It means we acknowledge the pluralism of our American existence—its unities and disunities. Plural teaching means "this and that"—that we examine the texts fully for the multiple contexts within them, using an interdisciplinary approach to acknowledge meaning and limitations, and that we examine how these texts coexist in relationship to each other. In my courses I acknowledge that texts and contexts make meaning together and that those meanings operate in concert with other texts that might be more familiar (call them canonical, traditional, etc., depending on how you center things).

Because of the context of teaching writing as part of the "literature, but generalist" reality of teaching at a regional campus, it's even more useful to help students understand this concept. In a course like beginning composition, students enter often feeling unprepared or underachieving for a variety of reasons; helping them to understand that all kinds of texts teach us—that many voices and stories better help us see the complexity of "us"—means that this also places an immediate value on what they *are* good at, comfortable with. Creating a space for bidialectics in original writing, for anecdotes and mythologies, reinforces in students the possibility of actually having something to say that matters and is valued in writing. For example, students who are deeply committed to their Appalachian, Latinx, Native or African American community may have a deep understanding of the cadences and nuances of speech and storytelling in their particular region that can be mined for their writing. Valuing voice and story—and the conventions that govern them—can lead to greater motivation to write, to share, and to then fine-tune their work toward new audiences.

Teaching in the plural means beginning in a space that doesn't say, "Look how diverse we are here; this is so important. Now, let's privilege someone else's cadence and rhythm so that you can be successful." Nor does it suggest that one's own voice is the only one that matters. Teaching in the plural means going beyond acknowledgement and articulating to students how who they are matters and that what they do is already working alongside multiple other ways of speaking, listening, and writing. Writing teachers teaching in the plural can allow students to share several ways of conveying information and story and discuss how those operate to accomplish their goals. Then, we can use those same operations to learn what the relationship is between texts, audiences, and conventions and how those reflect power and presence, rather than implicit value.

This could get further and further into multiple disciplines, however, and it requires developing the confidence and situating the time to allow students to pursue research into themselves, their regional and linguistic norms as well as certain histories. It requires the flexibility of choice and that instructors are willing to step back into facilitation, which can be uncomfortable.

Patrick: Are there any practical classroom strategies that have worked especially well for you as you have pursued teaching in the plural? The typical two-year college classroom is so rich and varied in terms of diversity and personal experience. Are there any strategies that we can use to make all our students feel welcome, honored, and valued?

Helane: I'd say beyond the example I mentioned before, that using multiple kinds/modes of texts has been most useful. Sometimes instructors choose texts to be representative, but this isn't ideal. I try to choose texts that are particularly keen or stylish in specific conventions, which sometimes requires stepping outside and inside different genres—and it requires that instructors are authentic about their own reading habits. As with any reading, when we find something useful that is striking, we share it differently, with passion and motivation. Always share lots of different texts with students so they can see how writing mingles, rather than separating texts into (un)stable categories. For example, if I want students to understand the use of a certain poetic or aesthetic (say imagery), I will find variations of that use in artistic, literary, and popular texts. That means I might examine Paul Laurence Dunbar alongside Etta James ("Swing Low, Sweet Chariot") or Louis Armstrong ("What Did I Do . . .") or Smokey Robinson ("Tracks of My Tears"). We take the time to not only look at these texts as representations of a particular convention, but we take the opportunity to understand connections and reception in terms of what these texts speak to and how we know (for example, imagery's use can be political, religious, and social at different moments). These are basic moves we make, but when they're made less as an urgency for representation and more because of what is actually found in the texts, I believe it has more impact—and that it encourages more critical thinking and analysis.

CELEBRATION

Patrick: Can you talk with us a little bit more about the idea of "celebration"? This idea appears to play a central role in your thinking about teaching and learning. Is there anything about celebration that teachers at the two-year college might find particularly useful, inspiring, and important?

Helane: Celebration shows up in how I contextualize student sharing, if that's what you mean. It's a part of ritual pedagogy that in our cycles of learning, there is birth, death, and transformation. In any of these, there is celebratory ritual for having moved from one part of that cycle to another. Many of our students are so used to having their writing picked apart that helping them to celebrate is a refreshing idea. Any time there is a sharing of final drafts of written work, there is celebration, from the small things like acknowledgement of sharing through clapping to the more formal celebrations that involve food.

Patrick: This seems like it might be an especially powerful pedagogical tool in an open-admissions context. Can you tell us just a little more about the theory behind this and how English teachers might apply this in their own classrooms?

Helane: So the idea of ritual pedagogy emerged from my research in ritual studies, which I use as a framework for literary analysis. Ritualizations are the repeated, public (meaning audience involved) performances that we use to mark the sacred as separate from the profane/secular or mundane. When I say ritual pedagogy, I am referencing a way of using repetition, performance, and recognition in the classroom associated with writing. (I have an article that will be helpful for this: "Birth, Death and Transformation: Ritual as Inquiry in the Classroom." *Pedagogy: Critical Approaches to Teaching Literature, Language, Composition, and Culture* 14 [2013].)

THE NATIONAL WRITING PROJECT

Patrick: As the director of a National Writing Project site at your institution, you have noted that "some of the most useful practices I have adapted into my classroom come from reflective pedagogical exchange with K–12 educators" (10). Can you tell us a little bit about your work with the NWP and what you have found most rewarding, interesting, and surprising about this work? Can you provide us with a few specific examples of those useful practices you have drawn from this work?

Helane: My interaction with K–12 teachers in the Ohio Writing Project (OWP, one of the oldest sites of the NWP) and broader NWP family really reminded me of the connections between instructors and learners across levels. Our students come from all levels and lifestyles, so it makes so much sense that we would find synergies among teachers across regions and educational levels. The NWP places a very keen value on that interaction. Having the opportunity to work directly with K–12 teachers in discussions about everything from choosing texts in classrooms to managing workload to maintaining student engagement was illuminating. We learned from each other daily in those exchanges because we ultimately have the same goals; our learning outcomes can differ based on content and level of expected critical thinking, vocabulary, and such, but our objectives are very similar and we need each other. The NWP manages to make a way for that conversation to happen about the teaching of writing without it being simply a Q&A about how to prepare students for college. That conversation is fine in some moments, but the real mutuality is found in the way that we think together about pedagogy based on shared objectives. I've always found myself around educators, so it wasn't necessarily surprising to me, but it was certainly refreshing that there was a space made for the sort of interactions that should always be happening.

For my own courses, I know I rethought discussions because of my interactions with K–12 teachers. It was Harvey Daniels' literature circles work that made me tweak my literature discussions to include specific tasks for reading and response that were more student-centered. The idea is by no means new; I think it emerged in the late 1990s in teaching literature, and it has been revised and rethought in a number of ways by many teachers since. The concept is that of task-oriented discussions (for example, someone who directs discussion, someone who creates a visual, someone who chooses sections of a text to discuss, etc.). I've found that providing students this sort of entry point into discussions about texts has granted them confidence and helped them to learn how to extend themselves. In my own version of these tasks, there is a leader of the discussion (Director), someone who researches contextual information (Contextualizer), someone who focuses the group on passages in the texts (Locator), and someone who helps the group to make connections to current events (Connector). It's not a far reach from the original concept, just with a higher level of expectation.

At first, I worried that it would seem juvenile to my students because I had borrowed from a supposedly lower-level approach to discussion. It was quite the opposite. Students were grateful for the guidance and the variation in their peers' responses because of the choices they could make based on specific tasks. The scholarship of teaching and learning that emerges from K–12 instruction informed how I decided to talk about texts as well. Slowing down to ask students what they noticed was a way of approaching reading that rubbed against some of my tendencies to jump to the "important parts." What this means is simpler than I'd like to admit: I start discussions by asking students what they noticed from whatever text we're dealing with—written or visual. It simplifies the language and automatically suggests to students that whatever they see is valid. So many times we get the blank stare back when we ask students to discuss texts expecting that they deploy the important terminology associated with critical analysis. But if we begin in that familiar space where we all experience texts, and build student confidence, they are always more willing to move forward with us. They end up feeling validated and participate in validating their peers' views of the texts because they speak candidly about how and why they noticed what they noticed. I discovered that all the important language would certainly come as that confidence was built and as I eased them into the use of the kind of critical discourse expected in the academy. I found that students appreciated so much the slow, steady approach to analysis of texts—even at the college level. Confidence is important and, again, using what students naturally notice as a gateway to discussion allows for their views and experiences to be acknowledged and celebrated.

SCHOLARLY ENGAGEMENT

Patrick: You are an active scholar and researcher while still teaching full-time at one of the open-admissions regional campuses at Miami. How do you do it? How do you find the time to stay actively engaged with the discipline? How does this work enrich your teaching practice?

Helane: There is never enough time. The trick to balance is integration and intersection. Each area of evaluation (for most of us there is teaching, service and scholarship or creative/research productivity) needs to feed into the others. Finding ways to link these and articulate those connections is really important. That way, no matter what you're working on, it's affecting all areas of your career life. The other trick is limiting and/or scheduling things that are typical time sucks—like answering email. Limit that to times of day that are least productive so that all of your real energy is spent addressing more important deadlines. Doing so results in responses that might be more thoughtful and less anxious.

INTERSECTIONALITY

Patrick: There has been considerable attention devoted recently in our profession to positionality, social identity, privilege, and race. I'm thinking of Asao Inoue's 2019 CCCC keynote address, and some great recent articles in *TETYC* including "The Risky Business of Engaging Racial Equity in Writing Instruction: A Tragedy in Five Acts" (2016) by Taiyon J. Coleman, Renee DeLong, Kathleen Sheerin DeVore, Shannon Gibney, and Michael C. Kuhne and "A Critical Race Analysis of Transition-Level Writing Curriculum to Support the Racially Diverse Two-Year College" (2019) by Jamila Kareem.

As a disciplinary leader, what are some key texts that two-year college teachers should be familiar with in relation to this ongoing conversation? And what recommendations would you provide to two-year college English teachers (and perhaps also the profession in general) for beginning to address issues related to positionality, social identity, privilege, and race in America in their classrooms?

Helane: There are many texts that help us teach well. For the most part, those that inspire us to reflect on who we are and why we do what we do are all important. What other texts can do, however, is show us the gaps in those reflections, how much we have yet to understand about the populations we serve, and how much really knowing, appreciating, and valuing the humanity of our selves and our students impacts what and how we teach.

I still believe that Paulo Freire's *Pedagogy of the Oppressed* is an important text that influenced so many other educators that it's a primary resource all instructors should work their own way through. I also think bell hooks's *Teaching to Transgress* helps us understand the impact of our practice. Virtually everything by bell hooks should be on a teacher's shelf, really. More recently, important books have emerged from exploring what the experiences of cultural practices mean in classroom contexts and student/local communities (e.g., culturally responsive/sustaining teaching practices).

There is no right way to teach every student; every student of color does not have the same story and teaching as though they do is just as problematic as rendering them invisible by centering a single identity. Therefore, I tend to suspect any practice that does not require the assumption of intersectionality as it's conceived in the United States. For that reason, I believe the work of Patricia Hill Collins and Kimberlé Williams Crenshaw is critical to any colleague's toolkit.

Finally, what I have found particularly valuable is the recognition of the sacred. Through opportunities for acknowledging what I see as a universal human triad—birth, death, and transformation—students can connect their own experiences to entirely different experiences of their classmates. This returns to my prior point about rites and celebrations. The mind is a sacred space that is intertwined with issues of the heart. Neither of these are easily separated from the tangible experiences of one's physical lived experience. Students show deeper respect for one another when they are presented opportunities for authentic and transformative connections. They need time to talk about transformative experiences that solidified or changed them in some fundamental way (I model and describe this further in "Invisible Layers of Labor: Ritualizing a Blackwoman Experience of Service" and "Birth, Death, and Transformation: Ritual as Inquiry in the Classroom"). Creating community requires acknowledgement of differences and similarities. And, everyone belongs. That is Beloved Community.

CONCLUDING REMARKS

Patrick: Did you always want to be a teacher? You've already told us a little bit about your journey to this place in your life and to your current position. Can you tell us a little bit more, especially who your key influences and inspirations were?

Helane: I never wanted to be a teacher. My mother worked in child development my entire life and I saw how hard she worked, how committed to children she was—and how we struggled. It's a bit complicated, but it boils down to this: I wanted to be a doctor of medicine and I was on that road, mostly for the wrong reasons. It was my mother who consistently returned my focus to what I loved, what I did in my spare time, which was reading and writing and listening (she would say talking—lots and lots of talking!). I worked in child development during the summers and as part-time jobs during college and was constantly getting positive feedback that made it back to her. She kept reminding me that I should do what I love and what I was clearly good at, but I was afraid that teaching wouldn't provide financial independence. I finally had a "come to Jesus" moment and discovered there were many things I could do that involved the skills and gifts that came most naturally to me. And then I discovered that teaching could happen in so many different ways . . . I also had that silly moment when you actually recognize the college instructors in front of you as humans who do what they do for a living. So my mother was this consistent, patient influence who helped me to trust that being happy doing what I was clearly called to do would be the best possible life for me. Is there anyone more right than a mom?

Patrick: It's hard to argue with that! My own mother, who was a third-grade teacher at a Catholic school on Long Island in New York (my Dad worked in the city), had a similar influence on my life and career. My final question is this: What parting words would you like to offer to your colleagues in writing classes across the nation doing the important work of teaching writing at open-admissions institutions? Thank you again, Helane. It has been a real pleasure talking about teaching and learning with you.

Helane: The work that we do is significant to those who haven't always had every privilege, or made every best choice along the way, and those who are on to new and next careers. Our students are capable of perhaps the greatest transformation and force in their communities. What they do and how they find success matters to many more around and behind them, so facilitating their journeys is a privilege. We must keep learning and working hard for their sakes and for the future of all of our communities.

Thank you so much, Pat, for this opportunity to think and share about teaching in these contexts.

REFERENCES

Gruwell, Leigh, and Renea Frey, eds. 2014. *Miami Composition Teacher's Guide.* Oxford, OH: Department of English, Miami University of Ohio.

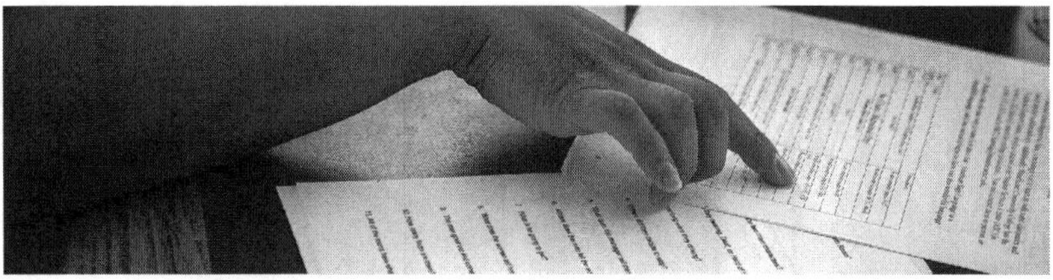

3

FLEXIBILITY

Student Perspective

Bridgette Stepule

Dear future teachers of two-year colleges,

I would like to start off with why they created the two-year community college. The reason, I believe, they created this type of college is for people who want to better their lives but do not have the time. They have the passion and devotion, maybe even more, of a student going to a four-year college. These people have jobs, kids, lives outside of learning, yet they still desire an education to find greater success. There is always an exception. There are also the students that don't know what they want to do with their lives but know that college will take them to a better place. As a teacher in a two-year college you have to deal with all of these types of people.

My personal story happens to be a mix. I was forced to go to college by my mother. I had no idea what I wanted to do or what I wanted to be. I began with studying business and entrepreneurship and then eventually changed my degree to accounting. I always desired to do well, even if it wasn't for anything. My first semester at MCC I got a 4.0 GPA, and this was for something I didn't want to do. I devoted myself to college. Not everyone is like that. As a teacher here, you need to understand that not everyone is the same and not everyone has the same goals. Yes, of course you should help your students do well in their class and not give up on them, but you also need to know that maybe they don't want

DOI: 10.7330/9781607329305.c003

to be here right now. Maybe they wish to become a mechanic instead, or a construction manager, but their parents are forcing them to attend each undesired class. I have encountered students in my classes of every kind. I have met kids that have been at MCC for four years and still don't know what they want to be. I have met people older than my parents, who want to change their careers. I have met people who have children and can only attend morning classes before their children come home. I have also met kids who have worked all day long and can only take night classes. I have seen a huge variety of people and I know how difficult it may be to teach a two-year college class. I know from all of my friends who have attended four-year colleges that their teachers are strict, and they are not flexible to people's schedules. I would not be able to handle that on top of the two jobs I have to pay for college, like most students here.

I have had many great teachers at MCC. The common thread is that they are all understanding. They are also very realistic. I had a business teacher who only accepted one-page papers because that is all they would take in the real world. He would not read your paper if it was longer than a page, just like a hiring manager in a big company. I also had a teacher that didn't care if words were spelled correctly or if punctuation was correct because it didn't matter in accounting. All of the little things that my teachers did for me made a world of difference.

My formal recommendation for new teachers is to embrace flexibility. When you become a teacher, I just want you to know that not everyone is the same. Also, that not everything goes the way you hoped.

Good luck with your future!

4

ENCOURAGEMENT

Student Perspective

Lydia Sekscenski

Students of the two-year college often have interesting, diverse, myriad stories—for example, students could be the first in their family to attend an institute of higher education. They could come from a lower socioeconomic background; perhaps they are simply trying to reduce excess expenditures before transferring to a more costly four-year school. There are students who are fathers and mothers, working to support their children and to create a better life for their family through higher education. There are students who have immigrated—perhaps even fled—to a new country, and they are learning a new language, a new culture, and a new way of life. There are students like myself, who may have had a very difficult start in life and did not want to attend college unless they felt they had a good reason to do so. When I was ready to continue my education, the two-year college was waiting for me. That is truly the best thing about the two-year college—when you are ready to return to school, the college is there to accept you. You do not have to come from wealth or prestige, you do not have to score high on standardized tests, and you do not need connections to be considered or accepted. The two-year college is an open and accepting environment in its very nature.

With this in mind, the two-year college professor must approach these students differently. Many of them are fully grown adults who have long

DOI: 10.7330/9781607329305.c004

since left the high school realm and their childhood homes, and have had a taste of "the real world." They do not need a crash course in the cruelties and realities of day-to-day living, and thus, should be treated with understanding and respect. While the student may take fewer hours at their place of employment to accommodate an increased course load and homework, the two-year college professor must take into account that most of the students are out there supporting themselves financially, and they usually cannot dedicate more than six hours a week studying or taking on large projects. Also, due to the various walks of life and perspectives of the students, the two-year professor should not focus on molding these students to a uniform way of thinking and belief, but rather cultivate and nourish creative minds. The goal of a two-year professor should be to help their students on the way to becoming the best and brightest version of themselves. There is no need to talk down or harshly criticize a student—constructive feedback, positive reinforcement, and encouragement will build bridges to academic and personal success. The greatest gift a professor can give to the two-year college student is self-confidence and the belief in their own strengths and possibilities.

PART II

Teaching Informed by Compassion and Theory

5

COMPASSIONATE WRITING INSTRUCTION

Brett Griffiths

Abstract: The author draws on her own experiences as a writer who lost her authorial voice and on similar experiences shared by students to advocate for a more intentionally compassionate and responsive pedagogy.

—For George Cooper, of course, and for Kate Lutes, Leah Bublitz, and the Macomb Reading and Writing Studios team, whose indefatigable compassion for our students inspires me daily.

LEARNING TO HATE WRITING

When I entered my doctoral program, I nurtured a Gordian knot of concerns about my potential. I was different in social class, formal training, and age from peers in my cohort. I had worked several jobs throughout my education. I had pursued an MFA rather than an MA. I had worked as a waitress, a social worker, and a fish wrapper—among other things—and I was about a decade older than my peers. The one resounding confidence I carried was that I could write. I could spin a lyrical thread into a narrative or a critique, I could braid images into a cause, and I could sew a double joint into the fingers of romantic metaphor, thus casting it into bitter irony. Then I began writing my first seminar papers for the doctoral program, and everything changed. Feedback

DOI: 10.7330/9781607329305.c005

like "your sentences require too high of a cognitive load" confused me. Definitional dialogues such as "what is 'access'?" and "what is 'rhetoric'?" and "what is 'diversity'?" made me question the validity of all of my prior knowledge and writing experiences.

My professors probably intended to develop my thinking, hold me accountable for defining concepts that are notoriously fickle in public and academic discourses, but that wasn't the effect this feedback had on me—at least not until years later. Instead, I found myself questioning the value of my worth as a human. I began to question the reality of what I had already learned about education and about writing instruction. This questioning was probably a useful part of my learning in the end, but it was stifling in the moment. When I sat down to write, I could hear only the voices of anticipated critique. My own voice seemed inert, muted, silenced against a cacophony of criticisms. To use the language of Jaqueline Jones Royster, the first voice I heard was never, ever my own (Royster 1996). For the first time, I also began to feel a visceral rejection of learning, of writing, and of the system of education that had once seemed beneficent, even essential, to my identity. Decloaked and rearing its scythe, education now intimidated me instead of motivating me. For the first time, I began to understand the experiences of so many students who had been nearly paralyzed by the anxiety of their transition into the academic world (see, e.g., Heller and Cassady 2017). Seeing education through my students' eyes taught me an essential lesson about the value of compassion in the teaching of writing—a lesson that has become central to who I am as a person and who I am as a teacher. My primary recommendation to new teachers of writing at the two-year colleges is this: To teach effectively and equitably requires that we hold compassion always at the center of our interactions with students. As I add final edits to this chapter amid the coronavirus pandemic, I am certain more than ever that compassion is not the antithesis to standards. It is the vehicle we share to attain them. And it must be foremost in our evaluation of the ways we execute and assess our teaching and learning.

Like my students at Muskegon Community College and Southern Illinois University, my energies during the years of my doctoral education were split between my academic, economic, and family responsibilities. I was helping to care for two terminally-ill family members in the final stages of their illnesses. My sister and her daughters lost their home, and I was assisting their navigation of the social safety nets, such as they are, while sharing with them whatever resources I could muster from my student life. By the end of my second year, my father's roof was caving in around him, his home had grown water-logged and mold-infested, and his health was failing.

The potential success or failure of each term paper or qualifying exam was inextricably linked in my mind to my ability to support and sustain my family members. Every critique, every revision was freighted with material and psychological implications. The increasing sense that my educational choices were inflicting physical harm on my family led to an acute, sustained case of writing anxiety. My hands trembled; I recoiled with every "pling" indicating a new email. I had developed a profound aversion to writing, like so many of our students have fostered (Sullivan 2011), and my intrinsic motivations—to heal and support my family—ran counter to both my development as a writer and a learner. I was drowning in the very same "life issues" Peter Adams describes in this collection. Those life issues submerged a writing voice I once had trusted, silenced what I knew, and interrupted the routines and practices that had shaped and been shaped by my love of language for years. I even stopped writing in my journal.

I share this story because it has underscored for me the importance of incorporating compassion into the practical strategies we use in the classroom. It reminds me of the many perspectives we *must* take as teachers, and the choices we *should* make to create learning spaces that deliberately position students as capable and powerful ambassadors for their own voices. I share it because I have come to recognize this experience—one which brought with it so much cognitive dissonance—as the experience that taught me what it was to see my students, to hear their voices, and to help them authorize their own stories (Bartholomae 1997). It reminded me what it means to teach within a system of power hierarchies, to be a part of those hierarchies, and to be mindful of the role I play in reproducing the harm they inflict on our students' sense of themselves and their potentials.

BOLD-LIFE FONT

After three years of abject panic, I made an appointment at the university's writing center. It was there that my tutor helped to introduce me to my own voice again. George generously invited me to hear my own thoughts and to disentangle my ideas from the many imagined readers I held in my head. He helped me to identify in **bold-life** font the ideas and arguments I intended to make and to separate them from the HIGHLIGHT-FONT family crises, personal doubts, and the economic disasters looming in the margins of my life. He pointed to moments where my own communications on the page seemed valuable, nuanced, or insightful. Most powerfully, he often uttered, "this makes sense to me . . . I wonder if . . ." He played what Peter Elbow has called "the believing game" with me once a week (Elbow 2008). In short, he used teaching strategies I had used with my own students before I forgot who I was. He brought a human voice of compassion and validity back into the writing situation.

Those weekly sessions initiated a long process of starting to write again; to believe in the questions I wanted to ask, in the students I wanted to support, and in the intellectual and social justice missions that had brought me to this point in my academic life in the first place. It was the process that helped me make room for my life issues to live alongside my intellectual identity—not in opposition, but as a core component of "self" that gave me unique authority. The yoking of these aspects of my identity began to give me permission to make vested claims. George persuaded me that I had the right to persuade others to care about the issues I found central to writing studies and the values that continue to shape my approaches as a teacher, tutor, and administrator—even if those scholarly interests were not historically central or recognized within an elite graduate preparation curriculum. He urged me to push my questions forward, to explicitly identify the disconnect I perceived between our disciplinary ethos and our treatment of two-year colleges—and the students who enroll in them (Toth and Jensen 2017; Lovas 2002; Townsend and Twombly 2007). Eventually, I found my writing voice (at least intermittently). That is the impact of compassionate writing instruction. It is the work of composition to which we are called.

MEETING STUDENTS WHO THEY ARE

An oft-repeated mantra of education is that teachers must meet students where they are, but perhaps it would be better to say we must meet students *who* they are. The students at the Macomb Reading and Writing Studios, which I now direct, represent a vast array of diverse backgrounds, and many of them are particularly vulnerable in the current moment. The college community in which I work boasts some of the largest populations of Chaldean and Arab immigrants and refugees from Iraq, Yemen, Syria, and Bangladesh now living in the United States. Situated in the county north of Detroit, we also serve a populous community of Black Americans from urban backgrounds. This community bears a disproportionate burden in terms of chronic health issues, poverty, and—most recently—coronavirus impacts, including high mortality rates and severe economic disruption. Portions of our geographic region were slowly beginning to emerge from a period of severe unemployment—nearly 20 percent at its height in 2009 ("US Census Bureau QuickFacts: Warren City, Michigan" n.d.). The college is positioned as a "way out" and a "way up" for all of these students seeking access to greater privilege and power. Yet, the very process of education is itself fraught with cultural, linguistic, and social roadblocks. As an academic literacy center, we serve as translators and scaffolds to the lives our students seek. We know our students bring great expectations, and we also recognize that some of their pasts have been peppered with trauma, including abuse, state violence, and the effects of intermittent or chronic poverty (Griffiths and Toth 2017; Broton and Goldrick-Rab 2018; Phillips, McDaniel, and Croft 2018). When strategies for teaching separate students from their stories, forcing them to write in a language that is not their own or to fear the telling of their lived experiences, it functionally cleaves their voices from their writing processes. This cleaving is an act of violence. It is a violation we need to avoid.

To better identify the kind of violence I mean to describe, here I share some of the kinds of responses we get from students[1] when we ask the seemingly innocuous question, "how are you doing?"

> *My house burned down last weekend, and my infant and I barely made it out. I have only the outfit I'm wearing right now. We are still looking for a place to stay.*

> *In my home country I have a college degree, but it doesn't transfer here. When my workplace there was bombed and some men from a militia threatened to harm our family, we escaped in the middle of the night. I've traveled through three countries in three years to get here, and I cannot write without thinking about the bombing; about my children. I schedule my classes around the times when I have transportation and when my children can be cared for. I am told my English is broken and bad, but I am learning as fast as I can. It is my fifth language, and I am tired, and I need rest, but I need a job so I can have money. I cannot learn English because my English is not good enough to learn English. I feel trapped.*

> *My mom and dad are addicts, but they've been sober—my dad seven years, my mom three. Last weekend, my mom got high and got herself sick, and I had to sit up with her while she worked it all out. When I got home to my dad's house, where I live because there's so much less drama, he was out pacing the street, yelling at the trees. I had to call him in and have him committed. This is how he is when he is not clean. Seven years sober. I had to turn him in. Now I don't know how I'm going to get groceries. I need to get this paper done, because I am not going to leave college until I have a degree and can move far away.*

> *In my home country, I was not allowed to go to school. When I was found trying to read, I was beaten with a stick. This happened many times. Now I live here, and I*

> *have a husband who supports my reading, but I know I have a lot to learn. And I want to write. I have things to tell people.*

In the Macomb Reading and Writing Studios, these conversations are foundational—not auxiliary—to our pedagogy. They define our work. Our tutoring hierarchy lives in service of Maslow's (1943) hierarchy of needs, so that part of a writing session may include a walk to the food pantry, to counseling, or a series of phone calls to other services and a rescheduling of an appointment during which we can get to the *writing part* of writing. We operate with the assumption that writers cannot write until their basic needs are met; then they can only authorize themselves when they believe their lives have value and their ideas, experiences, and language are worth sharing. In other words, my staff and I work with students to find ways to incorporate and represent their lived experiences through their use of authentic—sometimes multilingual—language construction, to fold their realities into the futures they are attempting to create. To this end, we also aim to incorporate any knowledge we have about the psychological and material realities of students' lives into our session. (*How is this semester going for you? Have you had a chance to eat today?*) And still, every time we work with others to help them hear and articulate their own voices, we are mindful that we are engaging a complex linguistic space in which power differentials are omnipresent and contested (see, for example, Anne Gere's "Whose Voice is it Anyway?" 2000). We are perpetually at risk of overwriting our students' voices, of silencing their experiences, of stoking that lifelong aversion to writing.

Admittedly, this tension is even stronger in a classroom setting, where students perform their identities not only for instructors but for their fellow students. In the classroom, tension arises because we need to assign an evaluation—a grade or a value—to a student based on performances (and sometimes, unfortunately, the individual intentions we assign to them, such as effort and investment). Such a tension—often described as one between holding up standards and accommodating students—is a common one instructors face, for example, when describing their experiences working with students whose learning is impacted by the availability of economic resources (Griffiths and Toth 2017). However, if we are dedicated to the potentials of access education and the mission of inclusion, we need to find new ways to make our classrooms spaces where students can embrace and perform many facets of their identities, even when some of the performances of those identities seem to conflict with good "studenting" behaviors we codify in our syllabi (see, Fenstermacher), even when they defy deadlines, absence policies, and the familiar font and spacing recommendations sometimes attached to each prompt. We need to find ways to affirm that they are valuable beyond words. Literally.

IT TAKES A VILLAGE

Writing instructional professionals have grown largely accustomed to our students' narratives. However, observing our students' complex lives and seeing them as actors within those lives call for different roles of us as teachers, tutors, administrators, and humans. I am fortunate to work at a college with an entire department dedicated to helping students navigate life issues. Our Student Options for Success (SOS) department helps students apply for medical insurance, financial subsidies for utility payments, etc. At the Reading and Writing Studios, we have cultivated relationships with SOS staff members, academic counselors, and classroom instructors with the goal of developing wrap-around team response to students who may otherwise fall through the cracks. It takes, as they say, a village.

Sometimes this is not possible. For example, when one of the students described above seemed to relive the trauma of her journey for refuge, including the bombing of her workplace and threats on her family, we attempted to set a meeting with the student, a professor, and a counselor. We knew we were unprepared to assist her with the kind of disruptive trauma she was experiencing, and we wanted to help her develop a social network; a net of resources for moving forward, regardless of what the outcome (read *grade*) for that semester might be. Unfortunately, the instructor refused to meet with the student present, explaining that the student needed to quit complaining and just move on with her life. We are—each of us, always—only one person in this system that shapes our students, but we must continue to expand our teams, to persist, and to ensure that our students and their voices are in the room.

This example is extreme—and it runs the risk of setting into too stark a light the kind of teaching violence we may unwittingly enact, thereby tacitly condoning lesser acts of teaching violence. That is not my intention. This example represents merely one extreme form of the kind of teaching violence we enact when we perpetuate narratives about our students that are incomplete and deficient. Here is another: as college campuses converted to remote learning in the spring of 2020 as a result of the Coronavirus crisis, I followed—as did many of you—the moves professors made to uphold standards during this unprecedented crisis, including a professor at a neighboring institution who decreased the exam times for chemistry courses from 60 minutes to 30 minutes in order to "prevent cheating" during online testing. Such moves achieve little more than reinforcing longstanding societal views that patronize students and criminalize learners, undermining the potential for sincere engagement with learning (see, for examples, Graff, 1991 and Falk, 2014). They are loaded with the underbelly of our meritocracy. They say, *if you are not like me, if you have not already achieved what I have, you do not deserve my compassion or respect.* If we look closer, these moves often highlight differences in social class, race, and experience.

In most cases, our difficulties as writing instructors and professionals result from the tension between upholding standards and tailoring learning to the individual needs of students (Perin 2018; Toth, Sullivan, and Calhoon-Dillahunt 2016; Klausman 2018). Rarely, however, in our graduate curricula on rhetorical theory and writing instruction is attention paid to the roles we play as first responders, confidants, and cheerleaders for such a diverse set of students as they muscle through fraught educational pilgrimages. Nor have we been prepared to manage the compassion fatigue that results from balancing so many roles. Nearly lacking in our professional scholarship is a thorough and pragmatic development of how we can support our students and ourselves—to validate the stories students tell and the language they use to tell it without prioritizing either the tale or the language of the tale one over the other. While our professional stances on language and race, articulated in "Students' Rights to Their Own Language" and elsewhere (National Council of Teachers of English 1974; Scott et al. 2009) have set forth clearly our moral responsibilities to language variation, the scruples of implementation fall through the cracks between the intellectual brothels of rhetorical theory and the first-year writing syllabus. While we are offered powerful examples of language inclusion and the reasons they are necessary in the scholarship of our field (Smitherman 1995; Lu 2004; Johnson Black 1995), we are sometimes left to devise trauma-informed teaching practices ad-hoc (see Perry; Gutierrez and Gutierrez for more about trauma-informed pedagogies for adult learners). We are not only teachers, but mentors for students who must navigate multiplicities in their language and learning identities while they are expected to perform these splits with the grace and authority of senior scholars. We assess their uses of academic language within our parlors, all the while counting the silverware remaining in the drawer. We set them up to fail.

During my transition as a student and scholar, the wall of panic and silence became scalable only after I analyzed and imitated the writing of my professors. I systematically copied their sentence cadences and borrowed their most common transitional terms. I began couching my own arguments in their discourse, not just rhetorically, but dialectically, switching the word "how" for the phrase "the ways that" and adopting other pet phrasal quirks of my readers. When teaching students, I aim to pull back the curtain on the mystery of academic writing. My students and I read and discuss the work of Smitherman, Lu, and Johnson Black, among others. We do this in first-year writing, and the exploration affords my students both a front-row seat to the making of academic discourse and a connection to their authentic purposes for participating in it. These discussions have helped students move beyond rhetorical analysis of essays to a greater recognition of the ways the writers we read elbow and claw their ways into their academic prose, how they insist on being recognized, how they earn their authority. In the classroom, we employ genre analysis to identify moves, compare them to other discursive models with which we participate, and then try them on (that is, Bawarshi 2003; Reiff and Bawarshi 2011; Rounsaville 2012). Sometimes, we discuss the problems of existing genre expectations and seek rhetorically effective ways to reject or negotiate them in our texts (see appendix 5.A: Advanced Genre Analysis Prompt for a scaffold to this kind of assignment).

At the Macomb Reading and Writing Studios, our tutoring strategies are limited by time constraints, but they are similar in kind. We invite students to think through the powerful texts they have read, the passages they have admired, the songs they sing in the waiting room, and encourage them to borrow generic moves that authorize them to interject, to disrupt their own academic writing with their powerful identities—to make agentive decisions about how to respond to confusing feedback, and even when to "play the game" until the next opportunity for them to shine.

RISK, RESISTANCE, AND THE DEFICIT NARRATIVE

Students meet us in layers. A name written on the board the first day, a syllabus, a welcome email, our favorite pair of jeans or suit and tie. They assess us the only way they can—by what we say and what we do. They make guesses about us—just as we make guesses about them. We mediate these assessments through course documents—syllabi and assignments, learning-management systems, and the textbooks we select (or are often selected for us). In every one of these situations, students' perceptions depend on schemas they have developed from experiences with previous instructors, and we perceive them through our schema of previous students. But we are—each of us—a single person in a moment in time, working within a system rife with structural inequities and inequalities and an opportunity to intervene.

It seems that, as we work within and through such a system, our students can only benefit if we disrupt some of the conventions of our teaching genre, push back against the "bad students" narratives we have inherited, and question what we have internalized about what writing is and how to teach it. We have an opportunity to help students reposition themselves with more authoritative footing and a sense of belonging, and we have the potential to change the structures, ever so slightly, through these interactions. We can begin by challenging cliché and insulting narratives about who students are, how hard they try, and what they can do. We can do this by rejecting memes on social media and faculty meeting complaints about "students these days." In so doing, we open greater potential for rigorous, linguistically reflective pedagogies. Our teaching environments become laboratories where students can take up writing and language as subjects of study, experiment and analyze their own writing processes, and articulate the philosophies that govern their own learning. I am arguing that this is more than an opportunity. It is the ethical foundation that grounds our work and makes true learning both safe and possible.

In this chapter, I have written from a place of failure and recovery. I have done so because I believe that failures—ours and those we witness among our students—are the most valuable lessons we have for writing and for living. In the end, as many times as I have considered and reconsidered teaching, I've come to embrace failure as a facet of learning and an invitation to forgiveness—of ourselves, our students, and even our teachers. As a colleague of mine once said while lamenting the attitudes of other instructors, "my students sometimes can't do the tasks I ask them to perform, but I'm not angry at them about it." Failure is a part of learning and a part of teaching, but it is never an opportunity to shame or disenfranchise our students.

The grounded evolution of writing studies from the fields of humanism and social sciences prepare us to do something extraordinary—to enact an interactive humanity of teaching and learning, to model an approach to teaching that embraces the foundational values of humanism and social interactions that our writing ultimately depends on. Teaching is hard. Like writing, there is no prescription for doing it right, but we cannot afford to burn out or turn off. Each student we fail teaches us to do better for the students who enter our classrooms the next semester. Thinking of teaching as a social, activist humanism may just open a new space, that mythical third space, wherein our identities are miraculously repositioned with respect to one another, where mulligans transform into lily pads, where the act of not knowing is not a mark of shame but a badge of learning. And maybe—through those interactions—we co-construct a new relationship of teaching and learning, a trajectory of possible selves, of possible educational systems. Maybe, in so doing, we can even evolve the structures that shape and limit our own teaching environments and the public discourses that shape them. With concerted and coordinated effort, such a compassionate pedagogy could even help change the very conditions and constraints that seem to bind us and our practice at this moment in history.

APPENDIX 5.A

ADVANCED GENRE ANALYSIS PROMPT

GENRE ANALYSIS

DISCUSSION: (Rooted in an ongoing class discussion and practice with concepts) In class, we have been discussing the concept of genre as a category for classifying texts, as well as a category for describing how texts behave socially with other texts, especially the kinds of social behaviors and conventions they solicit and reproduce in their construction. Understanding genre in this way can help students better understand how to write in their own disciplines.

PURPOSE OF THE PAPER: The goal of your next paper is to identify some of the "moves" writers in your proposed or exploratory discipline make as part of the generic conventions of your field.

STEPS YOU HAVE ALREADY COMPLETED: You have recently selected an article on a topic in your field. To get started on your genre analysis, I will ask you to observe and analyze how the article you have selected behaves. In order to write your paper, you will have to compose your observations into an overall analysis of the conventions of a scholarly, peer-reviewed article genre in your field. This analysis will mark your entrée into the social community of academic scholars and begin to identify for yourself what professors in your discipline expect. You will use this analysis to construct your own guidelines for writing future research papers and papers for publication.

PART I: (WORKSHOP OF ANALYSIS AND AS MUCH AS YOU HAVE DRAFTED, PLUS CONFERENCES THIS WEEK)

Begin by observing these aspects of your article. (Please use our class discussion to generate other kinds of observations you may make. This is just to get you started.)

1. Does the article you have selected contain sections? If so, what are they? How long is each? How long are the paragraphs? How long are the sentences (on average, in number of words per sentence)?
2. What words make up the subjects of each sentence? What words get repeated from one sentence to the next? Where do repeated words tend to appear in each sentence / subsequent sentence?
3. If your article contains an abstract, what information is contained there? In what order? What does each sentence in the abstract do?
4. How long is the introduction? What does each sentence of the introduction do? What is the main claim of the paper? Where does it appear? How does the author indicate to the reader that this is the main claim?
5. Highlight every citation your writer invokes. How is the source or idea introduced? What kind of statement follows the citation?
6. Where are counterarguments invoked? What language is used?
7. Where and how are rebuttals used? What language is used? (Or how does the author mark the counterargument and the rebuttals as different kinds of rhetorical work?)
8. What terms or concepts are defined? How are they defined? (Using dictionary? Using other articles? Describing behavior or criteria?) Where are they defined?
9. How does the writer support the argument? Logic? Citations? Methods? Combination?
10. How long is the conclusion? What kind of information is included? What kinds of additional arguments are made? Are any of these indicated earlier in the article? Where?
11. How are footnotes or endnotes used? What kind of information is contained there? Why not in the text?

PART II:

General Expectations:

- 4–6 pgs., single author; 5–8 pgs., two authors
- Subsections should keep with your disciplinary expectations
- Paper setup should follow citation guidelines from your field (APA, MLA, IEEE, etc. Please name them)
- Concepts, summary, paraphrase, and direct quotations should cite original authors

PROMPT:

Write an overall analysis of how this article is put together. Given that you only have one article, you probably lack the information to generalize to an entire genre. You may choose to (a) look at two more articles in your discipline to see if they operate similarly to the findings you have, or (b) simply write this as an analysis of a single article that *may* exemplify the genre.

ABOUT ANALYSIS GENRE:

In general, the genre of analysis gives an overall assessment of the object of analysis in the introduction, along with a reason for that assessment, and the ways the reader can benefit from understanding that assessment. Then, in general, an analysis will break down smaller components of the object for analysis into specific criteria of analysis. At the end of the analysis, the writer will make overall claims about the analysis and explain how they relate to the claims set up in the introduction about the benefits to the reader for understanding this analysis.

NOTE

1. These examples represent composite narratives typical of those we hear from students. As such, while the events described represent actual examples from students, they are synthesized to avoid conveying identifying information.

REFERENCES

Bartholomae, David. 1997. "What Is Composition and (If You Know What That Is) Why Do We Teach It?" In *Composition in the Twenty-First Century: Crisis and Change*, 11–28. Carbondale: Southern Illinois University Press.

Bawarshi, Anis. 2003. *Genre and the Invention of the Writer.* Logan: Utah State University Press.

Broton, Katharine M., and Sara Goldrick-Rab. 2018. "Going Without: An Exploration of Food and Housing Insecurity among Undergraduates." *Educational Researcher* 47 (2): 121–133.

Elbow, Peter. 2008. "The Believing Game: Methodological Believing." *The Journal of the Assembly for Expanded Perspectives on Learning* 5. Retrieved from https://scholarworks.umass.edu/eng_faculty_pubs/5.

Falk, Thomas. 2014. "Are Unmotivated Students Cultural Critics?" *JPSE* 2: 139.

Gere, Anne. 2000. "Whose Voice Is It Anyway." In *Writing and Healing: Toward an Informed Practice. Refiguring English Studies*, edited by Charles Anderson and Marian MacCurdy, 25–33. Urbana, IL: National Council of Teachers of English.

Graff, Harvey J. 1991. *The Literacy Myth: Cultural Integration and Social Structure in the Nineteenth Century.* New Brunswick, NJ: Transaction Publishers.

Griffiths, Brett M., and Christina M. Toth. 2017. "Rethinking 'Class': Poverty, Pedagogy, and Two-Year College Writing Programs." In *Class in the Composition Classroom Pedagogy and the Working Class*, edited by Genesea Carter and William H. Thelin, 231–257. Logan: Utah State University Press.

Gutierrez, Daniel, and Andrea Gutierrez. 2019. "Developing a Trauma-Informed Lens in the College Classroom and Empowering Students through Building Positive Relationships." *Contemporary Issues in Education Research* 12 (1): 11–18.
Heller, Monica L., and Jerrell C. Cassady. 2017. "The Impact of Perceived Barriers, Academic Anxiety, and Resource Management Strategies on Achievement in First-Year Community College Students." *Journal of The First-Year Experience & Students in Transition* 29 (1): 9–32.
Johnson Black, Laurel. 1995. "Stupid Rich Bastards." In *This Fine Place to Far from Home*, edited by C. W. Dews and Carolyn Leste Law, 13–25. Philadelphia: Temple University Press.
Klausman, Jeffrey. 2018. "The Two-Year College Writing Program and Academic Freedom: Labor, Scholarship, and Compassion." *Teaching English in the Two-Year College* 45 (4): 385–405.
Lovas, John C. 2002. "All Good Writing Develops at the Edge of Risk." *College Composition and Communication* 54 (2): 264–288.
Lu, Min-Zhan. 2004. "An Essay on the Work of Composition: Composing English against the Order of Fast Capitalism." *College Composition and Communication* 56 (1): 16–50.
Maslow, Abraham Harold. 1943. "A Theory of Human Motivation." *Psychological Review* 50 (4): 370.
National Council of Teachers of English. 1974. *Students' Right to Their Own Language.* https://www2.ncte.org/blog/2015/03/students-right-to-their-own-language/.
Perin, Dolores. 2018. "Teaching Academically Underprepared Students in Community Colleges." In *Understanding Community Colleges*, 2nd ed., edited by J. S. Levin and S. T. Kater, 135–158. New York: Routledge.
Perry, Bruce D. 2006. "Fear and Learning: Trauma-Related Factors in the Adult Education Process." *New Directions for Adult and Continuing Education* 110: 21.
Phillips, Erica, Anne McDaniel, and Alicia Croft. 2018. "Food Insecurity and Academic Disruption among College Students." *Journal of Student Affairs Research and Practice* 55 (4): 1–20.
Reiff, Mary Jo, and Anis Bawarshi. 2011. "Tracing Discursive Resources: How Students Use Prior Genre Knowledge to Negotiate New Writing Contexts in First-Year Composition." *Written Communication* 28 (3): 312–337.
Rounsaville, Angela. 2012. "Selecting Genres for Transfer: The Role of Uptake in Students' Antecedent Genre Knowledge." In *Composition Forum.* Vol. 26. ERIC.
Royster, Jacqueline Jones. 1996. "When the First Voice You Hear Is Not Your Own." *College Composition and Communication* 47 (1): 29–40.
Scott, J. C., Straker, D. Y., & Katz, L. (2009). *Affirming Students' Right to Their Own Language: Bridging Language Policies and Pedagogical Practices.* Routledge. https://books.google.com/books?hl=en&lr=&id=JleOAgAAQBAJ&oi=fnd&pg=PP1&dq=students+rights+to+their+own+language&ots=Wm2DrIIA43&sig=WCRuWooHvBC1BEB7jEP7vCg5DQE.
Smitherman, Geneva. 1995. "Students' Right to Their Own Language: A Retrospective." *The English Journal* 84 (1): 21–27.
Sullivan, Patrick. 2011. "'A Lifelong Aversion to Writing': What If Writing Courses Emphasized Motivation?" *Teaching English in the Two-Year College* 39 (2): 118.
Toth, Christie, and Darin Jensen. 2017. "Responses to the TYCA Guidelines for Preparing Teachers of English in the Two-Year College." *Teaching English in the Two-Year College* 45 (1): 29.
Toth, Christie, Patrick Sullivan, and Carolyn Calhoon-Dillahunt. 2016. "A Dubious Method of Improving Educational Outcomes: Accountability and the Two-Year College." *Teaching English in the Two-Year College* 43 (4): 391.
Townsend, Barbara K., and Susan B. Twombly. 2007. "Community College Faculty: Overlooked and Undervalued." *ASHE Higher Education Report* 32 (6): 1–163.
"US Census Bureau QuickFacts: Warren City, Michigan." n.d. Accessed February 16, 2018. https://www.census.gov/quickfacts/fact/table/warrencitymichigan/PST045216.

6

THE THEORY THAT REMAINS

Toward a Theoretically Informed Writing Assignment

Jeffery Klausman

Abstract: This chapter examines the importance of theory in grounding a pedagogically sound set of writing assignments that promote the social justice aims of open-admissions institutions. After sketching the author's emerging understanding of composition theory, culminating in his concept of "the flexible rhetor," this chapter analyzes the four major writing assignments that ground his newly revised first-year writing course. The chapter closes by acknowledging the incompleteness of any theoretical approach and suggests the next phase of development—a more racially conscious curriculum.

> *It's easy to create a course that is self-contradictory and thus baffling to students. We may teach one thing, assign another, and actually expect yet a third.*
>
> —Richard Fulkerson, "Composition at the Turn of the Twenty-First Century"

"Processing."

That was the one-word response to the question I emailed my friend, the Writing Program Administrator (WPA) at a neighboring university. I asked him, "How can we know that what we do in our comp classes has any lasting effect on our students?" Since I haven't heard from him on that question for fifteen years, I assume he's still processing.

The field has been too, and it has come a long way. I think we know much more about the effects—or non-effects—of what we do in our

DOI: 10.7330/9781607329305.c006

composition classes, and I think it's our responsibility to maximize that knowledge for our students' benefits. In what follows, I'd like to sketch out the development of my theory of teaching writing that grounds every class I design and then look at the major assignments that serve as landmarks for navigating my current first-year writing class. Through it all, I hope to show how what I do aspires to praxis—theory-informed practice—and how that praxis is always engaging the new.

Before I go on, let me say something about what follows: I purposely emphasize the research base of the course since I believe, as I suggested above, that we must know what we are teaching. And as academics, we rely on the best evidence and the best theory to know that—everything else is suspect. There is nothing more important than knowing what we are talking about—in this case, the field we work in—it is the basis of all wisdom, as Plato reminds us in both *Gorgias* and *Phaedrus*.

Having said that, I recognize that most two-year college faculty teach 15-credit loads, which allow for very little time to engage in scholarship; moreover, our colleges rarely demand such scholarship and only slightly less rarely reward it. And finally, I'll say that the graduate education most of us received did not prepare us for the breadth of scholarship necessary to keep abreast of the changes that affect our work. Tenured and tenure-track faculty have so many roles to play in their positions: writing program administrator and expert on placement, assessment, curriculum design, prior learning, as well as interpersonal relations and change management. In graduate school, I took on a subject and read deeply in it. The goal was exploration, immersion. On the job, we teach ourselves what we need to know to get things done: the exigence of work-scholarship is significantly different from the exigence of graduate school scholarship.

How to balance, then, the workload with demands of scholarship? It's not easy and I don't blame anyone for focusing their efforts on teaching their classes sometimes at the expense of the latest developments in the field. Nonetheless, there are ways to keep current without sacrificing one's home life or sleep.

I begin every morning reading through the WPA-L listserv, which I receive in digest form, just to stay abreast of developments in the field. Some threads I pay attention to, others I don't. I subscribe to three journals: *Teaching English in the Two-Year College (TETYC)*, *Writing Program Administration (WPA)*, and *College Composition and Communication (CCC)* and seek opportunities to make the reading mandatory—faculty reading groups with monthly meetings where multiple articles are discussed has been a useful, though difficult-to-sustain, practice. In one group, we divided up the recent issues of *CCC* and *TETYC* and reviewed the articles together. In another, each month, I shared with interested colleagues an article that was especially germane to issues we were facing on campus.

However, I've found more content-specific and time-limited focus groups far more effective, such as the teaching-for-transfer groups I discuss below. Over a period of six weeks, we read Kathleen Blake Yancey, Liane Robertson, and Kara Taczak's *Writing across Contexts* (2014) and discussed how their curriculum might play out on our campus in our curriculum. Based on our reading groups' work, a half-dozen of us developed and piloted a transfer-based curriculum, which formed the core of the course I currently teach and which I describe here. I was able to secure funding through a grant from our college's foundation to pay adjunct faculty for twelve hours of attendance, and I was able to run the faculty group twice, in successive quarters.

Also, I pay attention to recent publications through email announcements from the university presses of Utah State and Southern Illinois, as well as Parlor Press and National Council of Teachers of English (NCTE). Thanks to a small departmental budget, I buy those that look most useful to the writing program and share with colleagues. I have written book reviews regularly—another way of making the scholarship mandatory—prior to becoming review editor of *TEYC*. Finally, I attend my regional Two-Year College English Association conference and the Conference on College Composition and Communication (CCCC) every year, where what's new in the field is presented. I propose sessions, which further requires me to study. Finally, I have held a writing program administrator (WPA) position at my institution for a decade and built into that is the expectation of currency in scholarship. Getting a WPA position has transformed our department and program more than any other innovation we've attempted.

Personally, I cannot imagine my thirty years in college teaching without scholarship. It is what has transformed teaching from a job to a career, made the act of teaching part of a larger arc of scholarship, a pursuit of the "good and the just," again in a Platonic sense, which ultimately for me is manifest as an underlying social justice theme. It's what makes working at a two-year college so potentially rewarding: Nowhere else in higher education can we have such an important impact on the lives of those our social structures have, one way or another, deemed undesirable, deficient, incompetent, or "other." If we can make our courses not just pathways but energized experiences that engage individuals in their own informed lives, which then translates to college success, especially for the historically marginalized (the students of color, the first-generation students, the students with disabilities), then we've done something substantial in the world, however imperfectly, however infrequently.

These are lofty aims, of course, and I don't think of them often. But they're there, behind the administrative and pedagogical decisions I and my colleagues make, as do yours. And they underlie the decisions I make about designing the classes I teach, informing the small choices of texts and assignments, which I'd like to walk through now.

FROM ANALYTICAL WRITER TO FLEXIBLE RHETOR

As I mentioned at the opening, I have long been bedeviled by the basic question of whether we know that what we're doing works beyond our own classrooms. We've had some indirect evidence that first-year writing has a positive impact, such as Nancy Sommers' longitudinal study of student writing at Harvard, reported in "The Call of Research: A Longitudinal View of Writing Development" (2008). Sommers found that over time students got better at writing and appeared to apply what they had learned in their freshman writing courses later in their careers. However, no direct link was suggested. As Sommers notes, writing is an incredibly complex task performed across widely varied contexts in radically different settings by agents as changeable as the weather. Sommers had no way of knowing whether improvement was due to first-year writing instruction or a combination of other factors such as the undergraduate curriculum at Harvard or the prior knowledge of Harvard students, undoubtedly a different population than those I work with each year.

In 2004, David W. Smit, in *The End of Composition Studies*, argued persuasively that composition as then taught could not be supported on the assumption that it adds value to a student's education. Rather, he argued that writing is so context-dependent that no teaching of writing in general can have any value. Smit believes that only through immersion, augmented with instruction in particular discourse communities, can writers gain fluency. While his call to abolish first-year composition was, perhaps, hyperbolic or at least rhetorical (Davila 2006), I took it as a challenge. English 101 was not going away anytime soon, so how can we teach writing in a meaningful way? Even if we grant Smit's assessment, we don't have to accept his conclusion that there's no way forward, only that our current practices are insufficient. Others, with far more powerful and informed voices than mine, made similar points (Dickinson et al. 2006).

Then in 2007, Anne Beaufort published *College Writing and Beyond: A New Framework for University Writing Instruction*, based on her case study of a student writer as he progressed through a degree in history and then engineering and into the workplace. Beaufort found all kinds of problems with the transfer of learning. For instance, Tim, her case-study student, applied what he had learned in his first-year writing class to his history class, which turned out to be inappropriate. This "negative transfer," as Perkins and Salomon (1994) define it, was then followed by no transfer at all as Tim failed to apply what he had learned in his engineering courses to his work in the biomedical firm where he gained employment. Beaufort's response, unlike Smit's, was not to call for the end of first-year writing as currently situated in the academy, but rather to repurpose it around genre- and knowledge-transfer theory.

In my Cross-Talk review of the book in *TETYC* (Klausman 2008a), I placed Beaufort's argument in the larger discussion of knowledge transfer and first-year writing instruction; most notably, the challenge from Douglas Downs and Elizabeth Wardle and their writing-about-writing movement as articulated in "Teaching about Writing, Righting Misconceptions: (Re)Envisioning 'First-Year Composition' as 'Introduction to Writing Studies.'" Beaufort (2007) argues for teaching five knowledge domains that govern writing (process, subject matter, rhetorical, genre, and discourse), providing the framework that student writers need to effect positive transfer. However, Downs and Wardle (2007) emphasize making subject-matter knowledge explicit and transfer more implicit. They argue that any generalized view of academic writing constituting what Wardle (2009) elsewhere calls a "mutt genre" cannot be supported (2009, 770). Perhaps because Bartholomae and Petrosky's seminal work *Facts, Artifacts, and Counterfacts: Theory and Method for a Reading and Writing Course* (1986), which advocates the immersion in academic discourse, had formed the basis of my institution's writing program for over a decade, I was more persuaded by Downs and Wardle than by Beaufort.

Then, in the spring of 2016, I organized a faculty group to read together *Writing across Contexts: Transfer, Composition, and Sites of Writing*, by Kathleen Blake Yancey, Liane Robinson, and Kara Taczak (2014). A group of eight writing faculty met weekly to discuss the ideas Yancey et al. present and their applicability to our writing program. In brief, they present their teaching-for-transfer curriculum, which is grounded in three interlocking emphases—key terms, reflection, and developing a theory of writing. Based in part on *How People Learn:*

Brain, Mind, Experience and School (Bransford, Brown, and Cocking 2000), Yancey et al.'s book also presents their findings on how new knowledge of writing disrupts, augments, or replaces students' prior knowledge, which becomes an important aspect of the teaching-for-transfer curriculum.

Reading *Writing across Contexts* made clear to me how I could formulate a course in response to my concerns and perceived needs of my college's students. While Beaufort's model curriculum was intriguing, I had difficulty seeing how to structure my class to enhance student transfer. Perhaps I was simply not ready for it in 2008, but I think what was missing for me then was any direct evidence that emphasizing the five knowledge domains actually got the results we wanted. Yancey et al.'s approach was presented with supporting evidence, albeit debatable and far from conclusive. Still, their teaching-for-transfer approach offered the conceptual framework for students to become what I'd come to call "flexible rhetors," writers who can employ rhetorical concepts strategically to respond to different rhetorical situations.

Now, I had a home for much of what I wanted to bring from prior courses, especially an emphasis on multimodal composing (Selfe and Hawisher 2004; Shipka 2005; Yancey 2004). I had already experimented with students making short movies that presented an argument, and I had already required students to conduct studies of their own reading or writing practices and present their findings using graphs and charts. Moreover, I had shifted the writing-about-writing focus to emphasize texts of and about writing in the digital age. (This is what I'd been doing between 2008 and 2016.) All of this was meant to illuminate the intersection of students' own lived realities as competent and prolific readers and writers of digital texts and the academic analysis of reading and writing in the digital age.

This shift from analytical writer to flexible rhetor is not a subtle one. Rather than teaching an introduction to academic discourse with analytical writing at the center, my responsibility now is to create a learning space where students can adopt and adapt the theories and practices of composition and rhetoric to current and, I hope, future situations through the conscious reshaping of prior knowledge. This implies not emphasizing a particular set of rhetorical skills, however well embedded in cognitive or discourse theories, which students then apply, mysteriously, in their future academic settings. Rather, it aims to foster students' conscious awareness of their own ways of approaching and responding to a rhetorical situation so that they can more effectively adapt to new contexts and new demands.

There's a lot more to be understood in that shift from analytical writer to flexible rhetor that I hope to make clear in this chapter. However, my intention is not to convert anyone to this approach but rather to make visible what is often invisible in the design and delivery of a course.

DESIGNING THE COURSE

Three forces shape the design and delivery of any writing course I teach: the needs and abilities of the students; the current best theories on the teaching of writing; and the changing cultural and technological landscapes (for an accessible theory of course design see Beaufort's "College Writing and Beyond: Five Years Later" 2012). Of these three factors, I'll focus here on the design of new writing assignments.

I won't spend a lot of time looking at the cultural and technological landscape, though it heavily influences the evolving theory of writing in our field. Nor will I discuss how I tailor the presentation of those assignments and all the scaffolded work that supports them to the varied student body of a typical two-year college writing class, as Joanne Giordano and Holly Hassel (2016) so well describe it. I will say before I go on, however, that the diversity of students at my institution is significant.

This past quarter, in a single section of first-year writing, I've had students who were transferring to Ivy League and Public Ivies; a student in his late twenties who had been homeless the month before and became homeless during the semester; a woman in her early sixties returning to college after an absence of nearly forty years; students with various learning disabilities; a survivor of serious trauma; a veteran who had underperformed in high-school and was eager and yet worried about proving himself; international students from six different countries, one as young as sixteen years old; students who spoke one of eight native languages besides English; dual-credit students, some enrolled full time at the college and some taking only one class; a majority first-generation college students; and a number that could be classified as Generation 1.5.

How to shape writing assignments and the presentation of those assignments for such a diverse student body would require a chapter of its own. I'll only say that I always seek to validate students' prior knowledge and experience, encourage alternative-to-white discourses, and seek to demystify academic expectations as a means of empowering students to choose their own positionality. As I mention at the end of this chapter, a closer look at social justice issues, especially as expressed by a more racially conscious curriculum, is next on my agenda.

Here, I'd like to look at the major assignments that ground the class I developed and to show how they express my developing theory of composition.

Of course, artifacts of any course do not speak for themselves. A syllabus or assignment always represents more than it says. Anyone who has ever used the track changes feature in Word knows that revision after revision goes into the creation of any course document. What is it that we are trying to accomplish when we revise an assignment, never quite getting it right but merely abandoning it, as Auden says of poems (Auden 1966)? What drives us to tweak our grading schemes and rubrics every quarter or semester? It's my hope that analyzing the major projects of the course I designed can illuminate the theory that informs the practice, whose development I sketched above, as well as the theory that remains and challenges me to revise the course yet again. It's my hope that this will help all of us, in some small way, make better sense of the decisions we make in the designing and teaching of our writing classes.

THE CULMINATING ASSIGNMENT: A THEORY OF WRITING

Most of us, when we're thinking of putting a course together, start with the major assignments. They're like the navigational points for a long road trip, dividing the trip into manageable and significant stages. These stages serve both as stopping points and as determinants in choosing a path; that is, they create a roadmap. Similarly, as I was thinking about the course I was designing, I thought about the final destination: flexible rhetors. How could students learn to be flexible rhetors and what evidence can students provide to demonstrate that?

The culminating writing project that I developed, and which all the others move toward, is a comprehensive theory of writing (Appendix 6.B). Following Yancey, Robinson, and Taczak (2014) who put the theory of writing at the forefront as a key component of any teaching-for-transfer curriculum, I conceived of the theory as developing over the course of the quarter, drawing upon students' prior knowledge and encouraging, through active reflection, the integration of new knowledge. Yancey, Robinson, and Taczak (2014) identify three ways this new knowledge is commonly integrated by college writers, which they term assemblage, remix, and critical incident (2014, 104). They call for the explicit teaching of these concepts under the assumption that without the conceptual space the terms afford, students are less likely to make the most efficient use of the knowledge the writing course offers (2014,

126). In other words, without a mental map of the terrain to cover—in this case, the three main ways people learn—students will be less likely to identify their own experience and thus be unable to integrate their new knowledge.

This is an idea I missed the first time through the book with the spring 2016 reading group. While the concepts of assemblage, remix, and critical incident were heavily discussed in our group, I somehow did not see them as integral to instruction. It was not until I led a second reading group in the fall of 2016 that I caught the significance of the explicit teaching of how knowledge is integrated. So, my culminating assignment and my instruction in the fall 2016 course lacked that key component (see appendix 6.B). While I asked students to develop a theory of writing, I did not explicitly identify the ways in which that theory may change—and neither did I do so in the informal reflective writings that followed the completion of the major projects. Consequently, some students likely struggled to make sense of any discomfort they may have been feeling with new ways of doing things, such as more detailed planning or more systematic analysis of genre.

What that assignment did enact, however, were the three essential aspects of teaching-for-transfer, which are the explicit teaching of key terms, the essential role of reflection, and the development of theory. These three are usefully represented as an image of three interlocking gears, which I first encountered at the Conference on College Composition and Communication (CCCC) in Portland and which I recreated for my own purposes (figure 6.1). In my class, students developed their theory beginning the first week when I asked them to reflect upon a memorable school-related writing experience they had in their past and then to develop an answer to the question, "In general, how does good writing get done?" Students were asked to write about 500 words, but most wrote more.

Thereafter, with the completion of the three other major writing projects over the course of the quarter, they reflected again upon what they had written in prior reflections and upon their experiences in this particular writing project. In five hundred to one thousand words, students revised their understanding of "how does good writing get done?" revising some of their earlier claims, sticking with others, and expanding their understanding via use of key terms and aspects of process. In total, students wrote four informal reflections on how they approach writing in a college setting.

The culmination of these reflections was a roughly one-thousand-word assessment of how they understood college writing at the end of

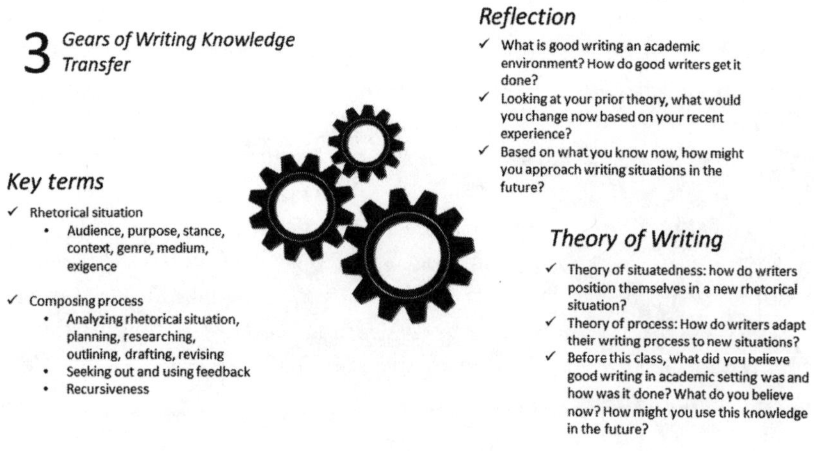

3 Gears of Writing Knowledge Transfer
Key terms
✓ Rhetorical situation
• Audience, purpose, stance, context, genre, medium, exigence
✓ Composing process
• Analyzing rhetorical situation, planning, researching, outlining, drafting, revising
• Seeking out and using feedback
• Recursiveness
Reflection
✓ What is good writing an academic environment? How do good writers get it done?
✓ Looking at your prior theory, what would you change now based on your recent experience?
✓ Based on what you know now, how might you approach writing situations in the future?
Theory of Writing
✓ Theory of situatedness: how do writers position themselves in a new rhetorical situation?
✓ Theory of process: How do writers adapt their writing process to new situations?
✓ Before this class, what did you believe good writing in academic setting was and how was it done? What do you believe now? How might you use this knowledge in the future?

Figure 6.1. Three interlocking gears driving writing knowledge transfer.

the course, based on their growing understanding as evidenced in their reflections. Students were asked to gather their four reflections in a single place, such as a Word document or a Google Doc or a WordPress site. They were to read through their reflections, talk a bit among their peers, and then write up a more-or-less formal theory of writing that presents their current knowledge about how they can and will approach college writing now and in the future, citing as many sources as appropriate.

THE FIRST OF THREE MAJOR PROJECTS: CONDUCTING PRIMARY RESEARCH

The first assignment, Conducting Primary Research (appendix 6.C), asks students to respond to an ongoing discussion in academic and professional circles about the effects of the ubiquity of digital text on the cognitive abilities of readers and the subject position of writers. In short, the question is the one Nicholas Carr (2008) posed as the title of his now-famous *Atlantic* article, "Is Google Making Us Stupid?" In addition to reading Carr, students also read Clive Thompson's "On the New Literacy" (2009) and an excellent and short response to Carr by Trent Batson (2009), in which Batson coins the term "hybrid orality" to describe the revolution to knowledge-making that the move from a print culture to a digital culture has made possible, especially as played out in social media and crowdsourced references like Wikipedia. Students are asked in the first assignment how they might legitimately join this conversation by identifying one area of tension, one area of uncertainty, one gap in knowledge, and bring something unique and valuable as a response.

As do many of us, I introduce the students to Burke's Parlor metaphor and ask the students seriously how they could say something that might actually further the conversation in a way that can be heard by people like Carr, Thompson, Batson, and others. I explain to students that these writers have expertise far beyond their own and yet, academic writing nonetheless compels us to speak. So, what can students bring? What do they have to offer that is unique? It takes some prodding, but eventually students realize that all the authors we've been reading were born before the digital revolution. The students, on the other hand, are mostly digital natives, and so perhaps they know something the authors don't about what it means to be someone whose mind has not been altered by digital media but has developed in the company of it. What of this can they bring to the table and how might they do it? As a nondigital native myself, I really want to know.

In my experience, students find this intriguing after the years of the mostly fake writing, as I call it, that they've done in school, such as giving both sides of an issue and then offering their opinion. I think deep down most students think their opinion doesn't really matter, that what they're doing is not real writing but "practice" writing; that is, writing for the teacher's sake, and this is why so many students loathe writing in school. It doesn't really count the way their writing on Instagram or their reading of YouTubers does. My assignment, while still constrained by the limited audience of the instructor and classmates, at least brings with it the possibility of being taken seriously and, more importantly, creating real knowledge.

Once the purpose of bringing something valuable from their own experience to the conversation is established, we turn to means. How will they bring it? Since this is the first assignment and I want to emphasize that all writing in the academy is real—none is fake, none is practice—I give students a genre that can shape their responses in a meaningful way. I introduce the IMRAD structure common in the sciences and social sciences. IMRAD is an acronym for introduction, methods, results, and discussion. Most students have not had experience writing in this genre nor, in fact, are they aware of any academic genre outside the five-paragraph essay, though they come to understand by the end of the quarter that they write in many different ones all the time. IMRAD provides a framework for a radical break from the strictures of the five-paragraph essay which, I've learned from watching my son progress through school, is taught as early as the fourth or fifth grade.

At this point I have students form what we call PFFs, which stands for project feedback friends. The acronym PFF is memorable for students, since it hearkens to BFF—best friends forever—and thus strikes both a familiar and humorous chord. I introduce PFFs by showing students the acknowledgements in their text, *Everyone's an Author* (Lunsford et al. 2016), which run several pages. I explain that no one writes alone, writing in the academy, as in most other places, is a social event, and writers get feedback on projects all along the way—a core threshold concept from Adler-Kassner and Wardle (2015), and which is reproduced on the assignment. We discuss what PFFs can do for one another in the process of completing this writing project: acting as a sounding board for idea development, as cocreators of the reading or writing study they are going to conduct, and as critical readers of outlines and drafts. PFFs, I tell them, will be acknowledged in the final draft of their writing project and will be partially responsible and credited for the work of the main author. I show them similar acknowledgements in edited collections of essays and in journals, where writers thank individuals who provided input on the writing project as well as, occasionally, anonymous reviewers. This is also a good moment to show them a generic feature of these acknowledgements, wherein the writer gives credit for the strengths of the piece to their colleagues while reserving the blame for the faults for themselves.

With their PFFs, students then define a more-or-less empirical study to test some notion suggested by the readings; for example, Nicholas Carr (2008) talks about his mind skimming along the surface of a text like a "guy on a Jet Ski." He makes this claim broadly, without nuance. Do students have this experience? When and how? How might that effect be mitigated or even controlled? Can it? Should it? A student might set up a study in which they observe and record distractions as they try to read a textbook in different situations, controlling for all variables but one, for example, studying with and without music. What's the effect of music on concentration? Have students known this, in a way, and used it as a strategy? What might that mean relative to Carr's argument?

They design and conduct the study, gather their evidence, and then write up the results in an IMRAD structure, which is beautifully effective in helping students see that genres are defined by common features because they respond to common situations where readers have common expectations. These features bring both constraints and affordances that can be exploited. Moreover, each section of IMRAD has its own purpose and expected content, which act as heuristics for the writer, an excellent opportunity to teach three of the key terms of the course: genre, audience, and purpose. An added value is that the IMRAD genre is so radically different from the five-paragraph essay, which many students come straitjacketed with, that it serves to break them free of seeing every writing situation as demanding a single, uniform response.

So, the first assignment serves to create a space for students to learn about genre, audience, and purpose, primarily. They also learn that a key feature of academic writing is joining the conversation legitimately, given one's level of expertise and unique position, which I use to augment understanding of writer's stance—a fourth key term of the course. It also focuses the writing on students' own reading and writing, giving them some space in which to find a foothold on their own study habits, including how they read and write, which they find somewhat empowering and, I hope, helpful in other academic settings.

Through the second informal reflection, which follows the completion of this project, students make sense of what they've learned in the context of their prior knowledge, which they laid out in their preterm reflection. In this way, the first major writing project serves both as a means of knowledge building and skill development and as a stage on the way toward the end point of the course: a developed and coherent theory of writing.

THE SECOND OF THREE MAJOR ASSIGNMENTS: DEVELOPING A POSITION

As I mentioned earlier, for nearly twenty years I structured my writing courses more or less along the lines first laid out by Bartholomae and Petrosky in *Facts, Artifacts, and Counterfacts* (1986). I augmented the design principles with more of the nuts and bolts of academic discourse as made explicit in David Rosenwasser and Jill Stephen's *Writing Analytically* (2014) and Laurence Behrens and Leonard J. Rosen's *Writing and Reading Across the Curriculum* (1996). Heavily influenced (as I still am) by Bartholomae's "Inventing the University" (1986), I sought to create reading and writing situations in which students could learn the rhetorical moves of academic discourse. I was committed to this position due to my own experience of having been a first-generation college student without a clue, wandering through his first two to three years at a large, urban public university, lost and without mentorship. I am committed to creating spaces where students, mostly first-generation or otherwise systemically disadvantaged, could gain the critical insight to the kinds of reading and writing moves that expressed the values of the academy. I believed that in so doing, students would gain power over their situations and be more likely to persist and excel.

Also, as I mentioned, I had no evidence at all, and quite a bit of evidence to the contrary, that students were benefitting from this instruction. It made sense that they would, but lots of things make sense that don't necessarily turn out to be true. Nonetheless, I had no intention of throwing out the baby with the bathwater, since in my years as the coordinator of writing across the curriculum at my college, I knew that much of the principles of academic discourse that I'd adopted is at least implicit in the kinds of writing that faculty in other disciplines assign and in the kinds of assessments they perform, though I can't say with any optimism that disciplinary faculty are necessarily adept at either assigning or assessing for it. Nonetheless, the question in designing the new course was how to carry these principles forward into the new paradigms of teaching for transfer and twenty-first-century writing.

In discussing with a colleague this move in our field beyond teaching academic discourse as if it were a second language best learned through immersion, not unlike the whole-language learning theories of Stephen Krashen (1987), I invoked the principles of dialectical phenomenology to suggest that this move was not necessarily a rejection of our earlier convictions but rather an overcoming of the inherent contradictions, between thesis and antithesis, that our teaching papered over but which Smit (2004), Beaufort (2007), Downs and Wardle (2007), and others exposed. While learning the moves that characterize academic discourse may be a worthy goal, our approach to teaching it as if it transferred automatically—similar to Krashen's theory of language acquisition, which does not require conscious attention to grammatical rules—had fallen far short of the ideal.

All of this is to say that the second major project, Developing a Position (appendix 6.D), focuses on academic argument but with a twist. While I still emphasize the distinction between persuasion and argument which, granted, need not always be absolute, I focus on different kinds of argument, suggesting that there is more than one way to make a claim and more than one purpose in doing so. That is, argument is best understood as a mode, and different kinds of argument can be considered genres. I introduced Rogerian argument, which was first brought to composition and rhetoric by Richard Young, Alton L. Becker, and Kenneth Pike in their seminal 1970 book *Rhetoric: Discovery and Change*, and which has been taken up by many since. I use our textbook, *Everyone's an Author*, which offers a brief overview of Rogerian argument as a useful starting point for discussion. I like to ground our consideration of Rogerian argument in Krista Ratcliffe's concepts as laid out in *Rhetorical Listening: Identification, Gender, Whiteness* (2006). Ratcliff says that the aim of rhetorical listening is to cross divides of race, class, and gender; I suggest that rhetorical listening, then, is a generative act that builds the knowledge base of the listener as well as affirms the humanity of the speaker, which is key to Rogers's person-centered psychology (1980).

Obviously, this is radically different from a debate-style argument which our students are familiar with. And it's a far cry from political argument, in which the goal is too often to beat down one's opponent. This is an important difference, I argue and believe, since in the digital age, so little listening seems to be done, and the purpose of argument seems far from generative. By contrast, Rogerian argument, grounded in rhetorical listening, frames the purpose of argument as humanizing different positions, finding commonalities, and where possible, forging both alliances and compromises. At its best, it's an expression of Buber's (1970) I-thou relationship, and thus expresses the underlying ethics of discourse, similar to Aristotle (see Lunsford 1979).

These are lofty ideas. More on the ground, Rogerian argument offers a kind of template for the construction of an argument that can serve as a heuristic. I won't go into the aspects of Rogerian argument here, but again, I link them to genre and purpose. However, now, with rhetorical listening as a starting point, I can emphasize context, which is a fifth key term that I teach, and which shapes the rhetorical situation. What is going on around the writer politically and socially? What are the linguistic and cultural forces at work on the writer and reader? How can a writer accommodate these forces and influences? Thus, I introduce context as an aspect of the rhetorical situation that influences all the other aspects.

Finally, I ask the students to answer the question, "Why now?" What makes their writing timely and important? What compels them to write in the first place? How might that shape their response? I introduce and explain exigence, a sixth key term of the course.

In this new frame, writing an argument as a key aspect of academic discourse and focused on the question of reading and writing in academic settings now has the chance to be both engaging and transferable. Again, a post-project reflection serves to both emphasize the new knowledge and skills, including the new terms students have learned, and place them onto the roadmap of their evolving theory of writing.

THE THIRD OF THREE MAJOR ASSIGNMENTS: CONDUCTING SECONDARY RESEARCH

In my experience as writing program administrator for my college for about a decade now, and as coordinator for writing across the curriculum for a half-dozen years before that, I've come to understand the tremendous demands that students' academic careers place upon them very rapidly. For various reasons—facing a research paper assignment in a gateway course, entering a professional-technical program, transferring to a four-year university—many students will be asked to conduct effective and ethical research with little to no training beyond, and sometimes even before, English 101. So, my third major assignment focuses on information literacy and conducting and writing research.

This assignment, Conducting Secondary Research (appendix 6.E), extends the first two assignments since many students choose to pursue some aspect of their growing understanding of reading and writing in a digital age. For example, one student studied her own reading with and without music in the first assignment, followed that with an argument on music and hyperattention, and then chose to conduct research on how music affects concentration. In this way, she was embodying the role of the researcher and scholar, pursuing her interests and her questions, broadening her scope and deepening her understanding. Other students, however, balked at further research on digital reading and writing and pursued other subjects, developing research questions far more varied and only tangentially related to the course theme.

However, in whatever manifestation, this assignment provided an opportunity for students to learn the first three key aspects of information literacy, as laid out by the Association of College and Research Libraries (2017): to identify what information is needed, locate and access that information efficiently, and assess the usefulness and credibility of the information and source. Information literacy is one of the course outcomes that I have added but which my department has not yet approved; nonetheless, for the reasons I stated above, I feel it is essential that students leave my class having developed their competence in information literacy.

This assignment also provides an opportunity for solidifying the students' understanding of their own writing process and how they can adapt it to different situations. While a few students come to my English 101 class with some training in a protracted writing process, often from an AP English course, most come with little or no conception of process beyond thinking about a topic and drafting a paper, usually in one sitting and with little preparation. Throughout the class, therefore, I scaffold assignments that move students from invention to revision, with spurs for recursiveness. I emphasize the importance of planning for professional and experienced writers, and require that students develop a research question, potential hypothesis, research plan, rough outline, and developed outline populated with notes from their reading, all before drafting. I have them work in conjunction with their PFFs throughout. Few students have ever conducted so much planning before, and many students were surprised and pleased at how easily the drafting process went, compared especially with the nightmarish tales they tell of writer's block, staring at blank screens, and all-night writing sessions fueled by energy drinks.

I'm also able to teach repurposing as part of being a flexible rhetor and ask students to create three-minute "flash presentations." I explain that scholars often conduct extensive research projects, culminating in books or journal articles, and then present some of their findings in short presentations. To be able to repurpose their findings for different audiences and in a different genre is a powerful ability. Students respond generally favorably, using Prezi, Google Slides, or PowerPoint, with visuals and text to present to the class or, if they choose, merely to their PFFs. The point is not necessarily to assess the quality of these presentations, but the students' understanding of repurposing as part of being a flexible rhetor. Finally, through reflection, students place this experience into their evolving theory of writing, which they then complete as the culminating project of the course.

THE THEORY THAT REMAINS

As I look ahead to teaching this class next fall, I can see areas where the theory and teaching of writing remain unfulfilled. Beyond simply making the assignments better, such as developing new approaches to teaching Rogerian argument so that the opportunities are made clearer, I have already revised the presentation of all the assignments using principles promoted by the Transparency in Learning and Teaching (TILT) project (Winkelmes 2014). And I have switched out *Everyone's an Author* for a draft-version of my own textbook (provided free to students) titled *Active Voices*, published by Fountainhead Press, which provides more explicit explanation of the academic environment while limiting the pedagogical apparatus. I have other additions that I believe will make the course more effective at creating the kind of flexible rhetor I hope students become. These are focused mainly on the culminating project, the theory of writing.

First, I'd like to leverage digital media more. Rather than a more-or-less analytical essay that presents the student's theory of writing, I'd like to use the spatiality and plasticity of digital media to encourage a more evolving theory. Inspired by Adam Banks' 2014 CCCC Chair's address, "Ain't No Walls behind the Sky, Baby! Funk, Flight, Freedom," in which he promoted the academic essay to the rank of "dominant essay emeritus" (2015, 272), I want to open my views to a much broader range of possibilities for composing. Heeding the call of Patrick Sullivan in his "UnEssay" essay (2015), I also want to think about creativity as an underlying and fundamental habit of mind that can inform the revision of this and many other assignments. While I already begin my course with a discussion of the habits of mind laid out in the *Framework for Success in Postsecondary Writing* (Council of Writing Program Administrators, NCTE, and National Writing Project 2011), I'd like to rethink those habits based both on Sullivan's entreaty and, someday, accomplish more of what Jody Shipka (2005) argues for in "A Multimodal Task-Based Framework for Composing," wherein she says that, in the ideal world, "composition courses present students with the opportunity to begin structuring the occasions for, as well as the reception and delivery of, the work they produce" (2005, 278–79). What would that mean, especially in considering the potential of online publishing to reach and create real audiences?

No doubt this would be a real challenge, as it would force me to go beyond merely an additive or, in Yancey, Robinson, and Taczak's terms, "assemblage" approach to curriculum revision (2014). Rather than add on multimodality, multimodality through remix would reshape the entire course and the theory behind it.

That sounds like a lot, but in actuality it can be effected at least partially by having students present their understanding of "how good college writing gets done" in spatial form. This might be nothing more than the drawing of stick figures on poster paper with word bubbles presenting key concepts. It might be a flow chart. Or it might be something more elaborate, like a Prezi with bubbles added and rearranged as new concepts are considered and new experiences incorporated. It might be an infographic, developed by adapting an online template. Regardless, it's my hope that these spatial visualizations of the student's theory of writing can then be the basis for their reflections as well as the platform, which allows them to rethink their theories. My suspicion is that such spatial writing better taps into the more-or-less natural literacies of digital natives.

Second, I'd like to emphasize a theory of process as a significant and distinct part of the theory of writing that augments the conscious application of the rhetorical situation terms. I already require a knowledge of writing process, convinced that students are far more empowered to write if they have a process they can rely upon. However, my current theory of writing assignment does not explicitly ask students to reflect upon and theorize about their own process. I intend to provide separate spaces in the assignment for a theory of approaching and analyzing a writing situation rhetorically and for adapting a process to respond to that situation.

Third, I'd like to do more with the threshold concepts that are meant to tie the assignments together into the broader field of writing studies. Borrowing and adapting some of the major threshold concepts as laid out by Linda Adler-Kassner and Elizabeth Wardle in *Naming What We Know: Threshold Concepts of Writing Studies* (2015), I listed a key threshold concept at the top of each assignment. Other than informal in-class discussions, I did not do much with those concepts and none found their way into student reflections or theories. At the same time, I'd like to pay more careful attention to the threshold concepts that actually seem to be present at two-year college campuses, especially metatextual practices, such as those that Theresa Thonney (2011; 2016) and Mark Blaauw-Hara (2014) show us.

Finally, there's an entire conversation going on about meaningful writing assignments and student engagement, which suggests to me a concept of self-authoring, which has been lingering beneath the surface of my interest in writing about writing and which will inform a move from teaching for transfer to learning for transfer. The recent book by Michelle Eodice, Anne Ellen Geller, and Neal Lerner, *The Meaningful Writing Project: Learning, Teaching and Writing in Higher Education* (2017), is on the top of my reading list this summer. Right below it is Dan Melzer's *Assignments across the Curriculum: A National Study of College Writing* (2014), which I hope will further contextualize the revising of the major assignments for my course. Finally, in a broader context, and closely aligned to the goal discussed next, is the inherent value of writing to the student as a human being, beyond what Keith Kroll (2012) warns is a dangerous neoliberal diminishment of the student writer to a customer or "economic entity" (2012, 119).

And so I hear the call for social justice, which in a way has founded my entire career, as I mentioned at the outset: I've attempted to create spaces for nontraditional students to excel in college and to avoid the kinds of paralyzing failures I experienced as a naïve and ignorant first-generation college student. I have plans to read *Code-Meshing as World English: Pedagogy, Policy, Performance*, edited by Vershawn Ashanti Young and Aja Y. Martinez (2011). Two recent *TETYC* articles, "Writing about Language: Studying Language Diversity with First-Year Writers," by Samantha Looker in 2016, and "Toward a Pedagogy of Linguistic Diversity: Understanding African American Linguistic Practices and Programmatic Learning Goals," by Staci Perryman-Clark in 2012, have got me thinking about the need to highlight linguistic diversity as a social justice issue but also as an academic literacy issue. That's more long-term, but I can see the emphasis of my current first-year writing course morphing away from reading and writing in the digital age toward languaging and self-authoring in the academy and the digital age. I think of Nancy Sommers and Laura Saltz's "The Novice as Expert: Writing the Freshman Year" (2004) and their call to help college writers see a larger purpose to their writing, as well as Adam Banks' recognition in *Race, Rhetoric, and Technology: Searching for Higher Ground* (2005) that marginalized students are forced to catch up again and again to technological advances and technological literacies in a context where it's people's lives at stake: "More than mere artifacts, technologies are the spaces and processes that determine whether any group of people is able to tell its own story on its own terms" (10).

I do not know what that course would look like but I am certain it would develop from the course I am currently teaching and revising, rooted in writing about writing and teaching for transfer, and grounded always in the belief that theory informs design which informs practice. And all of that is bound to the perceived needs and experiences of students in a two-year college, as widely varied as those students are and as in flux as is the role of college in our larger culture. As Joanne Giordano and Holley Hassel remind us, we cannot know who will or won't be successful in our courses (2016) since so many factors impact a student's performance (Sullivan 2013), but as a matter of social justice, and the two-year college's promise of democratizing education, we retain the opportunity to serve students who would be otherwise shut out of higher education. And this is an opportunity I think we all savor.

APPENDIX 6.A

KEY TERMS AND CONCEPTS

ENGLISH 101 KEY TERMS AND CONCEPTS

The English Department has agreed that the terms and concepts in the left column shall be shared across all sections of English 101. The terms and concepts in the right column are specific to this section of English 101 though are common in most first-year composition classrooms.

Departmental	*Class-Specific*
Rhetorical Situation[1]	*Composing Process*
1. Audience	1. Analyzing the rhetorical situation
2. Purpose	2. Planning
3. Writer's stance	3. Conducting research
4. Genre: common purposes, content, structures, linguistic features	4. Chunking, outlining, drafting, revising
5. Medium: types and affordances (that is, what is possible, allowed, etc.)	5. Seeking out and using feedback
6. Context: local, social, linguistic, epistemic	6. Reflecting and assessing
7. Kairos (or exigency)	
	Argumentation, Research, and Presentation
	1. Claim and evidence
Concepts[2]	2. Counterargument, rebuttal, concession, and qualification
1. Writers always engage a social and rhetorical situation.	3. Synthesizing sources
2. Writers respond to situations through recognizable forms.	4. Citing sources
	5. Ethos, logos, pathos
3. Writers enact and create identities and ideologies.[3]	6. Rogerian communication/ argument
4. Writers make knowledge and meaning for themselves and for/with others.	7. Active reading and note-taking
	8. Document design
5. Writers move toward expertise from a position of learning.	9. Information literacy: academic databases, Google scholar, Google, and types of sources

APPENDIX 6.B: CULMINATING PROJECT

DEVELOPING A THEORY OF WRITING

Threshold concept: Writers move toward expertise from a position of learning

INTRODUCTION

Dave is in the middle of his first year at Whatcom Community College (WCC) and completed AP English his junior year in high school. He is currently enrolled in first-year composition, biology, and a literature class. In each, he has to write often and in many different ways: a lab report and a short research paper in biology, a personal response to a short story and a presentation on a poem in his literature class, and an analysis of an online advertisement in composition. Dave sees each situation as unique and has trouble seeing the connections between what he is studying in his composition class, what he studied in AP English, and what he has to write in his other classes. Consequently, Dave struggles to make sense of what is expected of him and often receives grades on his written work that disappoints him.[4]

Sara is also taking first-year writing at WCC as well as American history and an art class. In each, she has to write often and in different ways. In composition she has had to analyze the situation she is in before she writes and then after the main writing project assesses how well she met the demands of the situation. In her American history class, before she wrote an analysis of how a current political event was connected to historical antecedents, her professor reminded her to consider her audience. This triggered the other ideas from her composition class, such as genre, medium, and context. Thinking about these helped her make conscious choices about how to respond to the writing she was asked to do in history. As a result, her project was much more enjoyable, and she received the grade she had hoped for.

Dave is a writer who is not yet able to transfer what he learns in his first-year composition to other classes, nor is he able to transfer what he already knows about writing from previous experiences. By contrast, Sara has developed a "metacognitive awareness" of herself as a practicing writer and is able to make more conscious choices about how to respond to different situations.

TASK

Develop a theory of writing that allows you to approach writing tasks in different situations confidently. A theory can be defined as "a set of principles on which the practice of an activity is based" (dictionary.com).

QUESTION

What is your "theory of writing"? What principles now guide your practice and will guide your practice in the future? How do the concepts, terms, and strategies inform that theory?

RESPONSE

Develop and present your theory of writing as an introduction for the writing reflections you complete this quarter. You may wish to refer explicitly to the terms, concepts, and strategies the class is based on (see the syllabus), concepts from *Everyone's an Author*, and specific instances in your reflections and your projects this quarter.

DELIVERABLES

A digital portfolio consisting of the introduction as described above, the four informal writing reflections, and any other texts (visual, alphabetic, etc.) on Google, WordPress, or any other (free) web-hosting site or as a stand-alone document.

TEXTS AND RESOURCES

- *Everyone's an Author*, chapter 36 (portfolio) and all other pertinent chapters
- Council of Writing Program Administrators and WCC English Department: English 101 Outcomes with Indicators
- CWPA, NCTE, NWP, *The Framework for Success in Postsecondary Writing* (executive summary)
- Mark McBeth, *Introducing the Framework for Success in Postsecondary Writing* (online video)
- Nancy Sommers and Harvard University, *Across the Drafts* (online video)

APPENDIX 6.C: MAJOR PROJECT 1

CONDUCTING PRIMARY RESEARCH

Threshold concept: Writers (and readers) always engage a social and rhetorical situation

INTRODUCTION

Tamara, a full-time Running Start student, has over 1,500 Twitter followers, and she tweets multiple times a day, writing the equivalent of a short novel every month. Moreover, she regularly receives dozens of tweets in response. However, in her college sociology class, she has been tasked with writing a research-based report and doesn't have any idea how to begin: "I'm not a very good writer," she says.

Jonas, an engineering student at Whatcom, is an A student who does all of his textbook reading in crowded places, like Starbucks: "I need the constant noise around me when I read," he says. "Otherwise, I can't concentrate on what the author is trying to tell me and I can't stay motivated to do the work." By contrast, when he used to read his textbooks in his apartment, his mind wandered off and he soon found himself playing video games.

Nicole, a returning student at Whatcom, uses Facebook and Instagram regularly, reading updates and posts from friends and responding throughout the day. At the same time, she uses email to communicate with family—especially her grandmother, who lives out of state and with whom she is very close—as well as the manager of the store where she works and her professors. When she was younger, she found writing difficult, but now she can switch from medium to medium easily. "I guess I just kind of figured out how to write to different people," she says.

Joe is a business major soon transferring to the University of Washington. Lately, he has switched all his reading to e-books so that everything he needs is on his MacBook. Not only is this more convenient, he has found that his reading is more effective, too. "I use Google docs to take notes on everything I read, and being able to copy and paste text really invites me to write responses, which makes me learn the material that much better."

What have all these students got in common? They all have found ways to read and/or write successfully though not necessarily in all situations.

TASK

Conduct a study of your own writing *or* reading activities to develop a hypothesis about the effects of the social and rhetorical situation on how your reading or writing is or is not more effective.

QUESTION

How does the social and rhetorical situation affect you as a reader or writer? Sometimes, as with Tamara and Nicole, the rhetorical situation and medium changes the way a person writes. Sometimes, as with Jonas, the social situation affects the way a person reads. And sometimes, as with Joe, the medium (part of the rhetorical situation), affects the way a person reads *and* writes. When you look at the way you read or write in a particular situation or for different tasks, what can you learn about yourself as a reader or writer? Why might that be helpful for you and others to know? *In short, what can you learn about yourself as a writer or reader engaging in social and rhetorical situations?*

RESPONSE

Develop a hypothesis about a reading or writing situation—something you do regularly—and set up either an *experiment* or *observation*.[5] *Conduct that study and record your findings*. Then, present those findings to your instructor and class. Use the IMRAD format common to the sciences and social sciences: introduction, methods, results, and discussion.[6]

Examples: You might consider one of these situations as a place to start:

Reading

- Reading for school vs. reading for pleasure
- Reading online vs. reading print
- Reading in different locations: public, private, home, bus, etc.
- Reading under different circumstances: time of day, with music or without, etc.
- Reading nonlinguistic texts: video games, Facebook pages, YouTube channels, etc.

Writing

- Writing in different situations: at work, school, or other.
- Writing text messages: in different circumstances, to different audiences, etc.

- Writing on social media: across different platforms.
- Writing online: blogs, comments, reviews, etc.
- Writing for pleasure: journals, poetry, fiction, etc., vs. writing for work or school.

DELIVERABLES

1. A brief memo to the instructor that proposes your project: focused subject of study, research question, hypothesis, and methodology.
2. A written text, augmented by visuals (images, graphs, charts) as appropriate, that presents what you studied and how, what you found, and what its significance is; recommended IMRAD format.
3. A digital poster of some kind with key ideas and images to be presented orally to a small group of classmates.
4. An informal "writing theory" reflective response to the project.

POTENTIAL TEXTS AND RESOURCES

- *Everyone's an Author,* chapters 1–3, 13 (pages 201–20, 231–39), 34 (illustrated essay)
- Nicholas Carr, "Is Google Making Us Stupid?"
- Trent Batson, "Response to Nicholas Carr"
- Sven Birkerts, "Reading in the Digital Age"
- Online videos on key terms
- *College Info Geek* on reading and writing (selected videos)

APPENDIX 6.D: MAJOR PROJECT 2

DEVELOPING A POSITION

Threshold concept: Writers respond to situations through recognizable forms

INTRODUCTION

In her early childhood education class, Jenn is presented with a number of theories of child development, each addressing different aspects of the social and cognitive development of children. As part of her training to become a preschool teacher, Jenn has to observe a preschool classroom and assess which of the theories helps her best explain a problematic social interaction she observes. To do this, she has to present her understanding of the different theories, describe the interaction she observed, apply the different theories to the situation, and then take a stand on which theory seems most useful and why. She has to present her understanding in an eight-page position paper.

For his political science class, Marcus has decided to analyze the use of social media in the Arab Spring of 2011, more specifically, the media's accounts of the use of social media. He looks at multiple resources: *New York Times* editorials, *Huffington Post* articles, a mainstream news story from the Associated Press, as well as two peer-reviewed journal articles. He synthesizes what he finds in his sources, looks at some of the actual postings on social media that he could find (primary documents), and takes a position, relative to that of experts, on the effects of social media in promoting change in the Arab world, primarily Egypt.

Both of these writers have to take a position on an issue relevant to their studies. They have to pull information from multiple sources, read in multiple genres, compare their knowledge to some object of analysis, and then state their position on the issue, all carefully qualified to what they can actually know and limited to the evidence they have gathered.

TASK

Inform yourself about the issues surrounding the effects of the digital revolution on education and develop a reasoned position on it.

QUESTION

What experiences have you had that intersect with and inform what professional writers and academics have said about the potential changes of the digital revolution to human understanding, knowledge-making, intelligence, and the role of education? What can *you* understand from a close analysis of your experience *and* these responses about how education has been affected by or should respond to the digital revolution? What do you think? *In short, what's your position on this issue and why do you take that position? What evidence do you have to go on?*

RESPONSE

Use an analysis of your own experience as a means to read and analyze various texts in various genres on the subject of the effects of the digital revolution on human intelligence, including reading and writing, and its relation to education. Look for patterns in the texts: similar and conflicting ideas, ideas that complicate other ideas, and ideas that seem anomalous. Develop a limited and carefully reasoned claim about your position on the subject relative to your deepening understanding of your own experiences and relative to the positions of experts.

DELIVERABLES

1. A written text, with relevant images as appropriate, that makes a reasoned argument by developing and supporting a claim through the careful analysis of source texts as applied to your own experience about your position on the subject.
2. A formal cover letter introducing the main text (one page, single spaced, 200–250 words).
3. An informal "writing theory" reflective response to the project, posted to WordPress.

TEXTS AND RESOURCES

- *Everyone's an Author*, chapters 10 (genre), 11 (arguing a position), and 24 (synthesizing ideas)
- Peter W. Cookson, Jr., "What Would Socrates Say?"
- N. Katherine Hayles, "Hyper and Deep Attention" (2007)
- Ken Robinson, "Schools Are Killing Creativity"
- Richard Miller, "Address to the Rutgers' Board of Governors"
- Clive Thompson, "On the New Literacy" (review)
- Nicholas Carr, "Is Google Making Us Stupid?" (review)
- Trent Batson, "Response to Nicholas Carr" (review)

APPENDIX 6.E: MAJOR PROJECT 3

CONDUCTING SECONDARY RESEARCH

Threshold concept: Writers make knowledge and meaning for themselves and for/with others

INTRODUCTION

For her English class, Jun, a student from Korea, is conducting research on cultural differences of student engagement between American and Korean students, a subject she very much wants to learn about. She argues that the differences, when left unspoken, can have a negative impact on international students' efforts to connect with professors and other students. She presents her research for her English class in a ten-page paper, drawing upon and synthesizing multiple sources.

Jun also attends a diversity conference at another college and, as part of a panel, presents to a group of students from around the state some of what she has found in her research, revising it into a short PowerPoint presentation.

At the same time, Jun is able to draw upon her research to develop a short, persuasive speech in her communications class on the need for cultural-awareness education in college classes. She uses some of the same images she used in her PowerPoint but augmented with charts and graphs from her research paper.

And finally, she emails a friend in Korea and tells her, informally, about the research she's been doing and how that has influenced the way she lives in America.

This writer has conducted ethical and effective secondary research and then shaped (repurposed) her results for different situations, finding new and effective ways to meet her audience expectations and her purposes.

TASK

Conduct some secondary research on an issue that intersects a personal experience or interest of yours and some aspect of education, possibly growing out of your expertise with technology and education and present it in different forms for different purposes.

QUESTION

How does some aspect of your lived experience, some real interest of yours, intersect with an issue surrounding education? For example, how might sleep patterns affect your performance? How might working impact a student's chances of success? How do learning styles and preferences and the demographics of students (for example, race, class, ethnicity, Generation 1.5, etc.) intersect with the perceived purposes of higher education? As a student, what can you tell your classmates, your instructor, and the college administration about this? *In short, what can you teach yourself about something you really want to know more about that touches upon your education and how can you present it to others?*

RESPONSE

Work with a small team to develop and focus a topic and then conduct research via the WCC Library's databases (Academic Search Premier and/or ProQuest) as well as popular search engines to gather several articles (peer-reviewed and popular) and other texts on some aspect of education, student success, and/or technology—we'll brainstorm and develop topics as a class, then present the current knowledge on the specific topic in multiple genres.

DELIVERABLES

1. A proposal, in memo form, outlining the paper plan and purpose (team or individual).
2. A research-based essay, with visual elements as appropriate, that presents and assesses the knowledge you've gathered and your assessment of it relative to your experience, and which tells WCC faculty and peers the value of your new knowledge (individual).
3. A formal cover letter presenting the paper and its salient points (individual).
4. A five-minute presentation (alone or with a partner) for the class using Google Slides, PowerPoint, Prezi, or another platform that demonstrates good document design and presentation principles (team or individual).
5. An informal "writing theory" reflective response to the project (individual).

TEXTS AND RESOURCES

- *Everyone's an Author,* chapters 19–26 (selected sections), 35
- Student-generated articles and texts (5–7)
- Any of the texts from Project 1 and 2, repurposed as appropriate

NOTES

1. We've agreed that "rhetorical situation" is most valuable as an umbrella term under which specific aspects of the situation interact.
2. These concepts derive from the five concepts that form the structure of the first half of Adler-Kassner and Wardle's *Naming What We Know: Threshold Concepts of Writing Studies.*
3. This will not be covered in depth in the class—students are not responsible for this concept.
4. Adapted from Lucille McCarthy's "A Stranger in Strange Lands: A College Student Writing across the Curriculum." *Research in the Teaching of English* 21 (3): 233–65, as reported in *Writing across Contexts,* Yancey et al. 2014, 28–29.
5. Note that an experiment involves manipulating a variable to measure the effect. An observation does not include manipulating variables but relies upon a systematic recording of data.
6. See *Everyone's an Author,* chapter 4.

REFERENCES

Adler-Kassner, Linda, and Elizabeth Wardle, eds. 2015. *Naming What We Know: Threshold Concepts of Writing Studies.* Logan: Utah State University Press.

Auden, W. H. 1966. *Collected Shorter Poems: 1928–57.* New York: Random House.

Association of College and Research Libraries. "Information Literacy Competency Standards for Higher Education." Last modified July 1, 2017. http://www.ala.org/acrl/standards/informationliteracycompetency.

Banks, Adam. 2005. Preface to *Race, Rhetoric, and Technology: Searching for Higher Ground,* xi–xii. Urbana, IL: National Council of Teachers of English.

Banks, Adam. 2015. "Ain't No Walls Behind the Sky, Baby! Funk, Flight, Freedom." *College Composition and Communication* 67 (2): 267–79.

Bartholomae, David. 1986. "Inventing the University." *Journal of Basic Writing* 5 (1): 4–23.

Bartholomae, David, and Anthony Petrosky. 1986. *Facts, Artifacts, and Counterfacts: Theory and Method for a Reading and Writing Course.* Upper Montclair, NJ: Heinemann.

Batson, Trent. 2009. Response to *Is Google Making Us Stupid?* By Nicholas Carr. *Campus Technology.* https://campustechnology.com/Articles/2009/03/18/Response-to-Nicholas-Carr-Question-Is-Google-Making-Us-Stupid.aspx.

Beaufort, Anne. 2007. *College Writing and Beyond: A New Framework for University Writing Instruction.* Logan: Utah State University Press.

Beaufort, Anne. 2012. "College Writing and Beyond: Five Years Later." *Composition Forum* (26). http://compositionforum.com/issue/26/college-writing-beyond.php.

Behrens, Laurence, and Leonard J. Rosen. 1996. *Writing and Reading Across the Curriculum,* 6th ed. Boston: Addison-Wesley.

Blaauw-Hara, Mark. 2014. "Transfer Theory, Threshold Concepts, and First-Year Composition: Connecting Writing Courses to the Rest of the College." *Teaching English in the Two-Year College* 41 (4): 354–65.

Bransford, John D., Ann L. Brown, and Rodney R. Cocking. 2000. *How People Learn: Brain, Mind, Experience and School.* Washington, DC: The National Academies Press.

Buber, Martin. 1970. *I and Thou.* Translated by Walter Kaufman. New York: Touchstone.

Carr, Nicholas. 2008. "Is Google Making Us Stupid? What the Internet is Doing to Our Brains." *Atlantic.* https://www.theatlantic.com/magazine/archive/2008/07/is-google-making-us-stupid/306868/.

Council of Writing Program Administrators, NCTE, National Writing Project. 2011. *Framework for Success in Postsecondary Writing.* http://wpacouncil.org/framework.

Davila, Bethany. 2006. Review of *The End of Composition Studies,* by David W. Smit. *Composition Studies* 34 (2): https://www.uc.edu/journals/composition-studies/issues/archives/fall2006-34-2/the-end-of-composition-studies.html.

Dickinson, Alan Chidsey, Jaime Armin Mejia, and Jeffrey Zorn. 2006. Responses to *Composition at the Turn of the Twenty-First Century,* by Richard Fulkerson. *College Composition and Communication* 57 (4): 730–62.

Downs, Douglas, and Elizabeth Wardle. 2007. "Teaching about Writing, Righting Misconceptions: (Re)Envisioning 'First-Year Composition' as 'Introduction to Writing Studies.'" *College Composition and Communication* 58 (4): 552–584.

Eodice, Michele, Anne Ellen Geller, and Neal Lerner. 2017. *The Meaningful Writing Project: Learning, Teaching, and Writing in Higher Education.* Logan: Utah State University Press.

Fulkerson, Richard. 2005. "Composition at the Turn of the Twenty-First Century." *College Composition and Communication* 56 (4): 654–87.

Giordano, Joanne Baird, and Holly Hassel. 2016. "Unpredictable Journeys: Academically At-Risk Students, Developmental Education Reform, and the Two-Year College." *Teaching English in the Two-Year College* 43 (4): 371–90.

Hassel, Holly, and Joanne Baird Giordano. 2013. "Occupy Writing Studies: Rethinking College Composition for the Needs of the Teaching Majority." *College Composition and Communication* 65 (1): 117–39.

Hayles, N. Katherine. 2007. "Hyper and Deep Attention." *Profession*: 187–99.

Klausman, Jeffrey. 2008a. Review of *The End of Composition Studies*, by David W. Smit. *Teaching English in the Two-Year College* 35 (4): 425–28.

Klausman, Jeffrey. 2008b. Review of *College Writing and Beyond: A New Framework for University Writing Instruction*, by Anne Beaufort. *Teaching English in the Two-Year College* 36 (2): 200–02.

Krashen, Stephen D. 1987. *Principles and Practice in Second Language Acquisition*. Englewood Cliffs, NJ: Prentice-Hall International.

Kroll, Keith. 2012. "The End of the Community College English Profession." *Teaching English in the Two-Year College* 40 (2): 118–29.

Looker, Samantha. 2016. "Writing about Language: Studying Language Diversity with First-Year Writers." *Teaching English in the Two-Year College* 44 (2): 176–98.

Lunsford, Andrea A. 1979. "Aristotelian vs. Rogerian Argument: A Reassessment." *College Composition and Communication* 30 (2): 146–51.

Lunsford, Andrea, Michal Brody, Lisa Ede, Beverly Moss, Carole Clark Papper, and Keith Walters. 2016. *Everyone's an Author*. 2nd ed. New York: W. W. Norton.

Melzer, Dan. 2014. *Assignments across the Curriculum: A National Study of College Writing*. Logan: Utah State University Press.

Perkins, D. N., and Gavriel Salomon. 1994. "Transfer of Learning." *International Encyclopedia of Education*, 2nd ed. Oxford: Pergamon Press.

Perryman-Clark, Staci. 2012. "Toward a Pedagogy of Linguistic Diversity: Understanding African American Linguistic Practices and Programmatic Learning Goals." *Teaching English in the Two-Year College*. 39 (3): 230–46.

Ratcliffe, Krista. 2006. *Rhetorical Listening: Identification, Gender, Whiteness*. Carbondale: Southern Illinois University Press.

Rogers, Carl. 1980. *A Way of Being*. Boston: Houghton Mifflin.

Rosenwasser, David, and Jill Stephen. 2014. *Writing Analytically*, 7th ed. Boston: Cengage.

Selfe, Cynthia L., and Gail E. Hawisher. 2004. *Literate Lives in the Information Age: Narratives of Literacy from the Unites States*. Mahwah, NJ: Lawrence Erlbaum Associates.

Shipka, Jody. 2005. "A Multimodal Task-Based Framework for Composing." *College Composition and Communication* 57 (2): 277–306.

Smit, David W. 2004. *The End of Composition Studies*. Carbondale: Southern Illinois University Press.

Sommers, Nancy. 2008. "The Call of Research: A Longitudinal View of Writing Development." *College Composition and Communication* 60 (1): 152–64.

Sommers, Nancy, and Laura Saltz. 2004. "The Novice as Expert: Writing the Freshman Year." *College Composition and Communication* 56 (1): 124–49.

Sullivan, Patrick. 2013. "'Just-in-Time' Curriculum for the Basic Writing Classroom." *Teaching English in the Two-Year College* 41 (2): 118–34.

Sullivan, Patrick. 2015. "The UnEssay: Making Room for Creativity in the Composition Classroom." *College Composition and Communication* 67 (1) 2015: 6–34.

Thompson, Clive. 2009. "On the New Literacy." *Wired*. https://www.wired.com/2009/08/st-thompson-7/.

Thonney, Teresa. 2011. "Teaching the Conventions of Academic Discourse." *Teaching English in the Two-Year College* 38 (4): 347–62.

Thonney, Teresa. 2016. "'In This Article, I Argue': An Analysis of Metatext in Research Article Introductions." *Teaching English in the Two-Year College* 43 (4): 411–422.

Wardle, Elizabeth. 2009. "'Mutt Genres' and the Goal of FYC: Can We Help Students Write the Genres of the University?" *College Composition and Communication* 60 (4): 765–89.

Winkelmes, Mary-Ann. 2014. "Transparency in Learning and Teaching in Higher Education." https://www.unlv.edu/provost/teachingandlearning.

Yancey, Kathleen Blake. 2014. "Made Not Only in Words: Composition in a New Key." *College Composition and Communication* 52 (4): 297–328.

Yancey, Kathleen Blake, Liane Robertson, and Kara Taczak. 2014. *Writing across Contexts: Transfer, Composition, and Sites of Writing.* Logan: Utah State University Press.
Young, Richard, Alton L. Becker, and Kenneth Pike. 1970. *Rhetoric: Discovery and Change.* San Diego: Harcourt, Brace, Jovanovich.
Young, Vershawn Ashanti, and Aja Y. Martinez, eds. 2011. *Code-Meshing as World English: Pedagogy, Policy, Performance.* Urbana, IL: National Council of Teachers of English.

7

FIND A PRACTICE THAT WILL SUSTAIN YOU

An Interview with Jeffrey Andelora

Patrick Sullivan

Jeff Andelora has taught writing and literature for thirty years, beginning in 1986 at Mesa High School. Ten years later he moved to Mesa Community College, where he taught for twenty years and served as English Department chair for nine. Since 2016 he has served as Dean of Arts, Humanities, and Social Sciences. He has also been active in NCTE, specifically CCCC and TYCA, chairing the latter from 2016–2018. He balances his work life by running, hiking, cooking, and practicing mindfulness.

VULNERABLE

Patrick: Jeff, thank you for speaking with me today. You have been an enthusiastic champion of the two-year college now for many years. What do you find most personally rewarding and meaningful about teaching English at an open-admissions two-year college?

Jeff: There are so many things I love about teaching at an open-admissions college, Pat. First, I love working with a diverse student population—and diverse in every way imaginable. I love working with students who don't yet believe in themselves as college students as they begin to realize that they can do this, that what they've been told or what they've come to believe about themselves may not be true. I also love the opportunity to be a positive influence in their lives, whether as a teacher, a mentor, or even someone who makes an effort to see and appreciate them for who they are. Even if they decide

DOI: 10.7330/9781607329305.c007

not to continue with college, I want them to leave knowing that they weren't just a name on a roster.

Patrick: Many newly minted teachers coming out of graduate school will be teaching at two-year colleges for the first time. Some readers of this book will also be seasoned teachers looking for new ideas and professional renewal. Can you give us three pieces of wisdom, perspective, or advice about two-year colleges and two-year college students that will help teachers at the two-year college thrive and enjoy teaching at these kinds of institutions?

Jeff: 1. Make every effort to connect with your students as real people, each with their own stories and their own struggles. Know that what they bring to the classroom and show you is probably their game face, the façade they hope will keep them safe in a place where they feel really vulnerable.

2. Be gentle with your commentary. Always find something positive and encouraging to say about their work—or, if their work shows no real effort at all, address that. Ask, listen, and offer suggestions on what they might do differently next time. Let them know that even if they don't earn a passing grade in your class, that's not a mark against their character or their ability. It may simply be bad timing. Either way, make sure they know that the real work belongs to them, and that if they're serious you'll help them at every step.

3. Remember that most English faculty were genetically predisposed towards graduate school in English. We loved reading and writing. That is not the case for most of the students we'll work with. Many won't yet have the work ethic or skills we want or expect in our students. The challenge is to meet them where they are and help them grow, succeed.

Patrick: That's a beautiful and inspiring answer. As a follow-up question: Are there any challenges specific to the two-year college that you think are particularly noteworthy that teachers new to the two-year college need to be prepared for?

Jeff: One of the biggest challenges new teachers will face is the shocking range of skills in any given class. They will have gifted students for whom this is the first step in what will be a very successful academic career. In the same class will be students who have a difficult time understanding and figuring out what to say about the readings you provide. Creating a meaningful experience for all students on this spectrum is one of the biggest challenges we face.

COURSE DESIGN

Patrick: You are now in your second year as the interim Dean of Arts, Humanities, and Social Sciences at Mesa Community College, but you have over twenty years of teaching experience in the writing classroom. Drawing on this experience, can you share with our readers how you put together a writing class? Can you talk us through what your basic writing class or FYC class looks like? How do you select readings? How do you put together units? What do students spend most of their time doing in your classes?

Jeff: This is a really hard question to answer, in part because my approach has evolved over the years, but I'll do my best. The writing classes I took as an undergrad were expressivist—in the lineage of Ken Macrorie, Peter Elbow, and others. And I ate it up. Writing this way not only helped me develop a voice, it also became a personal practice, much like a meditative practice. So, when I began teaching, that was what I wanted to give students. At some point I decided that first-year composition probably wasn't the place for personal and exploratory writing and began working with other genres and themes. While I continued to teach a personal and exploratory writing course, the WPA Outcomes statement really influenced the way I approached first-year comp and developmental writing.

Most recently, I (or the class) would decide on a theme for the semester, one that would be interesting to a diverse group of students and provide opportunities to read pieces together. I (and students) would choose a group of readings that addressed the topic, but that incorporated different points of view, different genres, and different audiences. My goal was to help students learn to read and write like scholars, so from week one I'd ask students to read, summarize, and respond. Because we were working with common readings, students could collaborate to make sure they were understanding key points, rhetorical strategies, etc. As the semester progressed, we'd look at other pieces that pushed against each other in some way, and we'd then begin to synthesize the ways people were writing about this topic. One of our writing projects would be a rhetorical analysis, another a synthesis. It's important to note that for better or worse, I never taught the same course twice. I've taught scores of sections of first-year comp, but it was never the same—and that's probably because I was never completely satisfied. It did keep me fresh, however! Sorry, I feel like I barely scratched the surface on this one.

Patrick: Fascinating. Can you give us an example or two of some semesters where the selection of topics and readings worked really well and engaged the majority of your students? Can you provide at least one complete reading list for an entire semester? Is there any trick to doing this effectively? Is there anything you've learned about this approach—especially ceding so much choice and control to your students—that you can pass on to teachers who may want to try this approach in their own classrooms?

Jeff: Ha! I was afraid you were going to ask that. I worked with themes like the impact of social media in our lives, strategies for student success, and personal responsibility. One pairing that I worked with for the latter began with Bill McKibben's "The Christian Paradox: How a Faithful Nation Gets Jesus Wrong." This was a really meaty piece—provocative, smart, and rhetorically sophisticated. We'd first look at the structure of the argument, the rhetorical function of each paragraph. This was new for students, and not easy. Most had never analyzed how a fairly long piece is constructed, but this was an important step in moving them way past the five-paragraph essay. They came to understand the logic of the organization, along with claims, evidence, and addressing opposing views. Needless to say, I had to be really careful teaching this, but that's part of what made it fun. I followed this with Peter Singer's "The Solution to World Poverty," an equally provocative piece. Students would write a summary/response for both, and then I'd ask them to find common ground between the two pieces. This led us to the rather broad question, "In an affluent society such as ours, what is our responsibility to others?" And here things get a little foggy. We'd read other pieces, talk about how McKibben or Singer would respond, and write a synthesis in which each person addressed some variant of that question. Needless to say, this wasn't a "clean" course, as I often wasn't sure where we would end up. But I love that I had the freedom to be creative and go in directions that seemed right for that class. On the downside, I never found the perfect combination, and that's partly why it was a different course each semester. If this gets me voted off the good-teacher island, I accept that.

If anyone wants to try a themed course like this, I'd say read Pat Sullivan's "A Lifelong Aversion to Writing" and do that instead.

BACKSTORY

Patrick: There is no chance you are getting voted off that island! Changing direction a little bit: How did you get interested in teaching English and find your way into this profession? Was it something you always wanted to do, even as a young child? Or was your path to this profession less direct? What were the important influences for you as you made this journey? Were there any courses, teachers, individuals, encounters, or books that were particularly important to you in this regard?

Jeff: I've actually been thinking about this question lately. As interim dean, I'm at a turning point in my career and am wondering what I want to do for the remainder. This has led me to think about how I got to this point in my life—how many decisions were deliberate and how many were more happenstance; deliberately not making a decision because I was afraid of making the wrong one. When all but one option is no longer available, is that making a decision? But back to your good question. No, it was not clear or easy. My first degree was in business—and this was due to a stunning lack of imagination on my part. Born in Buffalo, New York in the late 1950s, I was brought up to think that a man goes into business. So if one went to college, it was for that or some other career—medicine, law, engineering. By the time I finished my degree however, I knew that business was not the path for me, so, I worked in restaurants for a few more years not knowing what I wanted to do. Finally, it dawned on me. I always loved my English teachers in high school and college. One person in particular, G. Lynn Nelson at Arizona State University, became a friend and mentor, and I decided I wanted to be that person for other young people. So I went back to school to get certified to teach English. I then taught high school for ten years before moving to Mesa Community College in 1996, where I've been since. Looking back, I feel very lucky—even though there's still an unsettled feeling in me, never fully satisfied with what I'm doing. But that's something else for me to figure out. . . .

Patrick: As a researcher and writer, you have done perhaps more than anyone in our discipline to help theorize a professional identity for the two-year college English teacher. Can you talk us through how you became interested in this subject, how this interest and research may have affected your work in the classroom, and why you believe issues related to professional identity are so important for two-year college teacher-scholars?

Jeff: In the early 2000s I was working on a PhD in rhetoric and composition at Arizona State University, and I was also teaching full time at Mesa Community College. My department chair at the time was retiring and cleaning out his office. I saw a box of old *TETYC*s in the discard pile and asked if I could have them. I was curious about what people were writing about over the years and became interested in a few articles by Mark Reynolds and Keith Kroll encouraging two-year college faculty to write, to become scholars. Helon Raines also had an article about the need for TYCA, a professional organization to give two-year college English faculty more of a professional voice. I had worked at a high school for ten years, was then teaching at a community college, and was a grad student at ASU, so I started thinking about our professional identity. I noticed the lack of two-year college voices in the field of composition, and was struck by the fact that the theorists, the knowledge-makers, were those who for the most part didn't teach much composition, yet two-year college faculty were teaching five sections of it every semester. Where was our voice?

I started talking to people and asking questions. I emailed Keith Kroll, Mark Reynolds, Helon Raines, and others with questions about their work. They were all very helpful, and someone suggested that I reach out to Paul Bodmer, which I did, and doors started opening. I met Lynn Troyka, Jon Lovas, Nell Ann Pickett, and many others, and they all had really good stories to tell. All of this led to my writing an article, my first, and sending it to Howard Tinberg, editor of *TETYC.* I received positive feedback so decided to do a more in-depth study for my dissertation. Personal interviews with the people who made TYCA happen made it a genuinely fun and rewarding project. And the series on TYCA's history in *TETYC* is a distillation of the dissertation. Jeff Sommers was immensely helpful on that project.

And how did this affect my work in the classroom? I saw research and writing as real things—not an exercise, not an abstraction. It really was an opportunity to participate in larger conversations, and so I really believed in what I was teaching.

ENGAGEMENT WITH SCHOLARSHIP

Patrick: We sometimes hear two-year college English teachers say that they are too busy teaching and grading papers to have time for scholarship and research. How do you respond to that claim? Has your engagement with research and scholarship over the years helped make you a better classroom teacher in any way? If so, can you provide some specific examples of how scholarship or research translated directly into better teaching and learning in your classroom?

Jeff: I'm really empathetic to the lament that we are too busy to research and write. You need to be really excited about something or have a burning question in order to undertake research and writing. And, as you know, Pat, some writing projects, one article, can take a year or longer, which is a huge commitment when you're already very busy. Fortunately, plenty of people take up that call. The pages of *TETYC* are filled with articles that transfer directly to the classroom. I'm thinking of Holly Hassel and Joann Giordano's work that is pedagogically focused—and your own, Pat!—that help all of us. As I mentioned before, the WPA Outcomes Statement really changed the way I approached the teaching of writing. After that, I'm not sure where to begin. I wasn't the same as a teacher after reading Berlin and Bartholomae, as they both reoriented my theoretical understanding of what we do, but dozens more had a similar impact.

Patrick: You obviously stay personally engaged and current with scholarship. How do you do it? How do you find the time? What journals do you subscribe to and how do you keep yourself current?

Jeff: *TETYC* is my favorite, without question, but I also subscribe to *College Composition and Communication* and *College English.* I read what interests me. That includes topics I've long been interested in, but also new topics that spark something. I've also been going to CCCC for a long time and have made friends, so in some ways I'm part of a community of scholars. I know some of the people who write and want to read what they have to say and find out what they've been working on.

There's no easy way to stay current, but I feel it's incumbent on us as teacher-scholars, and so we need to find the time. I imagine we all got into this profession because we love reading and writing—so it's just staying true to that. I try to close my office door for at least half an hour a day and read something that honors the profession I've chosen, whether it's an article in *TETYC* or a piece about guided pathways or a poem. Part of my job is to read and think. That's not in the job description, but it's who we are, and to not keep that going is a mistake. Why not build that into our day at work?

Patrick: I know that you have been actively involved on your campus providing ongoing professional development for full- and part-time English instructors. Can you talk us through what you've been doing and what benefits you've seen from this work? Is there anything here that could perhaps be replicated in other English departments looking to add systematic professional development for full- and part-time faculty?

Jeff: This is a tough one. We have a terrific Center for Teaching and Learning that helps faculty with lesson and course design, outcomes mapping, and using technology to engage students, but the real gap I see is in discipline-specific professional growth. Anyone with an MA in English meets the minimum requirements to teach English at the two-year college, but that doesn't mean they have any coursework or experience teaching developmental writing or first-year composition. A few years ago, I developed a course for current and prospective faculty titled Teaching Composition in the Two-Year College, which provided an overview of post-secondary writing theories and pedagogies. I think the course was valuable, but it's probably not easily replicable, and we're no longer offering it. If someone could create an online version and find a way to offer it for free, or close to it, to colleagues around the country, that would be a terrific service to the field. A relatively easy, low-cost model I like is purchasing an institutional subscription to *TETYC* for $70. All members of the department can share the login info and form a reading group.

PARTING WORDS

Patrick: Finally, what parting words would you like to offer to your colleagues in writing classes across the nation doing the important work of teaching writing at open-admissions institutions? Thank you again, Jeff, for your leadership, vision, and great devotion to the two-year college and the students who attend them. This has been a real pleasure. I've admired you and your work for many years, so this is a treat to talk shop with you. Thank you!

Jeff: Wow, parting words . . . Take time to think about the trajectory of your career. No one sets out to be the burnt-out, grumpy teacher that we all wish had left the classroom years ago. But teaching a five/five load can be grueling and we may be more susceptible than most. So figure out how to stay fresh, how to bring something new to the classroom. We owe that to our students. Whether it's attending conferences, reading *TETYC*, writing and submitting an article for publication, going for a hike, or unfurling your yoga mat, find a practice that will sustain you over the long haul. The richness you bring to the classroom is only as deep as your enthusiasm for being there.

8

POTENTIAL

Student Perspective

Darlene Pierpont

I am a community college student in your English class.
I just finished high school . . .
I am retired . . .
I work several jobs . . .
I have a family . . .
I came to the United States for opportunity . . .
My parents want me to attend college . . .
I am changing my career . . .
I am struggling . . .
I am a wife and mother . . .
I have post-traumatic stress disorder . . .

(NOTE TO TEACHERS: Remember, students at a community college are from all walks of life, and are facing something they must overcome, but they want to succeed, and you have the power to teach them.)

I remember the first class I took when I returned to school. It was English 101. I had not taken an English class in several years, so I was extremely nervous but also excited. We had to analyze several stories, and the grammar alone was difficult for me, but I remember my English professor was kind and patient. (NOTE TO TEACHERS: Remember, when teaching your students, strive to be patient because it takes time

DOI: 10.7330/9781607329305.c008

and practice. If you see one of your students struggling, ask them if they need help. English is a difficult subject to learn.) I also remember my English professor was passionate about his work. I think English needs some passion when taught. (NOTE TO TEACHERS: Remember, when choosing assignments for your class, pick reading that you're passionate about, and that will encourage students to feel passionate about English too.)

In my second year at a community college I took Introduction to Literature. I'll never forget this class. I was terrified most of the semester, but I was determined to face my fears. The reading and writing were difficult because I had to face myself in ways I didn't completely understand or was ready to understand, but in time each assignment brought me closer to myself, and to understanding this world. My professor encouraged his students as well and was a compassionate man who also had a passion for his work. (NOTE TO TEACHERS: Remember to teach English with an open mind. It is a complex subject because it has endless questions.)

My journey continues throughout the classrooms of a community college, but I'll always remember my English professors for their patience and passion for teaching. They helped me to understand myself more, to not be fearful, and to love literature as they do. So remember, I am a community college student in your English class, I want to succeed, and you have the power to teach me.

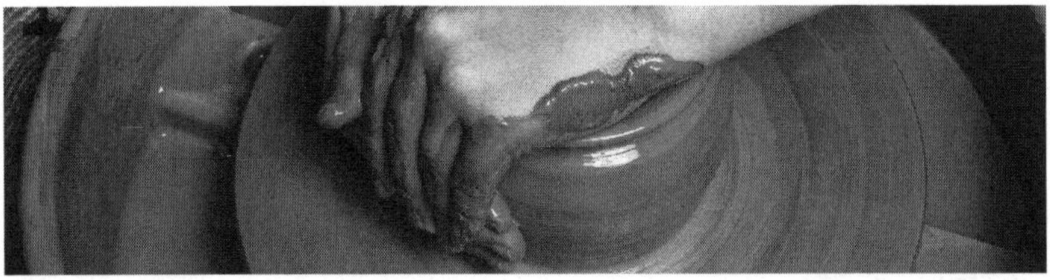

9

MINDFULNESS
Student Perspective

Kevin Rodriguez

My experience studying at a community college was great. Community colleges are usually small places in which the students get to know each other, and where the teachers remember most of their students when they see them walking around the campus. Students choose community colleges for many different reasons such as affordable tuition, credit transferability, location (distance from home), and proximity (to public transportation). The diversity of the student body is also a great bonus that comes from attending a community college as well as the interactions and teaching styles of the professors.

Community college tuition costs are accessible to a broader range of people than those at the university level. For instance, an individual making a minimum salary, looking to pay for their classes out of pocket, can afford to pay for classes and take them at their own pace in this more flexible learning environment.

Community college credits are widely accepted at many universities and alternative programs of study. Thus, most credits are transferable towards a bachelor's degree, which helps students save money. In fact, I just graduated from Manchester Community College in May of 2018, and approximately 98 percent of my credits transferred towards my bachelor's degree requirements. Additionally, community college continues to support my educational journey, as I am taking some extra

DOI: 10.7330/9781607329305.c009

summer and fall classes, which will also transfer towards credit for my bachelor's degree.

Community college locations are ideal, as for most students they are close to home, or within a reasonable proximity to public transportation. This allows for students to work and attend school without having to leave their family or job behind.

There is a significant amount of cultural diversity at the community college level, which comes along with meeting new people from different countries. Also, it is important to note that there is a more diverse range of nontraditional students. These nontraditional students vary in both age and previous college experience, and they bring with them many positive experiences and unique perspectives that enrich every other student's college experience. Also, because of the reliability of transferring credits, there are many students from other universities taking community college classes, which further enhances the nontraditional student population and the overall educational experience of the student body. I have seen many students from Central Connecticut State University, University of Connecticut, and even from Yale University taking classes at Manchester Community College.

During my community college experience, I learned many things about teachers and about myself as a learner. First, the accessibility of the professors at community college was great. If we saw a teacher walking around the campus, we felt comfortable enough to stop and ask them some questions about class, and even in this impromptu setting, without making a formal appointment, the teachers usually tried to help. Second, I experienced many different teaching styles. Some teachers told us many jokes to make us feel safe and to build our confidence, so we could do our class speeches and present our homework in front of the class without being too nervous. This was a great approach to help students relieve their feelings of insecurity and stress; however, I would not apply this to every single class environment, because some students did not take the class seriously or they lost interest in the class due to the teacher's casual approach. Another teacher was very engaging with the class, and she tried to be more informal by allowing more freedom in her class. It was good for us, in terms of it not being too stressful, but at the same time, the consequence of applying this technique was that it came at the cost of sacrificing the organizational structure of the class. The class was very disorganized, and it was hard to understand exactly what we needed to get done. One of the best teachers used an approach that actively engaged the class by having us share our stories and encouraging us to talk more about ourselves. He was also very organized, and we knew exactly what to do and when to get it done. Although this teacher's class was full of readings and assignments, the great environment created by the teacher helped us to overcome the great amount of school assignments. Nevertheless, encouraging students to talk about their personal experiences can be a dangerous path if there is not adequate follow up. For example, imagine a situation in which a student who feels confident and safe enough reveals that he has thought about committing suicide once before because of reasons that still presently exist. This situation comes with a significant risk of the teacher not being able to see that due to their great workload and many other duties that need to be completed by him. This situation can also be difficult for the student who just opened himself up to others by trying to reach out for help, or at least comprehension, and does not get a response. Sometimes, when we talk with others and encourage them to do something, we need to be aware of many possible outcomes. In other words, people react differently when they are being exposed to something that, otherwise, they would have never talked about in front of anybody. Therefore, although this last method of engagement with students was great for most, if not all, of my classmates, it can also be dangerous, especially with the many events happening around schools these days.

The main thing I learned is that the teachers who were both organized and engaging (found ways to connect with the students) created the most enjoyable, thoughtful, and memorable learning experiences for me.

Additionally, from a student's perspective, I would like to say that teachers should always consider the background of each student who is in front of them. For example, there are many foreign students who have already completed a bachelor's degree or who already have a law school degree from their country of origin; however, they are starting over in the United States and learning how to understand the English language. As a result, these students can get frustrated more frequently than other students who are just starting their college classes. Therefore, it would be beneficial if teachers could find a way to learn these things about their students, and thus show more empathy, to prevent them from quitting or taking a "long break" from this second educational journey in their life.

Over all, the community college experience, especially with access to the honors society (Phi Theta Kappa), and honors classes, helped me obtain scholarships during both my associate's degree and with the transition towards my bachelor's degree and was an outstanding journey.

PART III

Equity and Social Justice at the Two-Year College

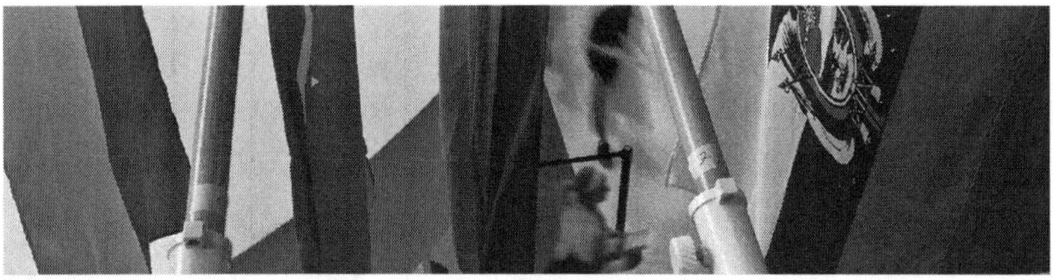

10

SOCIAL JUSTICE AND THE TWO-YEAR COLLEGE

Cultivating Critical Information Literacy Skills in First-Year Writing

Holly Hassel

Abstract: In this essay, I discuss the process of beginning to see more clearly the role that race and class play in access to higher education (including my own). It became more apparent to me how the stated social justice function of education that I studied in many of my graduate courses was actually a lived experience at the two-year college. Though my students at Southeast Community College, where I first started teaching, had fewer resources and more to do academically than their flagship peers, they were hard-working, scrappy, and wanted better for themselves and their families. I could connect with these ambitions, values, and culture as a person and teacher. I also found that my intellectual and philosophical values aligned more closely with the work of two-year college English than they did with the notion of working someplace closer to the top of the academic hierarchy. I saw the liberatory function of public higher education and I felt it in my own story.

When I was a high school student, I wouldn't have been caught dead going to Brainerd Community and Technical College, which was across the street from my high school in Brainerd, MN. As a working-class kid in rural Minnesota, I had a limited sense of what higher education looked like, but I had college aspirations with little accompanying knowledge of what that meant. As a bookish kid who read constantly and excelled

DOI: 10.7330/9781607329305.c010

in school and on standardized tests, academics were the one area in my life where I consistently felt a sense of unimpeachable achievement. Even though no one in my immediate or extended family had a college degree, I talked with friends' parents and teachers in general ways about a future of attending college. My dad in particular, a journeyman printer at the local newspaper, graduated high school and had ambitions for his six children to achieve more economic stability than he had enjoyed as the son of a house painter and stay-at-home mom. I aimed for the selective flagship university in my state, but after a year at the University of Minnesota in Minneapolis, a school of fifty thousand, struggling with a range of material challenges including the cost of tuition, lack of family support, a high number of paid work hours, and lack of reliable transportation, I transferred to a less selective regional comprehensive, graduating in three years and then starting on a master's program.

By the time I reached college and eventually graduate school, my assumptions about two-year colleges had not evolved significantly. I had only a limited sense of what distinguished different sectors of higher education. Starting in the writing center as a graduate assistant tutor, I gained a preliminary sense of what different students brought to college in terms of their learning needs. This was a foundational experience for me in part because, even though I was teaching in my MA program at a comprehensive regional university, we had a basic writing course and an English as a Second Language (ESL) program focused on international student learning, so I was trained to work with a wide range of students despite the structure of modestly selective admissions at the university. When I moved from the writing center to the classroom, I was assigned a book used by the program, given a week's training, and set out to teach a fairly structured curriculum with some ability to customize. This was true in my doctoral program as well, with an orientation and concurrently taught pedagogy and theory class as I taught two sections of first-semester college writing under the apprentice model that is typical of graduate teaching assistantships (GTAs). What that offered me was a structured opportunity to teach the kinds of students typically found at selective and flagship institutions—students who are motivated, well-prepared, and usually easy to teach—and in a program staffed primarily by GTAs. In such contexts, the intellectual work of curriculum development, professional development, and program assessment falls largely on a WPA or WPA-led committee. Though this provided me with a foundation of pedagogical content knowledge and disciplinary best practices, it did not help me anticipate the ways that most writing programs in open-access and less selective four-year colleges are not staffed, taught, or assessed in that same way.

When I reflect on how that transition to a new kind of workplace did or did not happen smoothly, I can identify two critical components that helped me prepare for teaching in a two-year college setting, both pivotal: the writing center experiences and formal writing center coursework I have already described, which helped me develop the ability to work in an individualized way a broad array of students in different courses and with different backgrounds. The second critical experience that was important to helping me bridge a gap between graduate education and working in different institutional contexts was, however, also extra-curricular.

It was also largely borne of material necessity: moonlighting at the local community college while I attended graduate school full time and taught two classes per semester as part of my teaching assistantship in the English Department where I was doing my graduate study. For three years, I taught one course per quarter, year-round, which gave me a wide enough range of interaction with students from developmental writing, Composition I and Composition II as well as a general education introductory literature course. This familiarized me with just how satisfying the two-year college teaching environment is (as someone who was already predisposed to valuing teaching as part of my future work). Like the students who I eventually taught for sixteen years in central Wisconsin, the Lincoln, Nebraska community college students were extremely diverse in myriad ways—all commuter students ranging from a student in his fifties who was retooling himself after working two decades as an over-the-road trucker to a student who attended classes when she wasn't a dancer in a strip club in town. I had traditional-age students with small children, students who were homeschooled for their entire K–12 experience and for whom mine was their first ever experience in a traditional classroom.

My two-year-college students had tangible goals and their material challenges were significant, including unreliable transportation, struggles to find money for gas, books, and food, or a lack of support from family, such as for the student in my English 102 course who would talk with me about her family's ongoing dissuasion of her college enrollment. Students in an introductory women's and gender studies course included a married couple, co-parents to a young toddler and one of whom worked an overnight shift at the regional airport. Typical students at the two-year colleges I have taught at enrolled in classes on top of working full time as carpenters, bartenders, CNAs and cashiers, to name just a few examples. But I also had a student with a perfect score on the ACT, another who had reversed transfer to our campus (in his hometown) from an elite private liberal arts college for family and personal reasons. Successful completion of college coursework—a two-year degree or a four-year degree—is, for these students, the difference between the reasonable possibility of earning a college degree and with it economic and civic progress and being lost to higher education altogether.

The diverse group of students I taught over the three years at Southeast Community College fundamentally shifted my teenage attitudes, as did the increasing levels of critical and feminist theory I was learning as a graduate student. I began to see more clearly the role that race and class played in access to higher education (including my own), and it became more apparent to me how the stated social justice function of education (and the Marxist theory I was reading) in many of my graduate courses was actually a lived experience at the two-year college. Though my students at SCC had fewer resources and more to do academically than their flagship peers, they were hard-working, scrappy, and wanted better for themselves and their families. I could connect with these ambitions, values, and culture as a person and teacher. I also found that my intellectual and philosophical values aligned more closely with the work of two-year college English than they did with the notion of working someplace closer to the top of the academic hierarchy. I saw the liberatory function of public higher education and I felt it in my own story.

What I mean to say is that by the time I graduated, I had the tools I needed to adapt to a new environment, and I was working toward refining my values as a teacher, scholar, and person, but my content knowledge base was inadequate to help me with the direct and specific task in front of me. In part, this was a gap between the academic and curricular preparation I had in my graduate programs and the actual work I was doing in the basic and first-year writing classroom in two-year college settings. My work as a graduate writing center tutor (and the accompanying writing center theory and practice course I took over a summer when I started tutoring) comes the closest to academic study that directly linked to the classroom work I ended up doing.

When I began working full time at an open-admission two-year college, I didn't know how to adjust my approach in curriculum, instruction, or assessment to the needs of these specific students. What stands out to me is that the experiences I had that ultimately made it possible for me to bridge that gap between graduate preparation and working in a new professional setting were essentially extracurricular. This is not the fault of the graduate programs I graduated from. It was that there were few, if any, structured opportunities that enabled me to integrate my teaching (or tutoring) and my academic studies. My MA program allowed me to take an internship class working with a local faculty member at a technical college, but with minimal academic or scholarly inquiry components that integrated the experiential learning with my intellectual and research interests.

It was only after I started learning about the Scholarship of Teaching and Learning—and seeing how program-level assessment had a role in the degree to which students were placed appropriately in courses and provided with the support they need to be successful. Only by doing the work that needed to be done to accurately assess student needs as they aligned with our admission practices, the types of preparation students brought with them to the writing classroom, and how to develop a curriculum that responded to those needs was I able to be the teacher my students required.

Like many teachers early in their careers, I started my career "importing" what I had learned about teaching first-year writing courses from graduate school. With experience from both the community college where I taught part time (and that had a fairly structured curriculum and assigned text) as well as more open-ended curriculum from the R1 program where I had received my degree, I had a couple of approaches to choose from, especially given that the institution I was joining had little in the way of curricular structure. Opting for an open-ended approach, I struggled to adapt to the needs of the student population that I encountered for the first few years of teaching. Failing to fully acknowledge the nonacademic and academic challenges my students brought, my flexible portfolio approach that relied heavily on process pedagogy with endless student autonomy had worked for the academically socialized students whose prior educational experiences were well-matched with the demands of college.

Unfortunately, for underprepared students, first-generation students, and the diverse students in my classrooms at UW Marathon County, this expansively flexible curricular approach did not work. It meant students were frustrated with what felt like a lack of direction, and I was frustrated that students didn't seem to be stepping up to the plate. Even though I knew on some level there were other factors at play, I couldn't help but personalize students' failures.

"TRANSFER INSTITUTIONS, TRANSFER OF KNOWLEDGE"

What ultimately changed my perception of two-year colleges and allowed me to reorient to the realities of the educational context I was in was to start to refocus my approach on the classroom. First, I moved from a teaching to a learning mentality. Through some professional and faculty development programming in the UW system—the Wisconsin Teaching Fellows program—I was provided an opportunity to reflect on and learn about pedagogical theory. I began to understand that the activity taking place in the classroom was not me doing a thing where then some other things would magically happen; it was a matter of recognizing that all thinking about teaching had to be complemented by accompanying thinking about learning. If I do X, then students need to do Y. What will make the relationship between those two things the clearest? And how can I structure a learning environment that facilitates the relationship between teaching and learning? Even though I was a first-generation college student, I excelled academically and had been well socialized to "perform" learning in formal schooling—something a lot of my students did not bring with them. I had to figure out how to make what I knew in an internalized and unexamined way about academics explicit to the students I taught who did not all share in that unstated knowledge. I had to surface and articulate the hidden curriculum and make it part of the explicit curriculum (see Freire 2007; Shor 1999; hooks 2000; Kozol 1991; Kozol 1995; Kozol 2005; Bourdieu and Passeron 2000; Delpit 1995).

Like Randy Bass (1999), I started to see classroom work as an interesting research problem to be investigated, which required an entirely different worldview. In "The Scholarship of Teaching: What's the Problem?" Bass poses:

> One telling measure of how differently teaching is regarded from traditional scholarship or research within the academy is what a difference it makes to have a "problem" in one versus the other. In scholarship and research, having a "problem" is at the heart of the investigative process; it is the compound of the generative questions around which all creative and productive activity revolves. But in one's teaching, a "problem" is something you don't want to have, and if you have one, you probably want to fix it. Asking a colleague about a problem in his or her research is an invitation; asking about a problem in one's teaching would probably seem like an accusation. Changing the status of the problem in teaching from terminal remediation to ongoing investigation is precisely what the movement for a scholarship of teaching is all about. How might we make the problematization of teaching a matter of regular communal discourse? How might we think of teaching practice, and the evidence of student learning, as problems to be investigated, analyzed, represented, and debated? (1999)

After reading other works like Ernest Boyer's *Scholarship Reconsidered: Priorities of the Professoriate* (1997) and Pat Hutchings's *Opening Lines:*

Approaches to the Scholarship of Teaching and Learning (2000), I began to see how as much as college writing is about a relationship between a teacher and a student, it's also about identifying and then anticipating the kinds of common issues that students will encounter, naming them, and building a class that responds to those.

Energizing me, then, as an instructor, is ongoing assessment of the changing needs of students—changes in student populations, degree requirements or structure, or other variables mean that there is no one-size, static curriculum and pedagogy I can deploy. These have to be matched with what I would call "constants" in terms of my instruction and assessment methods. These reflect my values and skills as an instructor and are built on the ongoing systematic inquiry that has informed my development as a teacher and what I know to be the needs of the students who choose a two-year college as their pathway to higher education.

A key project for me in identifying those constants was a research project with colleagues on the transition of students from English 101 to English 102. We recruited a number of students to track their growth as writers and success in moving from first-semester composition to second-semester composition, and then analyzed their writing across several key dimensions between the two courses. What we learned ultimately became the framework for my "course constants" that I adapt as needed to the courses I teach. All my pedagogical choices branch from these principles.

First, students need to develop **rhetorical adaptability,** as my colleague and research partner Joanne Baird Giordano and I coined it in our article that described the results of that research project, "Transfer institutions, Transfer of Knowledge: The Development of Rhetorical Adaptability and Underprepared Writers" (2009).

> Our classroom research reveals that students who straddle the basic/developmental writing and college-level writing borderland struggle to translate instruction into rhetorical adaptability. When faced with challenging new reading and writing tasks in the core, transfer-level composition course, students in our study reverted to rhetorical strategies typical of pre-English 101 instruction. Our findings emphasize the importance of cultivate students' metacognition as part of the writing curriculum, highlight the benefits of process pedagogy at all stages of pre-college and first-year college composition, and argue for text-based writing assignments in introductory writing courses. (2009, 26)

Specifically, when students write only in familiar genres and for specific rhetorical purposes (to summarize source information or to express an opinion) and in specific formats (the five-paragraph essay), they will struggle to develop the ability to adapt to purposes, genres, and audiences that require an on-the-spot or even deliberative assessment of how to make rhetorical choices that are suitable to that writing situation and task. Though this concept overlaps with the "WPA Outcomes Statement for First-Year Composition (3.0)" outcome of "rhetorical knowledge"—particularly working to "Develop facility in responding to a variety of situations and contexts calling for purposeful shifts in voice, tone, level of formality, design, medium, and/or structure" (Council 2014)—it is not identical. Knowledge implies something static, something that is known, whereas adaptability requires students to demonstrate in multiple ways their ability to write for different purposes, audiences, and goals. For me, the goal is to create structured opportunities with scaffolded instruction that will introduce students both to those writing opportunities and to the instructional materials and activities that will help them complete those writing tasks effectively.

Second, students need **structured opportunities to course correct** and develop metacognitive skills. For students who start their college writing courses within a basic writing/nondegree credit writing course, or those who begin in a first-semester course like our English 101, which includes students with borderline placement assessments, it's of critical importance to provide those students with lots of opportunities to try, to fail, and to course correct. Students in open-admission and two-year colleges often have educational experiences that are not well-matched to the demands of college writing, perhaps because they went to schools that emphasized literary analysis in their English courses; nontraditional students who have a gap in their education; home schooled students; students with non-college-prep coursework, and many other circumstances.

When subsequently asked to engage in complex rhetorical tasks that include synthesizing dense texts or analyzing the rhetorical choices of academic sources, students will often revert to informational or argumentative strategies (or sometimes evaluating sources). High stakes and low-feedback assignments only mean that students will (a) not want to take risks or (b) do the assignment wrong and receive a low grade. These are retention issues that can easily be addressed by structuring courses in a way that allows for students to try a hard task, then revise and redo it as needed. This means that several components are always key to my writing courses, including peer review and electronic submission of a draft with a revision plan to our Course Management System (CMS). Written feedback based on that submission (even brief notes on areas of revision), and then one-on-one conferencing (with class cancelled for the week as a workload management technique) all offer opportunities for students to refocus and reengage with a task. Last, portfolio assessment means that even if there is room for improvement at the midterm, the students can revise the draft before a final portfolio assessment, increasing the likelihood of doing the work and the learning that are required to pass a course and move on successfully to the next-level course or subsequent reading and writing intensive coursework.

Last, students in open-admissions contexts need to continuously work on their **critical reading skills**. This means that in all writing courses, students need structured opportunities to work through challenging texts across all ranges and registers. This also means that writing projects as I conceive of them are consistently text-based, and I ask students to employ critical frameworks as they read, unpack, analyze, or use sources. Most recently, I have worked hard on a "no intellectual shortcuts" philosophy, which means that the goal with teaching information literacy is to equip students with the ability to analyze and unpack sources—without relying on tropes or rules like "Wikipedia isn't reliable" or "scholarly journals are always credible" because sometimes Wikipedia *is* reliable (see Giles 2005) and sometimes scholarly articles have lots of problems (see Flaherty 2017; Jaschik 2017; McKenzie 2017). In the next section I describe my current English 101: Critical Reading and Writing course structure according to these three principles and how the assignment sequence aligns with and cultivates those skills which are also aligned with our writing program's outcomes and the WPA outcomes.

HOW THIS LOOKS NOW

Our department's structured curriculum and outcomes for English 101 calls for writing in several genres and for multiple purposes, and in keeping with that, my current course is structured around the themes of information literacy and Wikipedia as a source. My course description reads:

> "Don't Cite Wikipedia!" How many times have you heard this refrain? What it reveals is the tensions around how people access and use information, and the proliferation of the availability of information. Simultaneously, as critical readers, writers, and thinkers, we may struggle to identify what is or isn't quality information—or to identify what information we need to gather and evaluate for our particular purposes and audiences. In this

> course, we'll work on reading, writing, and researching for different purposes, cultivating your ability to assess and evaluate the quality of information and its relevance to your specific purposes as a writer. You'll also be writing for multiple rhetorical purposes and in different sites, including selecting a topic of importance to you and then actually drafting and posting a Wikipedia article on that topic. In this way, we'll be blending academic writing and new media writing in order to achieve the course goals, which are outlined below.

To achieve these goals, students complete a sequence of assignments aimed at engaging questions of information literacy throughout the course, but also through the lens of a particular topic they are passionate about. The departmental course sequence includes a literacy narrative, rhetorical analysis of a writer's arguments, synthesis of sources, and argument. I have adapted these to the course theme.

Assignment Purposes

First, instead of a traditional literacy narrative, students draft an information literacy narrative, in which they reflect on and apply the principles from the "Framework for Information Literacy for Higher Education," approved and published by the Association of College and Research Libraries (Association 2016). The framework, much like the "Framework for Success in Postsecondary Writing" (Council 2011), focuses on six core principles that students write about for the first paper but also continue to engage throughout the semester:

- Authority Is Constructed and Contextual
- Information Creation as a Process
- Information Has Value
- Research as Inquiry
- Scholarship as Conversation
- Searching as Strategic Exploration

In outlining both knowledge practices and dispositions, the document invites students to learn about different aspects of knowledge production including authority, creation processes, different media and formats, and appreciating the value of information. Their information literacy narrative asks them to reflect on the ways they have come to recognize and use authoritative sources, or the ways that they have or have not reflected the framework concepts of knowledge practices and dispositions. They use a series of prompting questions to start their drafting, including the following:

- What assumptions do you have about information—where you get it, what makes it credible, and how particular sources should and could be used?
- What are your primary "go-to" sources for information, whether academic or nonacademic needs?
- What kinds of formal writing assignments have you done in which you had to do research and/or evaluate information? What did you learn from those and how do they continue to shape your approach to information-gathering?
- What, if any, differences are there in the types of information you seek out for different purposes?
- What do you know (or think you know) or what have you been told about how you will use information/sources/research in college?
- What areas do you want to grow in as a reader and thinker as you move into your college career? How will information literacy and information management factor into those goals?

By reflecting on these distinct personal experiences and integrating them with the Information Literacy framework, students start to establish a benchmark of their prior knowledge as well as develop a foundation of understanding around how information is created and used and the appropriate and ethical ways of using it.

Building on this foundation, students start by doing a brainstorming list that focuses on generating a list of topics, activities, ideas, texts, sources, or interests that they have in their lives. They are preparing here to start finding sources—one must be a Wikipedia article—on something that is important to them in preparation for the rhetorical analysis of two sources on this topic. Topics last semester ranged from video games like Bioshock and League of Legends to Kurt Vonnegut novels to travel, physical fitness, waterfowl hunting, and gun calibers. The next task, then, is to "locate two sources—one should be a Wikipedia article on your topic or some subtopic, and another should be a scholarly (or peer-reviewed) article on that topic, if available. If your topic is very current, about an obscure figure or work, or about popular culture, you may not be able to locate a peer-reviewed article. In that case, another type of source will work—a magazine, newspaper, book, or website." They are called upon to ". . . move beyond comprehension of a text to analyzing the strategies that authors use to communicate messages to readers. Thus, you'll need to understand the author's rhetorical situation (audience, purpose, context), the different writing techniques the uses to reach the audience and achieve the purpose, and find specific evidence in the text itself to support your analysis about the text's rhetorical approach." As with the previous paper, students are given guiding questions:

- What is your first impression of text? Does it seem to take one side over the other?
- Pay attention to the essay's structure—where does it address which positions? Who speaks to and for those positions? Which are introduced and at what point? Which get more space?
- How does the writer select evidence to represent each point of view work? Do some sources seem more credible than others?
- What is the tone of the text? Identify specific textual examples where the writer seems to communicate a particular attitude toward the subject being discussed.
- Look carefully at the writer's word choice (diction). Where do you see words with negative or positive connotations? That is, which verbs seem to communicate a positive meaning and which communicate a negative meaning? Work carefully through the essay and try to identify specific examples of language that communicate the writer's tone or that characterize the topic in a particular way.

As part of this process, we spend two class periods learning about the distinctions between types of sources—again, in terms of author credentials, frequency of publication, review process, compensation of authors, and type of publication venue. They collect three sources in addition to the Wikipedia article on their select topic. The goal here is to figure out something about what makes an encyclopedia an encyclopedia and what makes a magazine article the thing that it is—and what makes a Wikipedia entry what it is. A key reading at the start of this unit is "Wikipedia: What Wikipedia is Not" (Wikepedia "What" 2018), a lengthy overview of all the source use, types, or functions that Wikipedia does not do. This is intensely illuminating to students who have mostly heard "don't use Wikipedia" even when they consult it regularly. They are also introduced to definitions of source material that are essential to information literacy but they haven't regularly learned, including the difference between primary and secondary sources, neutral presentation of ideas, and level of editorial control. Along with the "Five Pillars" of Wikipedia article (Wikepedia "Five" 2018), students use this as a foundation to understand how an information source they rely on regularly and heavily is distinct from other types of information.

Once students have cultivated a set of principles about what information is and how it is used, as well as some knowledge base on their selected topic, they are tasked with (a) learning how to write for the web, (b) learning to fulfill the rhetorical requirements of a writing task with specific purposes, audiences, and genre conventions, (c) evaluate the needs of a reading audience, and (d) participate in knowledge building and an attendant conversation with real readers and writers about that knowledge construction. That is, they have to write a Wikipedia article. The assignment instructions note this paper will "take on the form of an 'authentic' online text that will be used by other readers" and that "We'll read and discuss further documents that tell you about information literacy, source use, and writing for the specific audience of an online reference entry," and frames the task for students as follows:

> We've been working toward and talking about the ways that different kinds of sources have different types of audiences and purposes, and revising/editing formal texts that fulfill the expectations of those genres. You should be keeping in mind the principles of information literacy from the ACRL statement that we used for the Information Literacy narrative. Further, the multiple sources you collected for Paper 2—the rhetorical analysis—will *all* be sources you can draw from for your Wikipedia paper because, as we have read and discussed, good entries will be well-supported and draw from a range of appropriate primary and secondary research sources located by the writer(s). You will probably need to conduct additional research for your entry.

Students are allowed two options: "You may either (a) *substantively revise and add to an existing entry* or (b) *produce a new entry of at least 1000 words,*" and as they review the articles that already exist on their topic, they indeed find that either there is an information gap (potentially no article at all on the topic they have collected information about), or the article they have located is of poor quality or has incomplete information.

Lastly, students are poised to make their own independent argument about information literacy. Their final assignment asks them to select an issue we have explored throughout the course (within the topic of information literacy) and write an argument about that issue. This can be something related to information editing and management online, educational approaches to the topic, or some other claim they wish to support. In the end, the students are asked to locate sources on their topic (now that they've become familiar with the information literacy principles) and demonstrate both through the use of sources to support their claim and the position they take—a sophisticated understanding sufficient to argue for something.

Pedagogical Approach

The assignment sequence is intended to be built on critical reading tasks throughout the course, whether it's understanding and applying the principles of information literacy from ACRL or collecting and comparing the rhetorical features of several source types. And writing for the purposes of rhetorical analysis or synthesis (including the "neutral point of view" that Wikipedia calls for) is a surprisingly challenging skill for students who are well-versed in writing to inform or support an opinion but not analyze how texts work. As a result, a recursive writing and process portfolio pedagogy is essential to working with students at open-admission institutions.

Specifically, each paper is part of a unit that includes a peer review of the rough draft, submission of the draft to a CMS dropbox for holistic feedback from me, and then a conference before the midterm portfolio assessment and again at the end of the semester for course correction as needed. The specific pedagogical goals of these activities are as follows:

Peer review: Though there is no shortage of disciplinary research and evidence that supports the value of peer review in writing courses, it's not always an easy sell for students who are convinced that the only valuable feedback is that of a teacher who will tell them what to correct. Rethinking their relationship to other students as readers who can provide them with useful responses and to the text as something evolving in complex ways beyond punctuation or sentence-level issues can be challenging. Structuring and framing peer review—and cultivating a classroom culture in which texts are constantly evolving and improving based on feedback from real-life readers—is essential to making this a useful part of a writing course. The Wikipedia entry project is particularly well-suited to supporting this shift in perception because ultimately, they come to realize, the success or failure of their posted Wikipedia entry *ultimately depends on the review of Wikipedia readers*. Their article is only accepted or rejected based on its ability to conform to expected conventions and meet the expectations of readers/users of the online reference work. This is a powerful lesson for them.

Written holistic feedback: To also reduce the emphasis on punctuation and usage that so many students bring with them from high school to college, particularly students without a challenging college-prep high school curriculum, is feedback that focuses only on content and ideas for the first draft. In this way, submission of a draft through a CMS in which I as a reader only engage with content as well as global/higher order concerns is a crucial strategy to helping students focus their attention on the rhetorical dimensions of their text rather than the surface.

Conferencing: Likewise, a third layer of feedback on the same text (built into the course) is individual conferences. With multiple sections of writing, this can be tricky, but mandating them (portfolios are not accepted without participating in a conference) and providing verbal feedback on the first two papers of the course—one that has received written feedback from me already and another that has been peer reviewed—reinforces the notion that the writing process is recursive, and that revision is an essential component of an effective writing progress. In semesters where instructors are teaching multiple sections of writing courses (so, at two-year colleges this is all of them!) cancelling a week of class to manage these is a wise investment of time and energy. Mandatory conferencing also helps break through the anxiety and stress that many two-year college students feel about interacting with faculty. I know from conversations with students as well as my own experience as a first-generation college student with limited contact with educated or professional-class folks that the prospect of going to an instructor's office for a conversation was terrifying. Being accessible, setting the tone as conversational, and making it a required part of the writing and revising process has the advantage of helping students break through those anxieties, which means it is more likely they will use this valuable resource of interaction with faculty in subsequent semesters.

Portfolio assessment: Lastly, I can't emphasize enough the value of portfolio assessment (versus individual grades on individual papers) for two-year college students. Many students (not all) need an opportunity to course correct in the semester if they have had limited opportunity to write in these genres prior to arriving at college. Attempting a new task is always going to result in some failures—and being graded on first attempts to engagement with that task can mean the difference between passing or retaking a course—or failing out of college altogether. Portfolio assessment at the midterm and end of semester means that students get the opportunity to try, and fail, at a task and then fix those first efforts that missed the mark. This way, they aren't then trying to dig out of a hole that they created early in the course—or punished for trying new or unfamiliar things and rewarded for playing it safe.

These are structured and *required* components that make revision a learning goal of the course as well as a course requirement. In this approach, revision is normalized and expected—not something to do independently on one's own if desired, or as a task assigned by the instructor for increasing the grade on an assignment. Structured revision activities as part of the course send the message that revision as part of the writing process is necessary and valued, and in assessing through a holistic portfolio method, students hear the message that writing is something that can be evaluated systematically but isn't about nickel and diming points.

REFLECTIONS ON LOVE AND SOCIAL JUSTICE

As someone who had internalized a lot of the cultural messages about two-year colleges and without a critical framework provided in my family life about everything I now know to be true now, I have different ideas about access to public education as a pathway to social mobility. I can critically examine the toxic messaging around meritocracy and its myths (such as the bootstraps myth), and the ways that poor and working class people and people of color are encouraged to take a disproportionate responsibility for and to personalize their failures to advance in education, or work rather than to understand how they are situated in an existing power structure that reproduces privilege and rewards and compounds it. My work in the two-year college is the work of social justice, and that is why showing up every day to teach my students will always keep me energized and engaged. Every day in the two-year college I am helping students who might think they "aren't college material" or who are facing incredible material challenges and who are also showing up to work toward something better for themselves and their families. That will *always* keep me mission-driven.

The pedagogical strategies that I have described in this essay—and the reciprocal relationship between my teaching and my systematic inquiry into teaching—are one of the ways that I remain engaged in my work. Approaching first-year writing as inquiry-focused and in ways that are refreshed regularly in response to student needs means I'm not recycling the same assignments or reading the same papers on clichéd or shallow subjects—student interest in their topics in an academic way means we are partners together in cultivating intellectual curiosity along with rhetorical, research, writing, and college-learning skills. Further, projects and portfolios that students are engaged in—and that I can see they want to read about and learn about, make it a pleasure to participate in and not a slog through themes on topics that ultimately interest neither teacher nor student.

Refocusing in a real and substantive way—the work that we do as faculty from research with teaching as a secondary activity to teaching and research as mutually refreshing activities—is essential to creating a satisfactory career at a two-year college. Another part of the job is a willingness to recognize that many in academia have preconceptions and misconceptions about the work—and committing to helping correct those. This can be exhausting work, but it is necessary. Last, a genuine love for students and a willingness to do the social justice work of open-access higher education is required—and can be developed.

APPENDIX 10.A

Step 2: Select one of your source types and pair up with another student in the class who also has a source of that type (newspaper, website, magazine article, book, journal article). Discuss the following:

List source information:

What features apply to this source type?

Write your source type and info here:

Feature	Your assessment/analysis
Diction (complex and elevated or simple and accessible?)	
Structure (density of paragraphs, thesis-driven? Most information in intro? Traditional essay structure?)	
Jargon/technical language (specialist knowledge required?)	
Background info provided (lots of assumptions about what readers already know, or extensive explanations of complex terms?)	
Rhetorical purpose (inform, argue, persuade, move, reflect, or some other goal of the text?)	
Citations (footnotes, bibliography, in-text citations? Or signal phrase references?)	
Use of visuals (photos, images, tables, graphs?)	

Based on these qualities of that source type, what conclusions can you draw about the rhetorical features of that type of source?

REFERENCES

Association of College and Research Libraries. 2016. "Framework for Information Literacy for Higher Education." Association of College and Research Libraries Board. http://www.ala.org/acrl/sites/ala.org.acrl/files/content/issues/infolit/Framework_ILHE.pdf.

Bass, Randy. 1999. "The Scholarship of Teaching: What's the Problem?" *Inventio: Creative Thinking about Learning and Teaching* 1 (1). https://my.vanderbilt.edu/sotl/files/2013/08/Bass-Problem1.pdf.

Bourdieu, Pierre, and Jean-Claude Passeron. 2000. *Reproduction in Education, Society and Culture*, 2nd ed. Trans. Richard Nice. Thousand Oaks, CA: Sage.

Boyer, Ernest. 1997. *Scholarship Reconsidered: Priorities of the Professoriate.* San Francisco: Jossey-Bass.

Council of Writing Program Administrators. 2014. "WPA Outcomes Statement for First-Year Composition (3.0)." http://wpacouncil.org/positions/outcomes.html.

Council of Writing Program Administrators, National Council of Teachers of English, and National Writing Project. 2011. *Framework for Success in Postsecondary Writing.* WPA Council. http://wpacouncil.org/files/framework-for-success-postsecondary-writing.pdf.

Delpit, Lisa. 1995. *Other People's Children: Cultural Conflict in the Classroom.* New York: New Press.

Flaherty, Colleen. 2017. "'Colonialism' Article Flap Highlights Push for Transparency in Publishing." *Inside Higher Ed,* 12 June 2017. https://www.insidehighered.com/news/2017/09/26/author-third-world-quarterly-article-colonialism-wants-it-stricken-record-it-might.

Freire, Paulo. 2007. *Pedagogy of the Oppressed.* New York: Continuum.

Giles, Jim. 2005. "Internet Encyclopaedias Go Head to Head." *Nature* 438: 900–901. http://www.nature.com/nature/journal/v438/n7070/full/438900a.html.

Hassel, Holly, and Joanne Baird Giordano. 2009. "Transfer Institutions, Transfer of Knowledge: The Development of Rhetorical Adaptability and Underprepared Writers." *Teaching English in the Two-Year College* 37 (1): 24–40.

hooks, bell. 2000. *Feminism Is for Everybody: Passionate Politics.* London: Pluto Press.

Hutchings, Pat, ed. 2000. *Opening Lines: Approaches to the Scholarship of Teaching and Learning.* Pittsburg, PA: Carnegie Foundation for the Advancement of Teaching.

Jaschik, Scott. 2017. "How the Hoax Got Published." *Inside Higher Ed,* May 25, 2017. https://www.insidehighered.com/news/2017/05/25/publisher-explains-how-article-about-viewing-male-organ-conceptual-got-published.

Kozol, Jonathan. 1991. *Savage Inequalities: Children in America's Schools.* New York: Broadway Books.

Kozol, Jonathan. 1995. *Amazing Grace: The Lives of Children and the Conscience of a Nation.* New York: Broadway Books.

Kozol, Jonathan. 2005. *The Shame of the Nation: The Restoration of Apartheid Schooling in America.* New York: Random House.

McKenzie, Lindsay. 2017. "Journal Apologizes for Article Likening Transracialism to Being Transgender." *Chronicle of Higher Education,* May 1, 2017. http://www.chronicle.com/blogs/ticker/journal-apologizes-for-article-likening-transracialism-to-transgenderism/118084.

Shor, Ira. 1999. "What Is Critical Literacy?" *Journal of Pedagogy, Pluralism, and Practice* 1 (4): 1–30.

Wikipedia. 2018. "Wikipedia: Five Pillars." https://en.wikipedia.org/wiki/Wikipedia:Five_pillars.

Wikipedia. 2018. "Wikipedia: What Wikipedia is Not." https://en.wikipedia.org/wiki/Wikipedia:What_Wikipedia_is_not.

11

COMMUNITY

Student Perspective

Lauren Sills

When I was seventeen years old, I walked into my high school guidance counselor's office at Windsor High School in Windsor, Connecticut and told her I wanted to go to the University of Puget Sound, a small, prestigious liberal arts college just outside of Seattle that accepts only two thousand applicants per year. After flipping through my transcripts for about a minute, she looked over her desk at me and smiled,

"Have you thought about . . . a state school . . . ?"

"Not really." I said. "I want to be a writer."

Again, she smiled sympathetically and said, "I really think you'd do well at Eastern." With that, she slid an application for Eastern Connecticut State University (ECSU) across her desk at me and told me to have a good day. (Eastern is a local state school.)

I wasn't the best student in high school. I excelled in English but had little motivation for anything else. Looking back, I think I had too much going on in my personal life to be able to understand the importance of applying myself, and suddenly, there I was in an office being told that my "lack of ambition" had caught up to me and there was nothing I could do about it.

Later that night, I applied to ECSU and Puget Sound. When my acceptance letters came in, I sat staring at them for a while. I had gotten into both schools, but instead of feeling accomplished, I replayed that

DOI: 10.7330/9781607329305.c011

sympathetic smile over and over again in my head, feeling like there was still only one option. I began classes at ECSU in the fall of 2010 and found myself in an environment where everyone was there because they thought they were supposed to be. I failed out three semesters later.

Six years, two children, and a technical degree later I found myself sitting in a small classroom with no windows at a community college ten minutes from my house. After years of convincing myself that it would be different this time, I was apprehensive and quite honestly embarrassed. I was always fed the stigma that community colleges were for the kids who couldn't make it in "real" college. I was proven wrong by the end of the first hour.

In my opinion, the single most significant difference to note between the community college experience and the conventional four-year school experience can be found in the name itself: community. Community colleges create an environment that you won't find on any campus of any four-year school in any location. You will not find a four-year school with an environment that breeds unity and diversity the way a community campus does. Why? The answer can be found in the very reasons that community colleges are also discounted with the stigma of being the "last resort" or "only option." There are no GPA requirements for community colleges, no SAT score determinations, and no socioeconomic limitations. It is an open culture where the things that we have in common greatly outweigh those that we don't. From the young, single mother who is here on a grant, to the man who was a successful engineer in his home country only to immigrate here and start from scratch. We are all the same. We are all here for one reason: We want to be here. We aren't here because our guidance counselors told us we should be. We aren't here because our friends are here. We're here because community colleges offer us a way to achieve the things that we otherwise couldn't. They offer us an education; a future that is achievable without the threats of drowning in student loans or being overwhelmed in a lecture hall of 300 other people. There is no shame here, no judgment. We get each other, respect each other, and nurture each other. And that is nothing short of beautiful.

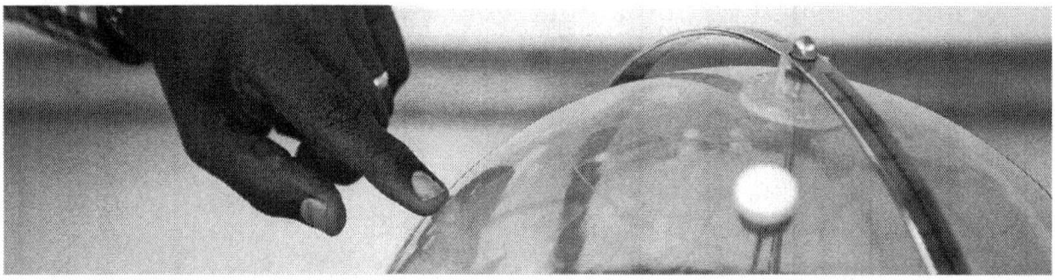

12
INVERSIVE TEACHING

Hope Parisi

Abstract: This article explores the non-normative potential of teaching in the community college, including the impact of our exceptional students and their struggles in the classroom and our teaching dispositions. It marks absences and presences as material starting points for thinking about the place-based context of our work.

COMMUNITY COLLEGE DAY ONE: YOU'RE HERE!

One of the most fundamental—and joyful—aspects of beginning a new semester at a community college is catalyzing those first encounters in which students and I, as well as students and other students, meet up in the classroom. That time of walking in, choosing seats, students checking out—but not checking out—whom else they're encountering, resonates a breath of celebration, of having made it to class, to this *very* class. Too small a victory to mark? I would say it is not. A greeting on my part, recognizing the struggles that have preceded this moment, feels fitting and natural. "Yes, we're here!" I like to acknowledge, "How fortunate for all of us! Let's look around. We're here." If I see faces that are familiar to me, typically from the prior semester or year, I say it: Even a large urban community college such as the one where I teach has its moments of feeling like a small town when students retake the same professor whom they know accepts their ways of working, their time constraints, and who will likely remember and celebrate their past successes. The presence of

DOI: 10.7330/9781607329305.c012

these types of students (this semester they make up more than 20 percent of my class), especially that first day, starts to shave back the traditional formality between teacher and student, infusing our beginning with the camaraderie from the end of a previous semester. Some students bring anxiousness with them, but there is also relief for having started, sensing welcome, in joining with others who, like them, are ready—when prompted—to acknowledge the hustle and just the *getting here.*

But for the community college student and teacher, an important question (should) also overwhelm(s) this moment: Where is *here?* Recent research in the place-based nature of literacy learning and literacy sponsorship has largely expanded the range of contexts by which to see and understand the classroom as one site competing among and overlapping others marking literacy. In her work on writing centers as storied and porous settings, for example, Wendy Pfrenger theorizes about relational space as a convergence of many immediate and small-town localities, each variously colored within and by their geographies, economies, histories, and demographics. Far from isolated, these localities cross-reference, influence, and (re)generate other sites where, it must be recognized, literacy is also sponsored. Social geographers such as Nedra Reynolds and Doreen Massey, whom Pfrenger cites, propose the "simultaneous multiplicity of [these] spaces" (Massey 1994, qtd. in Pfrenger 2017, 97), which present us with "the question of the social" (Massey 2013). Exciting intersections with literacy studies such as these reframe literate competence and classroom spaces not as marks along a flat surface (as we might say; now a student knows this or that academic "skill"—or thirty minutes ago was home but now is "here," in class), but as "cross space," where "you're cutting across a myriad of stories going on" (Massey 2013). This dynamic encompassing of "a myriad of stories" conveys the breadth of the community college classroom opposing its physical space, as well as identifies the rich, complicated, and *already literate* lives of community college students. That student with his head down in the back of the room? He will rarely be late, since working as an all-night warehouse stocker, he knows that being the first one in an empty classroom offers a convenient moment to rest. The hyper-focused student at the front of the room? She knows, as a sufferer of anxiety, she can more easily elicit the teacher's attention by engaging eye contact and speaking her questions close-range, rather than otherwise raising her hand. And the student who "waltzes in" (does it ever happen that way, really?) ten or twenty minutes late may have gotten up late, may not have planned the morning so well, but likely still felt something of that same urgency ("got to get there!") your other students felt who luckily managed to get there on time. All these students are "storied" individuals, with many lives in motion. And so for whom is it actually Day One?

Thus if there's a trace of victory in the air this first day, like a bauble, let it hang there. As essential a question as "Where are we?" or "Where is *here*?" is the question "Where are we *not*?" Within the repertoire of comparable experiences at four-year commuter colleges, residence colleges, or elite universities (there, I just answered my question), Day Ones are frequently elaborately planned affairs by administrations, programs, and resourced student teams overtaking campus greens and dormitory commons. These events function in fact very closely to those conventional markers Massey identifies "across [the] dead flat surface[s]" (Massey 2013) of time and space. By contrast, most community college students will not take on new and transformative roles particular to this campus this week. No one will become pledges. No freshman dean or other dignitary will host a reception to assure students that their particular applications stood out, or that they are—of their own doing—exceptional (and now among the elite). No mentoring junior or senior will cutely call any one in particular "my frosh," and no wavy archway of balloons will annunciate this new group's projected year of graduation. For community college students, the getting here and the coming back (attending, keeping up, doing well) is an alternate type of exceptional. The first days or weeks of a semester on a community college campus are likelier to feature extended hours by the advisement office than pledge parties or sports rallies; and one's momentous first walk onto campus can take place as easily in the spring as in the time of leaves crunching beneath new sneakers in the fall.

For these reasons, among others, the full and open classroom of Day One on a community college campus is unique for what it reflects about the perennial struggle for many students—nontraditional, low income, first-generation, students of color—to obtain their new beginning, which is what the community college promises. Even on the first day of a new semester (at a place where supposedly no one has accumulated more than sixty or so credits), a classroom of students entirely new to the college scene is rare. And not everyone comes back enthused; many are tired or discouraged. But all students seem to share this commonality: the fact that they are *more than* the traditional four-year select or residential college student in the compression of their academic lives into already psychically and materially well-occupied space. In this sense, they are the college student *exceptional*. They are the college student *plus*.

It's possible to understand the teacher of community college students, especially the teacher of community college writers, as the college teacher *plus* in that the range of considerations that comprise the daily getting-by and managing-it-all extends far past curriculum, pedagogy, and committee work. The professional life of a community college teacher encompasses not just the what to teach, but also the wherefore and how. Issues of student learning, motivation, access, inclusion, and engagement are the urgent basis of daily classroom activity and rapport. As a result of these exigencies, the students truly do become the focus, while the classroom becomes like a living text we must creatively break apart and resynthesize every day. As I have found, this text is so complicated, rich, and urgent that it can quickly engulf not only one's affective downtime, when one might (imagine it) relax, but also one's academic and research aspirations.

Like many community college teachers, as a graduate student I had been preparing for an academic career of scholarship—literature, history, and critical theory. From my dissertation on John Milton, I culled my first publications and saw a literature-based academic career burgeoning. During my job search, interviewers and advisers typically spoke to me of combining college teaching and a research-focused career. When the prospect was teaching in a community college, this talk touched on apportioning my time so that teaching would not crowd out my research. It included how I might advantage perks such as compressed teaching schedules and grant money that would make this most important work possible. And because my graduate program at the time did not encourage—because it did not yet formally include—education in the teaching of composition and rhetoric, it was assumed that I too would experience these two important aspects of my professional life as entirely separate spheres. Other members of the faculty, it was pointed out, had writing days apart from teaching days, presented at conferences, attended local reading groups and joined societies, and published in their field.

So, here's my Day One story: As I started out in the community college, I believed I could do those things too. Something I was not prepared for was how teaching—something I already knew I had a knack for—filled so much psychic space. My students became my curiosities, my challenges, my preoccupations; worse—or better—still, I began to see that the ways my graduate education had trained me to seek out contexts and theorize led me to experience the intentionality of teaching as inherently academic. Teaching was about so much more than lecture notes and novel ideas. I had to think bodies, movement, timing, spacing, affect, expression, rhetoric, and relating—all in equal parts matched to the bodies, movements, timings, spacings, affects, expressions, rhetorics, and relations of the students in my classes. This was dynamic and interactive; this was the presentation of selves, identities, and aspirations in active convergence, over and over again. The otherwise crucial aspect of subject matter, the what of teaching, paled in comparison to making a community college writing classroom a vibrant and transactional space.

It's difficult to imagine and plan at any point for the fact that one's professional aspirations—reflections not only of our expectations for ourselves but also of the expectations of others who have invested in us—will or must transform. Graduate students should understand that the decision to teach in a community college will rapidly speed up that transformation, impelling new personal and professional identities. I don't mean to suggest that pressing forward from the discipline-rich research interests of graduate school is much more difficult for those who teach in the community college; rather that the implacable questions of their relevance—to you, your students, and the social and political contexts of your teaching—will dog you in their pursuit. This is a positive thing; it means that the strands of personal and professional interests are of one cloth; difficult and marvelous, however, is that as researcher-scholars, we are in the constant company of our students, sustaining and provoking us to work even harder, dig even deeper for the questions that will matter most. Had we ever entertained any notion of scholarship as a stepping away from or apart from our work, and by work I mean our j-o-b-s of teaching, here's some news: coming to fully value that work changes us in our self-concepts and deepens our sense of mission. Then the fixed edges of our work disappear; it becomes *better* work, reorganized and "[re]arrange[d] . . . over [the] space of" (Massey 2013) community college teaching.

TEACHING IN THE COMMUNITY COLLEGE: THINK INVERSIVE!

Intentionality for the community college teacher means, for me, not only seeing these convergences of identity emerge, but also appreciating what I recognize as the inversions of the normative classroom, where students contend against long-held expectations for "good student" behavior due to racialized or insufficient educational backgrounds or policies, as they interact and collide with various systems. Inversive teaching, as a kind of queering, means uprooting assumptions and rebalancing priorities. And just as when components or properties of a progression reverse, switch, or alternate—or, loosely, *invert* (think music, atmospheric science, optics)—often that progression is revitalized. The result is not so much a contrast to the original as it is a new, richly signifying difference within it. These productive (re)arrangements of norms, priorities, or expectations regenerate our fields of meaning, compelling the crucial difference—something new and fresh!

As teacher-scholar professionals, we too operate within large, dynamic systems. How often are the inversions of our or others' expectations, whether of our teaching or of students' learning, translated down the road as insufficiency, failure, or disruption? Currently the community college is upending, or inverting, the discourse around what success means for its wide-ranging demographic. As a result, new conceptions of success are on the table, offering views on educational purposes—and *success*—from students' perspectives (McPherson and Schapiro 2008). I encourage all new community college teachers who uncritically subscribe to the biases of success as always passing or progressing (or being retained) to engage with this discourse. For example, adult students returning to school at a community college typically reenter with goals that are quite relevant to them at the time: goals related to work, legal status, or citizenship, or toward greater capacities in their families or communities (Harrell and Holcroft 2012). However, according to success metrics verifying "student persistence," these goals are not typically accounted for. As a result, much of our work with students—and statistically, many of these students themselves—becomes insignificant. Adult students' reasons for beginning, and often beginning again, are not explored for how they might offer "[a more] accurate image of the many ways in which our students succeed or how our colleges serve the state" (Harrell and Holcroft 2012), to say nothing of how our communities are served.

Thinking inversion, then, we can forget dealing with the myths of community college teaching—folding us against so much subtractive thinking of what community college teaching is "not," or how it is "less than." There's enough of that sentiment going around already, which too readily attaches to the students themselves. I can think of many inversions around how we could better recognize and reframe student learning and motivation. When can a behavioral disruption or missed assignment become an opportunity for refiguring students' needs or for recognizing the intrusion of scarcity, urging us to improve our outreach? We could do more to make our materials more accessible; co-create with students; ensure multiple means for students to engage with the course, even during periods of absence; and build access to support services across the institution within our courses. Community college and Basic Writing scholars likewise read the gaps that arise at the peripheries of our social spaces with students as anything but negative space. Deborah

Mutnick's research, for example, names and "explain[s] gaps in educational performance between upper- and lower-income children" in terms of "[c]oncrete, material conditions," that is, "racial resegregation, poverty, and cuts in federal and state educational spending" (Mutnick 2016, 45). For Susan Naomi Bernstein, the absences of austerity metrics likewise *fill* Basic Writing spaces. She observes "human beings enrolled in classes called 'Basic Writing'" demanding recognition as "human beings anywhere," who are "people who endure suffering."

> This suffering, so often invisible to teachers and others, may appear as excessive absences or late, incomplete, or unfinished homework—or it may appear as perfect attendance, stellar participation, and brilliant writing always submitted on the due date. (Bernstein 2016, 98–99)

Every class I have ever taught has evinced these words from both perspectives: from shortfalls to brilliant excess. The community college classroom encompasses both; and Bernstein, who passionately names Basic Writing as a call for social justice, leaves open that sometimes it will be the same student weaving both ends. Surely it's disappointing when the work of a good student falls off suddenly; and sad when a lagging student does not rally at the eleventh hour. But by linking austerity and trauma to absence and/or incomplete work, Bernstein cautions teachers against further voiding our classrooms by undervaluing the students who *are* present. "We need, as bell hooks long ago suggested, to teach the students who meet us in our classrooms—not who we think the students are or who we want the students to be, but the actual students" (Bernstein 2016, 99).

This is sound advice by which to sustain the ethos of a Day One welcome and catalyze inversive teaching. Notwithstanding the full and open classrooms of this Day One, the strains of trying to balance work and family obligations will result in frequent absence for many. Assignments will lag and student affect will change to reflect anxiety and discouragement. Some students will seem to "sign out" even as they attend class, or tread that fine line between barely enough and sufficient work to ensure good standing in the course. The more I can do to forestall this pattern from emerging, the better. I find that doing as much in-class informal writing as possible, which I collect, builds a base from which students can pick up where they left off if and when we need to search for reentry points later on. This foresight sometimes saves students from dropping out or repeating the level. Most community college teachers I know are patient, not dropping students or equating absence or lateness with disregard for the course. Some students, plagued by "good student" expectations, will out themselves even before I notice there is a problem. Here is one email that caught me by surprise:

> Hello professor,
> I do apologize for coming in late, in my previous email i did not elaborate on that. I was at therapy for my worst [wrist] since I have de quervain's tenosynovitis. My essay is in progress I will email you it this week for sure.

When I responded with a thank-you for letting me know, I got this note back:

> Thank you. I appreciate you a lot, i never had a patient and understanding professors. Also, it may look like I don't take your course serious but I do, I've never been intrigued by any [freshman English] class I've taken bc my previous professor weren't so interested in their own lessons as your are . . . I need to pass the semester so I really do try my best. . . .

And try her best she did, with work of B-plus to A-minus quality! My keeping hold of the student so she could keep hold of the course well enough to learn and acquire confidence as a writer manifested inversive teaching.

TURNING ABSENCES TO PRESENCE

We may regard turning absences to presences of all kinds as the critical work of the community college classroom. It is strenuous and inventive work with many implications, and here is how I see it happening.

Start with a resolve for success for all students present

Whether our goals for success reinforce big data's check on persistence or are tailored to students' purposes (possibly even concerning, of all things, *student learning* [Harrell and Holcroft 2012]), it's important to define success broadly: Regardless of passing or failing the course, all students will learn, and all students will succeed. This means understanding that progression is not linear and success in college is a varied acquisition: What happens in the classroom, what students feel they get out of it, is partly what keeps students coming back, and alongside other advocacy work, it's an area in which teacher agency has a great impact. As Bernstein reminds us, there are no basic writers, only "human beings . . . enrolled in classes called 'Basic Writing'" (Bernstein 2016, 98). Many returning students who have taken but failed a basic writing class could fill a book with what they have learned of writing expectations and course protocols. Likewise, there can be worlds of difference between a student who did not successfully complete a writing course due to work or family obligations and another for whom limited English or nonacademic styling was the cause. Casting a wide net for success means planning learning activities and experiences everyone has access to, no matter from where, how, or when they're starting out. Building a metalinguistic repertoire with students also helps them perceive and appreciate success for themselves, recognizing its many forms. This resolve toward success for everyone present is foundational and infectious.

Braid projects from separable strands

Most basic or introductory writing courses in the community college arise from complex ecologies of layered literacy/ies, reflecting students' already-acquired competencies on the way to writing-for-college goals. To catalyze these literacies, students should be encouraged toward varied types of writing—informal, expressive, reflective, as well as formal or genre-based—and formal assignments should begin in varied, even unpredictable ways. The variety of access into projects will ensure that most students will key into some prod for theme-based thinking and hop on board.

The use of freewriting throughout a course—whether as inkspills, completions of short essay skeletons, emotive responses to sentences on the board, and the list goes on—is invaluable for grounding students early in the arduous work of longer projects. To this point, I have come to rely on short, more-or-less informal writings to do most of the heavy lifting of my course. In recent years, I have drawn freewriting closer to the reading of the course by setting out a number of interesting longish quotes from our texts each framed by a prompt. These extended written responses (EWRs) provocatively isolate something unique from the text or resonate fuller textual themes. I choose six or seven of these as staple course writings and enclose them in a booklet posted to our course management system as well as packeted and handed out at the beginning of the term. Two to four paragraphs of response satisfy each of these assignments, but they can also grow to be more. In this sense, they are mixed-genre pieces: informal response; text-to-self, text, or world connections; quote analyses; or other modes I wish to highlight as students handle them. In the course of my responses to them via online exchanges, I prompt the "more" that these EWR's can become: suggesting, for instance, that in their next version of a particular EWR, they might lead with the quote (or sandwich it), or that the personal connection become more salient.

Students who are challenged by work and family obligations, needing to miss some classes, can be rooted in the course through this ongoing EWR model of informal writing. These EWRs typically mark the rhythms of the course as we navigate new units or topics and I can present what we are doing in class as challenges of mixed-discourse integration. When formal essays are required, as they are for our portfolio assessment, I can construct an assignment topic after the fact of our having written numerous EWRs and ask the students to create a blend of them as "the essay," including, if they like, any snatches of classroom dialogue or analysis, media-sharing, or cross-textual insights that might help foster these transformations. In this model, students gain the added experience of what Kim Gunter calls "rhetorical braiding," a type of academic literacy styling that mixes "selves, genres, and writerly purposes" (Gunter 2011, 76). Taking a page from Patricia Bizzell on "alt/dis" writing for the academy and Hannah Ashley's "queering" of academic voices, Gunter advocates "inviting student writers to braid together in the same document perspectives and experiences, for instance, with academic discourse community mandates" in order to "expand" academic writing "dialectic[ally]." Gunter's main interest here is "multifocal perspective within single texts" (Gunter 2011, 76), but such a value also suggests "contend[ing] with" a multivariate process of "new knowledge [being] . . . made" (Gunter 2011, 77). I hold that such an expansive discourse practice is especially valuable for students who will invariably miss some classes, and I share Gunter's confidence that students are already skilled in the weaving of forms and discourses. Students who return to class are generally happy to be reminded they have written pieces from which they can quickly build, and to know that, as they are, they are well-positioned in the course.

Find ways to connect with students: Easy pathways back in

A course partly mediated online also enables students to keep on despite gaps, whether in coursework or attendance. A course management site is essential not only for previewing assignments but also for gathering a view of what was missed, as instructors can post samples of students' classwork, links to videos, and photo snapshots of board work. A blog or Facebook page allows students to keep up with conversations. Most of all, online access to the teacher by way of email, messaging, and apps allows rapport to deepen, not disintegrate. For the nonpresent or struggling student, an instructor's thoughtful email summarizing where exactly that student stands in terms of completed or still-required work is a lifeline. It's also an easy venue for reformulating instructions in a pared-down way, which is critical for students who may be feeling overwhelmed. At the same time, there must be consideration for students who do not have all the tools of technology. Teachers must be willing to reiterate, but better, as if from the beginning, the essentials of even the most carefully worded handout already posted to the online blackboard, those times when students email or text you to say they still do not have access, and "cud u pls just let me no what essay 3 is about."

A recent communication to an earnest and struggling student went something like this:

> Hi there! I am resending you this [EWR] 4, which I found again in my emails, because you did a good job on it and you could still address the comments to create an essay for your portfolio. I realize you did not do the Shared Assignment, which is required as part of our link with theater class, but maybe you will still want to try submitting a portfolio, substituting a different essay. I believe you could create a very good essay using this [EWR] 4, even combining it with [EWR] 3, which has a wonderful story of personal experience, and pull together the required revised essay for your portfolio in this way. Your [EWR]s would serve as first drafts.
>
> Would you like to extend and combine your writings in this [EWR] 4 and another one and send me what you write this weekend? If there is enough time, as I think there might be, we can do a few drafts back and forth with comments. This way you will be able to turn in a portfolio for this course and progress to your next English class.

Invited to keep trying, students can pick up from somewhere they left off and feel included again, reminded they still have your confidence.

NORMALIZING ABSENCE AS PERCEIVABLE, RELATABLE STRUGGLE

Finally among inversion categories, I would like to step out of my own enclosure in sharing, through this article, one of the most difficult things I have found necessary to perform in the daily work of my classroom: the open, nonjudgmental, and normalizing acknowledgement of student absence. The risk as I have faced it is in accepting absence as fully recognizable by all students, beyond what teachers and even other students supposedly notice silently and merely tolerate. In other words, it is something to be spoken about, taken up as a thing materially seen and felt by others, so it might circulate as a co-constructive attribute of the community college classroom.

First, there was the issue of classroom authority for me: Was it possible that recognizing (and not bemoaning) absence could mean condoning it? And secondly, there was my part in maintaining students' identity investments for them: How were they associating attending, doing well, and even behaving well as college students? Together, these two concerns churned a thick potion of self-doubt within me. What might "good" students say or feel about such normalizing and acknowledgement? Would students who attend regularly perhaps resent those who were not meeting these expectations, and how would they think of me and how I regarded their efforts?

The absence of students in our classrooms, even in small numbers, strikes hard at teacher identities as institutional gatekeepers, while reflecting ("good") students' own ambivalences of having complied with these systems and done well.

By ascribing at least part of the problem to my own authority issues, I find that a lot more about socially just teaching practice opens up for me. This is especially the case as I grasp how my authority stands in for the white racialized authority of the writing classroom in general (Inoue 2015, 2016). Research on students' years in preschool through high school and beyond indicates that certain behaviors and dispositions link to "good student" identity and success (See Bank, Biddle, and Good 1980; Goodwin, Cheruvu, and Genishi 2012). While this research reinforces the "ideal behavioral qualities related to achievement . . . [as] time management, attention, engagement, and subject interest" (Souto-Manning, Dernikos, and Yu 2016), or more broadly, student *presence,* these qualities also reflect the privilege behind what race-critical composition scholar Asao Inoue describes as a "white racial habitus" within education. This habitus, Inoue contends, valorizing individual achievement, contractual fidelity, and objective, rational thinking, associates "ideal behavioral" qualities with an ethos of authority and control (Inoue 2016; Inoue 2015). From this standpoint, present students are in control of their lives and absent students, who likely struggle, are unmotivated or incapable. These associations are clearly wrong and prejudicial. While periods of "stopping out" or "non-enrollment" generally anticipate a decreased likelihood of degree completion for community college students (Fain 2013), some time out to question one's own purposes for education among students starting out in four-year institutions does not seem so alarming. Similarly, the effects of strict or explicit attendance policies versus no policy is still contested (Mancini 2017; Golding 2011) with generous policies linked to nonremedial courses and four-year liberal arts colleges.

Despite these racialized inconsistencies around attendance, some community college teachers still perceive absence as personal failing. Here is the posted response from one professor ("Longtime CC Prof") to the question of community college students' "stopping out" as reported in "Third Try Isn't the Charm":

> The reason many students fail to complete a college degree (2 or 4 year) is simply lack of tenacity. They give up too easily. They've never been required to persevere—there have been few genuine obstacles in their paths—so

> they've never learned or experienced how to overcome obstacles or meet challenges. They have a low threshold for frustration—finding it easier to walk away than face the challenges.
>
> This is especially true of students who grew up with a certain amount of privilege and financial security—no experience with difficulties—so no ability to deal with the work/study challenges: frustration, boredom, bureaucracy, long hours, little sleep, multiple deadlines, etc.
>
> In addition, they lack perspective: they are unable to appreciate that 4 or 5 or 7 years is a very small portion of a long life AND that the dedication now will pay off for many years to come. They just give up. I've been in the classroom for 30 years and see smart and motivated students every semester who just give up because they don't have the tenacity. (Longtime CC Prof 2013)

And here is a response from "Young CC Prof":

> I would hate to be your student. Lack of tenacity? Tell that to the man who's struggling to complete his online homework while he lives in a shelter. Or the immigrant woman who is raising two children, working full time and dealing with her mother's cancer. Or the one who spent two weeks in the hospital mid-semester, came back and got an A.
>
> Maybe your school is different. But here in the inner-city, we see students dropping out due to life, not lack of motivation. (Young CC Prof 2013)

Young CC Prof gives a tangible, material presence to these students' absences, and it seems that each of the students whom Young CC Prof mentions would undoubtedly deserve, as much as possible, some accommodation. What would some form of acknowledgement, visible to everyone, look like? Moreover, how could we help make such accommodation transformative for the classroom as a community? I suggest the following:

Be honest. Own your notice of people's absences.

It might be a simple acknowledgement, as in asking a classmate to collect the handouts and give them to the student when she or he returns. It might mean consistently setting out handouts on the desk where the student usually sits in case the student comes in late and mentioning publicly that that is what you are doing. More extended absences might merit these classroom announcements: "These handouts (shuffle, shuffle) I'm saving for Jan," or "I'm compiling a folder of materials for Jan," or "After class, I'll be in the English Office scanning copies of these materials for Jan." Sharing your own efforts to keep students included is part of the critical recognition of all students' struggles to keep up and the honored place such efforts hold in your classroom.

Involve students as exemplars, requesting to post or send their classwork to keep absent students in the loop.

Students who believe they are helping others succeed are much less likely to resent those students for receiving what, in other contexts, may appear as leeway to skirt the system. When help is recognized as impartial and distributive, students more closely identify with one another, confident that given similar circumstances, they would be afforded the same assistance. In addition, collaborating around a crisis point is very unifying. Not least, it builds confidence for a student to think that her or his classwork is exemplary.

Finally, when students return, acknowledge publicly the work they have been doing to keep up, or that the chance of catching up is quite do-able.

The implication: Their place in your class is (still) well-deserved. Quickly bring them back into the cycle of sharing their work with others. Use their return to have other students recapture the major points of emphasis or activity in the interim. Not least, publicly affirm their good standing in the class as well as your confidence in their ability to catch up, if need be, and based on affirming evidence. Thank publicly any students who have played a part in closing the gaps.

Overall, how we soften or extend the fixed edges of our classrooms speaks loudly and clearly to the value we place on all students' efforts to keep going, making it back to class and through the semester. In community college settings, the *getting here* and *coming back* are large recurrent moments for celebrating what student presence means, especially as we learn to recognize that presence—even in absence—in countless forms.

REFERENCES

Bank, Barbara J., Bruce J. Biddle, and Thomas L. Good. 1980. "Sex Roles, Classroom Instruction, and Reading Achievement." *Journal of Educational Psychology* 72 (2): 119–132.

Bernstein, Susan Naomi. 2016. "Occupy Basic Writing Pedagogy in the Wake of Austerity." In *Composition in the Age of Austerity*, ed. Nancy Welch and Tony Scott, 92–105. Louisville: University Press of Colorado.

Fain, Paul. 2013. "Third Try Isn't the Charm." *Inside Higher Education*, November 15, 2013. www.insidehighered.com/news/2013/11/15/students-are-unlikely-graduate-if-they-stop-out-more-once-study-finds.

Golding, Jonathan M. 2011. "The Role of Attendance in Lecture Classes: You Can Lead a Horse to Water." *Teaching of Psychology* 38 (1): 40–42.

Goodwin, A. Lin, Ranita Cheruvu, and Celia Genishi. 2012. "Responding to Multiple Diversities in Early Childhood Education: How Far Have We Come?" In *Diversities in Early Childhood Education*, ed. Celia Genishi and A. Lin Goodwin, 15–22. New York: Routledge.

Gunter, Kim. 2011. "Braiding and Rhetorical Power Players: Transforming Academic Writing through Rhetorical Dialectic." *Journal of Basic Writing* 30 (1): 64–98.

Harrell, Kim, and Carolyn Holcroft. 2012. "Searching for an Authentic Definition of Student Success." *The Rostrum*, Academic Senate for California Community Colleges, December 2012. www.asccc.org/content/searching-authentic-definition-student-success.

Inoue, Asao B. 2015. *Antiracist Writing Assessment Ecologies: Teaching and Assessing for a Socially Just Future.* Anderson, SC: Parlor Press.

Inoue, Asao B. 2016. "Afterword: Narratives That Determine Writers and Social Justice Writing Center Work." *Praxis: A Writing Center Journal* 14 (1): 94–99.

Longtime CC Prof [pseud.]. 2013. "Third Try Isn't the Charm." Discussion Thread. *Inside Higher Education.* November 15, 2013. www.insidehighered.com/news/2013/11/15/students-are-unlikely-graduate-if-they-stop-out-more-once-study-finds#disqus_thread.

Mancini, Tracy Janine. 2017. "First-Day Attendance and Student Course Success: Does Being There Make a Difference?—A Literature Review." *Community College Enterprise* 23 (2): 32–57.

Massey, Doreen. 1994. *Space, Place, and Gender.* Minneapolis: University of Minnesota Press.

Massey, Doreen. 2013. "Doreen Massey on Space: An Interview with Nigel Warburton." Social Science Bites Podcast Blog, *Social Science Space.* February 1, 2013. http://www.socialsciencespace.com/2013/02/podcastdoreen-massey-on-space/.

McPherson, Michael, and Morton Owen Schapiro, eds. 2008. *College Success: What It Means and How to Make It Happen.* New York: The College Board.

Mutnick, Deborah. 2016. "Confessions of an Assessment Fellow." In *Composition in the Age of Austerity*, ed. Nancy Welch and Tony Scott, 35–50. Louisville: University Press of Colorado.

Pfrenger, Wendy. 2017. "Cultivating Places and People at the Center: Cross-Pollinating Literacies on a Rural Campus." *Journal of Basic Writing* 36 (1): 87–119.

Souto-Manning, Mariana, Bessie Dernikos, and Hae Min Yu. 2016. "Rethinking Normative Literacy Practices, Behaviors, and Interactions: Learning from Young Immigrant Boys." *Journal of Early Childhood Research* 14 (2):163–180.

Young CC Prof [pseud.]. 2013. "Third Try Isn't the Charm." Discussion Thread. *Inside Higher Education.* November 15, 2013. www.insidehighered.com/news/2013/11/15/students-are-unlikely-graduate-if-they-stop-out-more-once-study-finds#disqus_thread.

13

THE RISKY BUSINESS OF ENGAGING RACIAL EQUITY IN WRITING INSTRUCTION

A Tragedy in Five Acts

Taiyon J. Coleman, Renee DeLong, Kathleen Sheerin DeVore, Shannon Gibney, and Michael C. Kuhne

Brand Agents and Blood Transfusions: A Postscript

Kathleen Sheerin DeVore

The authors (above, from left to right): Shannon Gibney (seated), Renee DeLong, Taiyon J. Coleman, Michael C. Kuhne, and Kathleen Sheerin DeVore (seated). Photo by Geoffrey Jones, Minneapolis College. Used with permission.

Race and writing instruction are not exactly a road untraveled.[1] Racial equity work in composition has had its moments of high visibility and has often been examined through a number of scholarly lenses: how to assess grammar or value students' primary languages, what curricular

DOI: 10.7330/9781607329305.c013

materials and assessments should be used within developmental education, and which hiring practices can attract more faculty members of color. However, many of these conversations have devalued the emotional components of racial equity work and diminished ways in which these conversations continue to perpetuate institutional and personal violence against black and brown bodies: students, faculty members, and staff. In fact, many of these innovations have continued to center around white masculinity while students of color continue to be failed by the institution.

This erasure of race is especially perilous for students and faculty of color. We reflect all of this—the erasures and the hesitancies, the perils and the pain—and as none of this is neat or orderly work, the piece reflects this roughly ordered, even fragmented, state. We align ourselves in this approach with educational researcher Gloria Ladson-Billings in that we are "attempting to speak to innovative theoretical ways for framing discussions about social justice and democracy and the role of education in reproducing or interrupting current practices" (1998, 9). That our primary mode of doing so is storytelling is not an accident; it underscores our belief in a foundational principle of critical race theory (CRT) to disrupt dominant racial narratives by "analyz[ing] the myths, presuppositions, and received wisdoms that make up the common culture about race and that invariably render blacks and other minorities one-down" (Delgado 1995, xiv).[2]

The contributors to this piece are members of an urban two-year college English department that has adjusted its curriculum to better reach our culturally diverse student population; a student body that has grown to 58 percent students of color at a site where over eighty languages are spoken ("Campus" 2015). As we broadened our work from curricular diversity to more diverse hiring practices, which later led to addressing our own persistent white privilege, things institutionally broke down. Three years later we are still broken and breaking. We attempt to shine light on those breaks both to aid in our own healing and to offer readers a kind of case study from which others might learn how to proceed in undoing the lingering race privilege shadowing all our institutions, as proceed we must.

ACT I. WHAT WE SAW AND WHAT WE DID: RACIAL EQUITY AND DEVELOPMENTAL WRITING

Michael Kuhne

Scene 1. "Old White Guy"

When I started teaching in 1995 at Minneapolis Community and Technical College, it wasn't even MCTC yet; it was still Minneapolis

Community College, a liberal arts two-year college that shared a campus with Minneapolis Technical College, a career and technical education institution (the two colleges would merge, by way of legislative mandate, in 1997). I joined the English Department when I was thirty-six years old, and I was the second-youngest faculty member; the youngest faculty member was a woman of color who stayed for two years before she left for another community college position in Massachusetts. At that point, the English Department was white, predominantly male, and older. Other than being relatively youthful, I fit in perfectly. Meanwhile, the students of color represented 34 percent of the student body (Coulter and Kuhne 1999, 11). However, this percentage of students of color was not mirrored by the employees of the college. At that point, only 10 percent of the college's administrators, 9 percent of the instructors, and 25 percent of the staff were people of color (41–45). Over the years, the percentage of students of color would continue to increase, becoming the majority of the students at the college in 2010, while the percentage of employees of color did not increase significantly (MCTC 2014). This snapshot portrays a history of inequity at our college. There was much that was wrong in the late 1990s. What we in the English Department saw—what we were willing and able to see—was an ineffective developmental writing curriculum. We worked to address this, as our training taught us. What we didn't see, however, was our colleagues of color struggling and frequently suffering within our department and institution.

Scene 2. High-Stakes Portfolio-Based Outcomes

In 1995, the college's developmental writing curriculum was a sequence of three courses, each based on a formal, structural approach to composition. The first course—Fundamentals of Written English I—focused on "parts of speech, sentence patterns, sentence combining, punctuation and spelling [with an] emphasis on writing and revising one-paragraph summaries of short essays." Student achievement was evaluated based on a timed writing test given during the final day of class (Minneapolis 1995). Students would not produce any writing that originated with their own experiences; rather, their goal was to write a one-paragraph summary of someone else's writing.

After Fundamentals of Written English I, another course followed in which students would continue to work on "grammar, punctuation and spelling rules . . . and effective sentences and . . . composition of the paragraph." Once again, student achievement was determined by a timed writing test (Minneapolis 1995). It was as much a test of endurance and persistence as it was of writing development, and the lucky few students who got through these first two courses still had one more hurdle between them and a college-level writing class: Fundamentals of Written English 2, in which students were to continue "to generate . . . a unified, coherent paragraph," which was—not surprisingly—evaluated at the end of the course with a timed test (Minneapolis 1995).

In 1995, we required three courses, three quarters, and ten credit hours before a student who tested into developmental writing could even start a college-level English course. While we do not have retention information from that era, one can predict the abysmal rates of completion just to get to a college-level English course. For instance, in Mike Rose's *Back to School,* Rose cites a study that indicates "only 16 percent of students at this level complete the entire remedial sequence" (2012, 84). That's not 16 percent of students who start in developmental courses who go on to get a degree; it's 16 percent of students who test into a developmental course and are able to progress into a college-level course. We have no reason to believe that our college's results would have been any more promising nor any less dispiriting.

There were many English faculty members invested in the three-course developmental writing curriculum, and it would take another six years, after many retirements within the English Department and additional hires who brought with them composition and rhetoric backgrounds, before we were able to make a change to streamline the curriculum. In 2001, the department invited Linda Adler-Kassner to lead us through a three-day curriculum revision workshop. We moved from a three-course sequence of developmental writing courses with high-stakes testing to one developmental writing course with a portfolio-based outcome. Students would now produce a body of their work from the developmental course (two revised essays and a reflection letter) that would then be evaluated by two other developmental writing instructors.

To many of us, this curriculum revision represented profound progress. While this change was no doubt an improvement over the old three-course sequence, it was not long before we began to realize that it was not going to be the answer to our problems of retaining developmental writers through the end of the semester. The new portfolio-based course worked remarkably well for students who made it to the end of the course and submitted a portfolio: time and time again, over 95 percent of those students earned passing evaluations. The problem, however, was that too few students were making it to the end of the semester. Term after term, completion rates averaged between 55 and 60 percent. Once again, students of color—in particular African American men and

Native American students—were disproportionately negatively affected. Portfolio-based outcomes, while certainly better than high-stakes testing, was still not effective enough in getting students into college-level writing environments.

Scene 3. Portfolio to Accelerated English

In 2012, Kathleen DeVore went to Baltimore for the Accelerated Learning Program Conference; she returned with the curricular innovation of accelerated English, an approach pioneered by the Community College of Baltimore County, and we began the necessary work to implement the model at the college. (Readers interested in learning more about the Accelerated Learning Program should view the data-rich website: ALP Accelerated Learning Program at http://alp-deved.org/). This approach enrolled students who tested into developmental writing into college-level English courses with a small cohort of other students. The ten students in the developmental writing cohort experienced the same course as the other fifteen students who had tested into college-level writing. Immediately after the first class ended, the cohort would meet for an additional fifty minutes with the same instructor. This support hour created an environment where students could continue the discussions they had begun in the college-level class and receive individual student-with-instructor writing assistance. (Also, these sections have always been scheduled for computer classrooms.) In the two years the college has offered accelerated English, we have seen retention and completion rates increase across all race and class demographics (see table 13.1).

Students of color in the accelerated curriculum completed the course and passed at a rate of 67 percent, which surpassed the traditional curriculum by 13 percent, and this 67 percent pass rate slightly surpassed students of color who were placed directly into the college-level writing course (64 percent). Comparable improvements can be seen across the board. Of particular interest are the success rates of African American males: within ENGA 0900/1110 (Accelerated English), African American males had a 53 percent pass rate. Compare this with only a 44 percent pass rate in ENGL 0900, and a 59 percent pass rate in ENGL 1110 (Cressman 2015). The 9 percent increase in pass rates for African American males who took the accelerated English instead of the more traditional developmental writing course was encouraging. However, the gap between African American males and other demographics has persisted, and frankly, a 53 percent pass rate is neither laudable nor acceptable.

Accelerated English has helped many students move into college-level writing courses more quickly and less expensively. It is not, however, the

Table 13.1. MCTE pass rates for ENGA 0900/1110, ENGL 0900, and ENGL 1110, spring 2013 to spring 2015

		ENGA 0900/1110			*ENGL 0900*			*ENGL 1110*		
Demographic Group		# Passed[3]	# Enrolled	% Passed	# Passed	# Enrolled	% Passed	# Passed	# Enrolled	% Passed
Gender	Female	215	288	75%	719	1,177	61%	2,441	3,502	70%
	Male	107	184	58%	556	1,124	49%	2,130	3,269	65%
Pell Eligible	Yes	263	402	65%	1,067	2,044	52%	2,782	4,452	62%
	No	29	35	83%	117	155	75%	788	1,075	73%
	Unknown	30	36	83%	94	107	88%	1,013	1,263	80%
Student of Color	Yes	267	401	67%	1,082	2,005	54%	2,685	4,168	64%
	No	51	67	76%	190	288	66%	1,876	2,589	72%
	Unknown	–	–	100%	–	–	46%	22	33	67%
First Generation (MN Definition)	Yes	126	174	72%	533	962	55%	1,246	1,928	65%
	No	182	276	66%	706	1,264	56%	3,244	4,735	69%
	Unknown	14	23	61%	–	–	49%	93	127	73%
African American Males		55	104	53%	311	713	44%	605	1,026	59%
Total		322	473	68%	1,278	2,306	55%	4,583	6,790	67%

answer; rather, it is but one answer to an ongoing and persistent set of questions about equity and developmental writing curriculum. As a group, the department is already considering further changes to move more students from developmental writing to college-level English.

That's what we saw.

SCENE 4: WHAT WE DIDN'T—OR COULDN'T OR CHOSE NOT TO—SEE

At the same time that the English Department was addressing retention and completion issues in its developmental writing curriculum, the department was also experiencing a number of searches for new hires. As a department, we worked hard to change our demographics as we assertively sought teaching candidates of color. On one level, we were successful in hiring a number of highly qualified faculty of color. On another level, we failed miserably to make important changes in the culture of the department and the institution (more on this later).

However, I have come to learn something about my role in the English Department specifically and the larger institution generally. When we started to change the developmental writing curriculum, I was active in making the changes. I was the department chair, for instance, when we made the change from high-stakes testing to portfolio-based outcomes, and I was one of the coauthors of the accelerated English curriculum change. What I saw was the abysmal rates of completion among all of our students. I saw the 2010 statistic that, frankly, haunted me: Only 9 percent of African American males would finish a certificate, diploma, or degree within three years at our college. We worked hard to make changes, and while the situation of many of our developmental writing students has improved, there is still much work left to do.

What I didn't see was born of my naïveté and white privilege, and this speaks more directly to issues of equity with and among my peers. Although I served on search committees, I was not able to see that simply hiring faculty of color without changing the culture within the department and institution would not move equity forward. Adding faculty of color to the department was not enough; we had to change the culture, one where white patriarchy had been an almost unquestioned way of doing things.

I think of the curricular changes we made and juxtapose that with the slow, inexorable, painful changes we have made among ourselves within the department. While making the changes to the curriculum took time and effort, and while those efforts continue in earnest, those changes were what I was trained as a graduate student to do. The equity work is harder in many ways because it demands that I connect my head with my heart, hands, feet, and voice. This kind of work was definitely not part of the graduate school curriculum.

And yet, without doing this hard work, many people will suffer. My peers have suffered and will continue to suffer. The students I teach will suffer. The communities from which our students come will suffer. While doing equity work is hard, not doing equity work will continue to produce misery and trauma.

ACT II. HOW WE BROKE

Kathleen Sheerin DeVore

Beyond the curricular changes to portfolio assessment and accelerated pedagogies, changes driven by a desire to increase student success—new practices that have been deep successes for the department—we then attempted cultural competency and white privilege work with English instructors as a community, and there we failed spectacularly. The student populations who had been most vulnerable in our basic writing (BW) curriculum were working-class students of color—particularly African American and Native American students. At great risk of oversimplification, we have found that recent immigrants from Somalia, Ethiopia, Mexico, South America, and South Asia had some access to communities where home languages and cultures were practiced, as well as English language learning (ELL) coursework prior to BW or college English, while African American and Native American students often had little or sometimes no access to either of these resources and had for generations lived under the heavy white dominance central to American colonial expansion. And so those students often arrived in their BW or college English classes with home languages and cultures that for generations have been deeply devalued, if acknowledged at all, by the dominant cultural practices surrounding them. It is no accident that these are the cultures most damaged by American settler colonialism and therefore most damaged by the ongoing colonization echoing through our white-dominant classrooms.

In hindsight, the curricular changes described in Act I perhaps served as a setup for the deeper white-privilege work we then undertook but failed at spectacularly, as that earlier curricular work, while considerable, engaged hardly at all with our own racial identity formation understandings as a white-majority faculty. Attending to patterns of racial exclusion in our curriculum did lead some of us to more intentionally ask why our faculty remained so white dominant, which then led to more racial diversity in our hiring and to new faculty of color naming persistent white privilege in the department and suggesting we attend to it. That last bit is where the breakdown occurred.

Here is a brief version of our racial equity story as I saw it, with a focus on points of breakdown and the consequences of these breaks reverberating still, as some of us have begun to dig through the wreckage and construct a strategy from the pain. I list ten parts here but focus more specifically on three. Bear with me, as my goal is to cover ten years in a couple of paragraphs:

A Tale in Ten Parts: A Racial Equity Story From 2005 to 2015 at MCTC

1. Some successful pedagogical shifts and a badly broken affirmative action committee: "We don't legally 'need' to do more in racial equity hiring."
2. A noose is hung followed by a college-imposed silence.
3. CRT hiring language leads to more racially diverse hires.
4. An equity program (a year of readings and discussions on race and privilege for the ENGL department) is created by a new hire.
5. A diversity VP position is created and a fantastic hire found.
6. Formal discrimination and harassment charges are made against four members of the English Department.
7. The new diversity VP departs after nine months due to an "unhealthy climate."
8. An approach, then a retreat from racial equity.
9. A colleague of color's third racial discrimination charge in three years; the first with a guilty finding and mandatory diversity training with the diversity manager in a position that faculty member herself pushed to create.
10. Now, there is much discomfort and deafening silence; personalizing of all racism, inability to address structural patterns that racial equity work generally and that CRT specifically allows us to dismantle.

Let me go back to just a few parts from this tale to offer some explanation, though seeing it condensed here reminds me that we really were in the midst of a kind of perfect storm. As student racial diversity reached nearly 60 percent students of color, our department tried to grapple with the persistent white dominance throughout the rest of the institution, but college and union leadership really had neither the skills nor the political will to address the issue and therefore could offer no support in engaging such complexity. We really were on our own, and particularly new faculty members of color were left largely on their own, as we lurched, inelegantly, forward.

Part 3: CRT hiring language. As the college's enrollment numbers grew—particularly with increasing numbers of students of color—our faculty hiring lines also increased, and so some of us became active on hiring committees. Once there, we asserted more intentional racial equity language, and honestly, it was then that we became more fully aware of CRT as scholarship that could push us past the largely ineffective boilerplate Equal Employment Opportunity Commission (EEOC) hiring language. For two years, our position descriptions for potential new hires requested "an awareness of critical race theory and demonstrated connection to communities of color," in addition to fairly typical community college English instructor requirements. There was some anxiety on the part of the largely white and white-identified committee about what exactly CRT was, and even though we mentioned it in the introduction, it may be useful to provide a definition here: "CRT begins with the notion that racism is 'normal, not aberrant, in American society' (Delgado 1995, xiv), and, because it is so enmeshed in the fabric of our social order, it appears both normal and natural to people in this culture. . . . Thus, the strategy becomes one of unmasking and exposing racism in its various permutations" (Ladson-Billings 1998, 7). And more specifically, on a critical race curriculum in the field of education, as Chican@ Studies professor Tara Yosso explains, "A critical race curriculum reveals the multiple layers of racialized inequality perpetuated by traditional curriculum processes. Therefore, it challenges educators to recognize deficit-based practices that deny students of color access to 'college bound' knowledges." And finally, Yosso notes, "A critical race curriculum exposes the white privilege supported by traditional curriculum structures and challenges schools to dismantle them" (2002, 93). Our use of CRT in hiring simply referred to the need for applicants who understand that we live and teach in a nation with a raced social order. The common white-dominance demand that pretends this is no longer the case with barely-conscious assertions that "slavery was a long time ago" could no longer suffice in a faculty responsible for educating a student body that is 58 percent students of color.

The position description language enabled interested candidates to look up CRT and tailor their applications to this stated preference, while simultaneously allowing a department-wide conversation on it as well—teachable moments all around, it seemed. That was not the case, however, in our department, where fear and an underdeveloped awareness of racial identity formation dominates, a lack of awareness not unique to our department. However, we were able to push the language through and found ourselves with more diverse pools of candidates than ever, which resulted in five hires of color and one white ally with demonstrated work in racial equity within a two-year time span. This was game-changing in a department of twenty-six full-time faculty unlimited (FTUs), as about eight of us—nearly one-third of the tenure lines in the department—were faculty members engaged in antiracist work. (We can at times have as many as twenty-five adjunct instructors, who serve at the will of the dean and whose voices are often restrained due to this vulnerability.) Due in part to the position description language and hiring committee discussions with applicants, most of the new hires saw a climate in which they could further antiracist and equity work, and so they began not only in their classrooms, but also by convening with panels among the broader faculty and workshops within the English Department. However, before long the charges of discrimination began to trickle in.

Part 6: Discrimination and harassment charges. Shannon Gibney writes below about the ways in which women faculty of color have been charged by students and institutions with discrimination at vastly greater rates than their white peers. Here I focus only on the discrimination and harassment charges filed against four members of the English faculty: one new hire of color, two white members of the hiring committee, and one supportive white colleague. As one of the charged, I can speak specifically to this instance where a white male job applicant, who was also an adjunct employee in the department, charged each of us with using language that discriminated against and harassed him as a white male. Our work generating the CRT hiring language and discussions of white dominance in the faculty had resulted in some tense department meetings. Given the low level of facility with discussions of race in our workplace, it was not surprising that anxiety was pretty high. Add that to the ongoing exploitation of contingent hires in our writing program, as well as the top-down and overtly legalistic leadership style of the administration at that time; we are aware in hindsight that we should have seen these charges coming.

The short version is that the four of us were charged with having said something that discriminated against and racially harassed our white male colleague. A yearlong investigation was initiated by our campus legal affairs officer, which included calling in sixteen English Department members as witnesses. The case required union representation for each of us, individual interviews with Legal Affairs for the four charged and sixteen witnesses, and so this involved twenty members of the department over ten months; and all were sworn to secrecy for the duration of the investigation. It was a very, very hard year.

Ultimately, we four charged were found not guilty, and yet the vice president overseeing the case made the determination that we could no longer use CRT hiring language, as it might exclude candidates "unfamiliar with this particular theory." We went through the looking glass here with institutional obfuscation, even idiocy when we were found not guilty but nonetheless punished in our innocence, and we were to go even further through that glass over the coming months. At the same time that half the English Department was being investigated or called as witnesses, one new hire of color had initiated a reading and discussion program on racial equity that would allow us to explore white privilege as a community of teachers for the first time in the college's one-hundred-year history and then think through ways to mediate that privilege to increase success for students of color. This would be hard work in the best of circumstances, but done during discrimination and harassment investigations, we found ourselves tumbling roughly across nearly unbroken ground.

Part 8: Approaching then retreating from racial equity. After six months of teaching with us, one of our new hires of color offered to pull together a panel for the college's fall opening days with colleagues she knew from the University of Minnesota whose work addressed racial equity and white privilege. The panel was very well received by most faculty, and some folks within the English department asked for ideas on continuing this work. Our new colleague with assistance from the department chair secured funding to bring one University of Minnesota colleague, Tim Lensmire, associate professor of education, to run a yearlong workshop series for us. Lensmire's work focuses on race and education and, he explains, "especially on how white people learn to be white in our white supremacist society. Grounded in critical whiteness studies, [this] work contributes to the ongoing effort to figure out how best to work with white people" ("Timothy" 2002). With Lensmire's assigned readings and two planned discussion sessions per term, we began a yearlong racial equity program.

After just one workshop a majority of faculty of color asked to caucus out into two groups, one for faculty of color, one for white faculty, as levels of experience, awareness, and understanding of white racial identity formation and white privilege were painfully low in the combined session. In short, white dominance persisted in the sessions themselves, which was taxing for faculty of color; however, this common move in racial equity work—caucusing out into affinity groups—was unfamiliar to most white faculty and one male faculty member of color. Feelings were hurt, anger surfaced, attendance dropped off at subsequent workshops, and for those who did attend, the focus became the fact of faculty of color separating off, and the shaming felt in the process, more than the readings Lensmire had assigned for discussion. We began to break. In May at our final faculty meeting of the year, the new hire who had led us into the white privilege work, who herself had dealt with student racism and harassment charges for teaching structural racism and who had grown ill from the tensions and hostilities at our institution, made the decision to resign, shared that decision at that final meeting, and named quite specifically and unapologetically what it had been like for her to work among us for those eighteen months. Two more women of color faculty then described their own struggles working among white-dominant teachers so little aware of the pain and damage our own unexamined privilege was causing colleagues and students of color. And this was in Minnesota, where a smiling passive aggression actually has a name: Minnesota nice. It was a tough meeting.

I don't have the space here to do justice to the complexity of emotion in that room; there was much silence, there were tears, there was a simmering anger. Some white colleagues tried to offer apology and emotional support; many remained silent, no doubt overcome with a range of emotions. The meeting ended very quickly, there were some hallway one-to-one connections, and that night my phone blew up. There were emails critiquing the tone of our resigning colleague's comments, urging the need for civility and collegiality. More emails supported the courage of those asserting civility, but there was silence regarding the substance of our peer's critique of the heavy white privilege she was leaving a tenure-track job to escape. Now, three years later, we still have not returned to antiracist work as a community, or even to that final department-wide conversation; the 2015 Conference on College Composition and Communication convention in Tampa was one of the first times we had spoken of it. Even writing of it here, my stomach freezes with the memory. We broke. We are still broken.

ACT III. CONTENTIONS: RACE, EVALUATION, AND RETALIATION IN THE CLASSROOM

Shannon Gibney

After my daughter died, I knew I had to go back to work. A stillbirth for reasons still unknown, she had decided at forty-one and a half weeks that she did not, in fact, want to come here. I had no choice but to respect her decision, but it was a devastating truth to face. My body still had not reconciled the loss when I stepped into my mass communications class that first day back from maternity leave. Everything was shiny—almost too shiny. Formerly blunt edges of desks became sharpened as I navigated past them, in my still-too-big postpregnancy body. And everything out of my mouth, all the *Hellos,* and *I'm okays,* and *Thank-yous* felt like they were balled up in knots in my mouth. Nothing came out right. But I knew it was just a day. One day out of a season of my life. A dead season, but one that would pass eventually . . . although never out of memory.

I don't know if she was with me when I began my class that afternoon, but I do know she was not not there. With her small head and brother's nose and long limbs. She was always beside me, if not inside me. I was a body divided that day—there with her, there with my students—but I had been divided in other ways and taught before. And I had always been a black woman instructor before. Which is why it was such a shock to meet the heat of a small group of students who became angry during a discussion initiated after another student's presentation on people of color in newsrooms nationally. What they said was, "Why do we always have to talk about this?" This meaning the legacy of ongoing racism in American life? This meaning something that they did not want to talk about? This meaning topics in mass communications? I blinked at them in confusion, and at the general energy of the class, which was not downright hostile, but could not be described as welcoming by any stretch of the imagination. The students had had a substitute—a very capable and kind white woman—for the first five weeks of the course, while I had been away. They were understandably a bit off-kilter, wondering how the course would proceed, with this whole new person at the helm. But there was something more to it, something that could be seen as intangible, but that was to me all too familiar in its ease of location: animosity at this black female body in front of them. Leading the class with authority. Determining the terms of the discussion and course content, deciding whether each of them passed or failed. That was the "this" they objected to. This was not the class, the world they had signed up for.

My body was tipsy with loss, my heart still far from healed, but I tried my best—what was my best in that moment, on that day, anyway—to moderate. I mentioned the ongoing history of white domination in newsrooms, as well as in every other aspect of American life. I said that I was definitely not talking about individuals, as in, "You! White person over there!" but rather, about whiteness as a system that privileges certain groups of people while it penalizes others. When mentioning the long tradition of newsrooms dominated by white, middle-class men,

I was conscious that my voice was not as solid as it could have been. I could see in their eyes that they weren't convinced. No, they were angry. And feeling dangerous. While I was tired and feeling broken.

The document that was issued after exhuming and examining the dead body of the classroom encounter—that is, the written reprimand that the college's vice president crafted after the legal affairs department had finished their investigation—certainly found that I had been in egregious error. The reprimand referred to my tone as "defensive, angry, and disrespectful" and took me to task for violating our college's nondiscrimination policy. The vice president said that he found it "troubling that the manner in which you led a discussion on the very important topic of structural racism alienated two students who may have been most in need of learning about this subject." I was directed to meet with our college's chief diversity officer for two training sessions on "managing diversity flashpoints" in order to help me learn to model civility.[3]

Perhaps I should not have been surprised by the letter, and the outcome of the institutional investigation, but I was. I can remember holding the letter in my dining room, reading it incredulously, my hand shaking. My faculty union grievance representative, who had represented many, many faculty members during institutional investigations like this, had assured me after our interview with the head of legal affairs that "they have nothing. This is completely ridiculous. It will come to nothing." And yet, out of around 172 student complaints of faculty that year, I was the only one that had been ruled in violation of policy, and the only one that had been disciplined. As tenured faculty in what was arguably the most powerful department on campus, I could not be fired out of hand. But what I could be was disciplined for not conforming to the status quo on another issue.

I appealed the policy violation determination, as well as the discipline, through my institution and the system's approved structures. Via breathtaking feats of illogical logic, misreading and misapplication of policy, and extreme structural violence, the appeal was denied. I then appealed everything via my faculty union's formal grievance process. Although the union fast-tracked my case, it still took seven months for it to reach the final step of the grievance process, arbitration, in which each side presents their case to an impartial adjudicator, who assesses all the evidence and later comes to a final and binding decision. Arbitration decisions and materials become part of the public record once a decision is reached, so my union grievance reps and legal counsel were not exactly surprised when the president of my college wrote me a letter stating that he was removing the letter of reprimand from my file, right before arbitration was scheduled to begin. I was surprised—flabbergasted, shaken to the core, more like—when, right before this, I was offered a "blank check" to leave MCTC altogether. I just blinked at my union representative when she told me this and asked her to say that again. Never, in all my years as a writer, teacher, and scholar, had I entertained the notion that it might be possible to get paid just for being me. Of course, if that were the case and I did take the money and run, it would have to be a very quiet version of me . . . which wouldn't be me at all, of course. All of which made the decision already determined. It just seemed that offers like this happened to people in other universes than mine. I could not fathom that I was that much of a liability to my institution and system. Then again, here I am, sharing this story here. . . .

We were facing around a forty-four-million-dollar system deficit, and the "leadership's" biggest priority was getting rid of a nonconforming black female faculty member who wasn't afraid of talking to the press? The whole thing was just profoundly demoralizing. But, as I hope this article has demonstrated so far, far from being an outlier, my story reflects all of the tensions and contradictions present in the (degraded) state of higher education and its classrooms today. This whole ordeal was my education, I slowly came to realize. And as painful as it was, it was also absolutely necessary.

***

For women of color faculty members who, like me, are extremely vocal advocates for our most vulnerable students (disproportionately first-generation college students and people of color), especially in institutions that have historically not served or even taken advantage of these students, our reputations inside the institution may become even more suspect than they might be for those who simply inhabit female and brown bodies but do not actively challenge the status quo. In the market-driven and extremely competitive higher ed landscape, in which diversity is seen as capital, we are expected to be grateful to be even granted entrance into the rarified, predominantly white, older, middle-class world of faculty, administration, and higher ed governance. The presence of our bodies themselves is supposed to be evidence of the institution's commitment to diversity. Our bodies are not supposed to act, speak, or, god forbid, contradict this narrative of sanitized "progress" in this sphere, and if we do, we are instantly labeled as unprofessional, not collegial, angry, aggressive, racist, or any other host of pejorative adjectives routinely used to keep women of color in our place. This was the context in which my story is located, the room into which I stepped on that fateful day in October.

My institutional reputation was peppered with the adjectives I just shared with you, and although all institutional players, and the so-called college and system leadership knew that our institution was, and, I would argue, still is, not a well-functioning one (sadly, not uncommon at many institutions of higher ed now), they saw me and my nonconforming black female body as a huge part of the problem. I had been disciplined for "not following procedure," I had been warned that I was "not collegial enough with colleagues." The first black female head of my department, I had been told in no uncertain terms that I would not be renewed in this position. After challenging the administration's mishandling of concurrent enrollment, I had received a written reprimand in my permanent file for representing my entire department's viewpoint on institutional letterhead. I had been issued a warning from my dean after sitting outside the meeting a fellow black female faculty member was having with administrators about her performance (I was there for support, and because she asked me to be). A few years before, a white male student at the student newspaper had filed a complaint of racial discrimination against me, for asserting that the fact that the staff was all white, as well as the fact that a noose had been hung there some years before, might have something to do with their lack of diversity, and the fact that few people on campus took them seriously. A few years after that, a disgruntled white male adjunct in the department had filed another complaint of racial harassment against me and three other colleagues (the rest of them were white) after we had lobbied hard to include the phrases "knowledge of critical race theory," and "demonstrated connection to communities of color," under "Preferred Qualifications" in the department's call for applicants during a hiring phase. Although I was eventually cleared on both counts, the Legal Affairs Department had slapped my hands by performing lengthy, fairly terrifying top-secret investigations and issuing me letters of expectation. In the last case, the administration ultimately pulled the preference for knowledge of CRT in the job call, stating that "it would be wrong to favor one theory over another" in our workplace. All of these incidents, as well as many more that it would take far too long to explicate here, are why I became an institutional target for moderating a discussion on structural racism and representation in a mass communications class. And also, they are decisively not why I became a pariah for such pedagogy. Very simply, the reason why I became an institutional target for moderating a discussion on structural racism and representation in a mass communications class was that I was a black woman faculty member who dared to demand that I be treated the same way as any other (read: white) faculty member.

***

In the end, each of us will have to begin where we are, naming and sharing our experiences as women of color faculty members in the Empire of the Academy as we go through them and building our networks of resistance as we live our stories. The professionalization of the academy, like the corporatization of the academy, has not benefited us, precariously located as we are, since these systems require absolute silence and compliance for membership. I was told while going through my ordeal that I should not speak, that I would lose my job, that I would be kicked out of higher ed forever, that my name would be mud. All by well-meaning, well-respected friends and colleagues at various institutions. And they were probably not wrong—who knows if I will ever be offered another job at an institution of higher ed after they have seen exactly what kind of person I am and, as my former dean said once, how little I care for "how things are done." However, I believe that I have something far more valuable, and that is the ability to sleep at night, secure in the knowledge that I have tried my best to live my values, and that I have stood with and leaned on community in every step of this journey. I will always be an outsider in the academy, and I will always find my worth from my community. As the *Presumed Incompetent* editors write, "the business of knowledge production, like the production of tea, spices, and bananas, has an imperialist history that it has never shaken. Inventing the postcolonial university is the task of the twenty-first century" (Gutierrez et al. 2012). This is not a task that will be completed lightly, but it is a task as urgent as any other on our national agenda, I believe. There will be tremendous losses and incremental gains, as there are in every social justice movement in history. What we cannot do is bow to the status quo, to capital, to white supremacy. We have to organize. We have to take courage, stand up, and risk something. We have to speak.

ACT IV. CHECK YOUR EGO AND OPEN YOUR MOUTH

Renee DeLong

Over the past fifteen years I've taught at schools that are majority-white institutions and schools that are over half students of color, and each institution has its own flavor of racist white dominance coated with a light veneer of diversity-speak. In each place, there has been a small group of people willing to talk about racial equity, and often this conversation happens among white women who see part of their work as allying themselves with people of color. In some ways, this conversation about racial equity feeds into the comfortable stereotypes around white heterosexist femininity and its caretaking functions. All of this makes me queasy—as a white, child-free lesbian. I feel alienated in this department for several reasons, and this outsider perspective allows me to analyze the ingrained culture of white heteronormativity.

It was May 2011, and we were preparing for the second-to-last department meeting. The day of the meeting, I read through the agenda and stopped short when I saw the associate of arts degree (AA) in creative writing was going forward. Before the department meeting, I cornered Shannon in her office to say that I was not comfortable endorsing this program and I didn't want to be quiet. I saw at another institution how the energy given to the creative writing program contributed to and stemmed from the race-blindness of the faculty members in the English Department. Part of the reason I applied for a job at MCTC was to work in a place where racism in higher education was being grappled with on a daily basis. When I saw that CRT was part of the job description, I figured that I could join colleagues who didn't need any schooling on the subtleties of racism. Then I saw this item on the agenda and decided it was time to say something about how unspoken racism within our field influences the decisions we make as a department. Before the meeting, my colleagues and I conferred. I elected to speak first because I was new and more likely to be heard. They warned me that people would get defensive but agreed to back me up.

It was the last agenda item, and I steeled myself to speak about race blindness and creative writing. Once I got my few sentences out, we had a short and tense discussion, and the decision was tabled until the final meeting of the year. When I read the notes from this meeting, my name did not appear as one of the people in the discussion, but Shannon's and Tai's names did. This was my tip-off that racial critiques are seen in this department as the work of black women—not white women. I was just erased.

At the final meeting we finally got more time to talk about the ways that creative writing is racialized in higher education, and the ways in which the writer is filled with assumptions about gender and race. This is a conversation that many of us have been having covertly in women's bathrooms and across café tables for years, and it was exhilarating to imagine how we can have it in a more public way. The rush to vote reminded me again that institutional processes always enforce the privilege of the comfortable majority—even when sustained and difficult debate about the values of the department reflect the spoken values of many of the members present. In other words, using an essay like "Poetry Is Not a Luxury" (1984) by Audre Lorde in your classroom is easy, and many white heterosexual instructors pat themselves on the back for their inclusivity. Now, how would you treat Lorde if she came back from the dead and in all her righteous glory told you that the department you shared was riddled with racism, sexism, and homophobia? Readers of this article, how willing are you to speak those difficult words and risk being seen as a troublemaker—within your own mix of privileges and oppressions? Too often, white and heterosexual faculty members assume that the people of color will talk about racism and the LGBT folks will comment on homophobia. Then the important/unimportant work is being done, and the faculty members with the most privilege sit back and watch the show.

Although I was surprised at how quickly the discussion at that department meeting became polarized, I'm glad that we spoke up. We lost the vote, but we forced everyone present to get on the record, and the rift it made forced some of the people who had been cruising on their privileges to realize that the political makeup of the department had changed. This vote also helped me see who my allies would be in this department.

This story is just one moment in which the racist and sexist hierarchy silenced a white lesbian, although I know that it disciplines faculty members of color, some of whom are also queer, in more nefarious and systematic ways. This happens in many institutions, though. We're really not special.

To short-circuit the ways in which white heteronormativity ignores racism, homophobia, and sexism, let's prioritize queers of color—particularly women—as we work toward equity together. This reformulation of who can be on our team and what our work can be may seem surprising in a classroom of presumably white, wealthy, and heterosexual students, but by reconfiguring our target audience and stretching our own pedagogical voices, we may create revolutionary space in seemingly mundane places. There are many precedents for this.

In the Combahee River Collective's Manifesto, written in 1977, the group explains that its organizing principle does not rest on diversity but on interwoven oppressions that constitute their lives. According to the statement, "we are actively committed to struggling against racial, sexual, heterosexual, and class oppression, and see as our particular task the development of integrated analysis and practice based upon the fact that the major systems of oppression are interlocking" (Combahee 1986, 9). This explanation of how interlocking and interrelated oppressions impact their lives and the unspoken disgust with the notion that oppressions can be ranked in order of importance or prioritized make the statement striking and complex. Dr. Kimberlé Crenshaw is credited with the first academic writing on intersectionality in the 1980s, but Combahee River Collective set up this analysis even earlier. As a discipline, we must be willing to examine the assumptions of our work with the lenses of both critical race theory and queer theory—especially if this makes the most privileged faculty members uncomfortable.

White faculty members also need to be willing to "stay in the room" when privileged white folks act out—and they will. White faculty, we need to take on the work of educating other white faculty about racism and asking tough questions on a regular basis. Our colleagues of color are already asked to be on more hiring committees than we are, their pictures are used to fill up the college's website, and they are mentoring many more students informally than you or I will ever see during office hours. The hypervisibility of faculty members of color also makes them more likely to endure more emotional mentoring work on top of the outward abuse and daily (or hourly) microaggressions. There are some useful passages in *Citizen: An American Lyric* (2014) by Claudia Rankine that can help white faculty understand how faculty of color are regularly reminded of their unequal status. Read it with other white faculty and host a public conversation about racism on your campus. Additionally, really use the texts that are likely already in your libraries and take up the challenges white readers so often leave unexamined. In "Eating the Other" bell hooks advises white people to analyze the racial politics of their daily interactions:

> That simply by expressing their desire for "intimate" contact with black people, white people do not eradicate the politics of racial domination as they are made manifest in personal interaction. Mutual recognition of racism, its impact both on those who are dominated and those who dominate, is the only standpoint that makes possible an encounter between races that is not based on denial and fantasy. For it is the ever-present reality of racist domination, of white supremacy, that renders problematic the desire of white people to have contact with the Other. (1992, 28)

This pedagogical desire to be close to people of color is echoed in every statement about teaching at my and most institutions. "I just love the students here," colleagues say over and over. "The students are the best part of the job!" White instructors, I ask that we problematize this reflex. Why do you love "the [black and brown] students here"? Because you feel like you get to atone for your white privilege by driving all the way across town to work with them? Because you imagine yourself as their white savior? Too much of the narratives around the work that involves students who have been oppressed by racism and classism is linked to a sense of noblesse oblige. Passion and teaching reaches a new level of dysfunction when white faculty members link their identities to their work "saving" minority students. Do not be deluded by good intentions and the sense that your identity is wrapped up in fixing "these" students. This grandiose vision of pedagogical prowess leads to the racist and patronizing interactions burdening, excluding, and even damaging the health and lives of colleagues and students of color alike.

ACT V. YOU CAN MISS ME WITH THAT, 'CAUSE PLANTATIONS WERE DIVERSE, TOO: A PERSONAL NARRATIVE AS A WINDOW TO POSSIBLE STRATEGIES FOR SUPPORTING AND ENGAGING EQUITY IN WRITING INSTRUCTION AND INSTITUTIONAL TRANSFORMATION

Taiyon J. Coleman

If you would have told me when I first attended college that I would end up teaching as a career and vocation, I would have said that you must be smoking crack. Dude. For real. Statistically, I wasn't even supposed to pass my first-year composition course as a first-generation college student born and raised in the inner city of Chicago, and I didn't. Statistically, I wasn't even supposed to be a black female tenured faculty writing instructor at a two-year college in Minnesota, but I am. For real, for real (Mike S 2014).

When I attended a professional discipline-specific conference a couple of years back (much like the conference at which this now-article was a presentation), I immediately felt an unease when I entered the convention venue and at first I couldn't understand why. Attendees seemed outwardly nice, and I had been teaching writing at the college and university level for over fifteen years. I had just completed my terminal degree in the field along with scoring a first-round job interview. By all accounts, it should have been good times. But while I walked around the conference venue politely seeking gentle smiles, hellos, and nondescript informal greetings with those who were now my colleagues, I had a hard time meeting their eyes, and most of the attendees, who were socially, historically, and institutionally constructed as white, rarely met mine.

On the second day of the conference, as I sat at an empty table to eat lunch, a black woman came to my table and asked if she could sit and eat with me. I said, "Sure." It was then that I realized why I was uncomfortable at the conference. I reremembered, reassessed, and reviewed back to the previous day when I first arrived. For the most part, I was among the few racially constructed blacks in attendance, and I reluctantly realized that the well-meaning eyes, demeanors, and dominant demographics of my colleagues facilitated a type of PTSD in me and, I surmised, in them too. For the first time, I started to confront the unlikelihood of me being in that space. I was not supposed to be there, and if my conference colleagues acknowledged me in any substantive way, I would actually "pop" materialize their (read, dominant) reality. (Isn't there some fable that if one doesn't believe in fairies, they cease to exist? It was like that.) So rather than confront the stressors that the social contradiction of the very presence of my black female body in that space created, the dominant collective, subconsciously or consciously, decided that I was not there. I couldn't be there; thus, it was like a Star Trek Ferengi cloaking device: sci-fi movie magic: poof! Now you see me, now you don't. (See Huber and Solorzano 2015 on racial microagressions.) Jazz hands, and I'm gone!

So, what happens when a group's actual invisibility, which can also be read as an absence or failure, is normalized, subsequently making that very invisibility central to maintaining a larger structural reality of dominant whiteness within institutional spaces? What departments and their institutions are constantly trying to place the Other back into the places and spaces (the trauma) that they thought they had survived by failing to recognize the micro- and macroaggressions experienced by the Other within the writing classroom, faculty spaces, and the larger institution?

Have you taught at institutions where poor, brown, and black students consistently fail writing classes or fail to successfully matriculate through the institution over semesters and then over decades and respond and act as if that is normal? Do you have that one other student, faculty, staff, or administrator, and you believe that your department/college is doing a great job at diversity? (To be read in a cheerleading voice, although I was a pom-pom girl, not a cheerleader, as even here there is a hierarchy.) Do you teach at an institution where the demographics of the students and the communities you serve are starkly different than the demographics of the faculty, staff, and administrators, and you believe that this is normal? Do you enter into a predominantly white classroom, faculty meeting, staff meeting, or administration leadership meeting and question if the racial makeup of the bodies in the room is equitable, or have you been desensitized and read the racial makeup of classrooms and other institutional spaces as normal, if you even notice it at all? Do you even see it, or do you even want to see it?

What does it do to the teaching and acquisition of writing when the experiences and identities of the Other are silenced physically and intellectually through the complicity of the very people who consciously claim (for example, through assigned readings and office and hallway posters of equitable writers) to support equity and inclusion? How can racial equity exist in writing instruction and student outcomes when equity does not exist among those faculty who teach writing nor within the institutions that house and serve them? What more explicit evidence of the historical legacy and contemporary status of the violent impacts of structural racism and its cumulative barriers than to enter into writing classrooms and other educational spaces and confront identity disparities, either through the actual disproportionate absence or presence of certain bodies relative to other bodies or the disproportionate, repeated, and patterned failure of certain students in writing classrooms and programs? To rationalize the disparity, consciously and subconsciously, is to actively perpetuate racism.

I get it, and I am compassionate. When Officer Ben Fields, a grown-ass man, "grabs . . . [the black female] student by the neck, flipping her backward as she sat at her desk, then dragging and throwing her across the floor" in Columbia, South Carolina (see Fausset and Southall 2015), it's much easier to cue the elevator music and wonder why, what happened, and to patiently ask and to be "deeply concerned" for the facts first, then to actually believe, accept, and take action regarding the daily physical, mental, and emotional realities, literally and analogically, for marginalized bodies within classrooms and other institutional spaces. I was not supposed to be a successfully matriculated college student, a college graduate, and a writing and literature teacher looking for a tenure-track faculty position. If I am not supposed to be there through the continued normalization of racially constructed and dominantly white spaces, places, and teaching positions, then who is still not socially, historically, and institutionally constructed to be in the writing or literature classrooms? I guess I got out of the Fields chokehold and off the floor (so I think), but there are countless others still not able to fully breathe . . .

I teach at a local college where the majority of my Writing Department colleagues (all excellent, well-meaning, well-intentioned, and good people) are institutionally constructed as white, but the majority of the students and the communities that we and the college serve are poor and of color. As at many writing programs and the institutions in which they are housed, the matriculation rate for students of color is challenging, and there are structural issues with the recruitment and retention of faculty of color. Although we (brown, black, poor, and gendered bodies) are in the classrooms and the institution, our marginalized bodies are systematically subjected to "macroaggressions": "institutional racism" and "racial microaggressions" (Huber and Solorzano 2015, 6). It is the failure of those with power and privilege within the discipline and the institution to actually look, see, recognize, and act to change historical and now contemporary patterns of exclusion of which we are all a part and perpetuate, consciously and unconsciously. As established by my colleagues earlier in this article, this willful ignorance continues the systemic oppression of brown, black, poor, and gendered bodies on every finger and thumb of the institution's hand: the students in the classroom, the faculty instructors, the staff, the administration, and the communities that the college serves.

In the Writing Department, I have witnessed faculty of color and their white allies metaphorically flipped out of their institutional chairs, accused of being noncollegial, incompetent, intimidating, angry, racist, and bullies because they have attempted to address issues of equity and the intersections of identity and experience as it relates to curriculum, pedagogy, student success, and faculty of color recruitment and retention. These disparaging and unprofessional insults and labels have become the subsequent consequences of those who dare to see constructed black and other marginalized identities and bodies and their experiences within the discipline of writing instruction and the larger academic institutions in which they are housed. Subsequently, these microaggression experiences of faculty members of color mirror the experiences of students of color in writing classes and within the larger college, and they also mirror the recruitment, retention, and experiences of staff and administrators of color within the college.

Walking around the conference and seeing my well-meaning and well-intentioned constructed white colleagues gave me flashbacks to my first-year composition class, when I was a first-generation student from Chicago's South Side attending a predominantly white public university in the Midwest. My well-meaning and well-intentioned white first-year composition teacher consistently told me, in her written feedback and final grade assessment of my paper assignments, that she could not understand what I was writing because it did not make any sense. Usually, I wrote about what I knew, which was being female, black, poor, urban, and being a first-time college student, away from home, attending a predominantly white college in the middle of the Midwest. Eventually, although someone like Officer Fields was not called to the classroom, I stopped attending class, and I failed my college composition course, although some of the essays were being published in campus-wide publications. A year later, after failing first-year composition like most students within my identity intersections, I dropped out of college. It would take five years before I would develop the courage and opportunity to return, let alone retake first-year writing. Sixteen years after completing my bachelor's degree, I can still walk into institutional venues for educators, and the educators are and were still primarily socially, historically, and institutionally constructed white, and no one seems or seemed uncomfortable or aware. This constructed and dominant whiteness in the field and discipline has been and is still completely normalized.

If we as teachers of writing normalize (read, accept) the dominant presence of constructed whiteness in the field and discipline among our students and colleagues, how might that consciously or unconsciously affect our teaching in the classroom and the assessment of students? What is the constructed identity of our students who are prepared for college writing and who successfully matriculate through our college writing classrooms? Is it that these numbers reflect a reality or reflect a constructed reality that we, being liberal, well-meaning, and well-intentioned educators, help to construct? Do we merely watch, show concern, and amass facts and other data? How might educators, writing instruction programs, and institutions work to get up from under this social, historical, and institutional bias that we have inherited through no fault of our own?

In response, I suggest the following steps as a start, not an absolute solution, toward equity in our classrooms and institutions:

- Fully understand what silence (lack of accountable, consistent, and transparent action) conveys.
- Avoid rationalization. There can only be one or two outcomes; either the failure of people of color and their infinite intersecting identities is normal inside and outside of the classroom, or there are institutional barriers that have prevented their very presence and success in the actual spaces that you and those of us with privilege inhabit.
- Don't ask and expect those who are the most institutionally and historically vulnerable among you to do the actual work of equity. The power of leading (big word) equity must reside within the leadership of the institution and must be embedded within its core cultural and institution-wide commitment—real, documented, and accountable pervasive policies and practices. If not, those who do equity work where there is no demonstrated and documented larger leadership institutional commitment become sacrifices like lambs to be slaughtered.
- There must be some other oversight body, which then has the power of holding individual institutions and instructors transparently accountable when equity situations are dire; this is not a system

of blaming, but don't just dance and listen to the orchestra while the Titanic is slowly sinking. This does not mean that individual programs are not free to construct their models relative to the communities and students that they serve, but to assume that individuals, who are well-meaning and well-intentioned, can autonomously maintain equity without a transparent checks and balancing system in the face of decades, and sometimes centuries, of exclusion is to underestimate (ignore) the legacy and power of structural and institutional unconscious and conscious racism and bias.[4]

- If you are in any space or room where there is a dominant majority, don't normalize their presence or lack thereof and ignore it; ask yourself what social, historical, and institutional actions might have happened that may have affected people directly and personally, which prevented them from being in that (read, your) time and space.
- Commit to working toward dismantling institutional and structural inequity as an institutional goal (practice) with a mission statement, hiring practices, curriculum development, and assessment and permeate it throughout the body and life of the institution.
- Recognize that institutional consequences are disproportionate for the same institutional actions. Because of cumulative and historical and structural inequities, any institutional practice that disparages any member works to disparage the more vulnerable members of an institution even more.
- As has been said numerous times in many other places, inequity is the canary in the coal mine. Recognize that achieving equity benefits all members of the institution and the communities that we serve.

The demographics of that conference space, like the spaces of my first-year composition course, our classrooms, our departments, our conference spaces, and our larger institutions, did not just happen; they are a result of the cumulative legacies of violent, historical, contemporary, and ongoing institutional exclusion and oppression. We will never get it right in these spaces until we first understand, acknowledge, respect, and synthesize this historical reality into our work, at every level, moving forward collectively.

"BRAND AGENTS AND BLOOD TRANSFUSIONS: A POSTSCRIPT"

Kathleen Sheerin DeVore

Firstly, thank you Patrick Sullivan for seeing the value in our *TETYC* article and requesting to use it in this book. This was not the first request to share the work, but it was the first to come not awash in entitlement. Thank you, too, for seeing the importance and utility in our "The Risky Business of Racial Equity in Writing Instruction: A Tragedy in Five

Acts" (*TETYC*, May 2016). As you might imagine, the reception at our home institution and in our broader statewide system of 37 colleges has been underwhelming. This really should not have been surprising as we're telling tales "outside the house," sharing long-kept secrets, and mostly asking a still-white-supremacist field, college comp instruction in America, to tell the truth about that ongoing colonizing violence, and to help us end it.

We shouldn't have been surprised, but the institutional silence, the underwhelming, almost total lack of interest, first in the article and later in the book-length version published in January of 2019, *has* surprised us. After all, our first title was *The Canary Is Dead: Failed Decolonization in the Two-Year College Comp Classroom, and the Risks of Equity in Writing Instruction.* So, when our Routledge editors advised us to soften this and we ended with *Working Toward Racial Equity in First-Year Composition: Six Perspectives*, we felt we had made the work less threatening, more inviting. Alas, not only did our home institution and statewide system both show little interest, our publisher also seemed uninterested in promoting their own book. Two months after the January release date, the Conference on College Composition and Communication (4Cs) was held, our field's largest national conference, and some members of our team were surprised to find no mention, no presence at all for our book at the Routledge booth.

As six two-year college (TYC) instructors at the time the article came out, all teaching five or six courses a term, we were novices in academic publishing, and so our first surprise was learning of the $140 pricing of the text, and then finding really no marketing or support in getting the book to its intended audience; composition instructors. We thought publishers were interested in selling books, but our experience suggests that they need to fill their catalogues and know that some, enough college libraries, will order the book to cover production costs. But interest in getting the work into the hands of college writing instructors? Somehow that seemed beyond their purview.

And so yes, the response to the book by institutions has been underwhelming, while the response of individual teachers like you—that has been deeply encouraging. Our hope is to continue to contribute to decolonizing classrooms one teacher at a time if need be, because this work—in a Trumpian America—is more necessary than ever.

Racism, especially in how it functions in writing classrooms and other institutions, is not just about meanness, ignorance, and/or inappropriate words. It's about very real policies and practices that have disparaging results to certain groups of people, that is, inequitable outcomes. Don't simply look at what we say and do, but also look at the results of what we say and do as the true (possibly only/best) measure of the equity of our actions/teaching (Freire 2014). As educators, and I include myself in this critique, we seem to have a cultural inability to use outcomes as the best measurement of inequality, access, and racism to the peril of our students and the future of a country whose democracy is dependent upon an educated citizenry (Mann 2010). This is evident in the *Precious Knowledge* documentary that demonstrates a link between the graduation rates of Latinx-American students from high school (outcomes) to racist, or homogenized at best, curriculum and pedagogy. We who teach in TYCs know how vulnerable the majority of our student population is; they are the most marginalized students in higher education. For readers unfamiliar with TYCs, here is a snapshot of who fills our classrooms: Nationally, the average age of a TYC student is 29, two-thirds of our students work, one-third work full time, 22 percent are parents, while 50 percent are first-generation college students and 25 percent are immigrants. While at our home institution, 60 percent are students of color, and we are a community rich in linguistic diversity, where eighty languages are spoken, yet we are challenged with the reality that 16 percent of our students struggle with housing insecurity. Given the under-resourced and materially and emotionally stretched nature of our student body, it has long been true for TYCs that, when the economy grows, our enrollment shrinks. Just as when the economy shrinks our enrollment rises, as folks unable to find work use the downturn to strengthen skills to increase their employability. Despite this long-known, nationally repeating trend, our college has directed increased funding to marketing initiatives, including urging all staff and faculty to become "brand agents." We are encouraged to wear college-logo apparel and logo-emblazoned name tags in order to increase the visibility of the college brand.

Were slaves brand agents for white supremacy and US capitalism?

Given the linguistic, cultural, economic, and resource-diverse environment I've just described, that our central response to current challenges is to further corporatize our staff with uniforms and name tags feels entirely beside the point. Because in the current political climate, where arguments for increased state and federal funding for public education are often nonstarters, we seem to have been hustled into strengthening our brand rather than materially strengthening our institution. This is particularly onerous given the rising anxiety of our low income, recent immigrant, and racially and ethnically diverse populations in border-wall, Muslim-ban, anti-immigrant 2019 America.

But here, let me start to wrap up this postscript not with more demographic percentages or even broad stroke racial and economic generalities. Let me tell you about one of my hardest-working, current summer-session college English students. I'll call her Rebecca—not her real name—and she is a DACA (Deferred Action for Childhood Arrivals) student brought to the United States as an infant by her undocumented parents wanting to escape generations of poverty in Mexico. She worked all through high school and continues working while in college, and has also developed a rare blood disorder, which recently has required blood transfusions to enable her to continue her grueling school and work schedule. Because her family does not have documentation, her health care has been inconsistent, but this summer she had been able to schedule a blood transfusion, which she told me about in the first weeks of the term. She then learned that the date of the transfusion was the same day a portfolio of her work was due to a committee for evaluation, as we use committee portfolio assessment for our BW (Basic Writing) course.

Because I teach six courses a term, and two in the summer—that's about 325 students a year—and because I am no longer young, when she missed a few classes and was in danger of missing the portfolio deadline, I sent her a terse email urging her to submit her work on time. Then the due date arrived, she was in class, but her work was not quite complete, and she could not stay to finish it. During a classmate's presentation she got up to leave, giving her work to a peer. I crossed the back of the room to catch her in the hallway; as I had put in extra time on her drafts, I was annoyed. I had also entirely forgotten her health issues. I asked, with some heat, why she was leaving; shakily she reminded me she had the blood transfusion in an hour. In deep shame, I remembered, promised I'd include a note in her portfolio, apologized for my forgetting, and wished her good luck with the procedure. I felt like—I was—an ass. Had I been wearing my college logo shirt or nametag I'd have been more of an ass.

We and our students at two-year colleges do not need uniforms or brand strengthening. What we need is material support for the most hard-working, committed, and economically and culturally marginalized students in the country. To address in part that cultural marginalization, we need college teachers to stop pretending that US colleges, and American education more broadly, are not part of the American colonizing enterprise. We need to acknowledge that they/we have been central to that enterprise, as during colonization, right behind the soldiers and the priests came the teachers, and so we need to radically decolonize our institutions yesterday. Critical Race Curriculum and antiracist pedagogies can help get us there, as well as nationwide support for hiring black and other faculty of color. White faculty are currently at 84 percent of full-time college faculty, so these practices must be adopted with *a quickness.* Our book, *Working Toward Racial Equity in First-Year Composition,* is part of this work, and this book, *16 Teachers Teaching: Two-Year College Perspectives,* promises to move the work further still. And we need these texts, and the decolonizing practices within them, to get into the hands of writing teachers across the country, one teacher at a time if necessary.

Thank you for furthering the work,
Kathleen DeVore

(For the writing team of Taiyon J. Coleman, Renee DeLong, Valérie Déus, Shannon Gibney, and Michael C. Kuhne)

NOTES

1. This essay originally appeared in *Teaching English in the Two-Year College,* vol. 43, no. 4, 2016, pp. 347–370. Copyright 2016 by the National Council of Teacher of English. Used with permission.
2. Much of this article began as a presentation at the 2015 College Composition and Communication Conference in Tampa, Florida. Thank you to those who came; sharing the story with an audience inspires our writing now.
3. Even here in the publication process, copyright law is the silencing of how white privilege functions, as we cannot include the letter in this article because we do not have the permission of the "writer" (who we suspect, as in many institutions, was merely a functionary signing off on a document someone else had produced in order to give cover to the institution). Even now, we have to hide the "evidence" to be heard at all.
4. Good times! For example, see the swift and subsequent suppression of voter rights in the United States after the Supreme Court struck down key provisions in the Voting Rights Act (Levy 2015).

REFERENCES

ALP Accelerated Learning Program. 2015. Community College of Baltimore County. September 2, 2015. http://alp-deved.org.

"Campus Fact Sheet." 2015. *About Us.* Minneapolis Community and Technical College. November 29, 2015.

Combahee River Collective. 1986. "The Combahee River Collective Statement." *Home Girls: A Black Feminist Anthology.* Edited by Barbara Smith. Albany, NY: Kitchen Table: Women of Color Press.

Coulter, Harold, and Michael Kuhne. 1999. *North Central Association Self-Study.* Minneapolis: Minneapolis Community and Technical College.

Crenshaw, Kimberlé. 2010. "Mapping the Margins: Intersectionality, Identity Politics, and Violence against Women of Color." *Stanford Law Review* 43 (1991): 1241–1299. Academic Search Premier, January 10, 2010.

Cressman, Leigh. 2015. "MCTC Pass Rates: ENGA 0900/110, ENGL 0900 and ENGL 1110, Spring 2013–Spring 2015." *Office of Strategy, Planning, and Accountability*. Minneapolis Community and Technical College.

Delgado, Richard, ed. 1995. *Critical Race Theory: The Cutting Edge*. Philadelphia: Temple University Press.

Fausset, Richard, and Ashley Southall. 2015. "Video Shows Officer Flipping Student in South Carolina, Prompting Inquiry." *New York Times*. October 26, 2015.

Freire, Paulo. 2014. *Pedagogy of the Oppressed*. New York: Bloomsbury Press.

Gutierrez y Muhs, Gabriella, Yolanda Flores Niemann, Carmen G. Gonzalez, and Angela P. Harris, eds. 2012. *Presumed Incompetent: The Intersections of Race and Class for Women in Academia*. Louisville, CO: Utah State University Press.

hooks, bell. 1992. "Eating the Other." *Black Looks: Race and Representation*, 21–40. Boston: South End Press.

Huber, Lindsay Pérez, and Daniel G. Solorzano. 2015. "Racial Microaggressions as a Tool for Critical Race Research." *Race Ethnicity and Education* 18 (3): 1–24.

Ladson-Billings, Gloria. 1998. "Just What Is Critical Race Theory and What's It Doing in a Nice Field Like Education?" *International Journal of Qualitative Studies in International Education* 11 (1): 7–24.

Levy, Gabrielle. 2015. "Congress Moves to Restore Cuts Supreme Court Made to Voting Rights Act." *U.S. News & World Report*. June 24, 2015.

Lorde, Audre. 1984. "Poetry Is Not a Luxury." *Sister Outsider: Essays and Speeches*. Trumansburg, NY: Crossing Press.

Mann, Horace. 2010. "From *Report of the Massachusetts Board of Education, 1848*." In *Rereading America*, 8th ed., edited by Gary Colombo, Robert Cullen, and Bonnie Lisle. Boston: Bedford/St. Martin's.

MCTC Data Shop. 2014. Office of Strategy, Planning and Accountability. Minneapolis Community and Technical College.

Mike S [pseud.]. 2014 "Marshawn Lynch, 'I'm gon' get mine more than I get got, doe.'" YouTube video. Minneapolis Community College Catalog, 1995–1996. https://www.youtube.com/watch?v=E5d0KXJMRWQ.

Rankine, Claudia. 2014. "Citizen: An American Lyric." *Minneapolis Community College Catalog, 1995–1996*. Minneapolis: Graywolf Press.

Rose, Mike. 2012. *Back to School: Why Everyone Deserves a Second Chance at Education*. New York: New Press.

"Timothy J. Lensmire: Expert Overview." 2002. University of Minnesota.

Yosso, Tara J. 2002. "Toward a Critical Race Curriculum." *Equity & Excellence in Education* 35 (2): 93–107.

PART IV

New Approaches to Teaching Developmental Reading and Writing

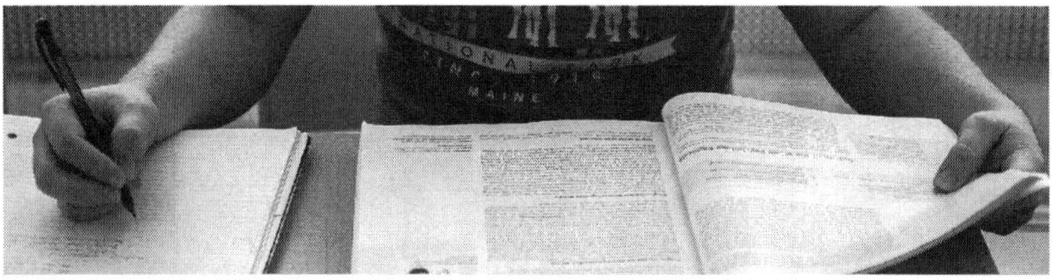

14

SETTING STUDENTS UP FOR SUCCESS

Teaching the Accelerated Learning Program (ALP)

Jamey Gallagher

Abstract: A teacher in the Accelerated Learning Program details the structure of the program, the benefits of ALP to both students and faculty, and how a shift toward an integrated reading and writing approach has affected pedagogy.

In 2011, I started my first full-time community college teaching position. When I was asked to teach in the Accelerated Learning Program at the Community College of Baltimore County, I had no real conception of what the program was, very little faculty development to teach the class, and, subsequently, no idea what I was doing. My PhD in composition and rhetoric helped me to know where to find resources, but I had never even heard of ALP before being hired by CCBC. My understanding of the program was this: Eight students from the English 101 section would meet with me for an additional class period, and I was charged with doing whatever I could do to help those students pass the credit class. My approach then was to simply try to figure out what those students needed and to give it to them. It felt strange to head into a class that was so small and that I didn't feel comfortable teaching.

Our class was held in a tiny, glass-wall-enclosed space in the middle of the library, which some teachers had dubbed "the goldfish bowl." During

DOI: 10.7330/9781607329305.c014

our first class meeting, I looked around at the eight eager young faces that had followed me into the room—all relatively recent graduates of either county or city public schools—and I asked them what they hoped to get out of college. One of them said he wanted to become a lawyer, another a doctor, a third a psychologist. I was impressed with their ambitions but daunted by how to get them to the level where they could pass a credit class, never mind enter a profession. But I quickly learned that believing in students was the key to success in the program. Although only three of those eight students in my first semester ALP class passed English 101, those three students, despite significant challenges, had progressed in almost unbelievable ways, becoming competent college writers, readers, and critical thinkers. They had progressed partly because they had spent more time with me, thinking about the writing they were doing, seeing the writing of other students in English 101, and working and reworking their sentences and paragraphs in small groups.

It was quickly apparent to me that ALP was *the* way to teach developmental writing. I become a supporter and a strong advocate of the approach, assuming the role of assistant director of the program under Peter Adams in the spring semester of 2012. My approach to teaching writing in general has been influenced heavily by my experiences teaching in the Accelerated Learning Program.

THE STRUCTURE OF ALP

When I began teaching at CCBC, the institution where ALP was started by a small group of faculty members spearheaded by Peter Adams, there were still separate reading and writing developmental classes. ALP was focused solely on writing instruction. Since that time, ALP has become responsible for reading instruction as well, but writing was the sole focus in the beginning.

As the assistant director of the program, I often traveled to other institutions and was frequently asked, "What do you do in the second, smaller class?" and, "How do you fill the class period?" I would rattle off a list of possible activities that had been brainstormed by Peter Adams and members of the ALP Steering Committee, but I think it's important to remember that at the beginning, ALP was flexible. The main goal, at all times, was to ensure that students could do the work in their credit classes. The more they felt like the two classes were one class, that the work they were doing in the developmental section was integral to their success in the credit class, the better. We took a "smorgasbord" approach to faculty development, basically promoting "whatever works for you."

We pushed teachers away from part-to-whole pedagogy and discouraged out-of-context grammar drills, but we didn't have a unified pedagogical approach. We encouraged teachers to think about reading instruction and workshopping, but nothing in particular was required of ALP instructors. We saw positive outcomes with this approach in terms of student success.

What worked for me as an ALP teacher was to think of each essay assignment in the credit class as a thematic unit. That was basically the way I had been teaching composition before coming to CCBC anyway, an approach that was basically aligned with the critical cultural studies approach of scholars like James Berlin. I tried to think of compelling issues that my students could write about, or genres that they could write in, and focus on those topics or genres for about four weeks. Students would write about equity in education or race in America, for instance. They would become, to the extent that it is possible in four weeks, experts in certain subjects, and they write from an invested viewpoint. I wanted the work not only to feel like but to *be* authentic intellectual work. So, in English 101 we focused on big ideas.

In the smaller ALP section, students would be working toward those essays or, occasionally, working on assignments that mirrored or deepened those assignments. Recently a colleague told me about how she sells the ALP section to her students as truly "accelerated," in that the students get *more* than the students in the credit class. They are able to dive deeper into the material and think in more complex ways. I love this way of thinking about ALP.

For most of the first two weeks in a unit, the ALP class does dive deeper, doing more informal writing about the topic, watching videos or reading articles that offer a different take on an issue, and writing short, low-stakes assignments that build up to the larger assignment. I will often have students mimic the writing style of articles we read, looking at sentences in isolation and replacing the author's content with their own content, getting a kind of mechanic's view of how sentences work and how a writer achieves rhetorical effects. There is a lot of brainstorming and a lot of discussion. Often, quieter students who don't feel comfortable speaking up in the larger credit class speak up in the smaller ALP class.

For the second two weeks of a unit, a good deal of workshopping happens in the ALP class. Either student papers are workshopped by the entire small group (something much more easily done in this smaller section than in the larger credit class) or students are split into small groups. Instead of working on grammar separately and out of context, we work on issues in students' papers as they arise. Students can cut up their papers into paragraphs and have other students put them back together.

Students can look at their own sentences in isolation to see where they are failing to connect ideas or how to work on subordination more effectively. While other students are completing a task, I am able to conference with individual students, spending time digging into both the ideas students are coming up with and the expression of those ideas. This second class is not a lab and it is not entirely a workshop—it is a flexible credit class that should have benefit to students beyond their English classes.

When one unit is completed, the process begins again with a new unit. I ask students to keep their writing in a portfolio so that no paper is ever "final." While I give students in the 101 class unlimited opportunities to revise, often I will require students in the ALP class to revise their papers for better initial grades. In this way, the two classes are always feeding off each other as we transition from one unit to the next.

THE BENEFITS OF ALP FOR STUDENTS

Given this structure, there are certain benefits to the Accelerated Learning Program. The most obvious benefit is that students are spending more time on task; more time reading, dissecting reading, writing, and thinking about writing. It is a more immersive approach to developmental education. While some people argue that accelerating students through their education is the wrong approach, since developmental writers need *more*, not *less*, time to work on writing, this approach to developmental education gives students the same amount of time as they used to get, but it compresses the time into a single semester. In my experience, that intensity makes a significant difference. Students have typically written and read for high school before coming to college, but because high school teachers are overburdened, often they do not get the intense feedback that an ALP instructor can provide. This intensity of their interactions with a faculty member leads to significant gains. At CCBC, we have seen that ALP students perform slightly better than their colleagues who placed directly into the credit classes in our three-year General Education Assessment projects, despite the fact that, ostensibly, they started behind those students. Clearly, students are benefitting from the program in academic ways.

The nature of the small classroom also gives students a chance to work on and think about their own writing in a different way. Whereas in a large class I often need a few weeks to determine what specific challenges my writing students face, in the ALP class I know within the first week what students need to work on, and I can point out those issues to them so they can become better self-editors. Very quickly, students see what challenges they face as writers, as well as the challenges other students face. They take on the habits and mindsets of writers.

Maybe the most important benefit of ALP, though, is relational. Being in a class with only eight or ten students is a very different experience, both for students and for community college instructors. In some ways, the class feels much more like a graduate seminar than a developmental class. Probably the first thing one notices when teaching in the Accelerated Learning Program is the kind of vibe that naturally develops in the cohort class. It is smaller, more intense, and more personal than the environment of a typical college class. Students become very comfortable talking in this setting. During my first semester, I had a student who told us that she was struggling in class because she was homeless. I was surprised that she was more than comfortable revealing that fact in the small classroom (she would never have done so in the larger class), but it has become less surprising to me now.

Part of the advantage of this small class is the noncognitive benefit, the possibility of talking about issues like lacking childcare, homelessness, losing a job, getting arrested, or getting pregnant (all of which have happened to my students), in a safe and respectful setting. As an open-access institution, the diversity of the student population is constantly evolving, with a robust international population, students with severe disabilities, autistic students, and students struggling due to a lack of resources. In ALP, relationships develop naturally, by dint of being in this communal space together for so long. Students form strong bonds among themselves, sometimes developing study groups, and during every semester I find us forming a kind of learning community that is focused on the same subjects, a community that is quick to tell me when I have taken a wrong turn.

This kind of classroom community-building is something I try to do in all my classes. There is a clear benefit to creating a community within the class. Since so many of our students fail not because of cognitive issues but because of life issues, it's important to open up all our classes to noncognitive issues. Sometimes simply talking to a student is enough to set them on the right path, while other times it's important to refer students to additional services at the college.

And this might be a good time to note issues of race and class—issues that I intentionally incorporate into the content for the course but that are also important when considering more relational aspects of the class. Our internal data has shown that, at our institution, African American students are far more likely to be placed into developmental classes, including ALP classes. As a White faculty member, it's important for me to acknowledge this. Elsewhere, I have written about using code-meshing as a way to value the language resources that students bring with them, but acknowledging the very real consequences of living in a racist society is necessary when considering noncognitive factors as well. For that reason, White faculty members should be open to discussions that revolve around race.

So, the benefit of the ALP approach for students is both cognitive and noncognitive. Students come to competence with writing and reading and critical thinking through their interactions with others. They become stronger members of the college community, which also leads to higher persistence rates.

THE NEW INTEGRATED READING/WRITING APPROACH TO ALP

In the past two years, the Accelerated Learning Program has changed significantly as we move to an integrated reading/writing model. It has been a challenging transition, but in the long run it will benefit students and the program. In the college, the Reading Department has transitioned into the Academic Literacy (or ACLT) Department, and reading classes have changed to focus on reading, writing, and critical thinking.[1] ACLT faculty teach both ALP classes and a lower-level integrated reading/writing class called ACLT 052. In the past few years, a second-level developmental reading class that many ALP students had to take either before or at the same time as taking English classes has been eliminated, and ALP has become responsible for giving these students the reading instruction they need to be successful in credit classes.

A small group, including myself, was set up to infuse ACLT pedagogy into the program. ACLT pedagogy mirrors a lot of what I came into the college doing. Students are asked to read and respond to complex academic texts. Thematic units focused on issues that are relevant to our students' lives are used. The focus is on bringing students to competence rather than on instilling discrete skills. One faculty member has called this approach "smuggling in the skills," a term I appreciate a good deal. We know students do not need all the grammatical terms that we might use in order to *use* grammar. They do not need to name rhetorical strategies in order to use those strategies. The lower-level ACLT 052 class is sold as "practicing college," which, in the ALP setting, becomes "doing college." I would argue that the approach is nothing new; it was what David Bartholomae and Anthony Petrosky argue for in *Facts, Artifacts, and Counterfacts* (1986) in the 1980s. We are seeing success with students diving deeper into the academic materials that will help them survive in future classes.

Naturally, this shift in pedagogy had to occur both in the credit class and in the developmental class, but the shift for me as a teacher occurred more in the ALP class, since I had already been teaching English 101 using this approach. The smaller class still follows the same basic structure, including ten students and meeting directly after the 101, and is still flexible and focused on noncognitive issues, but now I am much more intentional about ensuring that students are working with texts in meaningful ways. The work of Katie Hern has been instrumental in this shift. During a faculty development workshop with Hern, faculty members were introduced to the idea of the "reading-writing cycle," a simple schematic that has students working with texts beforehand, while they are reading, and after they read. Things like previewing activities and post-reading activities like speed dating, an activity that has students get into two rows, answer questions with a partner, then switch partners quickly until each student has interacted with all other students in the class, have been helpful in getting students to wrestle with texts in new ways, and has led to much better writing in the classroom. There are many places ideas for these kinds of activities can be found, from Katie Hern's work in the anthology *Deep Reading* (2017) and elsewhere, to programs like Reading Apprentice.

It has become clear to me that what faculty members need in order to teach an integrated reading/writing version of ALP well is self-reflexivity and a storehouse of possible techniques. The idea is not to bring isolated reading strategies to the classroom, but to determine what strategies will help students *in the moment*. This is a matter of art as much as craft. For instance, recently I had students read Ta-Nehisi Coates's *Between the World and Me* (2015), a book-length letter written to the author's son about what it means to grow up as a black man in America. It is a challenging but deeply rewarding read. I realized, after I had students read a section of the book, that they did not have nearly enough context to deal with the many names that Coates throws out in the section, the names of literary and cultural scholars focusing on race from the last two hundred years of American history. Many were names I did not recognize myself. One approach to this problem might be to introduce the names that students will need to know ahead of time, and I did some of that, but there were so many names I couldn't fully account for them all.

What students needed to do in that moment was to work with the text and see what the writer was doing in that section. It would have been easy to be distracted by the many names. Instead of the more traditional reading quiz I had expected to give students, I had students pair up, go through the thirty-page section, and trace Coates's thinking, mapping it with markers on large sheets of newsprint. It was really as simple as having students find Coates's take on race on the first page of the section and follow it as it changed, marking these changes on the newsprint like a river. Coates writes about what he thought about race when he entered Howard University, how his ideas were changed by the writers and ideas he encountered, and how he currently thinks about race. Students were able to follow the thread of his thinking, even if they didn't recognize every name mentioned. While completing this activity, they were writing, they were reading, and they were thinking critically. This activity is clearly not something that would work with every book, but it worked with Coates. What I am most interested in developing now as an ALP teacher are strategic, flexible, just-in-time reading activities.

There has been some concern at our college that an attention to reading instruction and a focus on the importance of the ALP class in doing *everything*—from reading to writing to critical thinking, preparing students for *all* of their classes—has led to a loss of flexibility and a lack of attention to noncognitive issues. This is a very real concern, and one I believe we'll avoid as we move forward. It is as important to attend to students' noncognitive needs as it is to attend to their reading needs. We can and should consider both.

BUILDING A UNIT

Currently in the program, we have unit plans that adjunct faculty can use in the classroom. These units cover issues like identity, food ethics, education, superheroes, and quite a few more. Each unit plan features a reading list that includes both complex academic texts and more accessible videos and readings, and a tentative class schedule that faculty are encouraged to modify to suit their needs and interests. The class schedules cover both the 101 and the ALP classes, though the ALP schedule is typically more flexible. We also encourage faculty to design their own units. I believe that the best teaching happens when teachers create their own material for the classroom, and I certainly always create mine, but this is difficult, time-consuming work. In order to help move the college along this path to integrated reading and writing, I designed a unit plan around language varieties and dialects. I hope that tracing my thinking as I developed that unit may be useful to others who want to take a more thematic approach in their classes. One benefit to taking this approach is that teachers can be free from the prepackaged curriculums of textbooks and, maybe more importantly, can attend to the interests and needs of students in their local area. A teacher in New

Mexico may want to find a different approach to a unit on language that would resonate more with her students. The best units, I believe, meet at a place where a teacher's interests intersect with students' interests, and new faculty need only think about what fascinates them and whether their students might also be interested to get started.

I have been interested in language and language varieties for a very long time. In the past, I had students think about the discourse communities they belonged to, which included everything from video gamers to followers of fashion to Hooters servers, and write mini-ethnographies, an assignment modified from one developed by my colleague Dr. Christy Wenger, then a graduate student at Lehigh University. Since then, I have developed an assignment that asks students to take on a persona in a hypothetical situation. The first thing I had to think carefully about was what ACLT teachers call the "essential questions" for the unit. I prefer to think of these questions as *guiding* questions, because they should guide students' inquiry. Guiding questions should be relevant to students, they should be complex enough that students can sink their teeth into them, and there should be enough on different sides of the issue that they are not forced into taking a stand with which they might not agree.

My essential question for this unit focused on the issue of whether other varieties of English, besides standardized English, should be allowed or respected in public places, places that include the work place, the classroom, the courtroom, and the public sphere. I wanted students to think about the language they had used, or heard being used, in their upbringing and whether that language had power or not. I wanted them to think about language and power and the value of what almost all my students call "slang." This obviously ties in with the positionality of my students. It allows many students to be the experts and places me in a novice position.

Then, following Katie Hern's reading-writing cycle, I had to determine ways to introduce students to the topic, "activating their schema" in the parlance of the discipline, so that they could work with the ideas. Language works well for a unit because it's something that students use all the time, but it's typically not something they have thought about in an academic way before. In a previous semester, a student had shared Kai Davis's spoken word piece entitled "Fuck I Look Like" (2011). I realized that that piece, very relatable to my students, could serve as a strong introduction to some of the ideas around language variety and the power of language. In the piece, Davis talks about the judgment she feels as a young black woman in an advanced placement class. She feels judgment coming from both directions; from black peers who find her use of "big words" pretentious and from white students who criticize her for using vernacular at all. My students particularly appreciate a section of the video in which Davis discusses the differences between the word "gargantuan" and the term "big as shit." The video has the added benefit of loosening students up. Since I use the video during my first class meeting with students, they are surprised by the language used in the video but put at ease.

I also thought that having students study language in the wild would be useful, so when I was on a large campus, I had students go to the cafeteria and listen to the language being used there. I asked them to be discrete eavesdroppers, something students initially raise concerns about but which they eventually agree to do—we are all eavesdroppers. In the cafeteria, students self-segregate, athletes sitting with athletes, gamers sitting with gamers. After copying down phrases that we hear among these groups, we come back and talk about the language used. We note how language both connects certain people and keeps other people out. Since I am no longer on a large campus, I have students do their observations outside of class now, going to malls or other public places. These two activities set up the language unit. Thinking of introductory activities is fairly easy. The bigger challenge is finding readings that can be put meaningfully into dialogue with each other.

As I built the unit, I thought constantly about how useful the material I was having students read would be as they put together their own essays. I wanted to immerse them in the subject and build their skills at the same time. I had to think about what would happen during each class period. I started with the essay assignment in mind, backward designing the curriculum to fit that assignment. The first week I wanted to introduce students to the ideas of the unit and get them to do informal writing. We watched the Kai Davis video and discussed language in the credit class. Directly following that, in the ALP class, we talked about students' fears and anxieties around reading and writing and started working on a student-created dictionary of terms; an activity students love, since it positions them as experts and me as a learner. After that, students were primed to read a chapter from bell hooks on language, a chapter that is very clear about how African American Vernacular English was developed and how it can have value in today's society. hooks writes: "An unbroken connection exists between the broken English of the displaced, enslaved African and the diverse black vernacular speech black folks use today. In both cases, the rupture of standard English enabled and enables rebellion and resistance." (1994, 224).

Students were then introduced to June Jordan's "Nobody Mean More to Me Than You" (1988), in which the following scenario is described:

A student in the author's class has a brother who has been murdered by the police in New York City in 1984. The class wants to write about the act and get the word out about what happened. They must decide whether to write in what Jordan calls black English or in standardized English. Obviously, there are connections to what has been happening in terms of police shootings in the past few years. Students are then given the chance to perform a short skit based on a scenario of their choice, as long as it deals in some way with language use in a public place. In the ALP section, we break the essays down in more depth than in the 101, we bring in other readings, we put readings into conversation with each other. Students do informal writings that compare hooks and Jordan.

Vershawn Ashanti Young's "Nah, we Straight" (2004) offers a more updated take on the issue of language variety, arguing for code-meshing over code-mixing. Code-meshing is the use of vernacular in everyday, public language, while code-mixing is the use of only one language in each setting. When one code-meshes, the barriers between languages are broken down, whereas when one code-mixes the languages are kept discrete. We broaden the discussion by bringing in Gloria Anzaldua's "How to Tame a Wild Tongue" (1990), which is written in an unapologetic mix of Spanish and English. Finally, students who choose to write about issues beyond African American Vernacular English are directed to Canagarajah's "The Place of World Englishes in Composition" (2006) or Horner and Trimbur's "English Only and U.S. College Composition" (2002).

Many of these works are very challenging pieces, especially for students who have been labelled "developmental." Getting students to read and truly understand these pieces takes time. Students have to reread. In some cases, I will start a difficult reading in class, we will talk about the first few paragraphs, getting some of the basic terminology understood, and then I will ask students to group up and tackle short sections of the text. Sometimes I will chunk the essays for students, asking them to find a certain number of ideas, or I will have students write a "difficulty paper," which gets them to think about *why* they were stopped by some of the writing. This is where activities like speed dating come in handy as well. Students should be reading the works both out of and in class. The more I can get them to work with the reading itself, the better their writing becomes.

As we get into the writing of the essay, we can begin to talk about academic moves that writers have to make. Students are asked to take on a role in this writing, imagining themselves as other people in a hypothetical scenario. Students definitely appreciate this more creative aspect of the assignment. In fact, sometimes the biggest challenge is to get them to spend less time on explaining the scenario and more time on transitioning to the very real work of connecting larger ideas to their personal opinions about the topic at hand. Students are able to argue either that other languages should or should not be used in public, but I certainly try to push for the value of vernacular languages.

The assignment is:

Language and the Politics of Proper English Essay Prompt

English 101

Consider one of the following scenarios:

- A shop owner refuses services to someone speaking Spanish.
- An employer has to choose between two different applicants with the same qualifications. One speaks Black Vernacular English (BVE), the other "standard" English.
- A young black man is brutalized by the police. To get the word out, his relative has to decide whether to write in BVE or Standard Edited English.

Take the point of view of one of the stakeholders in these situations. For instance:

- The brother of the black man brutalized
- The Spanish-speaking individual refused services
- The shop owner denying services

Your own personal view on the issue should align with the viewpoint you are taking.

Answer the question:

Should other varieties of English, or other languages, be allowed/acceptable in professional settings, schools, work places, etc?

Your essay MUST:

- Make a claim.
- Use at least three of the four essays we read together to either back up your claim and/or to offer the "other side."
- Take the opinions of others seriously.
- Consider counterarguments to your arguments.
- Take risks.

Your essay SHOULD:

- Take experience seriously.
- Use a mixture of first and third person. You should speak as a public intellectual.

Your essay MIGHT:

- Be adventurous in terms of language.
- Code switch/mesh.

Requirements:
4–6 pages
MLA format
Due dates:

Teachers may have concerns about students using vernacular language in their classroom, but it's my strong belief that having students use their own language in their writing, along with being in line with "Students' Right to Their Own Language," (CCCC 1974) helps students think in academic ways. A number of theorists in composition have written about the value of "bridge" pedagogies—approaches that bring people to academic writing through vernacular literacies. One of the criticisms of these bridge pedagogies has been that the bridge goes only one way—our students are expected to cross over to meet us, never vice versa. For example, Mary Soliday writes "by teaching students to manipulate the conventions and forms of academic language, writing teachers are unthinkingly acculturating students into the academy and glossing over issues of difference in the classroom" (1994, 512). My own approach to bridge pedagogies is to believe that we should allow more vernacular literacy into academic discourse, expanding our definition of what academic discourse means—and theorists, most notably Carmen Kynard (2012–2020), have already done that on a professional level—through the writing of our students. My hope is that by bringing more vernacular writing into the classroom, we meet the students halfway, and that academic literacy is invigorated and expanded as a result.

At the same time, by thinking about these different kinds of language, students become more aware of all their language decisions. For instance, during the course of the unit, I ask students to write a letter to a friend of theirs using their "home language." Students in previous semesters have done interesting work, and their reflections can be used as a window into what I hope to accomplish as a teacher by focusing on the value of vernacular and making my class explicitly about race. One student, a young woman who had been unsuccessful in earlier educational attempts, wrote the following, which she titled "Taming My Wild Tongue":

"We be talkin' bout whites and blacks, the shit really make me think frl. We sit there for a whole 90 minutes, expressing ourself and crazy thing about the shit, nobody pop off. The ova day yo gave us this paper and we had to annotate it, ion really like annotations but the stories he be givin' us make me wanna do my best and express how I feel. The professor inspiring fr, the fact that yo so comfortable talking about this typa thing. Sometimes we'll say something, and it's like he wants to really understand the concept of what's said."

This kind of informal writing has been useful in bridging this student to more academic language, in which she continues to sprinkle in some vernacular.

In developing units, it's important to think about the progression of readings. I try to start students with something very engaging and relatable, the Kai Davis video in this case, before moving to what I think of as touchstone texts for a unit—in this case the hooks and Jordan. I want at least one text that speaks in an academic way about the subject at hand, whether it's language or gender or monsters. Students should be able to see themselves doing real academic work, grappling with difficult ideas. They should also care about what they're writing about. This is certainly a tall order in a writing classroom, but I believe we can help students "own" their writing by sometimes allowing vernacular, by thinking creatively about assignments, and by sincerely listening to students' ideas.

THE BENEFITS OF TEACHING ALP FOR FACULTY

ALP offers many benefits for students, but there are just as many benefits for faculty members. I want to make a case for teaching ALP as a worthwhile intellectual activity. Because there are students of differing skill levels in this class (I would argue that there always are, though ALP makes this more explicit), sometimes it can be difficult to reach everyone in the same way. This is the challenge and the beauty of teaching basic writing in a community college.

There is an intellectual payoff in thinking about the units, in planning for how students will react to certain readings, and in rethinking units once they have been used in the classroom to make them more successful. There is also a sense of satisfaction in bringing up issues that are important to us and helping students see their importance. For instance, this semester I designed a unit on mass incarceration, an issue that I find to be momentously important. I was able to make that argument and immerse students in the subject, sharing with them writing done by top intellectuals like Ta-Nehisi Coates and Michelle Alexander. This is work that couldn't be done in a traditional modes-based basic writing class.

Beyond those intellectual benefits, working with students is incredibly exciting. We know that our placement policies are not equitable, that too many students of color wind up in developmental classes—see the work of the Community College Research Center, particular articles by Bailey and Hodara, Jaggars, and Karp. ALP is one initiative—along with culturally responsive teaching and placement reform—that is having a marked impact on these outcomes. It is truly a matter of social justice.

It is also personally satisfying to see students succeed. During the first semester I taught ALP, only three students passed the class. One of those three students was the student who started the semester claiming he wanted to be a lawyer. I didn't discourage him during that class, but deep down, secretly, I had some serious doubts. His skills coming into the class were rough. He struggled with sentence boundaries and essay structure. During that semester I saw him looking at other students' papers and emulating their openings, or their conclusions, or how they used sources. He never plagiarized; he simply modeled his papers on others' work until he was able to stand on his own. His progress was so impressive that I will remember him for years to come. I still occasionally hear from that student. He has graduated from Towson University with a bachelor's in public relations, and he has worked on several political campaigns in the city. He is a clear success story. Seeing students like this succeed is the most important and touching benefit of teaching ALP. It's why we are here.

I have now been teaching in the program for six years. I know that it works, and it works for those students who have been labeled as "developmental." It offers benefits for both students and faculty. It is setting students, like the ones mentioned in this essay and hundreds of others taught in other ALP classes, up for success.

APPENDIX 14.A

DAILY PLANS

(for an ALP that meets twice a week)

English 101	*Homework*	*ACLT 053*
Week One Day One • Watch "Fuck I Look Like?" by Kai Davis. Write informal response to video. Mini-discussion • Discussion: What *is* proper English? Who gets to decide? • Introduction to Integrated Reading/Writing. Working the Text • Read first paragraph of "Language" • Write informal response	• Read bell hooks "Language" • Annotate • Do a reverse outline, chunking the essay into four sections	• With a partner, begin reading and annotating "Language" • Discussion of first half of "Language" • Start compiling a dictionary of *their* language (modeled on *Black Talk* by Geneva Smitherman)

continued on next page

continued

English 101	*Homework*	*ACLT 053*
Week One Day Two • Quiz: bell hooks "Language" (appendix) • Discussion of concepts: Black Vernacular English, discourse groups • Pass out and go over first major writing assignment • Case study activity in groups: You are an employee who has to decide to hire one of two applicants. They have the same qualifications, but one speaks AAVE. Who do you hire? Why? Report out and discussion	• Read and annotate "Nobody Means More to Me Than You" • Eavesdrop: Go to someplace crowded and write down exact phrases you hear	• Field study of language—visit cafeteria • Write down exact phrases that you hear. • Discussion • Prewriting toward first assignment
Week Two Day One • Quiz: "Nobody Mean More" • Discussion: Eavesdropping. What did you learn about language? • Hand out four current controversies in language, discuss • Terms for next reading: unidirectional, monolingual, modernist, postmodern, multilingual and polyliterate	• Read and annotate "The Place of Global Englishes in . . . ," at least up to page 602, focusing on the introduction and "Focusing on Composition"	• Working with texts: Dialogue with bell hooks and June Jordan. (see sheet appendix) • Continue work on Dictionary of Students' Language
Week Two Day Two • Quiz: "The Place of Global Englishes" • What's the difference between an accent, a dialect, and a language variety? • Writing Activity: Write a piece in your home language.	• Read and write a "difficulty paper" about "How to Tame a Wild Tongue" • A difficulty paper is a response to the essay, concentrating on what you found difficult or confusing or troubling.	• Work with Canagarjah. • Find sources for "the other side"
Week Three Day One • Discussion of difficulty paper and "How to Tame a Wild Tongue" • Grading Activity: Grade a paper written in AAVE and a paper written in "standardized English" • Discuss standards	• Work on rough draft: Entire draft due next class	• Outlining vs. drafting • Prewriting toward first essay • Mapping out a plan • Time to work on essays
Week Three Day Two • Rough draft due • In-class workshops • Mini-MLA format lesson: Where to find resources, building a works cited page	• Write a writer's comment on your rough draft. What do you plan to do next? Begin working on the draft.	• Begin reading Anzaldua and grappling with the text together. Informal writing • Full-class workshop of papers for 101

continued on next page

continued

English 101	*Homework*	*ACLT 053*
Week Four Day One • Standard English vs. varieties of English: The Politics. What's at stake. Who's left out? • Case study: Business owner denying service to Spanish-speaker	• Work on final draft	• Preliminary collection of language from social media • Additional workshop of papers for 101
Week Four Day Two • Final draft of paper due • Setting up the next unit	• Reading toward next unit	• Workshop final drafts using grammar bingo (thanks to Nancy Murray) • Build grammar bingo sheets out of "errors" in student writing • Discuss the idea that grammar is contextual • Complete dictionary

NOTE

1. For more information, see Jeanine Williams and Sharon Hayes "ACLT 052: Academic Literacy—An Integrated, Accelerated Model for Developmental Reading and Writing" in *NADE Digest*, Winter 2016.

REFERENCES

Anzaldua, Gloria. 1990. "How to Tame a Wild Tongue." *Out There: Marginalization and Contemporary Cultures.* New York: New Museum of Contemporary Art.

Bailey, Thomas R. 2009. "Challenge and opportunity: Rethinking the role and function of developmental education in community college." *New Directions for Community Colleges* 145: 11–30.

Bartholomae, D., and A. Petrosky. 1986. *Facts, Artifacts and Counterfacts: Theory and method for a reading and writing course.* Portsmouth, NH: Heinemann.

Canagarajah, A. Suresh. 2006. "The Place of World Englishes in Composition: Pluralization Continued." *College Composition and Communication* 57 (4): 586–619.

CCCC. 1974, 2003. "Students' Right to Their Own Language." *College Composition and Communication* 25 (3).

Coates, Ta-Nehisi. 2015. *Between the World and Me.* New York: Spiegel & Grau.

Davis, Kai. 2011. "Kai Davis Spoken Word: Fuck I Look Like!" YouTube, November, 11, 2011. www.youtube.com/watch?v=DwvdOum4ed0.

Hern, Katie. 2017. "Unleashing Students' Capacity Through Acceleration." In *Deep Reading: Teaching Reading in the Writing Classroom,* edited by Patrick Sullivan, Howard Tinberg, and Sheridan Blau, 210–226. Washington, DC: NCTE.

Hodara, M., S. S. Jaggars, and M. M. Karp. 2014. "Improving Developmental Education Assessment and Placement: Lessons from Community Colleges across the Country." CCRC Working Paper no. 51. Community College Research Center, Columbia University.

hooks, bell. 1994. "Language." In *Teaching to Transgress: Education as the Practice of Freedom.* New York: Routledge.

Horner, Bruce, and John Trimbur. 2002. "English Only and U.S. College Composition." *College Composition and Communication* 53 (4): 594–630.

Jordan, June. 1988 "Nobody Mean More to Me than You and the Future Life of Willie Jordan." *Harvard Educational Review* 58: 363–374.

Kynard, Carmen. 2012–2020. "Carmen Kynard's Teaching & Research Site on Race, Writing, and the Classroom." *Education, Liberation & Black Radical Traditions for the 21st Century*. carmenkynard.org/.

Soliday, Mary. 1994. "Translating Self and Difference through Literacy Narratives." *College English* 56 (5): 511–526.

Young, Vershawn Ashanti. 2004. "Your Average Nigga." *CCC* 55 (4): 693–715.

15

SECOND-CHANCE PEDAGOGY

Integrating College-Level Skills and Strategies into a Developmental Writing Course

Joanne Baird Giordano

Abstract: This article traces my growth as a developmental writing teacher and the creation of an integrated reading and writing course as an alternative to the skill-and-drill approach to basic English courses that is still widely prevalent. I eventually came to the conclusion that even my students with the least experience as academic readers and writers needed to participate in classes that looked a lot like any other college classroom with challenging homework, intellectual discussions, and opportunities to take responsibility for their own learning as adults. This essay documents that personal and professional journey.

In my first semester teaching writing at a two-year college, a campus administrator asked me to create a developmental education program for underprepared students who struggle with academic reading. He had reviewed my job application and believed that I was qualified to develop the program based on reading pedagogy coursework that I had taken in my TESOL graduate program. I had absolutely no idea how to teach reading courses outside of an ESL program or design a developmental education program, but I told him that I would try because I needed the employment stability that came with the responsibility of creating a campus academic literacy skills program.

DOI: 10.7330/9781607329305.c015

I started the task of designing a single course that would become the starting point for working with colleagues to develop a cohesive statewide developmental English and writing program, but I felt like a total fraud. I had some relevant graduate coursework and experience as a curriculum developer, and I had a clear sense of how to teach first-year writing, but I had absolutely no idea how to design a course to help students develop the skills and strategies required for becoming proficient college readers and writers if their prior experiences with literacy both inside and outside of school had not yet prepared them for the demands of postsecondary education. I was an underprepared instructor attempting to not only teach but also design a program that would lay a foundation for first-year writing and general education courses. The stakes seemed especially high. I knew that my class was a last resort for students who had been left behind by a variety of complex factors that had interfered with their literacy development. Many came to my classroom as a condition of admission to the campus or as a requirement for avoiding suspension after a rocky start to college.

What I didn't know at the time was that most instructors who begin teaching developmental English at open-admissions institutions initially lack the training and experience required for navigating through the challenging and always-changing work of teaching students who are not yet ready for college reading and writing. There are very few doctoral programs dedicated to postsecondary literacy and developmental education (for example, the relatively new programs at Texas State and Sam Houston State University). Graduate programs in English typically focus heavily on literature and creative writing with minimal coursework in teaching college writing and typically no opportunities to study reading pedagogy. Even writing studies programs typically neglect to address the "meaningful professionalization" described in the white paper, *TYCA Guidelines for Preparing Teachers of English in the Two-Year College* (Calhoon-Dillahunt et al. 2017, 13). In particular, teaching literacy courses at an open-admissions institution requires "Familiarity with the distinctive history, missions, and institutional conditions at two-year colleges" and "Preparation for teaching the culturally, linguistically, socioeconomically, and academically diverse students who attend two-year colleges" (Calhoon-Dillahunt et al. 2017, 13). The knowledge and experience outlined in the white paper provide a starting point for teaching English at a two-year college; however, developmental English instructors also need additional training in evidence-based strategies for teaching postsecondary literacy (Boylan 2002).

After an initial rocky start to teaching developmental reading, I gave myself a crash course in developmental education and spent a year reading every textbook and article that I could find on college reading. However, so much of what I read didn't reflect what I knew about students, scholarship on literacy, or even how reading and writing work. I noticed a distinct gap between the textbooks for basic skills courses and what published scholarship said about students' literacy development. Most of the textbooks and online teaching materials that I found seemed to start with the premise that some students are so seriously deficient in reading and writing that they need to start over with sentence-level exercises before moving on to paragraphs and eventually writing essays and reading full-length texts. Then the next semester, these same students would miraculously be able to read challenging texts and write college-level essays in credit-bearing courses. It simply didn't seem possible to me that my own children were writing fully developed multi-paragraph texts in elementary school while adult learners inexplicably needed to limit their work as readers and writers to short, isolated pieces of acontextual texts.

I eventually came to the conclusion that even my students with the least experience as academic readers and writers needed to participate in classes that looked a lot like any other college classroom with challenging homework, intellectual discussions, and opportunities to take responsibility for their own learning as adults. In their preface to *Facts and Artifacts: Theory and Method for a Reading and Writing Course* (1986), David Bartholomae and Anthony Petrosky argue for an early-stage integrated reading and writing course as an alternative to the skill-and-drill approach to basic English courses that is still prevalent a generation later:

> . . . there was no reason to prohibit students from doing serious work because they could not do it correctly. In a sense, all courses in the curriculum ask students to do what they cannot yet do well. There was no good reason to take students who were not fluent readers and writers and consign them to trivial or mechanical work in the belief that it would somehow prepare them for a college education. It would make more sense, rather, to enroll these students in an exemplary course . . . and to provide the additional time and support they needed to work on reading and writing while they were, in fact, doing the kinds of reading and writing that characterize college study. (Bartholomae and Petrosky 1986)

Long before reading Bartholomae and Petrosky, I knew that I needed to create the type of course that they describe: "An exemplary course" that would give students an opportunity to experience college-level work even though they were not yet ready to do that work proficiently. However, I also felt overwhelmed by the daily challenges of teaching a diverse range of students who had experienced alternative pathways through secondary education to college. My classes included students who went to jail instead of high school, refugees who started their formal schooling as teenagers, students with disabilities who had never received K–12 accommodation plans, and students in the ninety-ninth percentile on the ACT exam and/or their high school graduating classes. Some had never written an essay or read a book. Others reported that they hadn't completed any assigned readings after middle school. It was clear that simply providing students with challenging basic skills courses to prepare them for even more challenging work at the next level would be insufficient unless I completely revised the way that I approached classroom teaching.

In this chapter, I provide an overview of a developmental writing course that I designed in close collaboration with colleagues at my previous two-year college institution to prepare students for the first of two credit-bearing courses in our first-year writing sequence. Students engage in challenging critical reading and writing tasks with intensive instructor support and scaffolded learning activities in the classroom. The work that students do both inside and outside the classroom looks a lot like what happens in a credit-bearing writing course except that students receive much more intensive individualized support through a workshop-style classroom learning environment. The teaching strategies that I describe provide underprepared students at an open-admissions institution with intensive and ongoing opportunities to engage with texts in a variety of different ways to prepare for source-based writing in credit-bearing courses.

It is important to note that the campuses for which I developed the course move as many students as possible to credit-bearing composition through lowered-placement cut scores, multiple measures placement with a portfolio appeal process, and corequisite support through a writing studio program (see Phillips and Giordano 2016). Students who would normally be in the top level of developmental writing at many other institutions start college in a credit-bearing first-year writing course. Because of institutional efforts to reduce nondegree coursework, most students in my developmental writing course have an academic profile that would require them to take two or more semesters of nondegree credit English coursework at other institutions. And yet those students are capable of doing challenging coursework in their first semester with strategic sequencing of course assignments and instructor support in the classroom.

GUIDED PRACTICE AND INDIVIDUALIZED INSTRUCTION

Before asking students to do difficult things that they had no experience doing, I needed to change my expectations about the quality of the work that students could produce. I began to structure developmental reading and writing courses around assignments and activities that were essentially carefully sequenced practice for the work that they would eventually do in other courses—but without the expectation that students would complete those tasks independently or do them well. Mike Rose describes the crucial role of practice and accompanying feedback in helping underprepared community college students develop proficiency: "As with any complex practice—from baseball to singing opera—you learn how to do it well by doing it and doing it over time, typically in some sort of formal or informal setting with guidance and feedback from others who are more skilled. The same holds for learning how to be a student in the formal setting of school" (Rose 2012, 43). What students need most from developmental English (and from subsequent credit-bearing composition courses at most two-year colleges) are repeated opportunities to read, write, and apply college learning skills through guided practice with frequent feedback. I believe that almost all of that work in an initial developmental writing course needs to be low-stakes with plenty of room for mistakes, new starts, reflection, and revision. Or, as one of my students explained his classroom community of writers, "This is a place for second chances."

In addition to opportunities to practice challenging academic tasks, classrooms that provide students with second chances for learning and literacy development require instructors to integrate individualized instruction and learning support into the classroom to address the significant barriers to academic success that vary considerably from one student to the next. My overall approach to classroom teaching at an open-admissions institution draws from the studio writing course model that Rhonda C. Grego and Nancy S. Thompson developed at the University of South Carolina in the early 1990's. Their efforts began as a way to re-envision basic writing and remediation. In *Teaching Writing in Thirdspaces* (2008), they describe an approach to writing course pedagogy that situates teaching and student learning within a community of writers:

> Writing Studio attaches, to an existing course or academic pursuit, a one-hour-per-week workshop, where students bring their work, sometimes to "work on it" but more often to present the work and obtain feedback so that they can go away and work on it further. This studio is a space for reflective communication. Presenting the work for one's own and other

> group members' reflection allows the writer to use the help of group members to generate ideas and refine not only approaches to content but also processes and attitudes toward the work. (Grego and Thompson 2008, 8)

Studio teaching completely disrupts traditional approaches to organizing a writing course. The teacher replaces formal instruction and planned lectures with in-the-moment teaching and workshop activities based on the issues that students identify as they work through the challenging process of completing college-level writing projects. In a studio learning environment, students have increased ownership of their own texts and responsibility for their learning.

In addition to developmental writing, I previously taught a one-credit corequisite studio course in which students met weekly in very small groups to share, discuss, and work on their projects for composition and any other writing-intensive courses taken concurrently in the same semester. Some students took developmental writing while others were concurrently enrolled in credit-bearing courses. We sat around a table together to discuss the work that students completed between sessions for other courses, their goals as writers, and their planned work to complete before the studio met again the following week. Students also completed guided process activities, sometimes together and sometimes individually. The studio courses at my previous institution permitted instructors to focus our teaching entirely on the individual learning needs of each student as we helped them make a transition to college-level reading and writing. Teaching in a space outside of a traditional classroom helps instructors model the processes and learning strategies that proficient postsecondary writers use while providing a structured learning environment for helping students figure out how college works.

My experience as a studio teacher helped me completely reimagine my work as a classroom writing instructor as a guide who facilitates discussions and writing-process activities. I wanted to provide students in my developmental writing course with the same kind of intensive one-on-one support that I use in studio teaching. I also wanted students to be able to reflect on their own work as writers, learn how to identify their own needs, apply their learning from one writing project to the next, and begin to use the strategies and processes that expert writers use to produce a text for an audience and purpose. I restructured my course around assignments and learning activities designed to give each student intensive experiences with practicing how to be a college reader and writer, and those experiences need to be different for each writer based on their educational, linguistic, and cultural backgrounds.

Obviously, it is unrealistic to fully implement the studio model in a classroom writing course of more than twenty students, especially when classroom teaching also requires instructors to support students in developing college-level reading skills and strategies. However, I realized that I could employ key components of the writing studio to address the individual needs of students through activities that help them become active participants in their own learning within a supportive community of other college writers. Grego and Thompson use the work of Bill Macauley to provide a definition for studio teaching that I believe can be successfully used (at least in part) for a classroom writing course: "a studio learning environment is one where activities of production are undertaken individually but in a place where others are working and discussing their work simultaneously, where teachers provide, along with other students, guidance, suggestions, input" (Grego and Thompson 2008, 7). The developmental writing course that I eventually designed and now teach brings student writers together to actively work on and discuss the texts that they are in the process of creating. Moving parts of writing assignments into the classroom (the "activities of production") provides students with guided support and practice for tasks that they would otherwise struggle to complete as take-home assignments.

COURSE DESIGN PROCESS

A developmental writing course that asks students to do challenging tasks is effective only with a carefully designed plan for the entire course that is situated within the context of a writing program. I initially had trouble designing my own developmental courses because no one in my writing program had a clear sense of what was supposed to happen in *any* of our courses. After my colleagues and I conducted a series of research studies and assessment projects on students' development as college writers at our own institution (for example, see Hassel and Giordano 2009; Giordano and Hassel 2016), we identified significant gaps between what students were learning in our first two writing courses and the final course that they needed to complete for a college degree. A lack of cohesion within and between courses created significant obstacles for our students. They arrived at college unprepared for English 102, the research-based course that is required for a college degree in the state system, and many were still not prepared for the course after taking developmental writing, followed by English 101.

To address barriers to academic literacy development for students, my colleagues and I used a backward design approach (Wiggins and McTighe

2005) to redesign our writing program curriculum around critical reading and source-based writing (see Phillips and Giordano 2016). We began the process by identifying the learning outcomes that we wanted students to achieve by the end of our writing program to prepare for general education coursework within our own institution and transfer to four-year universities in our state system. We developed learning outcomes and model assignments for each course by starting with the end of our final required writing course and worked backwards through the entire writing program sequence to the beginning of developmental writing.

I took the lead in redesigning the developmental writing course in consultation with colleagues. Here is an overview of how instructors can adapt that process to design a course that reflects the learning objectives, purpose, and mission of their own writing program:

1. Start by assessing the needs of students who enroll in the course. Examine institutional assessment data and program research (if available) about placement, student readiness, and the diverse populations that the course serves. To redesign an existing course, also take a close look at student writing from previously taught sections to identify their success and challenges.
2. Examine learning outcomes for the course (or develop a clear set of objectives in the absence of writing program learning outcomes). *What are the learning goals for developmental writing within the context of the writing program? What do students need to demonstrate at the end of the course to successfully enroll in and complete the first credit-bearing writing course? What reading, writing, and research skills do students need to develop across the entire writing program to successfully complete degree requirements and/or prepare for transfer to a four-year university?*
3. Develop a set of sequenced major writing projects that address the learning goals of the course. *Specifically, what assignments will help students achieve the course learning outcomes? What assignments will provide a way to assess student readiness for the next writing course? What do students need to do in the classroom and outside of class to develop the skills, strategies, and habits of mind required for becoming successful college readers and writers?*
4. Identify the reading assignments that students will complete. Select readings that can (a) become sources for writing, (b) invite students to engage in inquiry, and (c) serve as the basis for helping students achieve program learning outcomes for critical reading.
5. Break each assignment down into manageable, purposeful steps that students can complete both in the classroom and outside of class.
6. Starting with the last assignment, work backwards through the course to identify the learning activities that students will engage in during class to take them through basic reading comprehension and essay organization strategies to critical reading and independent writing.

7. Develop metacognitive learning activities (for example, reflections and self-assessments) that help students develop an awareness of their own processes as writers.

STRUCTURING ASSIGNMENTS TO PREPARE STUDENTS FOR CREDIT-BEARING COMPOSITION

In this section, I provide an overview of the sequenced assignments for my developmental writing course. Because I taught in a writing program with a university-transfer mission, all of the assignments in my developmental writing course focus on preparing students for critical reading and source-based writing in credit-bearing composition. For that reason, each assignment requires students to respond to one or more assigned nonfiction texts. However, I don't ask students to write about a particular reading assignment. Rather, I encourage them to identify ideas from readings that most interest them as readers and writers and then use the assigned texts as a starting point for identifying an issue that warrants exploration through writing.

Source-based writing courses require carefully selected texts that are sufficiently complex to generate ideas that turn into college writing projects. At the same time, the reading assignments need to be manageable for students who are still working toward becoming proficient college readers. Further, to stay engaged in their writing projects and have a stake in the issues that they explore, developmental writing students benefit most from assignments that they can connect to their own lives. For that reason, I center the readings in my developmental writing course around higher education and college success. The following semester in English 101, they explore issues related to twenty-first-century literacies. Every student can connect ideas from those sets of readings to their prior knowledge and learning experiences, and I can easily find texts on those topics that are accessible to students who are underprepared for college reading. My students don't do research in developmental writing, but they read texts that use research to support claims and arguments in preparation for reading more complex texts the following semester.

COURSE PORTFOLIO

In the middle and at the end of the course, students organize their writing into a portfolio of their work for feedback and a midterm and final grade. The portfolio includes a cover letter with a self-assessment, formal essays, a reflective note to introduce each piece of writing, and a self-selected set of their in-class writing. Students also create a title page and table of contents to gain experience with formatting a formal academic document. The portfolio is an especially important part of a developmental writing course that requires students to complete complex writing projects because it gives them time to work through non-graded low-stakes drafts and related classroom activities before receiving a grade. Although I provide students with a general sense of what their grades would be without revision, they don't receive a permanent grade until after submitting a portfolio.

WRITING PROCESS WORK

During each class period, students complete critical reading, writing, and workshop activities that lead to a longer writing project. Although the process varies based on the assignment, each writing project includes the following components:

1. Exploration of potential essay issues through writing and in-class discussion;
2. Discussion that helps students narrow a topic to a specific issue;
3. Discussion and in-class writing that helps students identify evidence from sources;
4. An essay-planning workshop to help students organize an essay around a main argument (thesis), key supporting points, and supporting evidence from readings;
5. Additional short discussions about their in-process draft work;
6. Peer review for a complete essay draft that includes in-class self-assessment writing;
7. A final revised draft with an author's note to introduce their writing process and the essay;
8. An instructor conference or written feedback;
9. A final revised and polished draft with an updated author's note for the course portfolio.

PROJECT 1: SUPPORTING AN ARGUMENT WITH EVIDENCE FROM SOURCES

Select an issue related to course readings on college students or higher education. Conduct informal research by interviewing at least one person who has experience with your chosen issue. Then write an essay that supports a thesis based on the findings of your interview research and evidence from course readings. You may also use evidence from your own experience.

Teaching Strategies

The first writing project is designed to help students begin to engage in independent inquiry and practice writing a well-organized college essay that supports a main point with evidence from sources. Students read a few short texts that use credible evidence to discuss issues related to college students. I select recent short articles that are relevant to students on my campus (for example, recent news articles for a general audience that discuss misconceptions about college students or that report on research about first-generation college students, returning adult learners, and rural students). As they discuss key ideas in the reading assignments, students also work together to identify issues that warrant further exploration through research and writing. Each student selects an issue and identifies someone who has experience relevant to that topic (usually second-year students, one of their professors, their campus advisor, or a family member). During class, students work through the process of identifying questions that will help them investigate their selected issues, which introduces them to very basic strategies for college-level inquiry that leads to the development of a writing project. Next, they conduct an informal interview, which gives them an opportunity for a discussion about higher education with someone who has more experience. During class, students then work through the process of using their notes from the interview and a course reading assignment to organize their ideas for an essay before drafting, sharing, and revising a formal essay.

It may seem strange to start a developmental writing course with a challenging multistage writing project, but this assignment is much less complex than other types of source-based writing, and even my students who have never written an academic essay can successfully complete it with classroom instructional support for each stage of the process. At the beginning of the course, most students are not ready to introduce multiple pieces of evidence from a reading assignment into an essay because they are still working through the process of learning how to read and take notes from a nonfiction text for an academic purpose. They can, however, more easily report on information collected from an oral discussion with someone who has experience relevant to a topic and then connect those ideas to class reading discussions. It's important to note that this assignment only works for developmental writing because students explore an issue that is relevant to their own lives and often to the lives of other family members. The assignment builds on their own prior knowledge and current experiences as a college student, and they start asking questions based on what they already know before moving to what they don't know but would like to find out. As students engage in the research and writing process for their projects and share them with the class through discussion and peer review, they learn about a variety of different perspectives on how college works.

Student Learning

This project helps students develop strategies for writing a well-organized essay based on sources. While they work on this project, students focus on the following reading and writing skills:

- Identify the audience and purpose for a nonfiction text;
- Identify main points, supporting points, and supporting evidence in a nonfiction text;
- Independently select an issue in course reading assignments to explore through writing;
- Identify evidence in readings that is relevant to an issue;
- Engage in discussion with others about complex issues from course readings;
- Organize a college-level writing project that uses basic evidence from sources;
- Begin to write a college-level thesis statement that presents a main point for an essay;
- Organize paragraphs around a clear main point;
- Identify evidence from sources to support the main point of a paragraph;
- Incorporate quotes and examples from a basic text into a paragraph;
- Distinguish between the writer's own ideas and evidence from sources;
- Participate in college-level peer review;
- Revise an essay in response to feedback from an instructor and classmates;
- Make progress toward following the basic conventions for college-level academic writing.

PROJECT 2: ARGUMENTATIVE ESSAY ON COLLEGE SUCCESS

Choose a complex issue from assigned course readings related to college success. Select an issue that will help you explore the social, academic, and/or personal factors that influence whether individuals go to college, achieve academic success, and receive a degree. You may choose to offer your own definition of college success that is different from how the course readings define college success. Write an essay that explains and supports your position on that issue, using evidence from at least three different course reading assignments.

Teaching Strategies

The main goal of the second writing project is to help students begin to make connections between ideas from multiple readings and use them to support a basic argument about a self-selected issue. Like the first assignment, this project encourages students to explore, discuss, and write about issues that are relevant to their own experiences as college students. They typically choose topics that are connected to achieving their own educational goals or addressing their current challenges as students (for example, how colleges can support first-generation students, becoming a self-directed learner, strategies for balancing work and school, or the relationship between proficiency in use of technology and academic success).

Working through the process of identifying and using evidence from shared readings helps students begin to develop the critical reading and writing strategies required for completing research-based essays in credit-bearing composition. Students draw from a set of readings that use evidence from research to discuss college success, including strategies for completing courses and overcoming barriers to persistence in higher education. Students do much of the reading for this project while working on the first essay. To help students build reading stamina, I gradually introduce longer texts but stick with shorter articles if the text is more challenging. In the class, the students identify and discuss specific quotes and ideas from assigned readings that they can use to support their arguments, and they help each other make connections between ideas from different texts. I work with students to help them move beyond summarizing information from readings to connecting each piece of evidence to a thesis and to the main point of a paragraph or section.

Student Learning

The second writing project addresses the learning skills and writing strategies from the first assignment while also introducing the following skills:

- Identify an author's arguments and supporting evidence;
- Write a thesis statement that takes a position on a multisided issue;

- Organize a paragraph around a supporting point that helps develop an argument;
- Support a thesis with evidence from more than one text;
- Connect the main point of a paragraph to the thesis of an essay;
- Begin to analyze evidence from course readings in connection to the main point of a paragraph or section.

ASSIGNMENT 3: EVALUATING AN AUTHOR'S ARGUMENT AND EVIDENCE

Select a course reading assignment. Identify the author's main argument, supporting points, and supporting evidence. Write an essay that analyzes and evaluates the writing strategies that the author uses to support the argument with evidence. Your essay should answer the following question: *Does the author effectively develop an argument with adequate, credible evidence for the audience and purpose of the text? Why or why not?*

Teaching Strategies

This third writing project helps prepare students for analysis assignments in credit-bearing courses while also teaching them how to evaluate sources in preparation for writing research-based texts. Unlike a traditional rhetorical analysis assignment that addresses a wider range of writing strategies, this assignment focuses only on how an author supports an argument with evidence. Students choose a text to analyze from a list of previously read course texts that use evidence to support arguments. During class, students work together to complete a series of critical reading discussions that focus on helping them answer the following questions as they write their essays:

- What is the author's main argument or thesis?
- What supporting points and other claims does the author make to develop the main argument of the text?
- What general types of evidence does the author use in the text?
- What specific evidence does the author present to support the main argument and other claims?
- What writing strategies does the author use to present evidence and develop an argument?

This assignment is the shortest but most challenging formal assignment that students write in my course. I purposefully assign it immediately after midterms because my students have difficulty managing a challenging project while they are preparing for final exams in other courses. At each stage of the writing process, students are doing college-level critical reading and writing. They aren't very good at that kind of work yet, but they receive substantial help from me during each class period. Through tackling a challenging project, they practice learning strategies that they will need to use in subsequent courses when they will have limited or no classroom learning support.

Student Learning

For this analysis assignment, students focus on a select set of writing skills from the first half of the course based on their midterm self-assessment writing and an instructor conference. They also practice the following new skills:

- Recognize the basic features of a text that make it an appropriate and credible source for academic writing;
- Identify an author's main argument and supporting points;
- Distinguish between main ideas and less relevant information in a text;
- Distinguish between a supported claim and an unsupported claim;
- Analyze and evaluate how a writer supports an argument with evidence;
- Identify some of the strategies that a writer uses to develop an argument;
- Evaluate the effectiveness of an author's writing strategies based on the audience and purpose for a text;
- Use quotes, examples, and specific details to support an analysis and evaluation of a reading assignment.

ASSIGNMENT 4: SYNTHESIZING IDEAS FROM MULTIPLE READINGS

Write an essay that brings together ideas from multiple assigned readings to answer the following question: What is the purpose of a college-level education? In responding to the overall essay question, your essay should also answer these additional questions:

1. What do the authors of assigned course texts say about the purpose of going to college and receiving a degree?
2. What is your thinking about the purpose of higher education in response to the authors' arguments?
3. What is the purpose of a college education in your own life? What do you hope to achieve and become by going to college and receiving a degree?

Support your answers with evidence from at least four assigned readings and your own experience.

Teaching Strategies

For the final writing project, students reflect on and bring together ideas from the entire course to analyze what assigned texts say about the purpose of higher education while also exploring their own reasons for going to college, including how their perspectives have changed over their first college semester. They know from the beginning of the semester that they will eventually write an essay on their thinking about the purpose of a college education, which provides a framework for making connections between readings throughout the course. The readings that students do in the last month of class are the most challenging and are similar to what they would read in English 101. For example, I assign selections from the *Framework for Success in Postsecondary Writing* (CWP, NCTE, and NWP 2011) because instructors in the writing program frequently assign that text near the beginning of English 101. I also assign William Cronon's "'Only Connect . . .' The Goals of a Liberal Education" (Cronon 1998), another frequently used text at my previous institution. Through discussions and in-class writing, students make connections between these challenging texts and the more basic readings that they have read, discussed, and written about earlier in the course. The process of identifying and connecting multiple pieces of evidence from different texts helps them begin to work toward being able to synthesize ideas from multiple research sources in more advanced courses.

Student Learning

The final writing project provides students with an opportunity to demonstrate their overall learning from the course and show that they are ready for English 101. They work on writing goals that they select through informal in-class self-assessment writing. They also work on the following skills that they will use in their next two writing courses:

1. Write a complex thesis statement;
2. Use a logical structure to organize an essay;
3. Make connections between ideas in multiple texts;
4. Use multiple pieces of specific, relevant evidence from different but related texts to support a thesis;
5. Connect multiple pieces of supporting evidence to the thesis and main

point of a paragraph;

6. Explain and analyze different writers' arguments on the same topic;
7. Begin to cite sources, using an established academic documentation style;

CLASSROOM TEACHING STRATEGIES

Students who are significantly underprepared for college reading and writing can successfully engage in the challenging critical reading and writing tasks that I have described, but they can't do that work independently without intensive learning support in the classroom. The following basic principles can help instructors organize a workshop-style classroom to provide students with guided practice and feedback that will help them develop the reading and writing strategies that successful college students use:

1. Students complete part of their coursework in the classroom in a structured and supportive learning environment. They have frequent opportunities to practice writing and discuss their own work as writers to support the work that they do outside of class.
2. Students work toward identifying their own needs as readers and writers in relation to the course learning outcomes and assignments. They often have agency over the work that they share with the class and choose what they would like to discuss about their own writing with peers and the instructor.
3. Students spend most of their time in the classroom engaged in hands-on learning activities, including discussing readings, participating in peer review, working individually on writing, and completing guided learning activities that lead to completion of their major writing projects.
4. The instructor spends minimal time lecturing, which frees up time in the classroom for facilitating activities, assessing student learning and providing corresponding feedback, and working with students individually and in small groups.
5. The instructor provides students with individualized learning support through one-on-one feedback in the classroom, small-group instruction, and both formal and informal conferencing outside of class. In the classroom, most direct instruction focuses on the needs of students in a particular course section in relation to their goals as writers and readers.
6. Most organized formal lectures or direct whole-group instruction teach students learning strategies and models what more experienced college students do.

Although it may seem counterintuitive, a significant increase in the individualized support that students receive from an instructor can help them take responsibility for their own learning. Individualized interaction with an instructor models for students the writing process and metacognitive learning strategies that more experienced writers use to make choices about their own learning. They receive instruction tailored to their individual needs and gradually learn how to reflect on their own writing, learning processes, understanding of texts, and habits of mind. They learn how to ask questions about their work and seek feedback. A workshop-style classroom also helps students work toward addressing the barriers to academic success that resulted in a placement in developmental writing.

STRUCTURE OF A TYPICAL DEVELOPMENTAL WRITING CLASS PERIOD

Although each class period varies, I typically use the following structure for a seventy-five-minute class that meets twice a week:

1. Before-Class Check-In
2. Introductory Whole-Class Discussion
3. Independent Writing
4. Small-Group Work and Individual Instructor Support
5. Whole-Class Reporting and Review

Before-Class Check-In

In the five to ten minutes before class starts, I welcome individual students, follow up with those who have missed class, and begin to talk with students individually and collectively about their writing projects. I sometimes use the time to meet briefly with students whose work schedules or family commitments prevent them from scheduling a longer appointment outside of class. Most of my students aren't initially prepared to navigate their way through the process of accessing help from an instructor or independently completing a challenging college writing project. Conversations at the beginning of a class period provide me with essential information about their progress in the course and their challenges with writing projects. I can then adapt instruction and learning activities to build on their successes and address potential barriers to successfully completing required coursework.

Introductory Whole-Class Discussion

The entire class often meets for about ten minutes to discuss topics that are relevant to most students in the class. This introductory whole-group meeting time typically includes a few of the following activities:

- A preview of the class period that connects in-class activities to prior course learning, upcoming take-home work, and major writing projects;
- Follow-up discussion on issues, questions, and concerns from students identified through learning activities in the previous class period or instructor conferences;
- A review of learning from previous discussions and homework;
- Time for students to report on and ask questions about their writing projects;
- Reading strategies instruction based on assigned course texts (usually connected to reading discussion activities for that day);
- Instruction on writing strategies addressed within the context of the current writing project;
- Brief mini-lessons on academic success strategies;

The main focus of the whole class discussion time is to help students make connections between their work as readers and writers in developmental writing and (a) activities in the course, (b) their experiences as new college students outside the composition classroom, and (c) their preparation for subsequent courses in the writing program sequence.

Independent Writing in the Classroom

On most days, students complete a structured low-stakes writing assignment that helps them prepare for the rest of the class period and connects their take-home reading assignments and/or writing process work to their major writing projects. Depending on the class period, the individual writing time takes place before or immediately after the introductory whole-group discussion. Students may choose to handwrite their responses or create an electronic document that they submit online. They also can choose to finish working on it outside of class if they need more time. I assign three different types of in-class writing assignments: (a) responses to readings that focus on course learning outcomes for critical reading, (b) prewriting for essay assignments (often also connected to readings), and (c) self-assessment writing focusing on their writing processes and products.

In-class writing in response to carefully designed prompts serves several purposes. First (and most important), many of my students have had limited experiences with writing before taking my class, and they become easily overwhelmed when they are assigned to do extensive out-of-class work beyond completing assigned readings and working on essay assignments. The in-class work provides them with practice that addresses specific learning outcomes for the course. Second, the in-class assignments prepare students for the reading discussions and writing workshop activities that they complete during the class period, which significantly improves the level of conversations that students have with each other about the readings and their own work as writers. Third, almost all of my students have had limited or no experience with timed on-demand writing, and they often experience high levels of anxiety about writing in a testing situation. Their in-class work gives them an opportunity to practice reading and responding to a prompt that they have never seen before. And finally, the in-class work frequently gives students a jump start on their homework, giving them an opportunity to write about and then discuss ideas that they can take home to explore through a more formal writing project.

Small-Group Work and Individual Instructor Support

Throughout much of the class period, students work in small groups or with partners, but sometimes they do individual work. For a typical class period, the work is split between discussions about their own writing and reading discussions or critical reading activities. They engage in longer formal peer review when an essay is due, but during almost every class period, they have an opportunity to discuss their writing and to work on process activities that help them work toward completing a project (for example, identifying issues in a text to write about, selecting evidence from a text, organizing source material around supporting points for an essay, discussing obstacles to completing projects and potential solutions, etc.). Students receive written prompts for the in-class activities, but as the class progresses they work toward identifying and asking their own questions both for the reading discussions and for peer review. During the group work time, I talk with each student, sometimes in groups but more frequently individually. In every class period, they have an opportunity to talk with me about their work, receive feedback, and ask questions about the course.

Whole-Class Reporting and Review

At the end of the class period, the whole class meets together for a review, reports on activities completed during the class period, and a preview of upcoming homework and class activities. Sometimes the class has a structured lengthy discussion about readings or writing project issues to bring together learning from the in-class activities. On other days, students give a quick report on their group discussions or I identify key issues that came up in my discussions with students. The final minutes of the class help students begin to see connections between that day's work and the take-home work that they will complete before the next class period.

ONGOING ASSESSMENT

Although it may seem like the workshop-style course that I have described requires less preparation than a traditional lecture-discussion class, the success of the course depends heavily on carefully planned and structured learning activities that can change substantially from one semester to the next and sometimes between different sections in the same semester. Adapting a course based on the strengths and challenges that students bring to the classroom requires me to assess student learning and carefully analyze their writing to identify the types of activities and individual support that a particular student group needs. However, I spend less time outside of class on assessing and grading student work because I spend time during almost every class period talking with students about their work and looking at their writing at every stage in the process from planning to a final edited draft.

Teaching a course that requires students to complete college-level coursework in developmental education with in-the-moment teaching is forever a work in progress. The overall structure is purposefully flexible, but that flexibility means that the course looks different every time I teach it because the students are different. The benefit to me professionally is that much more of my time is now spent working directly with students. I have learned that two-year college students are capable of tremendous growth as readers and writers in just a few short months and experiencing that learning in progress is the most rewarding part of my professional career as a teacher-scholar.

REFERENCES

Bartholomae, David, and Anthony Petrosky. 1986. *Facts, Artifacts, and Counterfacts: Theory and Method for a Reading and Writing Course.* Upper Montclair, NJ: Boynton/Cook.

Boylan, Hunter. 2002. *What Works: Research-Based Best Practices in Developmental Education.* Boone, NC: National Center for Developmental Education.

Council of Writing Program Administrators, the National Council of Teachers of English, and the National Writing Project. 2011. *Framework for Success in Postsecondary Writing.* CWPA. http://wpacouncil.org/files/framework-for-success-postsecondary-writing.pdf.

Cronon, William. 1998. "Only Connect . . . : The Goals of a Liberal Education." *The American Scholar* 67 (4): 73–80.

Calhoon-Dillahunt, Carolyn, Darin L. Jensen, Sarah Z. Johnson, Howard Tinberg, and Christie Toth. 2017. "TYCA Guidelines for Preparing Teachers of English in the Two-Year College." *Teaching English in the Two-Year College* 45 (1): 8–19.

Giordano, Joanne Baird, and Holly Hassel. 2016. "Unpredictable Journeys: Academically At-Risk Students, Developmental Education Reform, and the Two-Year College." *Teaching English in the Two-Year College.* 43 (4): 371–390.

Grego, Rhonda C., and Nancy S. Thompson. 2008. *Teaching/Writing in Third Spaces.* Carbondale: Southern Illinois University Press.

Hassel, Holly, and Joanne Baird Giordano. 2009. "Transfer Institutions, Transfer of Knowledge: The Development of Rhetorical Adaptability and Underprepared Writers." *Teaching English in the Two-Year College* 37 (1): 24–40.

Phillips, Cassandra, and Joanne Baird Giordano. 2016. "Developing a Cohesive Academic Literacy Program for Underprepared Students." *Teaching English in the Two-Year College* 44 (1): 79–89.

Rose, Mike. 2012. "Second-Chance Collegians: Inside the Remedial Classroom." *Dissent* 5 (4): 41–45.

Wiggins, Grant P., and McTighe, Jay. 2005. *Understanding by Design.* Expanded 2nd ed. Alexandria, VA: Association for Supervision and Curriculum Development.

16

REAL LIFE
Student Perspective

Jamil Shakoor

As a high school dropout, I did not learn the academic skills necessary to thrive in college. Upon entering community college, my reading, writing, math, and critical thinking abilities were very limited. This was confirmed when I was administered a battery of exams designed to gauge my reading, writing, and math levels. I believe I failed all but reading comprehension. As a result, I was required to attend several developmental English and math courses, and I was part of a group of students that entered community college with similar deficiencies. It was a hard pill to swallow—two-hour courses, three to four times a week. Despite the effort I put into earning a high grade in these classes, it would not affect my GPA, and the credits would not satisfy any college degree requirements. At first it felt like punishment—extra classes for failing several entrance exams. Not my proudest moment, but as I would come to realize, a necessary prerequisite for my success.

On my journey to acquire and develop basic academic skills—life skills—I was fortunate to be taught by a handful of professors genuinely interested in their students' success. The professors teaching developmental classes were particularly helpful. Their holistic approach to student development allowed them to understand students like myself lacked the skills necessary to do well in college, despite being in college. It enabled them to view immediate limitations as transitory, and

DOI: 10.7330/9781607329305.c016

not cast harsh judgment. When one is at the bottom of the student hierarchy, the expectation that they will thrive while operating within traditional and rigid parameters is unreasonable. Upon learning the background of many of my classmates, it was clear their lack of skill was a consequence of untraditional circumstances. Change is incredibly energy-intensive, and there is no wonder why institutional and academic policy makers would want to eliminate remediation—profit being a major factor. Which begs the question: is the top priority of policy makers and academic institutions to profit, or develop the education and skills of the students that entrust their education and future to them?

Having a developmental English teacher willing to work with students like myself with little writing experience or academic foundation was critical to my comfort and success in the classroom. In retrospect, it was crucial for me to be able to hand in an essay with almost no structure, typed in chiller font (it looked "cool"), and with no thesis and not be judged harshly. To still have the continued support of my professor despite the apparent leaps and bounds I would need to make as a writer, reader, and critical thinker. All in an effort to become a part of the general student body, graduate, break the cycle of poverty, and enter the professional work environment.

The extra help I received after class from my developmental English teacher also played an important role in my growth as a writer. I can recall spending time after class asking a fair amount of questions, all of which were always answered thoroughly. The amount of effort I put in to become a better writer was matched by my teachers. I would offer one or two extra drafts of a writing assignment for more feedback, and the extra effort was always supported and encouraged, and in my case, very much needed. Toward the beginning of my college experience, I would find myself discouraged, upset I was not further along in college. Upset at life. Support from my developmental English teacher outside of the classroom helped keep me on track, motivated, and focused. It was nice to have a positive and encouraging person in my corner.

After completing several developmental English courses, I then took on the general and required English courses. I can recall writing my first essay for freshman English. I thought it was my greatest writing yet, and I was certain I'd receive an A, but that wasn't the case. The professor at the time seemed to understand where I came from and took her time to explain why I did not earn a perfect grade. At the same time, she challenged me to go deeper, to write with more complexity, utilize more sources, and think critically. She was empathetic to my situation, but also maintained high expectations. This understanding coupled with challenge helped me grow into a more confident writer.

For me and many others I know, growth in reading, writing, and critical thinking has not been a linear progression. More often than not my motivation to learn was matched by my professors with an equal desire to teach. The developmental courses served as a necessary buffer between learning and performing. A much-needed one.

For those seeking to eliminate remediation from the college experience, it is clear to me they do not understand the struggle of attempting to complete a college curriculum not having gone through high school. Speaking from firsthand experience, I can honestly say my reading, writing, and math skills were not where they needed to be in order to pass (with a respectable grade, or perhaps any grade) college-level courses. In retrospect, despite all of the motivation to excel and turn my life around, despite all of the wonderful intentions I brought through the gates of Kingsborough Community College, I would not have been a successful student if I did not have the cushioning of remediation. Also, please keep in mind there is no smooth transition between remedial courses and regular college courses. The transitioning period has been a long and arduous one for me and everyone I know that has gone down the same path. Furthermore, becoming a fully capable college student can be complicated by cultural differences and familial and work obligations (factors that, in my experience, are typically associated with students in remedial courses).

If anything, I would like to see remediation programs become more comprehensive and intensified. Your typical college student starts college with a solid foundation in the basics: reading, writing, critical thinking, and math skills, and depending on the quality of their grade school and high school, has spent years practicing these skills to one degree or another. This is surely not the case of all students. Growing up in impoverished environments and schools, not having family support, and being surrounded with undereducated family and friends—this was my background prior to attending college. For one reason or another: be it societal, personal, or both, the only things I practiced prior to college video-game playing and skateboarding. I am not suggesting we enable poor decision-making, but we need to be aware that in many instances, being undereducated is not so much a choice, but a natural consequence of one's predicament and environment—in many cases, we don't know what we don't know. And when someone from an impoverished background manages to develop a sense of responsibility to himself and the world and has the courage to attempt to be the first in their family to end the cycle of poverty and deprivation, I believe academic institutions have a moral obligation to ensure these people are provided with all the resources necessary to help them succeed. It seems to me that any position contrary to this is founded on a serious lack of *real-life* experience.

17

PEDAGOGICAL EVOLUTION

How My Teaching Has Changed in Ten Years of the Accelerated Learning Program (ALP)

Peter Adams

Abstract: This essay traces my efforts over the course of ten years to design a developmental writing program that would be more successful than the traditional, multi-tiered model, which often takes students two or more years to complete before they are eligible to enroll in a credit-bearing English class. The Accelerated Learning Program (ALP), which developed as a result of that work, is a corequisite model for developmental writing that began in 2007 as a collaborative faculty initiative at my home institution, the Community College of Baltimore County. Since that time, ALP has consistently produced dramatic improvements in student success rates and has demonstrated that it can be scaled to a national level. More than three hundred schools around the country have adopted or adapted the ALP model, and six states have launched wide-scale ALP adoptions: Arkansas, Colorado, Connecticut, Indiana, Michigan, and Virginia.

The Community College of Baltimore County (CCBC) discovered back in 1993 what many English departments have discovered since: The basic writing courses we had established with the best of intentions to help students acquire the skills they needed to pass English 101 were having much less success than we had hoped. At CCBC only one student out of three who began in our upper-level basic writing course ever

DOI: 10.7330/9781607329305.c017

passed English 101. In the years since, schools across the country have discovered similarly disappointing results.

Through student focus groups and surveys, we at CCBC learned that the primary reason students in our developmental writing program were not succeeding was that they were dropping out of our courses, and often, out of school. They let us know that the most common reasons for this dropping out was that their challenging and stressful lives made it impossible for them to continue. Their children got sick, they lost their jobs, they were evicted from their apartments, they got in trouble with the legal system, they had to flee an abusive situation, and much more. Their presence in the college was so tenuous that all it took was one crisis—one medical bill they couldn't pay, one car repair they couldn't afford, one change in their working hours—and they couldn't continue in school.

And when these life issues didn't make coming to school impossible, their own psyches did. The most common comment we heard from our students went something like this: "I'm just not sure I'm college material." Too many arrived at college with doubts they belonged there, with fears they would be revealed to be impostors. And then their first experience at the college was taking a placement test and receiving the message, in effect, that *we're* not sure they're college material either. They were going to have to take a noncollege course for which they would receive no college credit until they could prove they actually were college material. No wonder their persistence in our developmental courses was so fragile.

Faced with these kinds of disappointing results, writing faculty across the country have been searching for models of developmental writing that will produce higher success rates. At Arizona State University, John Ramage, Dave Schwalm, and Greg Glau were first in the nation with their Stretch Program (Glau 1996, 79–91). At Chico State University in California, Judith Rodby and Tom Fox developed one of the earliest programs to mainstream basic writers into English 101. Rhonda Grego and Nancy Thompson, at the University of South Carolina, developed the writing studio model (Grego and Thompson 2008, 1–25).

At CCBC, embroiled in political struggles that involved a mandate to merge three independent colleges into one "megacollege," the elimination of tenure, censure from AAUP, and a no-confidence vote in our chancellor, we were slow to address the problem. But in 2006, our political issues having faded into the background, we designed a model for basic writing we called the Accelerated Learning Program (ALP).

Learning from Stretch that basic writers could succeed in English 101 with support, from the studio model that small class size can be very beneficial, and from learning communities the value of cohorts, a group of about six faculty at CCBC developed our model for basic writing. Here's how it works.

ALP students who, despite being placed in basic writing, enroll in an ALP section of English 101. That section includes ten ALP students and ten students whose placement is English 101. The ten ALP students also register for what I like to call a "companion course;" a three-hour course that immediately follows the English 101 class and is taught by the same instructor.

Under this ALP model, these ten ALP students spend six hours a week together, half of it in a very small section and all of it with the same instructor. After a few semesters of teaching in this model, we began to realize that ALP required more than just a change in the structure of the developmental program; it also meant a major rethinking of the goals for the developmental course. No longer was the course intended to *prepare* students for English 101. No longer was the course designed to *remedy deficiencies* in the students' K–12 education. No longer were we attempting to teach them what they either hadn't learned in high school or had learned but forgotten.

Those not familiar with the ALP model may be startled by the class size of just ten in the developmental section. At first glance, it may seem that class sizes that small are simply not possible in today's budget-strapped institutions. Let me explain why more than three hundred schools have found ALP, even with small class sizes, to be financially beneficial for the school. The results from a 2012 Community College Research Center (CCRC) at Columbia University quantitative analysis of the Accelerated Learning Program (ALP) "suggest that among students who enroll in the highest-level developmental writing course, participation in ALP is associated with substantially better outcomes in terms of English 101 completion and English 102 completion (college-level English courses)" (Cho et al. 2012, "Abstract"). Those "substantially better outcomes" are evident in table 17.2, below. Of the ALP cohort, 74.7 percent successfully completed ENGL101. Only 38.5 percent of the students who took the traditional prerequisite course (ENGL052) successfully completed ENGL101. ALP nearly doubles the success rate of developmental students.

This almost doubling of the success rate for ALP students explains why, even with the small class size, the model is financially beneficial to the college. The financial analysis in a 2010 CCRC study of ALP concluded, "Compared with the conventional approach in which students complete developmental courses before enrolling in college-level

Table 2
Raw Academic Outcomes of ALP and Non-ALP Students
(Fall 2007–Fall 2010 Cohorts)

Outcome	ALP (1)	Non-ALP (2)	Difference (1–2) (3)
Followed through end of fall 2011			
ENGL052 completion rate	82.77%	66.96%	15.8%***
ENGL101 attempt rate	100.00%	52.64%	47.4%***
ENGL101 overall completion rate	74.66%	38.50%	36.2%***
	. . . . .		
ENGL102 overall completion rate	37.50%	16.79%	20.7%***

Figure 17.1. Table extracted from CCRC Working Paper 53 (https://ccrc.tc.columbia.edu/media/k2/attachments/ccbc-alp-student-outcomes-follow-up.pdf)

courses, the ALP model provides a substantially more cost-effective route for underprepared students to pass the ENGL101 and ENGL102 sequence required for an associate degree ($2,680 versus $3,122 per student)" (Cho et al. 2012, 1).

In the ten years since I taught my initial ALP class, I have learned a great deal about teaching in this model. Through trial and error, listening to my colleagues, reading in our professional journals, and attending our conferences, I have gradually improved my pedagogy in ALP. Since retiring in 2014, I have done considerable consulting work with schools that are implementing ALP across the country. Some of the most important changes in how I teach have come from interactions with these schools. I am a much more effective ALP teacher today than I was when I started in 2007. In this chapter, I want to describe that evolution of pedagogy, an evolution that continues today, so this is very much a work in progress.

But first, I want to point out a serious weakness in the preparation graduate students receive for teaching basic writing in general and teaching ALP specifically.

When the six of us who began the redesign of our basic writing program in the early 2000s made an inventory of our graduate education, we discovered that not one of us had taken a single course to prepare us to teach basic writing. As I have been consulting with schools across the country, I have been asking some survey questions of participants before my visit. I have, thus far, surveyed 316 faculty teaching basic writing at forty schools:

- Community College of Baltimore County (MD)
- Six West Virginia universities (WV)
- Community College of Allegheny County (PA)
- Century Community College (MN)
- LaGuardia Community College (NY)
- Patrick Henry Community College (VA)
- Atlantic Cape Community College (NJ)
- Harford Community College (MD)
- Six Connecticut Community Colleges (CT)
- Rochester Technical and Community College (MN)
- Flathead Community College (MT)
- Fourteen Michigan community colleges (MI)
- Denver Community College (CO)
- Berkshire Community College (MA)
- NHTI Concord Community College (NH)
- Northwest State Community College (OH)
- Leeward Community College (HI)

Thus far, I have surveyed 361 basic writing faculty teaching at forty different institutions. The most significant question on the survey has turned out to be this one: "Which of the following best describes your graduate preparation to teach basic writing?" Of the 343 English faculty who responded to this question, 267—78 percent—had taken *no* courses in their graduate programs to prepare them to teach basic writing. Figure 17.2 shows the responses to this question.

Out of the 299 English faculty who responded to this question, 239 (80 percent), had taken *no* courses in their graduate programs to prepare them to teach basic writing. Today, faculty are not only being asked to teach basic writing, but they are also being asked to teach in radically revised formats like ALP, where they are expected to coordinate the developmental course with the composition course and to revise their pedagogy so it takes advantage of the small class size. In addition, they are expected to address those noncognitive issues that cause so many students to drop out and also to integrate reading and writing, for which very few have any preparation.

Of course, the solution to this problem would be for graduate programs to develop a robust collection of courses designed to prepare their graduates for this very challenging and very important work. However, most graduate programs in English are located at universities that decided more than a decade ago that students who needed developmental work would not be admitted. As a result, graduate students

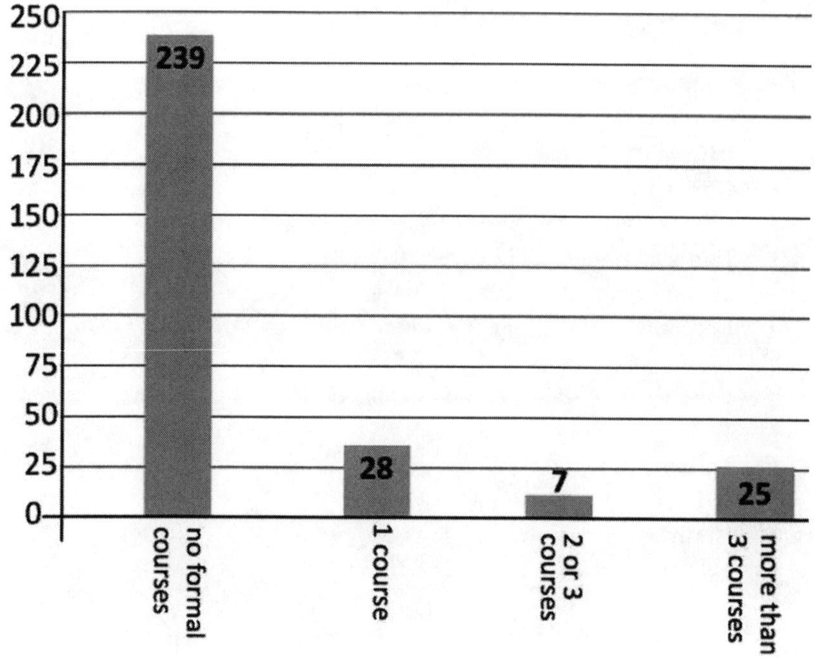

Figure 17.2. Graduate Preparation to Teach Basic Writing

are unlikely to experience teaching basic writing during their graduate program, unlikely to take any coursework in teaching basic writing, and unlikely to encounter graduate faculty who have taught basic writing.

The *TYCA Guidelines for Preparing Teachers of English in the Two-Year College* includes many important and useful suggestions, but the one most central for a school like mine that offers around seventy sections of ALP every semester often taught by faculty whose graduate program gave them no preparation for teaching those courses was this:

> Expand graduate course offerings to include topics valuable to faculty teaching in open-admissions and teaching-intensive colleges and universities, including two-year colleges. Such topics include basic writing, literacy education for culturally and linguistically diverse student populations, writing assessment, writing program administration, writing center theory, online pedagogy, and multimodal composition. (Calhoon-Dillahunt et al. 2016, 7).

I would only add one additional area to this list: preparation to address noncognitive issues. These issues are the primary reason students drop out of our courses, and faculty have had very little preparation for addressing them.

Rather than wait for graduate programs in English to produce a new generation of well-prepared basic writing faculty, the practitioners in the field, mostly at community colleges, have in the past decade developed an impressive panoply of innovations that are changing basic writing dramatically for the better. We are replacing assessment by multiple choice test with multiple measures and, in some cases, directed self-placement. We are abandoning traditional prerequisite models of basic writing and replacing them with corequisite models like ALP. We are integrating reading and writing. We are adopting the promising pedagogy of active learning. And we are developing ways to address our students' noncognitive issues.

As we have developed and adopted these innovations, we have been struggling and still are struggling to help faculty develop classroom pedagogies that will take advantage of these structural innovations. As I have visited schools across the nation, I have been amazed by the creative changes in pedagogy that faculty have come up with.

Some very smart English faculty from Jackson Community College in Michigan helped me to see that under the ALP model, the goal of the developmental course is not just to *prepare* developmental students for English 101. The goal is to help them *pass* English 101. The course is organized to help them accomplish the reading and writing tasks of English 101, not to remedy deficiencies from their seventh or eighth grade classes. In English 101, students are asked to read challenging texts and write college-level essays in response to them; in the ALP companion course, students are asked to do the same thing—read challenging texts and write college-level essays in response to them. The primary difference is that in the companion course they are given a lot more support, scaffolding, and opportunity for revision.

Changing the model for basic writing meant we needed to rethink how we taught the course. It was clear from the beginning that teaching in an ALP model was different from teaching in a traditional, stand-alone development writing course in several ways:

1. The ALP class had a different objective from the traditional developmental classes we had been teaching. No longer were we "remedying" deficiencies our students arrived with; instead, the goal of the course was to assist our students in passing English 101.
2. The developmental class was much smaller than any class most of us had ever taught—just ten students.
3. We were committed to addressing our students' noncognitive issues.
4. We were committed to integrating reading and writing.
5. The ALP class had to be coordinated with the linked English 101 class.

From the first semester we offered ALP, we were aware of these differences from the traditional courses we had taught, but we certainly weren't aware of how our teaching would change in response to this new model. In fact, my pedagogy, my approach to the course, has evolved each semester I taught, and is still evolving today.

Early on, I realized that the subject matter for the course was radically different. No longer was I trying to identify what my students had not learned or had forgotten from high school or even from seventh grade. No longer would the class consist of repeating what we thought students should have learned earlier. No longer would students be underlining the parts of speech, writing paragraphs, or reading paragraphs and underlining main ideas. Instead, the course would look at English 101 for its content; an approach often called "backward curriculum design." In English 101, students read challenging texts and write college-level essays in response to them, and we would be doing the same thing in the ALP, just more slowly and with more support.

This change in focus, in content, seemed pedagogically sound; students would be learning what they needed to become proficient college writers, but it also had noncognitive benefits. No longer would students arrive in college only to take a seat in a class that felt like they were back in seventh grade. Their attachment to the college, their sense that they really were in college would be enhanced.

Fairly early in the development of ALP, we realized that some of our colleagues were viewing the ALP model like this: English 101 is where we teach writing, and the companion course is where we teach grammar. As I visit schools around the country, I occasionally still hear this formulation. Most of us teaching ALP at my school came to surprising consensus on the grammar topic: First, the point of whatever we do under the umbrella of teaching grammar, the goal is not to turn our students into grammarians; the goal is to help our students become better *editors* of their writing. And most of us have also agreed that this means our students don't need to know the eight parts of speech or the difference between relative pronouns and reflexive pronouns. In fact, we have agreed that the amount of terminology, the number of grammatical concepts that our students need to master, is much smaller than we traditionally thought.

Instead, we give time for students to master conventions by working in groups to inductively discover them for themselves. We devote considerable class time to having students, again, working in groups to work on editing their own writing. And in the second half of the semester we introduce students to sentence combining. Working in groups, as they combine short, declarative sentences in different ways, they begin to see grammar as actually providing options.

You may have noticed the phrase "working in groups," which came up several times in the preceding discussion. A few years into the ALP program at CCBC, we were fortunate to have Michelle Zollars from the Southern Center for Active Learning Excellence at Patrick Henry Community College lead a faculty development workshop on active and collaborative learning. The idea that students learn better, are more engaged, and retain what they've learned longer if they discover what they are learning for themselves while working with a small group, has become an important part of our pedagogy. Having students work in groups to figure out for themselves the arcane requirements of MLA formatting or work in groups to discover what *The Immortal Life of Henrietta Lacks* actually says about racism and Johns Hopkins Hospital does take more time than it would to cover these topic in a lecture/discussion class, but students really do learn when they are actively involved, and they learn important group participation skills as well. Students learn how to organize themselves to work on a task and how to cope with the occasional "slacker" in their group.

The longer I taught ALP, the clearer it became that it was wrong to assume that my students could successfully read challenging texts; many of them needed help to develop into competent readers of the kinds of texts I was asking them to read. Bartholomae and Petrosky had made this same point back in 1986, but somehow I—and, I suspect, much of the profession—had lost sight of this important observation. When teaching an ALP class of only ten students, I was no longer able to ignore the problem. The "safe" atmosphere and the fact that my students came to know me not as a judge, but as a compassionate human being made it possible for them to reveal how much trouble they were having with the material I was asking them to read. Gradually, but inexorably, my developmental writing class became an integrated reading and writing class. Luckily, my reading colleagues at CCBC as well as the important work of scholars like Sugie Goen-Salter and Alice Horning were able to help me improve my understanding of what is involved in teaching reading.

After a half dozen years of teaching ALP, here's what I have learned about teaching this course: In addition to helping my students grow *as writers*, I address their noncognitive issues, engage them in active learning, approach their sentence-level errors without resorting to traditional grammar classes, help them mature as readers, and do all this in a way that is coordinated with what they are doing in English 101. A tall order.

My struggle to help students with all these issues gradually led me to a new way of structuring my ALP class, but also my English 101 class. To address all these issues and to coordinate the two classes, I gradually stumbled on a new way of organizing my teaching. The solution was to organize both classes around a lengthy series of reading/writing projects. When I had taught more traditional writing courses, I usually asked students to read a text or two and then write an essay in response to what they'd read. After perhaps a peer response session or some feedback from the instructor, the students turned in a final version of their essay, and then the class moved on to the next set of readings and the next essay.

Reading/writing projects take this two- or three-week cycle for an essay and stretch it out over twice as much time. Students read multiple texts related tightly to an issue or idea. They write short papers in response to these readings, watch a video or two on the topic, participate in group activities to explore the issue, and reflect on how the issue relates to their own lives. They conduct some independent research to find what others have said about the topic. After four or five weeks of reading, thinking, and discussing the same topic, they have enough knowledge and insight to write a thoughtful essay.

The following example of a reading/writing project may clarify how they work.

A READING/WRITING PROJECT ON WALTER MISCHEL'S MARSHMALLOW STUDY

In the 1960s and '70s, psychologist Walter Mischel conducted a series of experiments with young children at Stanford University. The children were given a marshmallow and were told that if they could wait and not eat the marshmallow for about fifteen minutes, they would be given a second marshmallow. Some children were able to delay gratification and wait for the second marshmallow; others were not. Mischel then followed these children for the next forty years and made some startling discoveries. The children who were able to delay gratification scored higher on their SAT tests, used drugs less often, reached higher educational levels, had a lower body mass index, and were better at maintaining close relationships.

In this reading/writing project, students explore Mischel's original study, consider alternative explanations for the results, examine delayed gratification in their own lives, locate and consider related articles, write many short papers and one major paper exploring the issue.

What follows is an overview of this reading/writing project.

Activity 1: Marshmallow Test Video (in 101 class)

Students watch a video re-enacting Mischel's original study: http://www.youtube.com/watch?v=Yo4WF3cSd9Q.

In this video, students watch as young children in an experimental setting are given a marshmallow but are also told that if they can wait a few minutes without eating the marshmallow, they will be given a second one. The variety of responses of the children to this situation are fascinating to watch.

Next, working in groups, students make a list of interesting observations about the video.

Activity 2: Previewing Mischel's Marshmallow Articles (in 101 class)

In Activity 3, students will read two articles on delayed gratification by Walter Mischel. Before they start any reading, however, I want them to spend some time previewing the articles. Working in groups, students have ten minutes to answer the following four questions about the articles (see Activity 3).

I use these four questions, sometimes with a couple more added, as a way of encouraging students regularly to preview any text before diving into it.

1. **Author.** We don't mean simply to find out the name of the author. What else can you learn about him? What evidence is there that the author really has some expertise? What biases might the author have? Is the author part of an organization? A corporation? What else has the author written?
2. **Purpose.** What does it appear that the author intended, or at least hoped, would happen as a result of this piece of writing? What did the author want the effect of this text on its audience to be?
3. **Subject.** What is this article about? What seems to be the main focus?
4. **Audience.** Whom does it appear that the author intended to be the reader or readers of this text? Whom was he addressing?

Activity 3: Reading about Marshmallows (101 homework)

Having previewed the articles in class, students read excerpts from two articles for homework. The excerpts I use in class are two or three pages each; here I've included just a paragraph to provide a sense of what the two excerpts are like.

Excerpt 1

Delay of Gratification in Children (excerpts)

Walter Mischel, Yuichi Shoda, and Monica L. Rodriguez

Science Magazine, May 26, 1989

For almost a century the infant has been characterized as impulse-driven, pressing for tension reduction, unable to delay gratification, oblivious to reason and reality, and ruled entirely by a pleasure principle that demands immediate satisfaction.[1] The challenge has been to clarify how individuals, while remaining capable of great impulsivity, also become able to control actions for the sake of temporally distant consequences and goals, managing at least sometimes to forgo more immediate gratifications to take account of anticipated outcomes. The nature of this future-oriented self-control, which develops over time and then coexists with more impetuous behaviors, has intrigued students of development, who have made it central in theories of socialization and in the very definition of the "self."[2] Such goal-directed self-imposed delay of gratification is widely presumed to be important in the prevention of serious developmental and mental health problems, including those directly associated with lack of resilience, conduct disorders, low social responsibility, and a variety of addictive and antisocial behaviors.

1.S. Freud, Collected Papers (Basic Books, New York, 1959), vol. 4, pp. 13–21.

2.S. Harter, in Handbook of Child Psychology, P. H. Mussen, Ed. (Wiley, New York, 1983), vol. 4, pp. 275–385.

Excerpt 2

The Marshmallow Test: Mastering Self-Control (Excerpt)

Walter Mischel

2014

It began in the 1960s with preschoolers at Stanford University's Bing Nursery School, in a simple study that challenged them with a tough dilemma. My students and I gave the children a choice between one reward (for example, a marshmallow) that they could have immediately, and a larger reward (two marshmallows) for which they would have to wait, alone, for up to 20 minutes. We let the children select the rewards they wanted most from an assortment that included marshmallows, cookies, little pretzels, mints, and so on. "Amy," for example, chose marshmallows. She sat alone at a table facing the one marshmallow that she could have immediately, as well as the two marshmallows that she could have if she waited. Next to the treats was a desk bell she could ring at any time to call back the researcher and eat the one marshmallow. Or she could wait for the researcher to return, and if Amy hadn't left her chair or started to eat the marshmallow, she could have both.

The struggles we observed as these children tried to restrain themselves from ringing the bell could bring tears to your eyes, have you applauding their creativeness and cheering them on, and give you fresh hope for the potential of even young children to resist temptation and persevere for their delayed rewards.

Activity 4: Thinking About Marshmallows (in 101 class)

After reading the two Mischel articles at home, in the next class, working in groups, students discuss the following questions. After fifteen minutes or so, the groups report out.

1. Describe the differences between these two texts. How do you explain the differences? Which is better writing? Why?
2. Who do you think the author of each article was writing for? What kind of a reader was he writing for?
3. "Translate" the first sentence in the scholarly article into more ordinary language: "To function effectively, individuals must voluntarily postpone immediate gratification and persist in goal-directed behavior for the sake of later outcomes."
4. Mischel finds a surprisingly strong relationship between the ability to delay gratification as a four-year-old and a number of positive outcomes later in life. Does this relationship surprise you? Why or why not?

Reading two articles by the same author written in vastly different styles helps students to understand the importance for a writer to think about audience. I have been surprised that many students find the scholarly article to be "better" writing.

Activity 5: Previewing the University of Rochester Marshmallow Study (in ALP class)

Working in groups, you will have just five minutes to answer the following four questions about the University of Rochester Marshmallow Study (see Activity 6).

1. Author. We don't mean simply to find out the name of the author. What else can you learn about her? What evidence is there that the author really has some expertise? What biases might the author have? Is the author part of an organization? A corporation? What else has the author written?
2. Purpose. What does it appear that the author intended, or at least hoped, would happen as a result of this piece of writing? What did the author want the effect of this text on its audience to be?

3. Subject. What is this article about? What seems to be the main focus?
4. Audience. Whom does it appear that the author intended to be the reader or readers of this text? Whom was she addressing? Were there other, more secondary, audiences?

After the groups report out on the first four questions, they will have another ten minutes to answer a fifth question:

5. Here is the second paragraph from the article: "Now a new study demonstrates that being able to delay gratification is influenced as much by the environment as by innate ability. Children who experienced reliable interactions immediately before the marshmallow task waited on average four times longer—twelve versus three minutes—than youngsters in similar but unreliable situations."

   What do you think the article means when it says children are influenced as much by the "environment" as by innate ability? What does the article seem to mean by the word "environment"? The article also talks about "reliable interactions" and "unreliable situations." What does it mean by "reliable" and "unreliable"? How did you figure out the answer to these questions?

Activity 6: More Reading About Marshmallows (101 homework)

For this activity, students read an article by University of Rochester psychologist, Celeste Kidd, which provides a very different insight into Mischel's conclusions in his "Marshmallow Studies." Kidd's research suggests that children's ability to delay gratification is at least partially a function of the environment they are living in, in particular, the amount of trust they have developed in that environment. The excerpt students read is three and a half pages; here I've included just enough to provide a sense of the article. Kidd finds that if children are promised something by the researcher which is later not delivered, those children are less likely to be able to delay gratification when given the marshmallow test.

THE UNIVERSITY OF ROCHESTER MARSHMALLOW STUDY (EXCERPT)

For the past four decades, the "marshmallow test" has served as a classic experimental measure of children's self-control: Will a preschooler eat one of the fluffy white confections now or hold out for two later?

Now a new study demonstrates that being able to delay gratification is influenced as much by the environment as by innate ability. Children who experienced reliable interactions immediately before the marshmallow task waited on average four times longer—twelve versus three minutes—than youngsters in similar but unreliable situations.

"Our results definitely temper the popular perception that marshmallow-like tasks are very powerful diagnostics for self-control capacity," says Celeste Kidd, a doctoral candidate in brain and cognitive sciences at the University of Rochester and lead author on the study to be published online October 11 in the journal *Cognition*.

"Being able to delay gratification—in this case to wait fifteen difficult minutes to earn a second marshmallow—not only reflects a child's capacity for self-control, it also reflects their belief about the practicality of waiting," says Kidd. "Delaying gratification is only the rational choice *if* the child believes a second marshmallow is likely to be delivered after a reasonably short delay."

* * *

The Rochester team wanted to explore more closely why some preschoolers are able to resist the marshmallow while others succumb to licking, nibbling, and eventually swallowing the sugary treat. The researchers assigned 28 three- to five-year-olds to two contrasting environments: unreliable and reliable. The study results were so strong that a larger sample group was not required to ensure statistical accuracy and other factors, like the influence of hunger, were accounted for by randomly assigning participants to the two groups, according to the researchers. In both groups, the children were given a create-your-own-cup kit and asked to decorate the blank paper that would be inserted in the cup.

In the unreliable condition, the children were provided a container of used crayons and told that if they could wait, the researcher would return shortly with a bigger and better set of new art supplies for their project. After two and a half minutes, the researcher returned with this explanation: "I'm sorry, but I made a mistake. We don't have any other art supplies after all. But why don't you use these instead?" She then helped to open the crayon container.

The reliable group experienced the same set up, but the researcher returned with the promised materials: . . . a rotating tray full of art supplies.

Activity 7: Annotating the University of Rochester Study (101 or ALP homework)

Students have previously been introduced to the idea that annotating a text doesn't mean just highlighting everything that seems important. Students learned that annotating can be used to comment on something they disagree with, to mark a reference to another text or book that they'd like to read, to add a thought of their own, to mark something they don't understand, to mark something they want to think about, to mark a powerful example, to add an example of their own to support or refute the writer's argument, or to make a connection to something else they have read or experienced.

With all these possibilities in mind, students are asked to annotate the University of Rochester Study for homework.

Activity 8: Thinking About the University of Rochester Study (in 101 class)

Working in groups, students discuss the following question and report out after twenty minutes:

> Does the article about the University of Rochester study change what you think about delayed gratification? Discuss any changes and the reason for them. Now what do you think about delayed gratification as a strategy in your own life?

Activity 9: Summarizing the University of Rochester Study (in ALP class)

Without any instruction about how to write a summary, students are asked in this activity to write a summary, to write something short—a half page is the suggestion—that summarizes the main content of The University of Rochester Study.

Activity 10: Analyzing Summaries (in ALP class)

Working in groups, students read over the summaries written by their group and make a list of the strengths and weaknesses of the summaries. After about thirty minutes, the groups will report out. Instead of reading about or listening to a lecture on what makes a good summary, in this activity students inductively derive a set of guidelines that are remarkably useful.

Activity 11: Writing about Personal Experience with Delayed Gratification (101 homework)

Students write a short paper about an experience they have had with delaying gratification. They are asked to think about whether they were able to delay gratification or not, why or why not, and what the results were.

We want them to apply what they've been reading and thinking and arguing about to their own lives.

Activity 12: Discussion of Short Writing in Activity 11 (in 101 class)

Working in groups, the students read the papers from their group. Then, for about a half hour, they discuss the following questions: Which kinds of strategies seem to work and which don't work? Are there times when delaying gratification is not the best strategy? Is there a middle ground between delaying gratification and not?

Activity 13: Researching Delayed Gratification (101 homework)

Students find at least three additional articles on the subject of delayed gratification, at least one of which discusses the work of Celeste Kidd, and then answer the following questions about each of the articles they find:

1. Who is the author(s)? What can you find out about the author(s)? How expert is the author on the subject?
2. Where was the article published? What kind of journal, book, or website?
3. Who seems to be the audience this article was intended for?
4. Does this article add anything new to the argument?
5. Which of the three articles would be the best resource for you to quote in an essay? Why?

In this activity, students are working on two important skills: locating resources and evaluating those they find.

Activity 14: Thinking About Audience (in 101 class)

Before students start working on the essay described in Activity 15, they work in groups to read the assignment for that essay and think about who the audience for this essay will be. They report out after about fifteen minutes. This is an opportunity to discuss how writing often has multiple audiences—in this case, next year's students, the New Student Orientation Committee, and, perhaps, their instructor for the course.

Activity 15: Essay 1 (101 homework)

For this assignment, students write a three- to four-page essay that grows out of their reading, their discussion, and their thinking about delayed gratification. The audience for this paper is students who will be arriving at the institution next year. They are also told that their essay, if accepted by the college's New Student Orientation Committee, will be included in a packet of information new students will receive to help them understand how to be more successful in college.

This sample reading/writing project is intended to demonstrate how an assignment can provide an opportunity for students to explore a focused topic in considerable depth and for students to spend extended time reading, thinking, arguing, researching, and writing about that topic before they actually write a formal essay.

In my thirty-six years teaching basic writing, one of my greatest disappointments, semester after semester, was that many of my students wrote papers that seemed not to have involved a lot of thinking. Sometimes they would play it safe and argue something that hardly anyone would disagree with, something like "child abuse is a terrible thing" or "communication is important to a relationship." Since their theses were so obvious, they wouldn't have to do much thinking to convince their audience to agree with them. At other times, they would clearly state some position that they clearly believed in strongly, but then wouldn't provide much evidence to support that position because they couldn't imagine how anyone could disagree. Perhaps most frustrating were the students who tried to make a strong case in support of an interesting thesis, but simply would not know enough about the subject to produce a thoughtful argument.

These reading/writing projects were an attempt to address this problem; to provide more time, more resources, and more activities that would help students think more deeply about the subject. I like to think we are helping students become "novice experts." As they work their way through the fifteen activities in the marshmallow project, they read articles taking a variety of views on delayed gratification; engage in discussions of the topic with their classmates; write low-stakes, short papers on various aspects of the topic; relate their reading and thinking about delayed gratification to their own lives; research the topic further; and, after all this thinking, they write a full-length college essay on the topic.

In my early days of experimenting with this kind of writing assignment, I was startled at the improvement in the reasoning in my students' papers, exactly the result I had hoped for.

However, as my experience with these extended projects evolved, I came to see that they allow many benefits in addition to more time for students to think deeply. For example, the project I outlined above provides many opportunities to help my students grow as readers, an important benefit as my school and many others across the country are integrating reading and writing. Particularly important is that, in a reading/writing project, reading is not simply *added* into the course outline; it is truly *integrated*, so it becomes an organic part of the project. In the project above, note that before we ask students to read Walter Mischel's scholarly article on his marshmallow test, in Activity 2 students work in groups to answer a series of questions about the author, the purpose, the audience, and subject of the essay. When the groups report out their responses to these questions, students begin to understand the multiple possibilities for previewing a text.

It's not easy to determine whether Activity 4 is a reading activity or a writing activity because the two are so well integrated. Students are asked to compare Mischel's scholarly article and a text from his popular book, written for a much more general audience. They compare the styles of the two texts and think about the audience for each. They are also asked to "translate" a sentence full of psychological terminology into one more accessible to a general audience, requiring that they make truly close reading of the passage.

In Activity 5, the students in the companion course get another chance to preview a challenging text. And in Activity 7, the entire 101 class is asked to annotate a text, another activity in which it's unclear whether the task the students are being asked to do is reading or writing.

In Activity 9, the ALP students are asked to summarize an article without any instruction about what makes a good summary. When they work in groups (Activity 10) to list the strengths and weaknesses of the summaries written by their classmates, they are inductively arriving at a sense of what makes an effective summary.

Even very traditional teachers like me have come to see, in recent years, that the old standby lecture-discussion is not always the most effective way for students to learn. Even though I can cover more material in less time with a well-constructed lecture, too often what students learn from a lecture is much less than what I cover. As active learning enthusiasts point out, when students discover insights and information for themselves through an inductive process, they seem to really understand and own the material in a way they don't when they simply sit and listen to a lecture. Furthermore, the level of excitement and enthusiasm when groups of students go to work on a problem or an issue far exceeds their enthusiasm for my lectures. And there is one more benefit of active learning that I've noticed: Joining these enthusiastic group discussions gives them a sense that they are part of the college, that they really do belong . . . a sense that is important to their remaining in school.

In addition to these benefits to their learning and their attachment to the college, learning to work in a group is a valuable skill that employers tell us is important in the workplace. Students working in a group to answer a question learn such skills as how to manage their time, to include diverse ideas, and to deal with a classmate who isn't "pulling his weight" in the group.

Somehow, the expansive format of these reading/writing projects provided the space and flexibility for me to include more and more of these active-learning activities. I still make use of the lecture-discussion format when it seems appropriate, but in the marshmallow project you can see that eight of the fifteen activities actually involve group work.

One feature of the ALP model that I had never experienced in my teaching before ALP is the need to coordinate two different courses. In the early years of ALP, I struggled to figure out how to make the most beneficial use of the extra class time in the companion course and how to coordinate whatever we were going to do in that course with what we were doing in the English 101 class. Some faculty faced with this puzzle have even resorted to using the companion course as a place to teach grammar in very traditional ways.

Once I transitioned to these extended reading/writing projects, I found coordinating the two courses much easier. For the most part, I use the time in the companion course to prepare students for what's coming next in English 101. For example, Activities 9 and 10 on summarizing in the companion course are designed to prepare students for work they'll be doing the following week in English 101 on summarizing, paraphrasing, and quoting.

At other points, I use the companion course to reinforce, practice, or clarify something we've just covered in English 101. In Activity 2, we worked on previewing a challenging text (actually, two texts) in the English 101 class. A little later, we review and reinforce that reading skill in Activity 5 in the companion course.

At the beginning of this chapter, I pointed out our early realization at CCBC that the reason most students in our traditional basic writing courses were unsuccessful had little to do with their writing abilities but resulted primarily from their giving up and dropping out of school for what are called noncognitive reasons—the feeling they are not "college material," the inability to overcome setbacks, the absence of a sense of belonging, and the stress caused by their lives outside college. While working on this project over four or five weeks, students are improving their abilities to think about a complex issue, read challenging texts, conduct research, and write about all of this, but they are also gaining a sense of belonging in college, establishing friendships, and thinking about an issue—the ability to delay gratification—that will help them persist in college.

This reading/writing project on the marshmallow test was the first of these that I have developed, but I now have ten others in various stages of development. To give an idea of the range of topics that can be used to organize reading/writing projects, here's a list of those ten:

- Choosing a career
- Grit
- Freedom of speech
- Truth, lies, and fake news
- Language and power
- The pursuit of happiness
- *Between the World and Me* (Ta-Nehisi Coates)
- What is art?
- *The Immortal Life of Henrietta Lacks* (Rebecca Skloot)

I want to talk a bit about how one of these writing projects fits into the syllabi of the English 101 course and the companion course. In the outline of the marshmallow test project, there are fifteen activities, but I don't want to give the impression that this list of activities is rigidly fixed. In fact, the list is extremely flexible depending on what else I am doing in the course and depending on the needs of the students each semester. When I first developed this project, there were only twelve activities, but as I worked with the project, I added additional activities. One semester I planned to work on summarizing a little later in the course, so I left Activities 9 and 10 out of the marshmallow project. The fifteen activities are there to choose from or add to, not to provide a rigid curriculum.

I'm not suggesting anyone treat this project as a rigid curriculum you should force into your syllabi. Modify it. Better yet, make up your own using a topic and texts you find interesting and that you think your students would too.

Finally, I want to talk about all the "normal" stuff we do in a writing course: work on thesis and unity, on providing support for assertions, on making smooth transitions, and even on editing skills. All of those "normal" topics are not replaced by the activities of a reading/writing project. They are integrated into the project. The attached appendix is a syllabus for the first four weeks of a semester and shows how this integration can be accomplished.

After ten years of teaching ALP and helping faculty across the country teach ALP, this is where I am today. I've learned a lot about teaching ALP, but I anticipate learning more in the future. I would not recommend that anyone adopt the marshmallow test writing project as it is or try to use the syllabus in the appendix as it is. I recommend that you do what I plan to do: continue to revise and improve these plans. To evolve.

APPENDIX 17.A

SAMPLE SYLLABI FOR ALP CLASSES

	ENG 101 Homework	ENG101 Class	Companion Course Homework	Companion Course Class
Wk 1 Tue		Quirky Questions (A) Review Syllabus (D) Marshmallow Test (V)		Interesting Interviews (A) Intro to Course (D)
Wk 1 Thu	Marshmallow Test Video (SW) Previewing (R)	Thinking about Marshmallow Video (D) Previewing Mischel 1 (A)	Reading is Thinking (V) Why You're In Dev Eng (SW)	Good & Bad English (A) Why You're In Dev Eng (A)
Wk 2 Tue	Writing Process (V) Mischel 1 (R) One Interesting Thing (SW)	Writing Process (D) Thesis & Unity in One Interesting Thing (A) Mischel 1 (D)		Thesis & Unity in One Interesting Thing (D) What Use Is a College Education? (A) Activating Schema (D)
Wk 2 Thu	Preview Mischel 2 (SW) Mischel 2 (R)	Being Interesting (A) Thinking about Mischel's 2 articles (A)		Annotating a Text (A) Previewing Kidd's Article (A)
Wk 3 Tue	Read "Being Concrete (R) Read Kidd's Article (R)	Revising for Concreteness (A) Thinking about Kidd's Article (A)	The Grammar in Your Head (V) Writing about Parking (SW)	Thinking about Parking (D) College Terminology (A)
Wk 3 Thu	Researching Delayed Gratification (SW)	Evaluating Sources (A)	Summarizing Kidd's Article (SW)	Analyzing Summaries (A) What Is a Sentence? (A)
Wk 4 Tue	Experiencing Delayed Gratification (SW)	Experiencing Delayed Gratification (A) Assign Essay 1 (D) Audience Analysis (A)		What is an Independent Clause (A) Punctuation with FANBOYS (A)
Wk 4 Thu	Essay 1 due	Peer Review of Essay 1 Difficulty with Pinker (A)	Editing SW from Wk4 Tue	Plan B (D) Run-Ons & CS (A)

A = Activity
D = Discussion
R = Reading
SW = Short Writing
V = Video

Figure 17.3. Sample Syllabi for ALP Classes (Reading/Writing Project Activities Highlighted in Yellow).

APPENDIX 17.B

THE PURSUIT OF HAPPINESS READING/WRITING PROJECT

ACTIVITY 1 (101 HOMEWORK)

The Pursuit of Happiness

Students write a short paper, about a page long, in which they explain what the word happiness means to them.

ACTIVITY 2 (IN 101 CLASS)

Previewing "A Better Kind of Happiness"

Working in groups, students answer questions about the subject, author, purpose, and audience of the article they will be reading for Activity 3.

ACTIVITY 3 (101 HOMEWORK)

Reading "A Better Kind of Happiness"

Students read an article by Will Storr from the *New Yorker* entitled "A Better Kind of Happiness." Storr argues that what we should really seek is not hedonistic happiness, but the "well-lived life," a life with purpose.

ACTIVITY 4 (ALP HOMEWORK)

Annotating "A Better Kind of Happiness"

ALP students work on their annotation skills by printing out and then annotating the Will Storr article.

ACTIVITY 5 (IN 101 CLASS)

Thinking about "A Better Kind of Happiness"

Working in groups, students think about Storr's terms eudaemonic and hedonic, attempt to understand the connections between happiness and health, and grapple with Storr's concept of the "good life."

ACTIVITY 6 (ALP HOMEWORK)

Believing/doubting "A Better Kind of Happiness"

ALP Students at home apply Peter Elbow's believing and doubting to their reading of "A Better Kind of Happiness," then share their notes in class.

ACTIVITY 7 (IN 101 CLASS)

What Would Make You Happy?

Students are asked to imagine themselves at age fifty or sixty. Working in groups, they make lists of what would be necessary in order for them to feel they had achieved Storr's eudaemonic happiness, to feel they had led a "good life." Putting these lists on large newsprint sheets and posting them around the room works well.

ACTIVITY 8 (IN 101 CLASS)

Previewing Aristotle's "Nicomachean Ethics"

Now we turn to the source of Storr's idea of eudaemonic happiness, Aristotle. Because the "Nicomachean Ethics" is such a challenging text, we spend extra time previewing it in class. After answering the standard previewing questions on subject, author, purpose, and audience, we will actually read the first couple of paragraphs together in class.

ACTIVITY 9 (101 HOMEWORK)

Reading Aristotle's "Nicomachean Ethics"

Students will finish reading the excerpt from "Nicomachean Ethics" as homework.

ACTIVITY 10 (IN 101 CLASS)

Thinking About Aristotle's "Nicomachean Ethics"

Working in groups, students will grapple with three questions: What big ideas did they get from the reading, what is Aristotle's argument for not considering wealth or honor to be an appropriate life goal, and what does Aristotle seem to mean by "happiness"?

ACTIVITY 11 (101 HOMEWORK)

The Happiness Survey

In Activity 7, students made a list of items they considered important to feeling that they had lived a "good life" at age fifty or sixty. For this activity, I will have compiled those items into a survey, asking for each item "how important, on a scale of 1 to 5, would this be in order for you to feel you had led a 'good life'?" Students will each survey six people using this form and we will compile the results in class.

ACTIVITY 12 (101 HOMEWORK)

Analysis of a Survey

I will give each student a copy of the survey compilation, and they will write a short paper, about a page long, in which they analyze what they learned from these data.

ACTIVITY 13 (ALP HOMEWORK)

Happiness in Sri Lanka

For this activity, students will read a short narrative about an extremely bright woman from Sri Lanka who won a scholarship in her country to a boarding high school and then to college in England. Her family is back in Sri Lanka living in a thatch-roofed house with a dirt floor, no glass windows, and no running water. She thinks about who is happier, her brothers and sisters back in Sri Lanka or herself with all the stress and anxiety involved in becoming an engineer. Students will write a short paper, a page or less, about what this story reveals about happiness.

ACTIVITY 14 (101 HOMEWORK)

Reading "More to Life than Being Happy"

Building on the life of Viktor Frankl, Emily Smith asks in this *Atlantic* magazine article whether a life with purpose is a more appropriate goal than a life of happiness. She also explores what counts as a life with purpose. Does it have to involve giving to others?

ACTIVITY 15 (IN 101 CLASS)

Thinking about "More to Life than Being Happy"

Working in groups, students will explore the questions Emily Smith raises in "More to Life than Being Happy"

ACTIVITY 16 (101 HOMEWORK VIDEO)

A Buddhist Monk Talks about Happiness

In this mesmerizing video, Gen Kelsang Nyema, a Buddhist monk, suggests that happiness is all in your head. Students watch the video at home.

ACTIVITY 17 (101 HOMEWORK)

Thinking about A Buddhist Monk Talks about Happiness

Students write a short paper summarizing Nyema's approach to happiness.

ACTIVITY 18 ESSAY (101 HOMEWORK)

Pursuing Happiness

Students write a three-to-four-page essay discussing their own pursuit of happiness. Now that they have read several essays from thoughtful magazines—the *Atlantic* and the *New Yorker*—their essays will aim to use the same style—a thoughtful discussion aimed at a general audience.

ACTIVITY 19 (101 HOMEWORK)

Researching Happiness

Before working on the Activity 18 essay, students will locate three books or articles, online or in the library, on the topic of happiness. They will write a brief evaluation of each.

APPENDIX 17.C

THE TA-NEHISI COATES READING/WRITING PROJECT

ACTIVITY 1 (101 HOMEWORK)

"'Between the World and Me': Ta-Nehisi Coates in Conversation on Being Black in America" (video)

Students will watch this video of the Coates interview as homework.

ACTIVITY 2 (IN 101 CLASS)

Responding to the Coates Interview (activity 1)

After watching the Coates interview (Activity 1), students will write a short paper, less than a page long, in which they describe the kind of person Coates seems to be.

ACTIVITY 3 (IN 101 CLASS)

Previewing Between the World and Me

Working in groups, students answer questions about the subject, author, purpose, and audience of Ta-Nehisi Coates' *Between the World and Me,* which they will begin reading for Activity 4. previewing for audience is especially useful for this book, because it is ostensibly a letter from Coates to his son, but it is also a message from Coates to America at large.

ACTIVITY 4 (101 HOMEWORK)

Reading Between the World and Me *(part 1)*

Students read the first 35 pages of *Between the World and Me.*

ACTIVITY 5 (101 HOMEWORK)

Annotating Between the World and Me

Much of the first 35 pages of *Between the World and Me* is a discussion of what it means to be black or white in America. Students annotate the text, particularly looking for discussion of these issues.

ACTIVITY 6 (IN ALP CLASS)

Education in Between the World and Me

Working in groups, students discuss what Coates says about education in the first 35 pages of *Between the World and Me.*

ACTIVITY 7 (IN 101 CLASS)

Speed dating Between the World and Me

Speed dating is an activity to provide a series of one-on-one discussions between students. Students sit in two concentric circles with the outer circle facing in and the inner one facing out so that each student is facing another student. On each chair is an index card with a question that the students will discuss for five minutes. Then, each student moves one chair to his or her right and faces a new student and a new question. This continues as long as time permits.

Here are some sample questions for this discussion of Coates:

On page 6, Coates writes, "Democracy is a forgiving God." Discuss what he means by this.

On page 7, Coates writes, "race is the child of racism, not the father." Explain what he means by this.

Near the bottom of page 26, Coates asserts that "the schools were drugging us with false morality." What does he mean by "false morality"?

At several points in this section, Coates refers to "the people who believed they were white." What does he mean by this?

ACTIVITY 8 (ALP HOMEWORK)

Annotating Between the World and Me

Students return to the first 35 pages of *Between the World and Me* and annotate those places where Coates explains what he means by "The Dream."

ACTIVITY 9 (101 HOMEWORK)

Reading James Baldwin's "On Being White. . . . and Other Lies."

Coates says he borrowed the phrase "people who believe they are white" from James Baldwin's essay "On Being White. . . . and Other Lies." For this activity, students read the Baldwin essay.

ACTIVITY 10 (ALP HOMEWORK)

Summarizing James Baldwin

Without any instruction about how to write a summary, in this activity, ALP students are asked to write a summary; to write something short—a half page is the suggestion—that summarizes the main content of this Baldwin essay.

ACTIVITY 11 (ALP CLASS)

Analyzing Summaries

Working in groups, students read over the summaries written by their group and make a list of the strengths and weaknesses of the summaries. After about thirty minutes, the groups will report out. Instead of reading about or listening to a lecture on what makes a good summary, in this activity students inductively derive a set of guidelines that are remarkably useful.

ACTIVITY 12 (101 HOMEWORK)

Explaining Race

Coates and Baldwin express their attitude on race using the phrase "people who believe they are white." Having read Coates and Baldwin, students write a short paper, about a page long, in which they discuss what is meant by this phrase.

ACTIVITY 13 (101 HOMEWORK)

Reading Between the World and Me (part 2)

Students read pages 39 to 71 of *Between the World and Me.*

ACTIVITY 14 (IN 101 CLASS)

Translating Coates

At times, some students may have difficulty with Coates's vocabulary, which gets much of its power from African American Vernacular English, as the following excerpt reveals:

> I first witnessed this power out on the yard, that communal green space in the center of the campus where the students gathered and I saw everything I knew of my black self multiplied out into seemingly endless variations. There were the scions of Nigerian aristocrats in their business suits giving dap to bald-headed Qs in purple windbreakers and tan Timbs. There were the high-yellow progeny of AME preachers debating the clerics of Ausar-Set. There were California girls turned Muslim, born anew, in hijab and long skirt. There were Ponzi schemers and Christian cultists, Tabernacle fanatics and mathematical geniuses. (Coates 2015, 40–41)

Working in groups, students translate this passage into language that would be more accessible to a broad audience. This activity provides a great opportunity for African American students to be experts on language.

ACTIVITY 15 (IN 101 CLASS)

Who Is the Tolstoy of the Zulus?

Coates first quotes Saul Bellow's question, "Who is the Tolstoy of the Zulus?" and then gives Ralph Wiley's reply, "Tolstoy is the Tolstoy of the Zulus." Working in groups, students explore this exchange.

ACTIVITY 16 ESSAY (ALP HOMEWORK)

Thinking About The Dream

In Activity 8, ALP students annotated references to The Dream in part 1 of *Between the World and Me.* For this activity, they annotate part 2 for references to The Dream again. Then, they write a short paper, no more than a page, in which they report how Coates's attitude toward this central concept changes from part 1 to part 2.

ACTIVITY 17 (101 HOMEWORK)

Reading Between the World and Me (part 3)

Students read pages 75 to 121 of *Between the World and Me.*

ACTIVITY 18 (IN 101 CLASS)

Advice to Samori

Working in groups, students sum up the main topic in this section of *Between the World and Me,* Coates's advice to his son Samori.

ACTIVITY 19 (IN 101 CLASS)

A Single Beige Race

In part 3, Coates discusses the suggestion that "the only way forward is a grand orgy of black and white, ending only when we are all beige and thus the same 'race.'" Working in groups, students summarize what Coates seems to think of this idea and decide what they think of it.

ACTIVITY 20 (101 HOMEWORK)

Reading Between the World and Me (part 4)

Students read pages 121 to 152 of *Between the World and Me.*

ACTIVITY 21 (101 HOMEWORK)

Final Thoughts

The final part of *Between the World and Me* focuses on the death of Coates's friend Prince and Coates's conversation with Prince's mother. Students write a short paper, no more than a page, in which they analyze how Coates is changed by these final events.

ACTIVITY 22 (IN 101 CLASS)

When Did You Realize Your Race?

In part 5 of *Between the World and Me,* Coates discusses the first time he realized what race he is and then asks his son when he first had this realization. Students watch a video in which a dozen or so people answer the same question, when they first realized their race. Then, working in groups, students discuss when they first realized their races.

ACTIVITY 23 (101 HOMEWORK)

Researching Race

Students find an authoritative source defining races in America and make reference to this source in their essay (Activity 26).

ACTIVITY 24 (101 HOMEWORK)

Essay

Based on their reading of *Between the World and Me,* their reading of other texts in this project, their reading of other texts they have located, their own short writings, and their participation in discussions and activities, students write a three-to-four-page essay in response to one of the following:

1. What does it mean for you to be black in America?
2. What does it mean for you to be white in America?
3. What does it mean for you to be Hispanic in America?
4. What does it mean for you to be Latino in America?
5. What does it mean for you to be Asian in America?
6. What does it mean for you to be Arabic in America?
7. What does it mean for you to be Native American in America?
8. What does it mean for you to be Pacific Islander in America?
9. What does it mean for you to be more than one race in America?
10. What does it mean for you to be some racial category not listed in the first nine choices in America?

REFERENCES

Bartholomae, David, and Anthony Petrosky. 1986. *Facts, Artifacts, and Counterfacts: Theory and Method for a Reading and Writing Course.* Upper Montclair, NJ: Boynton/Cook.

Calhoon-Dillahunt, Carolyn, Darin L. Jensen, Sarah Z. Johnson, Howard Tinberg, and Christie Toth. 2016. "TYCA Guidelines for Preparing Teachers of English in the Two-Year College." https://secure.ncte.org/library/NCTEFiles/Groups/TYCA/GuidelinesPrep2YCEngFac_REVISED.pdf.

Cho, Sung-Woo, Elizabeth Kopko, Davis Jenkins, and Shanna Smith Jaggars. 2012. "New Evidence of Success for Community College Remedial English Students: Tracking the Outcomes of Students in the Accelerated Learning Program (ALP)." CCRC Working Paper no. 53. https://ccrc.tc.columbia.edu/media/k2/attachments/ccbc-alp-student-outcomes-follow-up.pdf.

Coates, Ta-Nehisi. 2015. Between the World and Me. New York: Spiegel amd Grau.

Grego, Rhonda C., and Nancy S. Thompson. 2008. *Teaching/Writing in Third Spaces.* Carbondale: Southern Illinois University Press.

Glau, Greg. 1996. "The 'Stretch Program': Arizona State University's New Model of University-Level Basic Writing Instruction." *WPA: Writing Program Administration* 20: 79–91.

Mischel, Walter, Yuichi Shoda, and Monica L. Rodriguez. 1989. "Delay of Gratification in Children." *Science* 244: 933-938.

PART V

Conclusion

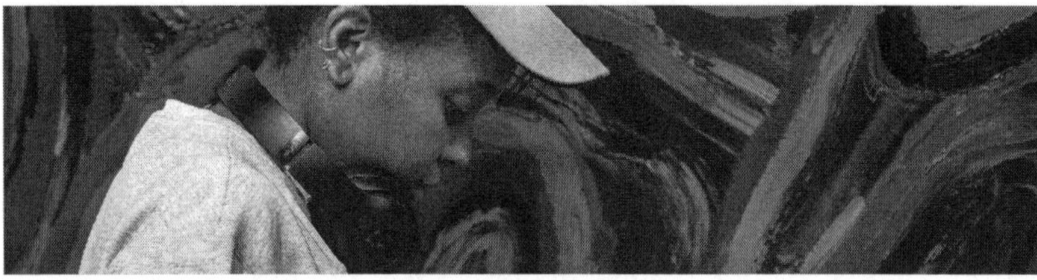

18
FOR NEW ENGLISH TEACHERS

Leah McNeir

"The learning process is something you can incite, literally incite, like a riot."
—Audre Lorde

Show me your passion. Invoke my senses to stand at attention in witness of the fire within you. A great teacher is one who can inspire their students, provoke their innate curiosity, and draw out and expand upon their understandings. As we consider what supports these goals, we must recognize that few things are more captivating and impactful than someone set alight by the flames of passion. So tell me, *why* exactly do you burn? What helped ferment the desire to teach in this field and what do you hope to achieve with your students? What was it about English that inspired you to pursue this degree? Was it in the way grammar, vocabulary, syntax, and style provide an infinitely chromatic palette of verbal tools? Was it the power of the written word and the timelessness of storytelling that drove you? Indeed, perhaps it was how language, when artfully and poetically expressed, can communicate the ineffable and deeply touch our souls. Perhaps it was in witnessing and recognizing how an adept wordsmith can forge and distill new ideas, manifest potent imaginings, illuminate new meanings, or reinterpret old dogmas in a way that forever alters the world—or, how through eloquent parlance, the written word can forever imprint upon us and alter our individual worlds and perspectives.

DOI: 10.7330/9781607329305.c018

> *"There is something about words. In expert hands, manipulated deftly, they take you prisoner. Wind themselves around your limbs like spider silk, and when you are so enthralled you cannot move, they pierce your skin, enter your blood, numb your thoughts. Inside you they work their magic."*
> —Dianne Setterfield

For those touched by the magic of the English language; who have reveled in its myriad of forms, applications, and repercussions, there's an intuitive recognition of the truth held in Pearl Strachan Hurd's quote, "Handle them carefully, for words have more power than atom bombs." Therefore, in acknowledgment of this power, take due care and time to carefully define for yourself your personal answers to these questions as you embark on this new chapter of your life. Reflect on what has fueled your passion and revisit these questions regularly throughout your career; especially as the inevitable challenges arise, or when you are faced with self-doubt, or if ever you find a sense of drudgery or stagnation creeping in. We have all had teachers for whom the fire has clearly smoldered into ash. Those weary educators who no longer bring their presence and energy to the classroom and instead emit a sense of cynicism, condescension, or apathy. Those are the classes where learning happens in spite of the teacher, not because of them, or, worse yet, where a spark within students can be extinguished. Take great care in your day-to-day interactions and realize your importance. Do not let your fire go out. Safeguard and tend it. Ceaselessly remind yourself why you were drawn to this field and recall all the rewards that English has brought you and what it can bring to your students' lives. In your off hours, take time for the things that kindle your enthusiasm and bring that energy to your classroom renewed and reinvigorated each day. Craft a classroom atmosphere that rejuvenates and inspires you. Let your love of English guide you and ooze out of you. Allow it to color and vitalize your lessons and lectures. Impart the flame and set alight each student's candle. By sustaining your inner fire, you will be more effective, driven, and committed to continually improving yourself as an educator.

> *"I've come to a frightening conclusion that I am the decisive element in the classroom. It's my personal approach that creates the climate. It's my daily mood that makes the weather. As a teacher, I possess a tremendous power to make a child's life miserable or joyous. I can be a tool of torture or an instrument of inspiration. I can humiliate or heal. In all situations, it is my response that decides whether a crisis will be escalated or de-escalated and a child humanized or dehumanized."*
> —Haim Ginott

As you define these answers and motivations for yourself and put ink to the proverbial paper, seek novel ways of materializing them in your teaching practice. When first clarified to yourself and consciously incorporated each day, your students will more easily read your manifesto, your face, your tone, and your methods to see, know, and be inspired by the passion within you. Many students will mirror your energy and presence—or lack thereof—and their reciprocal energy, in turn, can galvanize or dishearten you. We know that students learn best when they are engaged and motivated, and while your presence and passion can help set the tone, the stage must be set as well. So, what type of classroom do you desire? How will you create an atmosphere that supports deep learning for your students and ongoing rejuvenation for yourself? Will it be a classroom of rigidity or one of nuance? Will it be stern and cold or cheerful and open? Casual and lively or formal and quiet? Interactive or dictatorial? At every chance, demonstrate and discuss how the lessons hold relevance to your student's lives and allow students the chance to express the meanings and connections they are forming for themselves with each other. Allow your students to become storytellers and coauthors of their educational experience. Communication, after all, is at the heart of English and the greatest teachers are the ones who can inspire enthusiasm and engagement with their presence, presentation, and their classroom atmosphere.

> *"I've learned that people will forget what you said, people will forget what you did, but people will never forget how you made them feel."*
> —Maya Angelou

Will your class be viewed as a set of obligations and tasks the student must endure or will it be an exciting haven for student's personal development? The most memorable and impactful classrooms have been, for me, ones of open dialogue and debate that welcome creativity and shared exploration and reflection. They have been classrooms where the humanity of the content is recognized and takes center stage; where facts and figures come alive with human emotion, story, vitality, and continuity. Student engagement and interest is often closely tied to how they relate to, or connect to, the material. Connections to the material can be encouraged by exploring the relevance to students' lives and their worlds and by facilitating personal meaning-making through discussion and reflective exercises. Humans are natural, emotive storytellers and we strive to create meaning from our experiences. Allow students to openly explore what meanings, feelings, ideas, and connections they are making with you and with one another. Encourage creativity, flexibility of thought, diverse views, and intellectual risk-taking. Inspire participation by creating a welcoming, mutually respectful, and open classroom where your caring and concern for each student's development is apparent. Utilize Vygotsky's theory of scaffolding and carefully evaluate students' understanding on an ongoing and individual basis. Earnestly meet each student where they are. Be direct and clear with your pedagogical expectations and understand the various ways that students learn. Instruct in a way that incorporates and speaks to each of the seven learning styles. Be available to provide support and welcome student feedback on your methods. This information is critical to your ongoing development as an educator. Be flexible. Though you may only spend one semester with your students, they will remember your class for far longer. Make their time in your classroom an enjoyable experience and they will better remember both the content and their time with you for long after. As children, we instinctually learn best through play. I'd argue that this fact does not really change as we age. So, make your classroom fun!

> *"It only takes one person to mobilize a community and inspire change. Even if you don't feel like you have it in you, it's in you. You have to believe in yourself. People will see your vision and passion and follow you."*
>
> —Teyonah Parris

In two-year community colleges, your students will come into class bringing a wider range of personal and educational backgrounds compared to the student body of most four-year universities. Some may be adult learners returning to school after many years away. Others will be fresh out of high school. Their familiarity with, and preparedness for, college courses will vary. They will come from a broader range of socioeconomic classes, cultural or ethnic backgrounds, and will have differing levels of competing commitments and responsibilities outside of college. The more disparate nature of the two-year college's student body can result in more diverse academic challenges, as well as challenges to their sense of community or peer camaraderie. Therefore, double your efforts to establish a sense of community within your classroom. Bring your students together under a common banner and encourage connections and association between them. With student diversity comes great educational opportunity. Allow your students to share their varying perspectives and each will take away a broader and more considerate understanding. As students relate to each other or have their views discussed or expanded upon, they will be more likely to become engaged and interested. They will have a greater chance to hone their capacity for critical thinking, evaluation, judgment, and empathy. To quote Rollo Reese May, "Communication leads to community, that is, to understanding, intimacy, and mutual valuing."

> *"If you want to build a ship, don't drum up people together to collect wood and don't assign them tasks and work, but rather teach them to long for the endless immensity of the sea."*
> —Antoine de Saint-Exupéry

Above all else, strive to encourage a passion for learning, open-mindedness, and exploration in your students and use your course's content as a tool for this aim. Celebrate discoveries and guide student's natural curiosity. When students are enthusiastic about the learning process, they will not only retain information better, they will also be encouraged to become lifelong learners. With learning revered as a worthy goal in itself, students will face academic and life challenges with greater grit and determination as trials and growth are recognized as a natural part of the learning endeavor. As you face challenges, remind yourself of this as well. Strive for continual improvement and efficacy in your role as an educator and fan your personal fire for growth and development. Remember, you are not simply an English teacher. You are the keeper of the flame, the village storyteller, a vital link between the ages. Show me your passion and I'll find you intriguing. Allow me to explore ideas and take risks, and you'll allow me space to develop and grow. Fashion your classroom into a respectful community and I'll discover new ideas and shared values. Open my heart and you will open my mind.

Good luck to you on your journey.

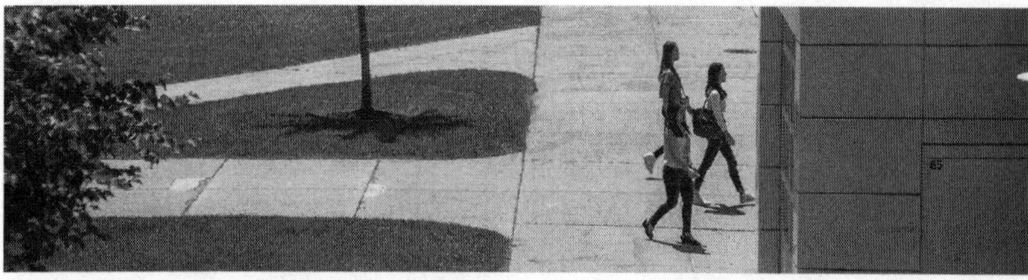

19

A PATH TO CITIZENSHIP

An Interview with Howard Tinberg

Patrick Sullivan

Howard Tinberg, a professor of English at Bristol Community College, has always had difficulty standing still. He must be doing something—as his wife readily observes—"work-related." Whether it's checking out student work (usually online), preparing for the week's class discussions, reading articles in academic journals (always a pleasure, no matter how challenging), and composing his own work for presentations or publication, Dr. Tinberg manages to remain busy—years ago that also meant being "counselor" at "Camp Dad" in the summer when his daughters were very young.

Before arriving at the community college where he has taught for thirty years, Dr. Tinberg was, one might say, the itinerant and peripatetic teacher; having taught as an adjunct at colleges in the Boston area, then as a full-time "foreign expert" in China for a year, and in a seventh-grade classroom in New Hampshire as well as an adjunct at a community college in the state, before arriving at a two-year college within Boston University.

From BU, Dr. Tinberg landed his current position at Bristol Community College. For fifteen years he served as the founding director of the college's writing lab—work that he found endlessly satisfying both for the opportunity to work one-on-one with students and for the chance to work with faculty committed to writing in the disciplines. During his

DOI: 10.7330/9781607329305.c019

tenure as writing lab director, Dr. Tinberg taught several classes, including first-year composition, a tutoring practicum, and surveys of British literature. He also developed and still teaches an honors course with a colleague from the history department on the literature and history of the Holocaust. For those of you thinking of pursuing a career at community colleges, consider the teaching possibilities that await you!

In 2004, Dr. Tinberg was honored to be selected as the US Community Colleges Professor of the Year. The next year, he received a fellowship with the Carnegie Academy for the Scholarship of Teaching and Learning—a year's residency at the Carnegie Foundation on the campus of Stanford University.

All this while Dr. Tinberg has been active in professional organizations, most notably in the Conference on College Composition and Communication, where he served as chair, and in the National Council of Teachers of English, having served as a member of the Council's Executive Committee. Dr. Tinberg is a former editor of *Teaching English in the Two-Year College* (*TETYC*), a national publication focusing on the work of English instruction in the first two years of college.

Dr. Tinberg is the author of *Border Talk: Writing and Knowing in the Two-Year College* and *Writing with Consequence: What Writing Does in the Disciplines.* He is coauthor of *The Community College Writer: Exceeding Expectations* and *Teaching, Learning and the Holocaust: An Integrative Approach.* He is coeditor of *What Is "College-Level" Writing?*, *What Is "College-Level" Writing? Vol 2*, and *Deep Reading: Teaching Reading in the Writing Classroom*, which was awarded by the Conference on College Composition and Communication the 2019 Outstanding Book Award for an Edited Collection. He has published articles in a variety of academic journals, including *College English*, *College Composition and Communication*, *Teaching English in the Two-Year College*, and *Change.* His article "Reconsidering Transfer Knowledge at the Community College: Challenges and Opportunities" received the Mark Reynolds Best Article of the Year in *Teaching English in the Two-Year College* for 2015. In 2015 he was also selected as a museum teaching fellow at the United States Holocaust Memorial Museum.

It has been one heck of a ride.

THE MISSION

PATRICK: Howard, one purpose of this book is to provide teachers of writing—teachers new to the profession along with seasoned veterans who will be looking to this volume for sources of renewal and inspiration—with a more personal, first-hand account of teaching at the two-year college. As a faculty member who has had a distinguished career as a teacher, scholar, and champion of the two-year college, what have you found most personally meaningful about teaching at a two-year open-admissions institution?

HOWARD: I'd answer your question in two ways: one, by way of an abstraction; the other by way of the very concrete.

What strikes me as unique about the two-year open-admission college is The Mission. Those who work at the public, open-access community colleges are reminded every day that our work is driven to achieve a public good. As you know, community colleges are "democracy's open door," providing affordable access to a college education for all. There is no underestimating the power of this idea; we are all activists in this sense, and we are all committed to the public good. Now, I realize that anyone who goes into education is committed to improving the lot of all. But the idea that animates open-access public community colleges, in my judgment, sets those institutions apart from other sectors in higher education.

Then there are our students; so varied, so interesting. In my thirtieth year of teaching at my own community college, I've been given the opportunity to teach at one of our urban campuses. I was struck immediately by the motivation of these students to succeed. Many—as they themselves admit—face terrific challenges, but I am inspired by their drive to succeed. Just yesterday I spoke to a student who had been put into state foster care at the age of twelve and, as she put it, ran away just about every weekend. At the age of fourteen, she was sharing an apartment and supporting herself by stealing. Now, she is in college. Not only that, she has started her own organization to assist others who need encouragement to face life's challenges. And, yes, this student had been thinking of dropping my 101 course because of the pressures of the work, but through the help of friends and mentors, she is hanging in there. To my mind, this student represents to perfection what awaits those who wish to teach at a community college: Be ready to be inspired.

As a teacher-scholar, I want to assure those thinking about working at a teaching intensive institution like mine that it is possible to do research and teach. In fact, one of the joys that I have discovered over the years is that research and teaching have gone hand-in-hand. I've truly enjoyed the opportunity to reflect on the work of the classroom and to engage other scholars on that work. For example, currently I am involved with colleagues on researching the teaching for writing transfer curriculum, which I have adopted in my 101. First of all, the adoption of this exciting curriculum has reenergized my teaching (as I had hoped it would) and engaged my students in wonderful ways. Secondly, the project has allowed me to share ideas about teaching with interested colleagues. And, third, I have engaged in thoughtful and rewarding interviews with students about what they are learning about writing. There is no divide between teaching and research: each engages and informs the others. I am becoming a better teacher as a result of this project.

ALL IN

PATRICK: I want to get back to some of the issues you raise here in a bit more detail, but before we do, I'd like to ask you this question and get your response on the official public record: Why would someone ever *choose* to teach at a two-year college rather than *settle* for working at one? What would draw teachers to these kinds of institutions?

HOWARD: First of all, let me come clean: Before I tell you why I chose the community college, I should note that while in graduate school at a research-intensive university several decades ago I imagined myself teaching at an RI institution having students engaged in the work of the British Romantics! I knew very little about "junior college," as it was then known to me (and, truth be told, I did have an ignorant and somewhat biased view of junior college). I make this admission to assure those current graduate students who have a desire to teach but who know little about teaching-intensive institutions and, frankly, are being given very little incentive to teach at such places, that there are ways to find out information about community colleges: various documents and position statements put out by the Two-Year English Association, for example. In the last several decades, prominent two-year college teacher-scholars have been committed to putting our story and our students' stories in print (I'm thinking of people like Lynn Troyka, Nell Ann Pickett, Mark Reynolds, Jeff Sommers, Jeff Andelora, Jeff Klausman, Carolyn Calhoun-Dilahunt, Holly Hassell, Darin Jensen, and of course yourself, Pat).

As for my own experience, I came to the community college via two important stages: First, I became engaged with the then-emerging field of composition studies, a field that unashamedly constructed itself both as a teaching and research subject. Next, after a couple of years teaching at a two-year college within a four-year university, I gained practical but guided experience in teaching rhetoric. I had wonderful mentors in the department at the university where I was teaching.

But I felt then that my students seemed somewhat homogeneous. I wanted greater diversity, especially among socioeconomic and cultural lines. That's when I saw the advertisement for the community college where I now teach. I researched the institution, saw its commitment to serve the community in a comprehensive way, and learned about the various ethnic and cultural groupings among students. I was hooked and have been here for, as I say, decades.

Applying to teach at the community college as a default move would be unfortunate because this kind of work requires that you go *all in.* I won't sugarcoat this: The teaching is demanding. Our students do ask a great deal of us. But in asking a great deal, they strike a bargain with us: Our students are essentially telling us that they will work (and I mean working full time out of school while taking several classes) extremely hard and will take their studies seriously; they expect us to be equally serious and committed in our work. I think that's a fair contract.

THE SCHOLARSHIP OF TEACHING AND LEARNING

PATRICK: Is it possible to love one's job at a community college even though there is a significant workload and a focus on teaching rather than research?

HOWARD: Good question and one that goes to the "heart" (and I use that word intentionally) of what we do at the community college. I believe that the short answer is yes. But I want to be frank—and, well, personal, too—here. The workload is exhausting, especially if we are committed to teaching to the best of our abilities. For the first time in several years, I am teaching a full course load of five courses, four of which are ENG 101s (I had a modest course reassignment of a single course for a semester when I was serving as program chair of CCCC and later as president of our Faculty and Staff Senate). The teaching of writing courses, as you know, places a special strain on the instructor (and on our students), if it is done well—with plenty of writing assignments and with prompt and effective feedback on that writing. Yes, all this is true. But what an opportunity we are given—both through class discussion and the steady stream of written responses from our students—to learn so much about our students. I have felt for many years that despite the challenges of teaching writing—the persistent view that writing is merely a "skill," the apparent lack of standardized "content," and the steady stream of writing to be assessed—first-year composition is the one course in the entire college curriculum where teaching (pedagogy and teaching practice) and the students themselves occupy space as the subjects of the course.

And then there is the opportunity for research. I want to be clear about this, Pat. For me, the teaching and the research are coequal. Now, if what I say were taken out of context (as, perhaps some might be tempted to do), the statement might be construed as evidence of my own bias in favor of research *over* teaching. But that would be a misrepresentation of my meaning. What I mean is that teaching and research (as I have understood it—the "Scholarship of Teaching and Learning") must of necessity be equally important. I would not be a tenth of the teacher that I am now if I had not continued to read about, to inquire about, and to write about my teaching. To graduate students, I say this: If you are serious about teaching, I would hope that you are serious about continuing to study, reflect on, and research teaching. You must continue to learn on the job—for your students' sake but also for your own development as a community college teacher and scholar. As long as you are intellectually curious, your students will respond positively to you. I learned this about my students long ago: They will understand if an assignment did not work as well as planned—if I come clean and show them what it means to learn from failure. And what a lesson that provides for these students, whose lives have so often been marked by failure.

IT CAN BE DONE. IT MUST BE DONE.

PATRICK: You have been a scholar and disciplinary leader now for many decades, and many of us are inspired by your example, but we also wonder: How do you do it? How do you stay so involved, fresh, engaged, and positive and still balance this important work with other areas of your life—especially being actively involved with your family, raising your daughters, and having a personal life. How do you find the time to do your reading and research? What does an average weekend look like for you? What would you say to a graduate student who is seriously considering teaching at a two-year college but may be worried about this?

HOWARD: I'd ask the same of you, Pat, since, to my mind and that of others, you have been most prolific over the years; publishing articles in major journals, single-authored monographs, and (several) edited collections.

Listen, I'm a child of immigrants who came to this country as refugees with very little but a conviction that this country that provided them with safe harbor would yield so many benefits if my parents only worked hard. I and my siblings have taken our parents' work ethic and run with it. Do we always achieve a work-life balance? I can't say that is the case—I'm always reading student writing and journal articles! But my wife and I have been married thirty-five years and have raised two loving and smart daughters.

But let me answer your question more directly: At our college, we have one day away from campus. That day happens to be Fridays. Now, much of the time I'm using these days to read student work since there is precious little time during the week to do so (if I am to spare my weekends). But I do use those days to read journal articles and to think through some projects that I may be involved in. Now I try to keep Saturday as time for family. The same goes for the early part of Sunday. But late Sunday I prepare for the week's work.

Most of my writing and research are done during intersession and especially the summer. I can't stress enough the importance of using summer to do this sort of work. I do not teach in the summers anymore, although I recognize that younger faculty may not have this "luxury." Still, this is essential time for the kind of work that I'm describing.

Finally, I have obtained sabbaticals during my career: In one sabbatical, I researched and authored a textbook; in another, I cowrote a book; and in yet another, I researched and wrote up an article for a journal. Not all of us have access to a sabbatical, but if you do, I strongly urge you to make use of it. They are not luxuries but rather necessities for extended research and writing. And they benefit our teaching and our students.

In all candor, I was blessed early on to serve as director of our college's Writing Lab, a position that allowed me significant course reassignment to lead what I felt then and feel now was a de facto Writing in the Disciplines program. I loved the work and produced my first book based on the work, but again, I was able to do much of this in part because of the space and time afforded by my unique position.

Have I stopped writing and researching over the five years or so since I stepped away from the position? I don't think so. I've cowritten two books, and coedited (with you) three collections.

It can be done. It must be done.

ADVICE TO NEW TEACHERS

PATRICK: I want to pose a very pragmatic follow-up question: What kind of advice would you give to new and veteran writing teachers at the two-year college about staying fresh and engaged? The issue of finding the right balance between work and life seems like such a pressing professional concern for teachers—in any subject, of course—but perhaps particularly so for writing teachers at two-year colleges because of workload issues and all the drafts and essays we have to read, offer feedback about, and grade. What pragmatic advice can you give writing teachers about maintaining balance and finding ways to stay as positive and enthusiastic about our work as you are?

HOWARD: I wish there were an easy answer to the question that you ask, Pat. But here I am, in my thirtieth year of teaching at my college, and I have embarked on a transformation of my ENG 101 curriculum! Before getting involved in the teaching for transfer project, I remember thinking to myself that my approach to ENG 101 was far from perfect. I was pleased by my emphasis on genres (which remains a vital approach for me both in the classroom and in my scholarly work), but I felt that my teaching needed rejuvenation. For one thing, I didn't believe that the readings were holding my students' interest—all from the textbook. In fact, the most interesting reading was usually the sample student writing that we focused on during workshops. How could I give my teaching of 101, which has always been challenging, a shot in the arm? That's when I became interested in the idea of "threshold concepts" and writing transfer—two areas that you also have been thinking and writing about.

So, in reference to your question as to what advice I would give new teachers of writing, I would recommend that they view ENG 101 or Basic Writing as long-term projects and that they view their own careers as having a teaching and research trajectory. Now, here's the payoff, in my judgment: As we make our courses more interesting to students, they will produce more engaged and interesting work. Seems obvious, doesn't it?

But let's get pragmatic, as you suggest. Each of us needs to find a way to manage the paper flow and assessment protocols effectively. For me the godsend has been the web. Now I don't use learning management systems (for reasons that are partly philosophical, partly practical). Instead, I have created my own course site, easily found, easily navigable. On that website I have placed the links to blogs created by all my students. Students maintain and organize their writing electronically. I comment directly onto their blogs. Now I have colleagues who use Google Docs or similar platforms in the same way. The point I'm trying to make is that no longer do we need to lug our papers in suitcases and backpacks. And by the way, responding via the keyboard or as Jeff Sommers taught us years ago via recorded comments is much faster than commenting by hand. A comfort with digital technology is pretty much assumed these days and allows us to manage the "paper" flow. While adopting new software is an ongoing challenge for me, I never regret learning new ways of delivering instruction or allowing students (who have such busy lives) to deposit their work from a distance.

SCHOLARLY ENGAGEMENT AND ITS REWARDS

PATRICK: Staying current with scholarship and disciplinary conversations appears to be a vitally important part of your teaching practice. This work also appears to be linked in powerful ways to your ability to stay fresh and rejuvenate your energy. Can you give skeptical readers some specific examples of how scholarly engagement has made you a better teacher? And what would you say to a colleague who says, "I don't have time for reading research. Scholarship has nothing to offer me"? What kind of recommendations would you offer to teachers who wanted to try some first steps?

HOWARD: I'm glad you asked what examples might be provided of scholarship that improves my teaching. After all, I have encountered deep skepticism among colleagues whom I respect about the efficacy of scholarship and research as a practical matter. And yes, I have heard those colleagues doubt that they have the time to do this kind of research and scholarship as if this kind of work—the scholarship of teaching and learning—were an "add on" or something that I and others do for reasons that have little to do with our own teaching.

So, here are exhibits A and B, one reflecting recent change, the other change some years past:

Exhibit A (Recent Transformation of Teaching)

I have assumed for a very long time that my ENG 101 had little to do with reading as a teachable and relevant subject. I would assign readings from the textbook and, as I noted in my last email, expect students to (a) be engaged and (b) know how to actually work with the reading. Of course, what I was encountering was writing that reflected only the most superficial connection with what students were supposed to have read. And the writing showed that level of disengagement. Now, this ignorance on my part regarding importance of reading spilt over to my writing instruction because I believe I spent precious little time showing students how to engage and dive deep as readers into their own and classmates' writing, nor had I sought readings that would cross modes and speak to diverse students' interests. So, what I have recently discovered—through study of your work, in fact, and the work of composition scholars who have been interested in reading for a very long time—are approaches to bringing into my 101 a way of reading and a modeling of that reading that enriches classroom instruction and engagement as well as students' written performance. To be perfectly practical, for the first time I am demonstrating—with the help of colleagues from our information science area—how to synthesize sources when writing with research. Yes, I know there are textbooks out there that attempt to do just that, but I had not personally known how to incorporate that kind of instruction into my teaching. By the way I have taken some of the research done by Mariolina Salvatori and Patricia Donoghue (and before them David Bartholomae and Anthony Petrosky) and routinely ask students to reflect in writing on what they find difficult in a reading and why. Finally, I have incorporated an array of web-based, freely available mixed-genre works into my courses: TED Talks, essays from popular online magazines, profiles, and obituaries.

Exhibit B (Transformation from Long Ago)

Commenting on student writing is, so the cliché goes, where the rubber meets the road. When I first started teaching composition, I was essentially an editor; making changes on student work myself, a grader, offering rationales for my grade. The comments that I customarily had been giving would mark the end of that student's work on the paper. Now, while I believed that my comments would magically transfer lessons that students could apply to future writing in the course, I was inevitably disappointed—in part because (a) I was doing the editing and perhaps even revising of the papers and (b) I had used the comments as summative rather than formative (to use our technical language). The comments were not having a practical effect; they were not instrumental.

Now you know where I am going with this. Sensing the problem but unable to put my finger on it, I read scholarship about response. I read the work of colleagues like Nancy Sommers, Lil Brannon, and Richard Staub and began to see a different purpose for commentary. I began to see that teacher commentary had rhetorical purposes that I had never thought to consider. I needed to rethink my purpose in commenting. I needed to think of my reader. I needed to think of my voice. I need to think of my comments as more than a "rubber stamp," and rather to be meaningfully linked to the students' writing and ideas. I have tried since then to become, and I believe I have become, a more effective conversationalist through my comments on students' work. And I believe that students' writing has improved as a result. I have become, in short, a better teacher of writing.

CORE VALUES

PATRICK: On a related but perhaps more foundational level, what are your core values and guiding principles now as a writing teacher at a two-year college? Have these changed or remained constant over the course of your career? When you think about entering a writing classroom at a two-year college this week, what are the three things that are most important to you or most in the forefront of your heart and mind as you begin engaging students? What do you hold to most enthusiastically and passionately as you enter a classroom today?

HOWARD: Currently, I hold these truths/values to be essential to what I do in the writing classroom (since we are focusing on first-year composition):

1. Respect our students as learners: Shouldn't that be self-evident? In my judgment, not so—especially at the community college. What I'm about to write likely will offend some, but here goes. I believe that while our intentions as community college faculty may be to assist our students to succeed in college and beyond, our efforts may in fact be providing obstacles. Now, please don't assume that I am one of those "upholders of standards" who decry what is often described as the lazy thinking of students and society writ large. No, I'm talking about challenging our students in ways that they can achieve success but that make them stretch for that success. But it's not just about keeping the bar high. I really do mean that we should respect our students—especially our community college students—for the hard-bought wisdom that they bring into our classrooms and the tough resilience that they display in just, well, being there.
2. Model behavior that expresses creativity, curiosity, inquiry, and problem-solving: Why should our students write when we don't as professionals? You know I was going to ask that question. But the question is not just whether we should write for publication. The question begs other questions: Should we write creatively (I define that in the broadest sense possible, including academically)? Should we continually ask questions that are meaningful to us,

especially about our classroom and our students? Should we display resilience when faced with seemingly intractable problems and push toward possible answers? The answer to all three is "yes!" I have a student who over the last couple of weeks asked me, "What is it like writing a book?" and "What was the most difficult thing about graduate school?" I thought to myself, I am more than my syllabus. I am a person whose experience, both recent and more distant, matters.

3. Aspire, innovate, and demonstrate a willingness to learn from failure: Do I need to make the obvious point that many of our students come to us having failed in school and, so they may think, in life itself? Don't I see routinely students admitting such failure without excuse? Don't I see a willingness in them to learn from mistakes not only to better themselves but to do so for others (children, parents, classmates)? Students at the community college can be so understanding when we ourselves fall flat, as long as we honestly acknowledge our effort and learn from our mistakes. That was one of the first things I learned at the community college: Students will forgive us if we (a) admit our mistake and (b) learn from it.

THE DESIRE FOR JOY AND AN EPIC WIN

PATRICK: Wow. That's inspiring and beautifully put. You've commented about students at two-year colleges already, but I wanted to explore that subject a bit more fully because I think it's a vitally important one. A great deal has been said, written, and theorized about students at open admissions institutions. Not all of it has been flattering. What do you find particularly enjoyable about working with two-year college students? What should someone new to teaching at the two-year college know about the students who attend two-year colleges that is not usually highlighted or acknowledged in public accounts and perceptions?

HOWARD: To begin with: I don't want to overgeneralize, nor do I want to idealize our students. They are each distinct and complex human beings, each with compelling life stories to tell. Those stories often carry a heavy weight. I can see many bearing the weight when they enter my classroom. To be honest—and sometimes I even say this in front of the class—I wish I could see more smiles on their faces when they come into my classroom. I would like to see more joy. Like anyone else, I respond with a smile when I see a smile. It's just human nature. But I need to recognize that many of my students bring experiences very different from my own (I remember liking the classroom, experiencing joy at learning). I should not *ever* confuse my own experience as a student with theirs—despite the fact that, as a child of wartime refugees who were really among the working poor for a very long time, I could, in theory, sympathize. But my students don't need or want my sympathy. They want, as I mentioned earlier, my respect. And they have it.

Here's what I think about community college students—and, yes, I am now hopelessly generalizing as I mentioned I wouldn't: I believe that as a group they have an intense hope and desire for what I, even as an immigrant's kid, took for granted—joy in this life. The other day we were watching a TED Talk in class on how "gaming can make a better world." The speaker, Jane McGonigal, mentioned that the joy that she and other gamers feel, especially on the verge of an "epic win," is nearly indescribable. She realizes that for many gamers outside of the game and many of us who don't have an obvious source of joy currently in our lives the opposite seems to be true: we feel that we are "not good" at life. Well, her point—and the point that I want to make as well—is that our students aspire, in their own way, to achieve that goodness and joy. It is our job to tell them this: You can succeed. You are more than good enough.

PATRICK: There has been considerable attention devoted recently in our profession to positionality, privilege, and race. I'm thinking of Asao Inoue's 2019 CCCC keynote address, and some great recent articles in *TETYC* including "The Risky Business of Engaging Racial Equity in Writing Instruction: A Tragedy in Five Acts" by Taiyon J. Coleman, Renee DeLong, Kathleen Sheerin DeVore, Shannon Gibney, and Michael C. Kuhne (2016, reprinted in this volume) and "A Critical Race Analysis of Transition-Level Writing Curriculum to Support the Racially Diverse Two-Year College" (2019) by Jamila Kareem. Jamila notes, for example, that

> [n]one of the available key disciplinary volumes that center on high school–to–college transitions consider social identities, including *What Is "College-Level" Writing?* (Sullivan and Tinberg), *College Credit for Writing in High School: The "Taking Care of" Business* (Hansen and Farris), and *Naming What We Know: Threshold Concepts in Writing Studies* (Adler-Kassner and Wardle) (276). Instead of arguing for making race a central theme of these texts, I suggest that scholars take note of what they leave out by not giving any attention to racial cultural identity of students. Taking a critical race lens to the transitional moments from secondary to postsecondary writing experiences gives the field a critical opportunity to address deeper societal issues that often makes transferring literacy practices across institutional cultures seemingly impossible for many students, specifically those from "underclass" (Wilson) communities. (276)

As a disciplinary leader, what are some key texts that two-year college teachers should be familiar with in relation to this ongoing conversation? And what recommendations would you provide to two-year-college English teachers (and perhaps also the profession in general) for beginning to address issues related to positionality, social identity, privilege, and race in America in their classrooms?

HOWARD: It is so interesting that you would raise the issues of positionality and privilege, Pat, since those of us who teach at community colleges often promote the narrative that open-access institutions like community colleges can assist students in achieving success no matter the backgrounds they bring with them or the barriers that confront them. I will be the first to admit that many of the stories that we tell each other and that our students have shared with us are fairly remarkable accounts of success achieved despite the odds. But such accounts should not blind us to the reality that our students face each day when they enter our classrooms: that many of them come having come from schools ill-equipped and neglected by an educational system and a complacent public. In our commitment to the grand narrative of open admissions—as in my own college's vision statement, "We change the world, learner by learner"—we lose sight of the vast disparities and inequities even among our own students and most certainly between our students and those from well-endowed private universities and the affluent school systems which produce them. We want to believe that our efforts can enable all of our students, no matter how disadvantaged. But the reality is far different.

Our capacity as educators to come to grips with the reality and to engage in a pedagogy that is suited to confront privilege and inequity is contingent on our own radical transformation. You mention that heart-breaking and poignant essay by Taiyon Coleman and her amazing colleagues on the pain of raising race consciousness in one department. The passionate commitment of the authors to effect change is met by fierce pushback and the resulting alienation of the progressive educators from their department. That essay should be required reading not merely because it so poignantly chronicles the struggle to transform one department but because it stands as a testimony to the authors' passionate commitment to social and racial justice. The essay reminds me of another piece of writing—one that has influenced my own thinking about race and pedagogy over the years: bell hooks' *Teaching to Transgress.* In that key work, hooks persuasively argues that faculty need to "offer something of ourselves to the students" in order to teach in a truly progressive fashion (139). In other words, we faculty need to recognize our own subjectivity and our own position of privilege before we can claim to teach in a socially just way. We must walk the walk and not merely talk the progressive talk. Our pedagogy must be examined and, if limited, must be broadened and transformed.

A PATH TO CITIZENSHIP

PATRICK: This has been a wonderful conversation, Howard. Thank you for being so generous with your time, energy, and expertise. It has been an honor. I have just a few final questions that I'd like to pose. I will ask them and then step back and let you have the final words: Is there anything that we haven't discussed that you want to comment on or address? What would you like to say to America as a nation, to the voting public, and to politicians and state legislatures who make funding decisions about community colleges? And finally, what parting words would you like to offer to your colleagues in writing classes across the nation doing the important work of teaching writing at open admissions institutions? Thank you again, Howard, for being an inspiration to us all.

Howard: Is it too much to ask that ENG 101, a slender courier that holds so much hope, make not only better writers and readers but also better citizens? That is certainly my hope, while admittedly a very tall order. Over the past year, I admit, I have been less than sanguine about students' ability—and the ability of the voting public at large—to work through to the truth of things and thus become informed and active citizens. But I remain faithful to the promise both of ENG 101 (which I see aiming at the Truth of things) and of the mission of the community college, as expressed in my own college's vision statement to "change the world, learner by learner."

REFERENCES

Coleman, Taiyon J., Renee DeLong, Kathleen Sheerin DeVore, Shannon Gibney, and Michael C. Kuhne. 2016. "The Risky Business of Engaging Racial Equity in Writing Instruction: A Tragedy in Five Acts." *Teaching English in the Two Year College* 43 (4): 347–370.

Inoue, Asao B. 2019. "How Do We Language So People Stop Killing Each Other, or, What Do We Do about White Language Supremacy?" *College Composition and Communication* 71 (2): 352–369.

Kareem, Jamila M. 2019. "A Critical Race Analysis of Transition-Level Writing Curriculum to Support the Racially Diverse Two-Year College." *Teaching English in the Two-Year College* 46 (4): 271–96.

ACKNOWLEDGMENTS

"I am what time, circumstance, history, have made of me, certainly, but I am, also, much more than that. So are we all."
James Baldwin

This book is dedicated to James Baldwin's essential message, articulated so eloquently here, about the luminous potential that resides in us all. The open admissions community college is devoted to precisely this inspiring proposition. Anyone working at an open admissions two-year college is engaged in revolutionary social justice work, endeavoring to spread hope and opportunity more broadly across our nation. This work helps build strong families and communities across America, and it strengthens and renews our democracy.

I thank all of you who are engaged in this noble enterprise.

As John Dewey suggested,

> It is no accident that all democracies have put a high estimate upon education; that schooling has been their first care and enduring charge. Only though education can equality of opportunity be anything more than a phrase. Accidental inequalities of birth, wealth, and learning are always tending to restrict the opportunities of some as compared with those of others. Only free and continued education can counteract those forces which are always at work to restore, in however changed a form, feudal oligarchy. (1980 138–139)

There is no way to adequately measure or quantify what this "equality of opportunity" means to individual students other than to say that it is incalculable. It is a gift beyond measure.

This book, though humble, was made with great joyfulness, love, and hope, and it has benefitted tremendously from the help of many. It is with sincere gratitude that I offer these brief words of thanks to the people who have made it possible.

My thanks to our awesome group of contributors, including our student authors. It has been a great pleasure working with you on this project. It is an honor to share the pages of this book with you.

My heartfelt thanks to the editorial team at Utah State University Press, especially Rachael Levay and my anonymous field reviewers. Thank you for your encouragement and your excellent constructive feedback. It has guided and inspired me and helped me to make of this book something much better than I could have ever produced on my own. Thank you.

Sincere thanks to my awesome colleagues at Manchester Community College, where I have taught now for many years. I would especially like to thank my colleagues in the English Department: David Caldwell, Alina Ciscel, Lois Coleman, Jeanine DeRusha, Kaarina Finegan-LaBella, James Gentile, Kim Hamilton-Bobrow, Wanda Haynes, Tanya Millner-Harlee, Linsey Muldoon, Lois Ryan, Lisa Sandoval, Andrew Sottile, Gail Stanton, Steve Straight, Steven Torres, and Charlie Wilcox. You are an inspiration to me every day.

I would also like to thank my close friends and colleagues Andrew Paterna, George Ducharme, Pat Beeman, Kurt Ravenwood, Don and Joan Kelsey, Gordon Plouffe, Lucy Hurston, David Nielsen, Duncan Harris, Bettylou Sandy, Brenda St. Peter, Julie and Wes Larkin, and Michelle and Jeanne Nickerson.

A special word of gratitude to Dan, Dennis, and Molly—extended family members who I hold close in my heart.

I also wish to extend my heartfelt thanks to my great teachers at Mohegan Community College in Norwich, Connecticut, where this improbable journey began many lifetimes ago, especially Jim Coleman, Jim Wright, and John Perch. A special thank you to John Basinger, my lifelong friend and mentor.

Thank you to my inspiring friends and colleagues in the profession affiliated with NCTE and TYCA including Howard Tinberg, Sheridan Blau, Jeff Sommers, Christie Toth, Carolyn Calhoon-Dillahunt, Holly Hassel, Joanne Baird Giordano, Jeffrey Klausman, Darin Jensen, Brett Griffiths, Cheryl Hogue Smith, Jason Courtmanche, Amanda Greenwell, Jessyka Scoppetta, Peter Adams, Mike Rose, John Pekins, Mariolina Salvatori, Patricia Donahue, Mark Reynolds, Hope Parisi, Emily Schnee, Cheryl C. Smith, Kathi Yancey, Muriel Harris, Alfredo Lujan, Ellen Carillo, John Schilb, Leslie Roberts, Jody Millward, Sterling Warner, Lois Powers, Lawrence McDoniel, Frost McLaughlin, Miriam Moore, Jonathan Alexander, and Christine Vassett.

I would also like to thank my amazing students, especially my English 93 and English 101 students, who have taught me so much.

I offer my deepest thanks to those I have lost who would have been delighted by this book. This includes my mother and father, Barbara and Donald Sullivan, and my mother-in-law, Mary Classen. And my lifelong friend and mentor, Victor Kaplan, a writer and professor of English at Eastern Connecticut State University, who taught me how to write. I miss you all very much.

And finally, I offer my deepest thanks to my wife, Susan; my children, Bonnie Rose and Nicholas; and my granddaughter, Marigold Hope. None of this would have been possible without you.

I am, of course, what time, circumstance, and history have made of me, but I am also, thanks to all of you, so much more than that. Words cannot adequately express the debt of gratitude I feel for the many gifts you have given me over these many years.

ABOUT THE AUTHORS

Peter Adams taught at the Community College of Baltimore County—mostly basic writing—for thirty-six years before retiring in 2014. In 1993, a longitudinal study he conducted revealed that only 33 percent of the students who were placed in the basic writing class one level below first-year composition ever passed composition. Over the next decade or so, Peter developed the concept of mainstreaming basic writers into first-year composition and, later, the model for redesigning basic writing now known as the Accelerated Learning Program (ALP). A Community College Research Center study in 2012 revealed that 74 percent of students who enrolled in ALP were successful in first-year composition, more than double the success rate under the traditional program. As of fall of 2017, CCBC has integrated reading and writing into ALP and scaled it up to 100 percent.

For the past eight years Peter has travelled extensively around the country presenting on ALP to individual schools and to statewide gatherings, and he has conducted faculty development workshops for schools that have decided to adapt the ALP model. As of fall of 2017 more than three hundred schools are offering sections of ALP, and seven states have made large-scale adoptions. Peter is dedicated to improving the success of students placed in basic writing, but he is also dedicated to improving his backhand before his wife starts beating him at tennis.

Jeffrey Andelora: See chapter 7's headnote.

Helane Adams Androne: See chapter 2's headnote.

Taiyon J. Coleman earned a BA and an MA in English from Iowa State University, and she holds a MFA in creative writing and a PhD in English literature and culture with a minor in African American and African Diaspora studies from the University of Minnesota, Twin-Cities as an Archie Givens Collection of African American Literature Research fellow. Taiyon is a 2017 recipient of a McKnight Foundation Artist Fellowship in creative prose, and she is one of twelve Minnesota emerging Children's Writers of Color selected as a recipient of the 2018–2019 Mirrors and Windows Fellowship funded by the Loft Literary Center and the Jerome Foundation. Taiyon is an assistant professor of English literature at St. Catherine University in St. Paul, Minnesota.

Renee DeLong earned her PhD in English from the University of Minnesota with a minor in literacy and rhetorical studies and teaches first-year composition, creative writing, and LGBTQ literature at Minneapolis College. She lives in Minneapolis with her wife Laura and their precocious cat Mimi. Her karaoke song of choice is "Kiss" by Prince.

Kathleen Sheerin DeVore has taught writing as well as topics in the African diaspora since 1986, first in Lesotho, Southern Africa; next, beginning in 1991, in Minneapolis following her completion of a PhD at the University of Minnesota; and currently, beginning in 2000, at Minneapolis College.

Jamey Gallagher: As a former community college student himself, Jamey is deeply invested in the community college. He is humbled to have worked with community college students over the past ten years; students who have taught him far more than he has taught them.

He hopes to continue to teach at a community college for the rest of his working life. He is interested in changing academic writing from the inside, so that someday it may match the style and verve of the writing of his best students. He is also a creative writer, and his novella *Midwinter*, a fundraiser for a friend with a bad heart, is available as a Kindle download.

Shannon Gibney has taught critical and creative writing, journalism, and African diasporic topics at Minneapolis College since 2007. Her second novel, *Dream Country*, was published by Dutton in 2018. She coedited *What God is Honored Here: Writing on Miscarriage and Infant Loss* with Kao Kalia Yang. It was published by the University of Minnesota Press in 2019.

Joanne Baird Giordano is a faculty member in the writing program at Salt Lake Community College. She previously coordinated the statewide developmental reading, writing, and ESL program for the University of Wisconsin system's two-year colleges. Her work on two-year college writers and teaching has appeared in *Teaching English in the Two-Year College*, *College Composition and Communication*, *College English*, and edited collections. With Holly Hassel, she is a corecipient of the Council of Writing Program Administrators Outstanding Scholarship award and the *TETYC* Best Article of the Year award in 2010 for their coauthored essay, "Transfer Institutions, Transfer of Knowledge: The Development of Rhetorical Adaptability and Underprepared Writers," which appeared in the September 2009 issue of *Teaching English in the Two-Year College*. Her professional service includes chairing the first TYCA national conference, serving on the CCC editorial board, and coauthoring white papers on placement and developmental education reform as a member of the TYCA Research Committee.

Brett Griffiths directs the Reading and Writing Studios at Macomb Community College, where she serves as a teacher-scholar-activist of inclusive and empowering writing pedagogy. When she is not researching, writing, teaching, or tutoring, she is terrified of the act itself. Brett developed writing anxiety late in her education, having identified as a writer and poet from the days of her earliest memories in elementary school through her first decade as an adult. Brett shares her daily life with three humans; her husband Sebastian and sons Aaron and Raphael and two dogs; Khaleesi and Padfoot. Her husband and two sons remind her every day that balancing our love for one another and engaging the struggle for a better, more dignified world in which to love each other is the defining work of being human at this time. Days spent camping, swimming, and hiking with the full "pack" makes the necessary balance possible—or at least imaginable. Brett aspiringly calls herself a "once and future poet" and looks forward to reengaging the writing of poetry and creative nonfiction alongside scholarly publications in the coming years. Her academic work appears in *Pedagogy*, *Teaching English in the Two-Year College*, and *College Composition and Communication*. Creative work has appeared in Ohio State's *The Journal* and *PoemMemoirStory*.

Holly Hassel: I was raised in Brainerd, Minnesota and attended the University of Minnesota, St. Cloud State University, and the University of Nebraska–Lincoln. I have taught at multiple two-year colleges in multiple states. For lots of reasons that were not academic, college was a hard and terrible experience for me. My love of reading and writing sustained me. What I have tried to bring to my students is rooted in both of those realities: knowledge that will help navigate college culture, which can be opaque, implicit, and unwelcoming and how to navigate those challenges, but also cultivating a love of engaging with complex ideas, texts, and problems. I have published a lot of writing, but what I care most about is making college accessible, purposeful, and achievable for students who have historically been underserved by higher education.

Darin Jensen is the son of working-class parents and is a first generation college graduate. He has been working in two-year colleges since 2003. He has been an adjunct, an administrator, and a full-time faculty member. Currently, he is an instructor of English at Des Moines Area Community College. He teaches at the rural Carroll, Iowa campus. He is the incoming editor of *Teaching English in the Two-year College*, an NCTE journal, as well as the editor of the Teacher-Scholar-Activist-Blog, which won the 2018 John Lovas Award for best academic blog from Kairos. When he isn't teaching, he's in the garden, feeding birds, reading comics. Darin is a committed advocate for open-access education centered on helping people improve their lives and communities. His scholarship often centers on creating a more equitable profession for two-year college English faculty.

Jeffrey Klausman is a professor of English and WPA at Whatcom Community College in Bellingham, Washington, where he has worked since completing a Doctor of Arts in English at Idaho State sometime in the last century. In addition to promoting program-related work at the local, state, and national level, Jeff has decided to treat his impending sixties as a chance to reconnect with kayaking, backpacking, and cycling, regardless of the sore knees and hips and despite the fact that his sixteen-year-old son has to wait for him all the time. His wife, Sherri Winans—a writing center director and fellow compositionist—if she's not participating in activities, greets him with a cold beer or glass of wine upon his return.

Michael C. Kuhne is a former high school English teacher and coach. He has an MA in language and linguistics, as well as a PhD in English with a composition and rhetoric studies emphasis, both from the University of Minnesota. He has taught at Minneapolis College since 1995. His writing (almost always done in collaboration with others) has appeared in *Teaching English in the Two-Year College*, *Communitas*, *Minnesota English Journal*, and *Antipodes*, and chapters he has written appear in numerous books. His decision to teach at a community college was driven, in part, by a desire to work with students who are too frequently at the margins of higher education.

Dan Long is a professor of photography at Manchester Community College in Connecticut. He is a first-generation college student who studied art and photography at Bennington College, R.I.S.D. and Purdue University. He also studied higher education administration at the University of Connecticut. He lives in Connecticut's "quiet corner" with his wife of many years, who is also a community college art professor at a different college in a different state. Dan and his wife have spent twenty-eight years discussing students, faculty, administration and curricula during breakfast, in bed at night, while hiking trails, while stuck in traffic jams, on the beach in July, and on Christmas morning while unwrapping gifts. Dan likes to garden, hike, bike, and travel and still likes books printed on paper. Dan and his friends started a book group in 2002, and the group has been a reassuring constant over the years—they still have the same thirteen (lucky) members. They have read more than 100 wildly different books and the free-form book discussions before, during, and after dinner have been provocative, sometimes loud, and often hilarious. Reading with friends: sweet.

Leah McNeir is a first-generation, nontraditional college student who was born and raised in Baltimore City, Maryland. She currently lives in southeastern Connecticut with her fiancé, Jason. After nearly fifteen years of running her own art and graphic design small business, and driven by a growing desire to be more directly involved in helping others, Leah's priorities and outlook shifted and she returned to college at age thirty to pursue a new career in a therapeutic field. She found success, maintaining a 4.0 GPA and achieving an induction into an honor society and a writing contest award. Coming from a tumultuous upbringing that culminated in her dropping out of high school, she takes pride in her recent academic accomplishments and credits several teachers and mentors that assisted her through their support and guidance. During her freshman year, her fiancé was diagnosed with thyroid cancer. He was successfully treated and has an excellent prognosis, thanks to the expert care at Yale Medical Hospital. During her sophomore year, Leah was diagnosed with autoimmune disease. These challenging experiences crystallized her academic and career goals and she is now pursuing a degree in health care with an aspiration to become a medical practitioner. When she's not working, studying, or delving into literature on whichever topic has taken her fancy that month, you can find her exploring hiking trails, camping, fishing, gardening, contributing to online patient education groups, or spending time with her loved ones. Leah hopes to inspire others with her writing by reminding readers that they are alchemists of meaning and are truly the authors of their life story and its direction. She seeks to encourage others to meet life's challenges with resolve and gusto, to revel in life's beauty and embrace each precious moment, and to empower others to live a life of health, happiness, and authenticity.

Hope Parisi is a professor of English and faculty mentor for part-time and new faculty at Kingsborough Community College, City University of New York. She teaches mostly basic writing and freshman composition, enjoying the confluence of pedagogy and conversations around access in the blending of teaching modes as part of the Accelerated Learning Program. One of her recent projects sets assistance for basic writers in a studio workshop model that combines support from TRiO Support Services and the college's writing center, where Hope served as the academic director for many years. She has published articles in *Teaching English in the Two-Year College*, *Journal of Developmental Education*, *Open Words: Access and English Studies*, and *Journal of Basic Writing*. Hope is coeditor, with Cheryl C. Smith (Baruch College/CUNY), of *Journal of Basic Writing*.

Darlene Pierpont lives in a small country town in Connecticut with her husband, six-year-old son, and her two cats, Fred and Ginger. She is pursuing a degree in liberal arts and sciences and she hopes to continue to inspire others through her writing. While Darlene is not tormenting her husband and son with her indecisiveness, endless questioning, and contemplating the meaning of existence, you can find her studying, playing her piano, or getting lost in the pages of endless tales of adventure and wonder from horror stories to children's books. Her passion for reading comes from her son, and she enjoys reading children's books the most. The fun thing about children's books is that my son and I get to explore our imaginations together. It doesn't matter how old you are; We all have an imagination and it takes work, but you just have to find it hiding beneath your layers of age and time, and children bring that out of you!

Kevin Rodriguez came to the United States in May 2012 to start a new life and, at that time, he had never spoken or written English before. He decided to start over and enrolled at a college to start learning English. In 2015, after a hiatus time from school, he enrolled in the Criminal Justice program and Homeland Security certificate program at Manchester Community College. On May 2017, he earned a Homeland Security Certificate from MCC. In May 2018, he graduated from MCC with an associate's degree in criminal justice with honors and as a summa cum laude student. During his time at MCC, he earned multiple scholarships while trying to keep his full-time job. Kevin also received the President's Award from MCC, an award given to only one student at the commencement ceremony in recognition of exceptional efforts and unusual perseverance. Additionally, because of his outstanding academic achievements, Kevin was one of the two students selected to represent MCC on Phi Theta Kappa's All-Connecticut Academic Team of 2018. While focusing on academics, Kevin also enjoyed indulging in a chocolate muffin from the cafeteria each day.

One of Kevin's passions is to give back to his community by participating in several community service activities both locally and overseas. Kevin loves bread, but for health reasons he has unsuccessfully tried to quit eating bread. In fact, he discovered that it was easier to get an A in math than abandoning his love for bread. Kevin has a hunger for learning that will never stop, as he is continuing to pursue his educational goals. By the way, many thanks to Professor Sullivan's morning English classes, with snacks and music, which will never be forgotten.

Lydia Sekscenski is a self-identified nerd, trivia buff, poetry enthusiast, and music lover, raised by musicians. She is the eldest of five children and returned to college after a nine-year hiatus in the working world. She is a student of occupational therapy with a heart and passion to encourage people to live their best lives and follow their dreams. She is also involved in civic engagement, lending support to local and national candidates for political office who share her vision of promoting good, sustainable, and healthy living for every individual. She also knows the lyrics to a mind-boggling number of songs from many genres that were recorded decades before her time of birth—just ask her.

Jamil Shakoor is currently in the process of reinventing himself and searching for meaning in life. He was brought up in an impoverished environment with a single mother. He beat the odds as a high-school dropout by being the first to attend and graduate college in his family and working professionally for four years. All of this before entering the navy to materialize his dream of many years of becoming a Navy Seal. Soon after entering the navy, he ended up leaving, disillusioned with the grandeur of it all. After many years of his pursuit, he now works in research and is training to run ultramarathons while cultivating a kinder and humbler new paradigm of himself and the world. He enjoys exploring culture and pushing the boundaries of his mind and body. Some of his inspiration comes from David Goggins, Whim Hoff, and Daron Malakian.

Lauren Sills grew up in Batesburg-Leesville, South Carolina before relocating to Windsor, Connecticut in 2001. She comes from a family of educators, including both of her parents. She is studying English with the hopes of becoming a high school English teacher. Prior to starting at Manchester Community College, she worked as a dental assistant for four years. She is a lover of cat-themed coffee mugs, Pablo Neruda's love poems, and attempting to keep plants alive. She is currently living in South Windsor with her two children, two cats, and her husband, Patrick. Her hobbies include reading, building blanket forts in the living room, and cooking.

Bridgette Stepule is the daughter of two business owners. She originally began to study entrepreneurship because of her parents and quickly decided to create her own path. She is now studying accounting and enjoying every moment of it. When she is not calculating balance sheets or income statements for class, she is not who you would think she is. Bridgette has many hobbies, including sailing, learning new things, crocheting, reading, target shooting, hiking, and just about any DIY project there is. Bridgette also worked as a barista at her grandparents' coffee shop for about two years, and also worked as a pet sitter and managed a pet store. Bridgette likes to try new things and keep an open mind about life. She believes that trying new things builds character. Bridgette and her boyfriend are currently planning on moving to Vermont after she finishes her two great years at MCC. This will be an adventure because she is the fifth generation in her family to grow up and live in the Glastonbury-East Hartford area. Bridgette's academic success includes attending MCC and achieving a 4.0 GPA for her first year. This got her the honor of being part of the Phi Theta Kappa honor society. Bridgette wants to remind everyone to be who they choose and always be open to new experiences because you never know where they may lead you.

Howard Tinberg: See chapter 19's headnote.

ABOUT THE EDITOR

Patrick Sullivan teaches English at Manchester Community College in Manchester, Connecticut. He believes deeply in the mission of the community college, and he is very grateful to have had the opportunity to work with so many amazing community college students over the years.

Patrick has taught a wide range of reading and writing classes, and he has published scholarship in a variety of journals, including *Teaching English in the Two-Year College*, *College English*, *College Composition and Communication*, *Academe*, *Liberal Education*, *The Journal of Adolescent and Adult Literacy*, *The Journal of Developmental Education*, *The Journal of Basic Writing*, *The Community College Journal of Research and Practice*, *Innovative Higher Education*, *The Chronicle of Higher Education*, and *English Journal*.

In 2011, Sullivan received the Nell Ann Pickett Award for outstanding service to the two-year college. His article "'A Lifelong Aversion to Writing': What If Writing Courses Emphasized Motivation?" received the Mark Reynolds *TETYC* Best Article Award for 2012.

He is the editor, with Howard Tinberg, of *What Is "College-Level" Writing?* (NCTE, 2006) and, with Howard Tinberg and Sheridan Blau, of *What Is "College-Level" Writing? Volume 2: Assignments, Readings, and Student Writing Samples* (NCTE, 2010) and *Deep Reading: Teaching Reading in the Writing Classroom* (NCTE, 2017). He is also the author of *A New Writing Classroom: Listening, Motivation, and Habits of Mind* (Utah State University Press, 2014) and *Economic Inequality, Neoliberalism, and the American Community College* (Palgrave Macmillan, 2017). Patrick has also edited, with Christie Toth, *Teaching Composition at the Two-Year College: Background Readings* (Bedford/St. Martin's, 2016).

In addition to teaching and writing, Patrick enjoys running, biking, walking, reading, and spending time with his family—his wife, Susan, and his children, Bonnie Rose and Nicholas.

INDEX